# Advancing the Frontiers of Heterodox Economics

This collection of essays honors the life and work of one of the most prominent and fervent heterodox economists, Frederic S. Lee, who has been at the heart of the heterodox economics movements for the past three decades. Authors in this book demonstrate that heterodox economics has transcended the criticism of mainstream economics and, more importantly, that constructive developments are in the making by way of cross-communications among various heterodox economics traditions.

Frederic S. Lee's contributions to heterodox economics are centered on three themes: the making of a history and identity of heterodox economics, heterodox microeconomics, and the heterodox analysis of social provisioning. Part I addresses the importance of history, theory, research methods, and institutions in the making of the identity of heterodox economics as an alternative to mainstream economics. Part II delves into heterodox microeconomic theories—in particular, investment, pricing, competition, markets, and market governance—as foundations of heterodox macroeconomic analyses. Part III expands the analysis of the capitalist social provisioning process with an emphasis on its subsystems and their relationships over historical time. Part IV encapsulates the life and work of Frederic S. Lee.

Throughout his intellectual life Frederic S. Lee has shown to many that the development of heterodox economics is rendered possible by unselfish and ceaseless efforts to build both theory and institutions. Essays in this book attest that establishing an alternative critical theory to the status quo is not only possible but also serviceable to the majority of the population.

**Tae-Hee Jo** is Associate Professor of Economics at the State University of New York, Buffalo State, USA.

**Zdravka Todorova** is Associate Professor of Economics at Wright State University, USA.

## Routledge advances in heterodox economics

Edited by Wolfram Elsner
*University of Bremen*
and
Peter Kriesler
*University of New South Wales*

Over the past two decades, the intellectual agendas of heterodox economists have taken a decidedly pluralist turn. Leading thinkers have begun to move beyond the established paradigms of Austrian, feminist, Institutional-evolutionary, Marxian, Post Keynesian, radical, social, and Sraffian economics—opening up new lines of analysis, criticism, and dialogue among dissenting schools of thought. This cross-fertilization of ideas is creating a new generation of scholarship in which novel combinations of heterodox ideas are being brought to bear on important contemporary and historical problems.

*Routledge Advances in Heterodox Economics* aims to promote this new scholarship by publishing innovative books in heterodox economic theory, policy, philosophy, intellectual history, institutional history, and pedagogy. Syntheses or critical engagement of two or more heterodox traditions are especially encouraged.

This series was previously published by The University of Michigan Press and the following books are available (please contact UMP for more information):

# Advancing the Frontiers of Heterodox Economics

Essays in honor of Frederic S. Lee

Edited by Tae-Hee Jo and
Zdravka Todorova

Routledge
Taylor & Francis Group

LONDON AND NEW YORK

First published 2016
by Routledge

2 Park Square, Milton Park, Abingdon, Oxfordshire OX14 4RN

52 Vanderbilt Avenue, New York, NY 10017

*Routledge is an imprint of the Taylor & Francis Group, an informa business*

First issued in paperback 2020

*British Library Cataloguing in Publication Data*
A catalogue record for this book is available from the British Library

*Library of Congress Cataloging-in-Publication Data*
Advancing the frontiers of heterodox economics : essays in honor of Frederic S. Lee / edited by Tae-Hee Jo and Zdravka Todorova. – First Edition.
 pages cm
 Includes bibliographical references and index.
 1. Economics. I. Lee, Frederic S. 1949–2014. II. Jo, Tae-Hee, editor. III. Todorova, Zdravka K., editor.
 HB119.L44A38 2015
 330.1–dc23                                         2015008181

ISBN: 978-0-415-73031-0 (hbk)
ISBN: 978-0-367-59852-5 (pbk)

Typeset in Times New Roman
by Wearset Ltd, Boldon, Tyne and Wear

# Contents

# Figures

# Tables

# Contributors

**Tuna Baskoy** is Associate Professor in Politics and Public Administration at Ryerson University, Toronto, Canada. His research focuses on business competition, market governance, information and communication technology industry, and the European Union. He is the author of *The Political Economy of European Union Competition Policy: A Case Study of the Telecommunications Industry* (Routledge, 2008). His articles have been published in *Journal of Economic Issues* and *Journal of Electronic Democracy*.

**Lynne Chester** researches and teaches in the Department of Political Economy at the University of Sydney, Australia. Her research is grounded in using the theoretical to develop methodological frameworks for empirical analysis of contemporary issues such as the economic-energy-ecological relation, energy impoverishment, the restructuring of production from financialization, the structure and operation of markets, and Australian capitalism's institutional architecture. She is the author of *Neoliberalism and Electricity Sector Restructuring: A Régulationist Analysis* (Routledge, 2016), and co-editor of the *Review of Political Economy, Handbook of Heterodox Economics* (Routledge, 2016), *Challenging the Orthodoxy: Reflections on Frank Stilwell's Contributor to Political Economy* (Springer, 2014), *Proceedings of the Annual Conference for the Australian Society of Heterodox Economists (Refereed Papers)*, and a special issue on heterodox economics for *On the Horizon* (2012). She has contributed chapters to *A Modern Guide to Rethinking Economics* (Edward Elgar, 2016), *Handbook of Research Methods and Applications in Heterodox Economics* (Edward Elgar, 2015), *Neoliberalism: Beyond the Free Market* (Edward Elgar, 2012), and *Readings in Political Economy* (Tilde, 2011). Her research has also been published in the *American Journal of Economics and Sociology, Australian Journal of Social Issues, Economic and Labour Relations Review, Energy Policy, European Journal of Economics and Economic Policies: Intervention, International Journal of Green Economics, Journal of Australian Political Economy, Journal of Economic Issues*, and *Review of Radical Political Economics*.

**Fabiano Dalto** is Associate Professor at the Federal University of Parana, Brazil. He received his Ph.D. in Economics from the University of Hertfordshire, UK, in 2007. His research interests concentrate on money and finance, and economic development from both Keynesian and institutionalist perspectives. Recently, he has studied the institutional structure of monetary policy decision making in Brazil, fiscal policy, and financial instability.

**Erik Dean** is an instructor of economics at Portland Community College, USA. He has presented papers on heterodox microeconomic theory, institutional economics, and methodology at meetings for the Association for Institutional Thought and the Union for Radical Political Economics, and has contributed book reviews to the *Journal of Economic Issues* and the *Heterodox Economics Newsletter*. Dean received a Ph.D. from the University of Missouri–Kansas City under the supervision of James Sturgeon and Frederic S. Lee.

**Carlo D'Ippoliti** is Assistant Professor in Political Economy at Sapienza University of Rome, Italy. He is the author of *Economics and Diversity* (Routledge, 2011, winner of the 2012 EAEPE-Myrdal Prize) and assistant editor of *PSL Quarterly Review* and *Moneta e Credito*. His research has been published in both mainstream and heterodox journals, and he is editor of NEP-HME, the weekly report on Heterodox Microeconomics within the RePEc project.

**Sheila C. Dow** is Emeritus Professor of Economics at the University of Stirling in Scotland and Adjunct Professor of Economics at the University of Victoria in Canada. Her main research interests lie in the history and methodology of economic thought and the theory of money and banking. Recent books are *Foundations for New Economic Thinking: A Collection of Essays* (Palgrave Macmillan, 2012) and *Economic Methodology: An Inquiry* (Oxford University Press, 2002). She is a co-editor of the World Economic Association's online journal, *Economic Thought*, and a co-convenor of Stirling Centre for Economic Methodology (SCEME). Past roles include Chair of the International Network for Economic Method, Co-Chair of the Post Keynesian Economics Study Group, and Special Advisor on monetary policy to the UK Treasury Select Committee.

**Ruslan Dzarasov** is the Head of the Department of Political Economy at Plekhanov Russian Economics University (Moscow) and a senior research fellow at the Central Economics and Mathematics Institute of Russian Academy of Sciences (Moscow). His main research interests lie in economic theory, problems of development, corporate governance, and investment behavior of firms. His recent publications include: *The Conundrum of Russian Capitalism: The Post-Soviet Economy in the World System* (Pluto Press, 2014), "Eichnerian Megacorp and Investment Behaviour of Russian Corporations" (*Cambridge Journal of Economics*, 2011), "Werewolves of Stalinism: Russia's Capitalists and their System" (*Debatte: Journal of Contemporary Central and Eastern Europe*, 2011).

**Ramón Fernández** is Full Professor of Economics at the Federal University of ABC, Brazil. He worked at the Escola de Economia de São Paulo–Fundação

Getúlio Vargas (2004–2011) and at the Department of Economics of the
Federal University of Parana (1993–2004). He is Argentinean, and has lived
in Brazil since 1976. He received a Ph.D. in Economics from the University
of São Paulo in 1992. Ramon identifies himself with the original institutionalism in economics, as well as with the substantivist view in economic history
and anthropology. His research and teaching areas include the methodology
of economics (chiefly from a rhetorical perspective), heterodox microeconomics, institutional economics, and economic history. He has published
in journals such as *Journal of Economic Issues, American Journal of Economics and Sociology, Estudos Econômicos, Brazilian Journal of Political
Economy*, and *Economia & Sociedade*, as well as in volumes edited in Argen-
tina, Brazil, Spain, and the USA.

**John F. Henry** was Visiting Research Professor at University of Missouri–Kansas City (2005–2014) and Professor Emeritus, California State University,
Sacramento (1970–2004). He obtained his Ph.D. from McGill University in
1974 under the supervision of Athanasios (Tom) Asimakopulos. Henry has
made enormous contributions to heterodox economics, in particular in the
fields of history of economic thought, economic history, and political
economy. He is the author of two seminal books, *John Bates Clark* (Macmillan, 1995) and *The Making of Neoclassical Economics* (Unwin Hyman, 1990;
reprinted by Routledge, 2011). He has published over 50 journal articles and
book reviews in *Journal of Economic Issues, Journal of the History of Economics Thought, History of Political Economy, Forum for Social Economics,
Review of Social Economy, Review of Political Economy, Journal of Post
Keynesian Economics, History of Economics Review*, and *Studi e Note di
Economia*. Henry has served various economics associations for many years
including presidency of the Association for Institutional Thought, membership of the Steering Committee of the International Confederation of Association for Pluralism in Economics, and membership on the editorial boards of
*Forum for Social Economics* and *Journal of Economic Issues*.

**Therese Jefferson** is Associate Professor at Curtin University in Perth, Western
Australia. Her research focuses on gendered aspects of work and labor
markets, particularly links between lifetime earnings and access to economic
resources in later life. Her research has been published in a range of national
and international journals and other forums, including the *Cambridge Journal
of Economics, Australian Bulletin of Labor, Feminist Economics, Journal of
Economic Methodology, Economic Record, Journal of Australian Political
Economy, Labor and Industry, Journal of Industrial Relations*, and the *Encyclopedia of Political Economy*.

**Tae-Hee Jo** is Associate Professor of Economics at the State University of New
York, Buffalo State, USA. He is the former co-editor of the *Heterodox Economics Newsletter* (2010–2013). He is also co-editor of the *Handbook of Heterodox Economics* (Routledge, 2016), *Marx, Veblen, and the Foundations of*

*Heterodox Economics: Essays in Honor of John F. Henry* (Routledge, 2015), *Heterodox Analysis of Financial Crisis and Reform* (Edward Elgar, 2011), and a special issue of *On the Horizon* (2012). He has also published articles and book reviews in the *American Journal of Economics and Sociology*, *Journal of Economic Issues*, *Forum for Social Economics*, *Review of Social and Economic Studies*, *Bulletin of Political Economy*, and *Review of Political Economy*. Frederic S. Lee was Jo's Ph.D. dissertation supervisor and mentor. Following Lee's theoretical legacy, Jo has been working on various theoretical issues in heterodox microeconomics.

**Jakob Kapeller** is an economist, who accidentally became a philosopher. He is working as a post-doctoral researcher at the Department of Philosophy and Theory of Science at Johannes Kepler University Linz in Australia and has served as editor for the *Heterodox Economics Newsletter* since 2013. He is also affiliated with the Institute for Comprehensive Analysis of the Economy (ICAE) at Johannes Kepler University Linz, which facilitates research on alternative economic theories, critical evaluations of mainstream analysis as well as sociological accounts of economics as a scientific field. His research interests include the epistemology of the social sciences, the history of political and economic thought, heterodox economics, and the distribution of income and wealth.

**John E. King** is Emeritus Professor at La Trobe University and Honorary Professor at Federation University Australia. His recent publications include David Ricardo (Palgrave Macmillan, 2013) and *The Microfoundations Delusion* (Edward Elgar, 2012). He is currently working on an English translation of Otto Bauer's 1936 book *Zwischen zwei Weltkriege?* (Between Two World Wars?) for Brill and is writing *An Advanced Introduction to Post Keynesian Economics* (Edward Elgar).

**Jan A. Kregel** is a senior scholar at the Levy Economics Institute of Bard College in the US and director of its Monetary Policy and Financial Structure program, and holds the position of professor of development finance at Tallinn University of Technology. He is also the co-editor of the *Journal of Post Keynesian Economics*. In addition to over 200 journal articles Kregel's major works include *Ragnar Nurkse: Trade and Development* (with R. Kattel and E. S. Reinert, Anthem Press, 2009), *Origini e sviluppo dei mercati finanziari* (Banca Populare dell'Etruria e del Lazio, 1996), *Theory of Capital* (Macmillan, 1976), *The Theory of Economic Growth* (Macmillan, 1972), and *Rate of Profit, Distribution and Growth: Two Views* (Macmillan, 1971). Kregel previously directed the Policy Analysis and Development Branch of the UN Financing for Development Office and was deputy secretary of the UN Committee of Experts on International Cooperation in Tax Matters. In 2011 he was elected to the Accademia Nazionale dei Lincei, also known as the Lincean Academy, the oldest honorific scientific organization in the world. He is a life fellow of the Royal Economic Society (UK), an elected member of the Società Italiana degli Economisti, and a recipient of the Veblen-Commons Award (Association for Evolutionary Economics, 2010). Kregel studied under Joan Robinson and Nicholas Kaldor at the University of Cambridge, and received his Ph.D. from Rutgers University under the chairmanship of Paul Davidson.

**Frederic S. Lee** (1949–2014) was Professor of Economics at the University of Missouri–Kansas City, USA. He received his Ph.D. from Rutgers University. He taught at UMKC from 2000 to 2014; and before that he taught at De Montfort University in England (1991–2000), at Roosevelt University in Chicago (1984–1991), and at the University of California-Riverside (1981–1984). Lee authored and edited 16 books, including *A History of Heterodox Economics* (Routledge, 2009) and *Post Keynesian Price Theory* (Cambridge, 1998); 56 articles; and over 100 book chapters, book entries, book reviews, and notes of one sort or another. His articles appeared in various heterodox journals, including the *Journal of Economic Issues, Journal of Post Keynesian Economics, Review of Social Economy, Review of Radical Political Economics, Review of Political Economy, Cambridge Journal of Economics, Capital and Class, Bulletin of Political Economy, Metroeconomica,* among others. Lee was the president in memoriam of AFEE (2015) and the president of AFIT (2012), a former executive director of the International Confederation of Associations for Pluralism in Economics (2006–2010), and the founder and honorary president of the Association for Heterodox Economics in the UK. He was a member of the editorial board of *Journal of Economic Issues, Journal of Post Keynesian Economics, Review of Social Economics,* and *Forum for Social Economics*; was the founder and editor of the *Heterodox Economics Newsletter* (2004–2009) and the book series *Advances in Heterodox Economics* (University of Michigan Press and, later, Routledge); and was an editor of the *American Journal of Economics and Sociology* (2009–2013). His primary research areas included heterodox microeconomic theory, history of heterodox economics, the research assessment exercise in the UK, and the ranking of journals and articles; and his areas of teaching were microeconomics, advanced heterodox economic theory, American economic history, and radical political economics. Lee died on October 23, 2014.

**Nuno Ornelas Martins** is Lecturer in the School of Economics and Management and CEGE, Universidade Católica Portuguesa, Porto, Portugal. He is also a member of the Cambridge Social Ontology Group, and the author of *The Cambridge Revival of Political Economy* (Routledge, 2013). His main research interests lie in the history of economic thought, the philosophy of economics, and social economics.

**Andrew Mearman** is Associate Professor in Economics at the University of the West of England, Bristol, UK, having previously taught at the University of Lincoln, UK and Wagner College, NY, USA. He is a former coordinator of the Association for Heterodox Economics (2004–2007). He has published on economic methodology, pedagogy in economics, and the economics of the environment in journals including *Cambridge Journal of Economics*, *Oxford Economic Papers*, *Metroeconomica*, *Economic Issues*, and *Journal of Economic Methodology*. He is a graduate of the University of Leeds, UK.

**Jordan Melmiès** is Associate Professor of Economics in the Clersé Research Department at the University of Lille 1, France. His main research interests lie in the theory of prices and competition, and the link between competition and profit margins from a Post Keynesian perspective.

**Huáscar Pessali** is Associate Professor at the Federal University of Parana, Brazil. His main research interests are institutional economics, institutional design, the design of public policy, and the rhetoric of economics. He has published articles and book reviews in *Review of Social Economy*, *Journal of Economic Issues*, *Journal of Institutional Economics*, *Brazilian Journal of Political Economy*, *Journal of Developing Societies*, and *Economia & Sociedade*. He has also published chapters in volumes edited in the US, Brazil, and Spain. In 2011 he was the recipient of the Hellen Potter Award, presented by the Association for Social Economics, for the best article in the *Review of Social Economy*.

**Bruce Philp** is Head of the Department of Strategy, Marketing and Economics at Birmingham City University, UK. He is a former coordinator of the Association for Heterodox Economics (2011–2013) and is presently Secretary. He is author of *Reduction, Rationality and Game Theory in Marxian Economics* (Routledge, 2005), and has published on heterodox labor economics and macroeconomic distribution in journals including *Review of Political Economy*, *Cambridge Journal of Economics*, and *Journal of Economic Issues*. He is a graduate of Manchester Metropolitan University and the University of Manchester.

**Alessandro Roncaglia** is Professor of Economics at Sapienza University of Rome. He is a member of the Accademia Nazionale dei Lincei, and has been President (2010–2013) of the Italian Economists Association. He is the editor of *PSL Quarterly Review* and *Moneta e Credito* and is a member of the editorial board of the *Journal of Post Keynesian Economics*. His recent books, translated into various languages, include *Piero Sraffa* (Palgrave-Macmillan, 2009) and *The Wealth of Ideas* (Cambridge University Press, 2005).

**Henning Schwardt** is a Post-Doctoral Fellow at the Institute for Institutional and Innovation Economics at the University of Bremen, Germany. He is the author of *Institutions, Technology, and Circular and Cumulative Causation in Economics* (Palgrave Macmillan, 2013) and co-author (with Wolfram Elsner and Torsten Heinrich) of *Microeconomics of Complex Economies* (Academic Press, 2014). He has published articles in the *Journal of Economic*

*Issues, Journal of Institutional Economics, Forum for Social Economics*, and *Games*. Schwardt received a Ph.D. from the University of Bremen in 2012.

**Bruno Tinel** is Associate Professor of Economics at the 'Panthéon-Sorbonne' University of Paris, France. He has participated in the creation of the French Association of Political Economy and the International Initiative for Promoting Political Economy. His first research was on the emergence and transformations of radical political economy. Now he works on labor and industrial relations and on public finance. He has published articles and book reviews in *Review of Radical Political Economics, Review of Political Economy, Cadernos EBAPE.BR, European Journal of Economic and Social Systems, Revue de l'OFCE, Revue Française de Socio-Economie, Economie et Institutions, Economie Appliquée, Cahiers d'Economie Politique, Revue Economique, Economies et Sociétés*, and *Actuel Marx*. He met Frederic S. Lee for the first time in 2006 at the Ninth International Post Keynesian Conference in Kansas City. He translated one of Lee's articles into French for the *Revue Française de Socio-Economie* in 2011.

**Zdravka Todorova** is Associate Professor of Economics at Wright State University, USA. She obtained her doctorate degree in Economics in 2007 from the University of Missouri–Kansas City, where she wrote her dissertation under Frederic S. Lee's supervision. In 2007 Todorova received the International Veblen Prize awarded jointly by the European Association for Political Economy and the Association for Evolutionary Economics, for her dissertation. Her book *Money and Households in a Capitalist Economy: A Gendered Post Keynesian-Institutional Approach* (Edward Elgar, 2009) was selected as a 2010 Outstanding Academic Title by *Choice magazine*. Todorova has published articles in *Feminist Economics, Journal of Economic Issues, International Journal of Political Economy, American Journal of Economics and Sociology, European Journal of Economics and Economic Policies: Intervention*, and *The Elgar Companion to Post Keynesian Economics*. Currently Todorova serves as President of the Association for Institutional Thought (2015–2016).

**Andrew Trigg** is Senior Lecturer in Economics at The Open University in the UK, where he has worked since 1993. He has published widely in refereed journals and edited volumes; his 2006 monograph, *Marxian Reproduction Schema: Money and Aggregate Demand in a Capitalist Economy*, is published by Routledge. In collaboration with colleagues at The Open University, Andrew has edited and contributed to four textbooks: *Running the Economy* (OU, 2013), *Personal Investment: Financial Planning in an Uncertain World* (Palgrave, 2010), *Microeconomics: Neoclassical and Institutional Perspectives on Economic Behaviour* (Thomson 1998), and *Economics and Changing Economies* (Thomson, 1996). His most recent research is on the role of the Pasinetti model of pure labor in understanding the foundations of Classical, Marxian, and Post Keynesian economics.

**L. Randall Wray** is Professor of Economics at the University of Missouri–Kansas City and a senior scholar at the Levy Economics Institute of Bard College, USA. He is currently a co-editor of the *Journal of Post Keynesian Economics*. Wray's research focuses on providing a critique of orthodox monetary theory and policy, and the development of an alternative approach. He also publishes extensively in the areas of full employment policy and, more generally, fiscal policy. Wray is the author of *The Rise and Fall of Money Manager Capitalism: Minsky's Half Century from World War Two to the Great Recession* (with Eric Tymoigne) (Routledge, 2014); *Modern Money Theory: A Primer on Macroeconomics for Sovereign Monetary Systems* (Palgrave Macmillan, 2012); *Understanding Modern Money: the Key to Full Employment and Price Stability* (Edward Elgar, 1998); and *Money and Credit in Capitalist Economies* (Edward Elgar, 1990). He is also the coeditor of, and a contributor to, *Money, Financial Instability, and Stabilization Policy* (Edward Elgar, 2006) and *Keynes for the 21st Century: The Continuing Relevance of the General Theory* (Palgrave Macmillan, 2008). Wray received his Ph.D. from Washington University, where he was a student of Hyman Minsky.

# Foreword

*Sheila C. Dow*

This volume is a fine testament to a remarkable man who played a unique role in heterodox economics. The range of contributors to the volume and the enthusiasm with which they and the editors have sought to honor Fred is testament to the extent to which he touched and shaped not only the thinking but also the lives of so many people.

Fred was above all an activist. Having formed strong views as to what he saw as the best way of approaching economics, he then sought to promote this approach by argument and by action. The aim was not only to encourage others, but also to facilitate the development of their work in the face of the substantive obstacles placed in their path by the dominant orthodox approach to economics. This he did through numerous activities, ranging from the formation of the Association for Heterodox Economics (AHE) to promoting the education in heterodox economics of new generations of heterodox economists at University of Missouri–Kansas City (UMKC) to gingering others up to activism. Fred latterly displayed remarkable courage and the depth of his convictions by continuing in his activism in spite of his declining health.

The approach that Fred promoted so effectively was not so much a specific methodology (although he did that too) as an overall approach to economic theorizing and discourse. Specifically he advocated and promoted pluralism in the sense of openness to a range of methodologies and theories, an obligation to engage in debate and the need for justification by reason and evidence. Pluralism is often misunderstood as 'anything goes,' but this is clearly contradicted by Fred Lee's approach and by the aims and practices of the AHE. The AHE was developed under Fred's influence as a forum which welcomes and facilitates a wide range of methodological and theoretical approaches to economics, the common factor being a willingness to engage in both collaboration across approaches, and critical debate.

The heterodox critique of orthodoxy is fundamentally a critique of its refusal to engage with other approaches—or worse, where there has been active suppression of heterodoxy. But engagement within heterodoxy means an ability and willingness to defend one's own approach to methodology and theory. Nobody could accuse Fred of holding back from direct criticism of positions with which he did not agree. Indeed his challenges were posed within heterodox economics as a means of fostering constructive theoretical developments. His theoretical focus was much less on challenging mainstream economists who refuse to engage—but he did sustain a continuing challenge to mainstream economics, at the level of academic politics, to engage with heterodox economics. The (pluralist) point is that Fred engaged and expected others to do likewise. Indeed, thinking further about Fred Lee's approach suggests to me what may be a new term to capture this robust form of pluralism: 'critical pluralism.'

The definition of heterodoxy in terms of a shared pluralism was central to Fred's account of the history of heterodox economics (Lee 2009). This history is valuable in its own right. But it is also strategically important in that it further cements the identity of the heterodox approach which Fred did so much to foster. This strategy was additional to the setting up of institutional structures and using them to good effect. In the UK Fred made a particular contribution by running successful heterodox sessions alongside the annual Royal Economic Society conference and by documenting the damaging effects for heterodoxy in the UK of the Research Assessment Exercise which guided research funding. Overall Fred Lee was a pluralist in the strategies he employed to promote heterodox thinking.

As if this were not a sufficient contribution, Fred also made a substantive mark on methodology and theory within heterodox economics, notably in his 'grounded theory' approach and his development of microeconomics, drawing on and contributing to the Post Keynesian, Institutionalist, Marxian-radical political economy, and social economics traditions. Fred also made his own contributions to the history of economic thought. He used history of ideas, as well as economic history, in order to generate more grounded developments for application to emerging contexts. But his interests and contributions were broader still. The various chapters in this volume not only provide fine indications of this breadth of interests, but also demonstrate the fruitfulness of pluralism. The pluralist engagement across approaches, which has become increasingly evident in heterodox economics, leads to productive cross-fertilizations which take heterodox economics forward. The range of approaches used and topics addressed in this volume admirably reflect the scope of Fred's own contributions to heterodox economics.

Fred was tireless in his efforts to promote heterodox ideas and those who sought to develop them. His career exemplified his approach to economics: developing theory, forming institutions, focusing on education, and encouraging debate, all drawing on real experience and a strong sense of social justice, and all with a view to action. We owe him a great debt.

## Reference

Lee, F. S. 2009. *A History of Heterodox Economics: Challenging the Mainstream in the Twentieth Century*. London: Routledge.

# Foreword

## Fred Lee, heterodox economist extraordinaire

*John F. Henry*

In 2005, Fred organized a small conference at the University of Missouri–Kansas City (UMKC) to commemorate the hundredth anniversary of the founding of the Industrial Workers of the World. As conferences go, this was a piddling affair and the papers presented would hardly advance one's standing in traditional economics departments. Yet, notable members of the heterodox community were in attendance, several traveling from Australia, England, and lengthy distances in the US. Curious, I asked a few, "why?" Why undertake the journey and expense of coming to Kansas City for such an event? To the letter, the answer was, "we owe it to Fred." The *Heterodox Economics Newsletter* had been organized by Fred the previous year, and people were so grateful for this sole means through which economists of our persuasion could communicate in a structured fashion that they "owed it to Fred" to participate.

I shall make a claim: no one sharing our theoretical orientation(s) is more important to heterodoxy than Fred. No one has worked harder to build a heterodox community; no one has provided more encouragement and guidance to students in advancing heterodox economics. Fred has been the center, the Northern Star of the attempt to organize a viable, effective, activist public face of heterodoxy. In this, he has pleaded, cajoled, and—yes—pressured people into doing what is necessary to advance this cause.

As is well known, Fred has been active in almost every heterodox organization extant—AFEE, AHE, AFIT, ASE, EAEPE, URPE. (Please excuse the acronyms.) In particular, Fred was the main force (along with Alan Freeman) in the formation of the Association for Heterodox Economics. As well, Fred has always been active in Post Keynesian circles, in both the US and the UK. Additionally, he has been involved in the major history of economic thought associations (HES, ESHET), which clearly spill over into the heterodox community. He has served as editor of the *American Journal of Economics and Sociology*, president of AFEE and AFIT, and has received numerous awards for his work in promoting heterodoxy. In particular, in 2009, he was the recipient of the Ludwig Mai Service Award given for exceptional service to the Association for Social Economics. One should also mention his efforts in supporting the International Confederation of Associations for Pluralism. In addition to participating in conferences hosted by the organization, he was (in typical style) often the organizer of the ICAPE booth at the Allied Social Science Association meetings. In this, Fred's ability to pressure people into doing their duty will be recognized by those reading this tribute: for one holding quasi-anarchist views, he's quite the disciplinarian!

Something must be said about Fred's work in the Association for Heterodox Economics and his relationship to the Industrial Workers of the World (IWW). The IWW originally was structured along the lines of the 'Chicago' form of organizing. No single orientation was demanded of its members, but all members had to adhere to a general position that the main objective of the organization was to emancipate labor from 'wage slavery' through the elimination of capitalism. Hence, the IWW enlisted Marxists, anarchists, radical trade unionists, etc. in the formation of industrial (rather than craft) unions in working toward that objective. All were loosely socialists or adherents of a 'cooperative commonwealth,' but no specific political program was put forward as the only 'correct' path to follow. The main point was to bring the disaffected, the discontented, the outcasts together to work for social change.

Fred is a long-time member of the IWW, and the AHE has adopted this approach in attempting to fulfill its mission. It does not restrict its membership to those hewing to a Marxist, institutionalist, Post Keynesian, Sraffian, or any other theoretical orientation, but welcomes all—with the exception, of course, of straight-arrow neoclassical economists (though even those adhering to a neoclassical line are welcome *if* they are willing to engage in pluralist discussion and debate, and to learn from heterodoxy). That is, the AHE, through open discussion and debate seeks to develop something of a synthetic approach to heterodoxy, one that will advance this program through an ongoing dialogue among non-mainstream economists. As long as the main objective of emancipating economists (and other social scientists) from the intellectual slavery of conventional economics is accepted, 'all are welcome.' After all, we are the disaffected, the discontented, the outcasts of the economics order. It might be noted that it's difficult to categorize Fred himself. On some days, he's mainly a Marxist; on others, an institutionalist, a Post Keynesian, a Sraffian. (I've even accused him of being a quasi-Austrian!)

Fred's work on ranking economics departments and journals, in concert with his critical analysis of the UK Research Assessment Exercise, should not go unmentioned. While the massive effort that has gone into this work is likely to be underrated, it is important. From the neoclassical perspective, heterodox economists make no contribution to the discipline, and thus, publications by these economists should receive little or no respect. Fred has been able to demonstrate that neoclassical rankings are subject to an internal bias, and, applying a similar bias to heterodox departments and journals produces a ranking order much more favorable to heterodox economists. This conclusion, buttressed by the data collection and statistical analysis that lies at the foundation of the argument, has proven (sometimes) useful in fending off attempts to denigrate our efforts and eliminating heterodox courses and faculty from academic curricula and departments.

All the above which speaks to Fred's efforts in building a heterodox community should not overshadow his work as a heterodox theorist. His 1998 *Post Keynesian Price Theory* in particular, coupled with his *A History of Heterodox Economics* (2009), along with many edited collections and journal articles have established Fred as a leading contributor to the theoretical approach he so tirelessly promotes. In honor of his theoretical work, Fred received the 2000 Gunnar Myrdal Prize, awarded by the European Association for Evolutionary Political Economy.

Since affiliating with UMKC, I've lived down the hall from Fred's office. As we both tend to be in our respective offices five days a week, we've spent a goodly amount of time discussing theory, politics, the administration, students, and the future of heterodox economics. While we certainly don't agree on any number of specific issues, we do know where the other is coming from and don't have to undertake what can be fairly heated exchanges in merely establishing foundations for our respective positions. This speaks to a certain quality in Fred's approach to heterodoxy. Fred does have strong positions, and has no fear in expressing these. But he is respectful of others' positions—assuming they're defensible—and enjoys lively debate. Thus, while he promotes heterodox economics in general, he does want to move people toward a theoretical stance that is on firm ground, coherent, internally consistent, and better equipped to both engage neoclassicism in intellectual combat and to advance our understanding of the economy and the larger social order in order to promote the social provisioning process. One thing that he will not tolerate is the sneaking of neoclassical theory in whatever form into the heterodox camp. Pluralism can be carried just so far, and pluralism does not include dogmatic neoclassicism.

I close by mentioning his work with students, for students represent the hope for the future of heterodoxy. When I first arrived at UMKC in 2001, Fred had very few students with whom to work directly: most came to work in modern money theory. Over the last five years or so, an increasing number began working with Fred, influenced by his modeling of the economy based on Leontief and Sraffa. Fred's approach has attracted the attention of students as it allows a conjoining of money, production, and distribution, shedding much needed light on the fundamentals of a monetary production economy.

Fred has always been very generous with his time, has always been encouraging—and demanding!—and has imparted an ethic to 'do your duty' in the promotion of heterodoxy, not uncritically to be sure, but to advance the argument by drawing on the various branches which constitute this alternative to conventional economics. To this end, he and his wife, Ruth, have established the 'Frederic S. Lee Heterodox Economics Scholarship,' in the 'hope for the future of heterodoxy.'

In April of this year (2014), when it was clear that Fred could not carry on, graduate students organized a tribute to Fred. Student after student spoke to how much Fred meant to their academic and personal lives, and promised to carry on in his tradition. No finer accolade could honor Fred's work in the service of heterodox economics.

# Preface

This book project started in late 2012 upon knowing that Professor Frederic S. Lee was planning to retire in 2015. As first two Ph.D. students of Fred Lee, we wanted to pay homage to his unparalleled contributions to heterodox economics. While a typical festschrift volume is a collection of essays written by already-established and renowned scholars in the field, we decided to make this volume distinctive and special (or 'heterodox' in a sense to honor a truly 'heterodox' economist of our time) by asking young and rising heterodox economists around the world. The rationale was that Fred was always concerned with the future of heterodox economics, and hence that we wanted to show him that what he had done over the past 30 years started producing fruit. Essays collected in this volume certainly attest to this. Heterodox economics in the near future would be different from the previous three decades. It has entered into a new phase in which there are many important contributions transcending (mere critiques of) mainstream-neoclassical economic theories. The volume is designed to show-case the beginning of a new phase of heterodox economics as an alternative to mainstream economics.

To our sadness, his life ended too early. Fred Lee died on October 23, 2014 after suffering from lung cancer. If Fred were alive, he would be happy to read (and comment on) all the essays in this volume. He deserves much more than one book. Our initial plan to surprise him at his retirement event did not work out. In March 2014, we told him that we were working on this book. He was most thankful to all the contributors.

We are most honored to edit this book in his honor. We are extremely fortunate to be his students. We are tremendously grateful to Fred Lee for his guidance, comments, encouragements, and support. Without him, we might have become totally different heterodox economists. From his work we have learned that a heterodox economist should not behave like a self-interested neoclassical human being; a heterodox economist should know more deeply and widely than neoclassical economists; a heterodox economist should not be afraid of being critical of the status quo (be it heterodox or orthodox); and a heterodox economist should not be lazy if we are concerned about the future of heterodox economics.

This volume is a festschrift for and tribute to Frederic S. Lee. In addition to three themes derived from Fred Lee's work—history and identity of heterodox economics, heterodox microeconomics, and the social provisioning process, we have added Fred Lee's short autobiography and complete bibliography, two forewords, and two tributes. We wish to thank Sheila Dow, John Henry, John King, Jan Kregel, and Randy Wray for writing such wonderful tributes to Fred Lee. Thanks must be given to all the contributors of this volume for their excellent contributions to the book. The overall quality of the book has been improved significantly by constructive comments given by reviewers. They are Tanweer Ali, Tuna Baskoy, Natalia Brancarense, Lynne Chester, Thomas Dallery, Erik Dean, John F. Henry, Jordan Melmiès, Tara Natarajan, Huascar Pessali, the late Robert Prasch, Matias Vernengo, and William Waller. We are grateful to Louis-Phillippe Rochon and Edward Elgar for allowing us to reproduce an abridged version of John King's obituary that first appeared in the April 2015 issue of the *Review of Keynesian Economics*, Vol. 3, No. 2. Lastly, we would especially thank Ruth Lee for allowing us to include Fred Lee's autobiography in this volume.

Tae-Hee Jo and Zdravka Todorova
February 2015

# Introduction

## Frederic S. Lee's contributions to heterodox economics

*Tae-Hee Jo and Zdravka Todorova*

### Frederic S. Lee: personal recollections

We are still coming to grips with the reality that we won't see Fred Lee, our advisor and mentor, at the next conference. It is hard to imagine that he has departed. Our e-mail boxes are emptier and our hearts are heavier. But we know that he will always be with us in the work of heterodox economists.

After graduating from the University of Missouri–Kansas City (UMKC) in 2007, we were always excited to meet and talk to Fred at various conferences, at least three times a year. He showed up wearing his checkered shirt, three or four pens of different colors in his chest pocket, holding a paper or two in his hands, either reading or commenting, and with a ton of energy to spread. He always came to the conference before the beginning of the first session and stayed until all the sessions ended. He certainly enjoyed talking to and debating with other heterodox economists—especially young ones. Whenever he found a young heterodox economist whom he had never met before, he approached her or him and asked: "Who are you? What are you working on? How did you know about heterodox economics? Are you subscribing to the *Heterodox Economics Newsletter*?" Besides, one night at every conference we had a big UMKC dinner organized by Fred Lee. Not only UMKC students and faculty but also any friends and heterodox economists were welcomed to the dinner. We always had interesting conversations with each other as if we were a big family.

These episodes tell us only a partial view of Fred Lee. He was, above all, a heterodox economist who cared much about the future of heterodox economics and, therefore, who always tried tirelessly to organize heterodox economists, often at the expense of his time and energy for his own research. He, together with others around the world, worked hard to build heterodox economic theory, and, equally importantly, heterodox communities and networks. Because of his contributions, heterodox economists have a better chance of getting hired, getting published, and getting recognized (although his contribution is not always recognized; nor did he expect it to be recognized). This is the legacy that Fred Lee has left to all of us—his students, colleagues, and friends. It is never too many times to repeat: Fred Lee has been, is, and will be an inspiration!

We asked Fred Lee to be our dissertation adviser because we were inspired by his lectures, research, and personal conversations. We believed that his approach to heterodox economics was something to be developed further. He taught us not only heterodox economic theories but also how to do heterodox economics in a pluralistic and integrative manner. His encouragement and support helped us to become responsible and open-minded heterodox economists.

He had a constructive vision of heterodox economics—that is, developing an integrated theoretical framework of heterodox economics drawing on various heterodox approaches. He was never hesitant of putting his vision into practice; and never afraid of entering into debate on theories. Yet, he was always ready to hear different ideas. He was not dogmatic or sectarian. Nor was he eclectic in terms of theory. Over the years we saw him evolving, and opening up even more. He had high standards—not only for his students, but also for his colleagues and himself. He had high expectations for everybody's involvement and efforts, he wanted to see people being energized and driven.

It is somehow mysterious that Fred Lee was able to engage in a number of projects simultaneously and persistently as if time was not scarce. Consequently, Lee's contribution to heterodox economics goes beyond a typical economist's life-time achievements. In what follows we shall highlight his most important contributions to (1) the making of a history and identity of heterodox economics, (2) heterodox microeconomics, and (3) the heterodox analysis of social provisioning. The main argument of each essay collected in this volume is incorporated into this introduction.

## Making history and identity of heterodox economics by developing theory and institutions

Fred Lee spent a great deal of his time working for others, in particular, younger heterodox economists and students, and for the community of heterodox economists. His conviction that institution building—for example, organizing and/or running social networks, conferences, and academic programs—is as important as theory building (Lee 2009, 15–18) was bequeathed to him from his mentor, Alfred Eichner. In his tribute to Eichner, Lee recognizes Eichner's "unflagging energy to establish Post Keynesian economics in the United States" from the early 1970s towards the end of Eichner's life in 1988 (Lee 1991, 26), which helped establish Post Keynesian economics. More importantly, Lee notes that

> because of these [Eichner's] efforts we young and newly minted Post Keynesians have had a much easier time getting published, giving papers at the ASSA sessions, and even finding an academic position in which we can teach Post Keynesian economics. While these efforts often go unnoticed, I think that for Al they represented his commitment to the belief that if you think Post Keynesian economics is the best then you are in a sense obligated

to push it where you go, and you must do it in a manner that will let others who follow you get published, get recognized, and to develop the discipline.

(Lee 1991, 27)

There is no doubt that Fred Lee continued and extended Eichner's legacy in terms of theory and also of service to the community of heterodox economics. While in the UK, he played an essential role in the making of the Association for Heterodox Economics (AHE, founded in 1999). He served as the first coordinator (1999–2000) and became one of two Honorary Life Presidents of AHE (the other is Victoria Chick). Notably AHE is the first pluralist association promoting all heterodox economics traditions. In its constitution, it is stated that AHE "aims to promote open and tolerant debate in economics through pluralism in theory, method, and ideology, and to promote heterodox economists and perspectives in the academic, governmental and private spheres of the discipline of economics" (Association for Heterodox Economics 1999; Lee 2009; see also Andrew Mearman and Bruce Philp's chapter in this volume for the history of AHE and the detailed account of Lee's involvement with AHE). The aim of AHE partly reflects Fred Lee's long-time argument for building heterodox economics as a coherent and comprehensive explanation of the social provisioning process that is an alternative to mainstream economics. It should also be noted that his support for pluralism does not mean all heterodox theories are compatible with each other. In other words, Lee notes that "pluralism is compatible with the development of a coherent economic theory in which some views get discarded" (personal communication, April 1, 2014; see also Henry and Lee 2009 and Sheila Dow's Foreword in this volume).

Along with its successful annual conferences, AHE has also organized Postgraduate Research Methodology Workshops in which Fred Lee actively participated.[1] Therese Jefferson, a participant of the 2004 Workshop while she was a doctoral student, recalls that "one of the few economists who had critically discussed and analyzed the methodological basis of grounded theory and its potential use in economic research was Fred Lee" (see Jefferson's chapter in this book). Influenced by Fred Lee and others at the workshop, Jefferson demonstrates in her chapter that the grounded theory approach combined with other research methods offers specific insights that cannot be found by deductive modeling.

An importance of the establishment of AHE and its workshops is that the term 'heterodox economics,' referring to a wide range of theoretical traditions alternative to mainstream economics as well as to a community of economists generating alternative theories has been received by many economists around the world.[2] For example, the Society of Heterodox Economists (SHE) was established in Australia three years after the AHE was formed. Major heterodox associations such as AFEE, AFIT, ASE, EAEPE, IAFFE, and URPE[3] have explicitly included 'heterodox economics' in their calls for papers for conferences and for journal special issues. Many authors have used 'heterodox economics' in their book titles (see the list of books and journal special issues collected in the

*Heterodox Economics Directory* website.[4] *The New Palgrave Dictionary of Economics*, one of the essential reference books in economics, has included an entry on 'Heterodox Economics' (Lee 2008b) in its second edition published in 2008. Recently, summer schools with the heading of 'heterodox economics' have been organized—e.g., Pozań Summer School of Heterodox Economics (2012 and 2013, Poland), PEF (Progressive Economics Forum) Summer School in Heterodox Economics (2011 and 2014, Canada) (Lee 2009, ch. 10; see also Chapter 2 of this book).

The above movements indicate that heterodox economics has established its identity as a pluralistic or diverse set of alternative theoretical traditions by way of making institutions—associations, conferences, workshops, summer schools, journal issues, books, and social networks. Doubtlessly, in the process of making the identity of heterodox economics, *Heterodox Economics Newsletter* (the first issue published on September 29, 2004) and *Heterodox Economics Directory* (the first edition published in 2005) created and run by Fred Lee have played an important role. The *Newsletter* and *Directory* not only promote heterodox economics, but also give heterodox economists around the world the feeling that they are part of a global heterodox economics community; otherwise they would have been isolated 'loners.'[5] In his recent book, Marc Lavoie lends credence to our observation:

> I decided to adopt the denomination 'heterodox economics.' Over the years, in particular since the late 1990s, but even more so since the mid-2000s, the term 'heterodox' has become increasingly popular to designate the set of economists who view themselves as belonging to a community of economists distinct from the dominant paradigm. Indeed, there is now a huge *Heterodox Economics Directory* (Jo 2013), which provides useful information to all those young scholars looking for an alternative economics. As a result, I shall speak of 'heterodox economists,' as has been suggested in particular by Frederic Lee (2009).
>
> (Lavoie 2014, 6)

Fred Lee's commitment to heterodox economics is also demonstrated by his book, *A History of Heterodox Economics: Challenging the Mainstream in the Twentieth Century* (Routledge, 2009). He spent over 15 years completing this book (and once he said that he did it because someone had to do it). This is the only book ever published that deals with the institutional history of heterodox economics from 1900 to 2006 in the US and UK. Essentially, the purpose of the book is to show that not only did/does heterodox economics exist, but also it offers radical (in the sense of challenging the status quo) insights into the social provisioning process under capitalism. His work on history is also coupled with other important works, such as research assessment and the ranking of economic journals and departments (Harley and Lee 1996; Lee and Harley 1998; Lee 2006, 2007, 2008a; Lee and Cronin 2010; Lee *et al.* 2010; Lee *et al.* 2013). These works aim at providing the historical and empirical ground that heterodox economics is a well-articulated and robust research paradigm (independently of neoclassical economics) that should be an integral part of the economics curriculum. The importance of these works is that they open up an array of positive possibilities for the future of heterodox economics.[6] In a nutshell, for Fred Lee the notion and practice of a heterodox economics community bears a reciprocal relationship with theory development.

Although the connection between theory and community (or institution in general) is well analyzed by many heterodox economists (institutionalists, in particular), not many heterodox economists actually practice their theory. To paraphrase Marx's famous saying: many heterodox economists have only interpreted the world in various ways; the point is to change it. For Fred Lee, building a heterodox economics community and developing heterodox economic theory were akin to his work with Industrial Workers of the World (IWW). In other words, "advancing heterodox economics is not enough; the world needs to be changed as well" (Lee and Bekken 2009, 8). In this regard, Fred Lee was an extraordinary heterodox economist (see John Henry's Foreword in this book). Fred Lee's view of the community of heterodox economists as "a social system of work" is clearly addressed in his 2009 book:

> For the community of heterodox economists to exist, it must be grounded in a social system of work that produces economic knowledge that contributes to a heterodox understanding of the economy and the social provisioning process. Since a social system of work implies that participants are dependent on each other for the production of scientific knowledge, how strong or weak the community is, in part, a function of how dependent heterodox economists are on each other's research and on the extent to which they work on common research goals, and, in part, is dependent on the degree of integration of their social activities.
>
> (Lee 2009, 192)

This vision of the community runs parallel to his definition of heterodox economic theory:

> Heterodox economic theory is an empirically grounded theoretical explanation of the historical process of social provisioning within the context of a capitalist economy. Therefore it is concerned with explaining those factors that are part of the process of social provisioning, including the structure and use of resources, the structure and change of social wants, structure of production and the reproduction of the business enterprise, family, state, and other relevant institutions and organizations, and distribution.
>
> (Lee 2009, 8–9)

If the economy is understood as the "historical process of social provisioning," economic theory must inquire into the system as a whole that is historically constituted by actors and their agency, durable structures, and causal mechanisms.

Such an approach to heterodox economics could be articulated by taking core theoretical claims into account. In their chapter Carlo D'Ippoliti and Alessandro Roncaglia address this point. In particular, they argue that theories of price (and their historical development) embody competing (and incompatible) visions of a capitalist economy. That is, the theory of price from the heterodox perspective is anchored in the monetary-surplus production economy, whereas the neoclassical theory of price (or the market price mechanism) promotes a vision that the capitalist economy is an efficient market exchange system. Two important implications follow from this. First, price theories demarcate the contours of economics—heterodoxy and mainstream. Second, the history of economic analysis is an integral part of doing economics, since the historical development of theory is the reflection of a particular vision of economy.

The future of heterodox economics lies in the development of a distinct, internally coherent, comprehensive, and empirically grounded theory. In their chapter, Bruce Philp and Andrew Trigg emphasize that the concept of class conflict is a core element of heterodox economic theory that enables the challenging of the ethics of distribution within the system of social provisioning. They also argue that there are commonalities within the variety of heterodox approaches to conflict over distribution, and show that the development of heterodox theory benefits from a variety of approaches.

The foregoing discussions with respect to Fred Lee's contribution to the making of history and identity of heterodox economics imply that heterodox economics is a constructive research paradigm. However, we still find many economists saying that the label 'heterodox' connotes merely the opposition to the mainstream, or segregates dissenting economists from the entire discipline (often with an implication that heterodox economics is inferior to mainstream economics). We would argue that such a view lacks an understanding of heterodox economics in historical context. Heterodox economics (with various streams therein) has changed over the past three decades and the further development of heterodox economics is open-ended, as we continue building theory and institutions.

## Heterodox microeconomics and the foundations of heterodox macroeconomics

Let us now move onto Lee's theoretical contributions to heterodox economics. Throughout his academic career he had a "grandiose project" that was formed while doing his doctoral study at Rutgers University. His lifetime project was developing "heterodox microeconomic theory as a complete alternative to neoclassical microeconomics" (Lee 2014b, Preface; see also Fred Lee's autobiography in this book). Unfortunately, this project was only partially successful due mainly to constant interruptions, such as organizational activities described in the previous section. Although he always wished to spend more time on developing heterodox microeconomic theory, Fred Lee would never regret what he had done for the community of heterodox economics.

vantage point of social agency (for example, megacorps in Eichner and going concerns in Lee). Thus in Eichner's and Lee's theories of investment and pricing (although there are differences between their respective theories) the distinction between micro and macro becomes irrelevant; instead, they offer how price and investment decisions are actually made within the business enterprise, and how such actions give rise to macro-outcomes. This is an important theoretical as well as empirical argument that escapes many macroeconomists' notice (see Lee 2010, 2011a).

In the Post Keynesian tradition, investment is linked to pricing (through profit margins) and market competition. Jordan Melmiès' chapter articulates this issue. He points out two theoretical positions on the link between competition and profits margins—one being Kalecki's degree of monopoly principle, the other being the investment-financing tradition developed by Eichner (1976) and Adrian Wood (1975). While Lee was critical of the Kaleckian position since there is no empirical evidence that profit margins are functionally tied to the structure of the market, he developed the Eichner–Wood position arguing that going enterprises make strategic decisions on profit margins, price, financing, and investment so as to allow them to grow and expand over time; this is done regardless of the structure of markets or the degree of competition since enterprises are able to 'manage competition' by establishing market governance organizations (Lee 2011c, 2012a, 2013a).

Lee's account of enterprise activities and market competition in the context of monetary, circular, surplus production economy is reinforced by the institutionalist notion of the going concern. Erik Dean, in his chapter, demonstrates that the business enterprise as a going concern (composed of the going plant and the going business) is a key to understand complex and evolving nature of the social provisioning process. Examining the history of the US software industry from the 1950s to the 1990s, Dean argues that historical changes in the size and structure of the going concern and of the industry is not the outcome of the pursuit of efficiency as in neoclassical theory, but the consequence of the deliberate agency exercised by the going concern. Therefore Dean's study lends empirical-historical support to Lee's heterodox theory of the business enterprise as an alternative to neoclassical theory of the firm.

Since the business enterprise and other organizations are going concerns in the sense of making decisions and pursuing actions in the social and historical context, the analogous concept of the market in which going concerns operate in the real world needs to be developed. In her chapter, Lynne Chester provides an analytical framework that helps to systematically analyze real world markets. Her framework overcomes the abstract and rhetorical concept of markets in neoclassical economics, and more importantly, sheds light on essential aspects of the market—that is, structure, operation, behaviors, rules, price setting; or in Lee's terminology, 'structure–organization–agency' (Lee 2013b)—which are germane to the well-being of the public in the social provisioning process.

These six chapters attest that Fred Lee's contributions are conducive to the development of heterodox microeconomic theory, and also that his legacy will continue to be influential as long as young heterodox economists develop Lee's incomplete grandiose project.[8] In a nutshell, Lee endeavored to advance a heterodox microeconomic theory that is free of relative scarcity, optimizing individual behavior, equilibrium, market-clearing, the distinction between short-period and long-period, the split between micro and macro, and the laws of supply and demand, as all of them have no resemblance to the real world. In his alternative theoretical framework, it is social agency in historical time that makes the entire system open (as we observe in history) by way of changing existing structures of the economy. More specifically, it is business enterprise and state's expenditure decisions generating effective demand that drive economic activities in the monetary production economy.

## Advancing the heterodox analysis of social provisioning

In the course of developing heterodox microeconomic theory, Lee was influenced by various heterodox streams. Initially he was a Post Keynesian economist taught directly by Alfred Eichner, Paul Davidson, Jan Kregel, Nina Shapiro, among others. Later, while at the University of Missouri–Kansas City, Lee found that Modern Money theory was compatible with and complementary to his microeconomic foundations of macroeconomics (see Jan Kregel and Randall Wray's chapter in this volume). Thus it was inevitable for him to develop a micro-macro integrative framework with a concentration on microeconomic issues.[9]

As we observed for the past decade or so (particularly after the publication of John King's *A History of Post Keynesian Economics since 1936* in 2002 and following debates among Post Keynesians), Post Keynesian economics has been divided into smaller groups—Fundamentalist Post Keynesians, Sraffians, Kaleckians, Kaldorians, among others (and growing discord between them). Lee was never happy about such a 'sectarian' movement. Moreover, many current Post Keynesians erroneously assume that Post Keynesian economics is only macro. This is something Fred Lee could not accept, since his mentor, Alfred Eichner and Lee himself played an important role in the making of Post Keynesian economics since early 1970s (see Lee 2009). Due to such a sectarian movement (as a negative push factor) and also to broader influences from various heterodox traditions (as a positive pull factor)—for example, original institutionalism, Marxism-radical political economics, feminist economics, and social economics—he gradually became a heterodox microeconomist, instead of staying within Post Keynesianism.[10]

In his heterodox microfoundations of macroeconomics, Lee was putting together compatible heterodox theories to build a general theoretical framework that could offer a comprehensive and realistic understanding of corporate capitalism. In doing so he revived and promoted the concept of the social provisioning process that was originally conceptualized by institutional economists (notably, Gruchy 1987, 21).[11] In Lee's general heterodox framework, the social provisioning process means "a continuous, non-accidental series of production-based, production-derived economic activities through historical time that provide needy individuals and families the goods and services necessary to carry out their sequential reoccurring and changing social activities through time" (Lee and Jo 2011, 859). More specifically,

> [t]he social provisioning process is a view of economy, which stresses the flow of goods, services, incomes, and both tangible and intangible resources taking place in historical and social context—cultural values, class/power relations, norms, ideologies, and ecological system. Economic activities under capitalism, such as production, consumption, employment, and exchange, are part of the provisioning process, which is controlled by the ruling capitalist class empowered by (and at the same time creating) a particular ideology, norm, cultural value, and class ethos.
>
> (Jo and Lee 2015, 6)

In contrast to the narrow neoclassical definition of economics, which is centered on rational choices given scarce resources, such a broad heterodox view of economy and economics has potential for integrating various heterodox theories that are concerned with explaining corporate capitalism in historical context. In light of Marxian, institutional, Post Keynesian, and other heterodox economics, the social provisioning process is theoretically equivalent to the monetary, circular, surplus production economy. Therefore, the theoretical core of heterodox economics, in Lee's vision, is composed of three organizing principles: the theory of monetary production, the surplus approach, and the principle of effective demand. Lee has shown that these theoretical cores can be augmented by Sraffa–Leontief input–output matrix, Marxian social accounting matrix, institutionalist social fabric matrix, and Post Keynesian stock-flow consistent modeling (Lee 2011b, 2012c) as well as a critical realist-grounded theory method (Lee 2002, 2005, 2015a, 2015b).

In particular, Lee has developed a heterodox surplus approach that is consistent with his commitment to a general heterodox framework rooted in various heterodox approaches. His surplus approach, however, does not mean to return to the classical surplus approach. In place of the classical (and Sraffian) surplus approach, Lee proposes a heterodox surplus approach that integrates Leontief input-output analysis, Sraffian circular production schema, and Keynes's principle of effective demand in a selective manner. Therefore in his surplus approach, self-replacing economy, the total product, and the long-period price (and convergence to this) are not 'assumed givens'; instead, it is capitalist class agency that determines the volume and composition of the social surplus, which in turn drives the production of basic goods, employment, income, and the total social product. Class conflict is explained in the production process of the social surplus—that is, the ruling class agency drives the production and distribution of surplus goods. Whether there is an inverse relationship between wages and profits, a point central to the Marxian-Sraffian analysis is an empirical issue, not something that is taken for granted from the heterodox surplus approach developed by Lee (Lee 2012c, 95).

This suggests that the concept of labor commanded and the exploitation of labor are restricted to the Sraffian and classical social surplus approach. In particular, workers are not exploited in the labor theory of value sense in that they get less than what they produce. Rather, they are directed by the ruling class to produce surplus goods and services for them and as a by-product produce their own goods and services. The end result is the same but the analytical narrative is different.

(Lee and Jo 2011, 871, fn. 15)

An important implication for the development of heterodox economics can be drawn from this. While many heterodox economists criticize neoclassical economics, they often refrain from challenging heterodox theories. If heterodox economists wish to move their approach forward, it is imperative for them to engage in theoretical debates, which would promote critical pluralism and intellectual dynamism within heterodox economics (Lee and Jo 2011, 870; see also, Lee 2012c). A focus on the social provisioning process sets the tone of a general framework encompassing various strands in heterodox economics. In a tactical sense, this promotes cross-communication among compatible theories and, thereby, challenging theoretical sectarianism and dogmatism.

Another implication is that, as Nuno Ornelas Martins argues in his chapter of the book, the heterodox surplus approach, as opposed to the demand-supply framework, would help better analyze present socio-economic problems (in particular, distribution and inequality) since it uncovers the complicated process of reproduction and allocation of surplus (and incomes) under capitalism.

The social provisioning process in connection to various heterodox theories analyzing the capitalist economy is, however, still in need of further articulation and elaboration. For example, while the production process is well articulated in heterodoxy (and also in Lee's framework), households and consumption need further attention.[12] In her chapter, Zdravka Todorova builds on Lee's conception of the economy as a whole and offers a theoretical formulation of consumption as a process that is part of social provisioning under capitalism. In other words, consumption is viewed as a process in conjunction with other delineated processes that constitute social provisioning. As a result of this formulation, an analysis of consumption could start with any institution, not just the household or the individual consumer. For that reason heterodox economic analysis of consumption should not be limited or reduced to either an aggregated macro analysis or a micro theory of consumer choice.

Todorova's micro-macro integrative approach implies that the concept of the social provisioning process transcends a conventional individualistic or holistic analysis by incorporating the historical interrelationship between agency, organization, and structure, and that any economic activity should be explained in a larger social context beyond the narrow market mechanism. Of these three analytical constituents of the social provisioning process, it is agency as socialized, class-based individuals vested in the acting persons or organizations that create, maintain, and reproduce structures over historical time (Lee 2011a, 17; 2011b,

1304–1305). The role of agency is central to the dynamics of the social provisioning process and, therefore, makes Lee's analysis distinctive from both holistic (in the sense of concentrating on given structures) and individualistic analyses.

Conventionally, market competition is viewed as a structural issue in both mainstream and heterodox economics—that is, the structure of the market determines price and quantity in neoclassical theory, or the degree of concentration or monopoly is proportional to the level of profit-markup and price (in Post Keynesian theory). However, if market competition is interrogated in the context of the social provisioning process, the market structure-competition logic is replaced by the regulation-competition logic. In his chapter, Tuna Baskoy, drawing upon Lee's contribution to Post Keynesian theory of competition, argues that in the real world market competition is regulated mainly through the market governance organizations—e.g., trade associations and cartels. That is, competition and control are two sides of the same coin. Therefore, not only do market structure and the market price mechanism have little relevance in the real world market, but also both stability (induced by control) and instability (induced by competition) present themselves as a consequence of strategic activities undertaken by the business enterprise. The conventional market structure-competition theory in this respect obscures and legitimizes the appropriation of profits by dominant class agency in the capitalist social provisioning process (see Lee 1998, 2011c, 2012a, 2013a, 2013c; and also Melmiès' chapter in this book).

The regulated competition thesis derived from the social provisioning perspective implies that there is no competitive equilibrium in the historical process. History is replete with examples of competition and control taking place either simultaneously or consequently. This is one of the arguments addressed by Bruno Tinel in his chapter. Through the writings of Norbert Elias, a German sociologist who is not well known to heterodox economists, Tinel argues that the formation of the modern state even before the emergence of capitalism shows that bellicose competition led to the monopolization of power (that is, military force and taxing authority), which was maintained by the control of 'pacific' competition in the name of 'democracy.' Thus the state under capitalism or feudalism has always been embedded in the process of social provisioning. If this is the case, a model of the economy without the state is either misleading or deficient (Lee 2011a, 2011b).

Even though the state is included in the account of the economy as a whole, its role is often misguided by creating a false analogy that the state is a household (especially in the mainstream analysis of economic policies in the name of 'sound finance'). As Huáscar Pessali, Fabiano Dalto, and Ramón Fernández argue in their chapter, if fiscal policy is framed in the state-as-household analogy it legitimizes fiscal austerity and a scaled-back welfare system as we have observed in many economies across the world. The social provisioning process perspective coupled with the surplus approach and the theory of effective demand eradicates such false reasoning. In his model of the economy as a whole, Lee demonstrates that the state's deficit expenditures help generate private business enterprises' profits by way of creating a demand for government goods and services—that is, "the more the state spends, the more profits (given tax rates) the capitalist class receives" (Lee 2011b, 1296). Thus the causation runs from spending to revenue (taxes and profits), rather than the reverse. What this implies is that it is not the lack of resources but the lack of effective demand by the ruling class (both the capitalist class and the state) that hinders the development of the provisioning process.

How is the structural dynamics of the social provisioning process explained? Henning Schwardt in his chapter provides a broader framework in which technology and institutions developed and maintained by acting agents play an integral part in the historical changes in the social provisioning process. He, in particular, singles out five development effects—Smithian, Veblenian, Schumpeterian, Arrovian, and Solovian effects—that interact with each other and, hence, form a development path a provisioning process can take. A path is determined in a circular and cumulative manner; and also it is open-ended since a particular path is determined by agency embedded in historically formed institutions. Therefore, Schwardt's chapter shows a way to advance heterodox theory concerning the dynamics of the social provisioning process.

## Concluding remarks

In this introductory chapter we have striven to delineate Fred Lee's wide-ranging contributions to heterodox economics focusing on the making of the history and identity of heterodox economics, on heterodox microeconomic theory, and on the analysis of the social provisioning process.

What do these contributions mean for heterodox economics? Throughout his intellectual life Fred Lee has shown to many heterodox economists that the development of heterodox economics is made possible by unselfish and ceaseless efforts to build both theory and institutions. The opposite is also true. If heterodox economists stop making historically grounded theory, stop engaging with each other and with other heterodox traditions, stop participating in scholarly activities, stop teaching heterodox theories to their students, there will be no future for heterodox economics—that is, "Death by Failure of the Will to Live" (Lee 1995, 2).

Essays collected in this festschrift for Fred Lee are on the optimistic side. Indeed, the objective of this volume is to demonstrate that heterodox economics has transcended the criticism of mainstream economics and, more importantly, that constructive developments are in the making by way of cross-communications among various heterodox approaches.

The community of heterodox economists has lost Fred Lee, one of its fervent leaders, who has been at the center of the heterodox movement for the past three decades. He, however, has left us his theories, institutions, and goodwill that will continue developing in the work of economists who are concerned with establishing an alternative critical theory to the status quo.

# Notes

1 Fred Lee attended all the workshops except one in 2007. His presentations were mainly on the grounded theory approach: "Grounded Theory and the Empirical Opportunities for PhDs in Economics Today" (2001), "Grounded Theory and Economic Research" (2002), "Grounded Theory in Heterodox Research: Pricing Theory" (2004 and 2005), "Grounding Theory in Historical Evidence" (2009), and "Critical Realism, Method of Grounded Theory and their Applications to the UK Research Assessment Exercise" (2014). Fred Lee's critical realist grounded theory approach is the ontological and methodological basis of his heterodox theory. Trained in history before he got interested in economics, he emphasized that any historical analysis ought to be theoretical, and that any theory ought to be historically grounded. He also wanted to see heterodox economists engaging in various research methods, both quantitative and qualitative methods. For his methodological standpoint, see Lee (2002, 2005, 2012b, 2015a, 2015b).

2 Before 2000s 'heterodox economics' was mainly used by institutionalists in a narrower sense (for example, Ayres 1936; Dorfman 1970; see Lee 2009, 189–190, for other references).

3 Association for Evolutionary Economics, Association for Institutional Thought, Association for Social Economics, European Association for Evolutionary Political Economy, International Association for Feminist Economics, and Union for Radical Political Economics, respectively.

4 http://heterodoxnews.com/hed/works.

5 Not until I [Jo] took over the *Newsletter* in 2010 did I realize that a single issue required about two hours of work every day. Heterodox economists highly appreciate such a service to the community of heterodox economists.

6 In his response to Andrew Mearman and Bruce Philp's question on the history of AHE, Fred Lee says that

> If you think I really liked devoting the last 15–20 years working on ranking journals and departments and on the RAE, you got to be kidding. I would have rather worked on developing heterodox microeconomic theory. I put my own research aside and did research that benefited others—others can do the same.
>
> (Jo's personal record dated July 24, 2014)

7 Like other early Post Keynesians trained in the 1970s and 1980s, Lee had never agreed to the separation of Sraffian economics from Post Keynesian economics, although he was theoretically critical of the Sraffian concept of the long-period position and the convergence to this position.

8 In his Preface to the unfinished manuscript, *Microeconomic Theory: A Heterodox Approach*, Lee notes that

> the microeconomic theory presented in the following pages is incomplete because the possible contributions of ecological, feminist, and social economics as well as other heterodox approaches are largely absent and because not all subject areas are covered, most notably distribution of income and workplace control. Their absence in the book is not due to unimportance on their part, but to recognition by me that my grandiose project is indeed too grandiose for me to complete.

9 If Lee had enough time, he might have moved onto such issues as financialization as it pertains to enterprises' investment-financing behavior. This is hinted at in a personal conversation with Ruslan Dzarasov and John King. See their chapters in this volume.

10 Also note that in 2000 Fred Lee made a contract with Routledge to write a book on *Post Keynesian Microeconomic Theory*. Later he changed the title to *Microeconomic Theory: A Heterodox Approach*.

11 As President-Elect of the Association for Evolutionary Economics, Fred Lee organized the 2015 AFEE-ASSA program with the theme of "Theorizing of the Social Provisioning Process under Capitalism." An interesting and important question raised by Lee in this call for papers is

> Can institutional economics look beyond the ideas of Keynes, Kalecki, Sraffa, and Marx edifice and engage with other 'institutionalist' traditions such as the related research programs of the Social Structure of Accumulation, Social Ecological Economics, French Régulation and French Convention schools?

This implies that Lee was envisioning a broader heterodox economics community in which various heterodox traditions work together. To this end, Lee also organized several joint sessions among heterodox associations—that is, AFEE-URPE, AFEE-ASE, and AFEE-IAFFE.

12 In a personal conversation between Lee and Todorova (July 27, 2014), Lee notes that "in a sense neoclassical economics got right that the end of economic inquiry is consumption." That is to say, if social provisioning is the object of study in heterodox economics, consumption and provisioning for human needs should be fully analyzed in the context of the social provisioning process.

## References

Association for Heterodox Economics. 1999. "Constitution." Accessed February 12, 2015. http://hetecon.net/division.php?page=about&side=constitution.

Ayres, C. E. 1936. "Fifty Years' Development in Ideas of Human Nature and Motivation." *American Economic Review* 26 (1): 224–236.

Dorfman, J. 1970. "Heterodox Economic Thinking and Public Policy." *Journal of Economic Issues* 4 (1): 1–22.

Eichner, A. S. 1976. *The Megacorp and Oligopoly: Micro Foundations of Macro Dynamics*. Cambridge: Cambridge University Press.

Gruchy, A. G. 1987. *The Reconstruction of Economics: An Analysis of the Fundamentals of Institutional Economics*. New York: Greenwood Press.

Harley, S. and F. S. Lee. 1996. "Research Selectivity, Managerialism, and the Academic Labor Process: The Future of Nonmainstream Economics in U.K. Universities." *Human Relations* 50 (11): 1427–1460.

Henry, J. F. and F. S. Lee. 2009. "John Davis and the Recent Turn in Economics." Paper presented at the Association for Institutional Thought Annual Conference. Albuquerque, NM.

Jo, T.-H., ed. 2013. *Heterodox Economics Directory*, 5th ed. Buffalo, NY: Heterodox Economics Newsletter.

Jo, T.-H. and F. S. Lee. 2015. "Marx, Veblen, and Henry." In *Marx, Veblen, and the Foundations of Heterodox Economics: Essays in Honor of John F. Henry*, edited by T.-H. Jo and F. S. Lee. London: Routledge.

Lavoie, M. 2014. *Post-Keynesian Economics: New Foundations*. Cheltenham and Northampton: Edward Elgar.

Lee, F. S. 1984. "Full Cost Pricing: A New Wine in a New Bottle." *Australian Economic Papers* 23 (42): 151–166.

Lee, F. S. 1985. "Full Cost Prices, Classical Price Theory, and Long Period Method Analysis: A Critical Evaluation." *Metroeconomica* 37: 199–219.

Lee, F. S., ed. 1991. *Tributes in Memory of Alfred S. Eichner*. Leicester, UK: Leicester Polytechnic. Accessed February 12, 2015. http://heterodox-economics.org/archive/eichner/1991-eichner-tributes.pdf.

Lee, F. S. 1994. "From Post Keynesian to Historical Price Theory, Part 1: Facts, Theory and Empirically Grounded Pricing Model." *Review of Political Economy* 6 (3): 303–336.

Lee, F. S. 1995. "The Death of Post Keynesian Economics?" *PKSG Newsletter* 1 (January): 1–2. Accessed February 22, 2015. http://postkeynesian.net/downloads/PKS-GNews1.pdf.

Lee, F. S. 1996a. "Pricing and the Business Enterprise." In *Political Economy for the 21st Century: Contemporary Views on the Trend of Economics*, edited by C. J. Whalen, 87–102. Armonk, NY: M. E. Sharpe.

Lee, F. S. 1996b. "Pricing, the Pricing Model and Post-Keynesian Price Theory." *Review of Political Economy* 8 (1): 87–99.

Lee, F. S. 1997. "Philanthropic Foundations and the Rehabilitation of Big Business, 1934–1977: A Case Study of Directed Economic Research." *Research in the History of Economic Thought and Methodology* 15: 51–90.

Lee, F. S. 1998. *Post Keynesian Price Theory*. Cambridge: Cambridge University Press.

Lee, F. S. 1999. "Market Governance in the American Gunpowder Industry, 1865–1880." Unpublished working paper.

Lee, F. S. 2002. "Theory Creation and the Methodological Foundation of Post Keynesian Economics." *Cambridge Journal of Economics* 26 (6): 789–804.

Lee, F. S. 2005. "Grounded Theory and Heterodox Economics." *Grounded Theory Review* 4 (2): 95–116.

Lee, F. S. 2006. "The Ranking Game, Class and Scholarship in American Mainstream Economics." *Australasian Journal of Economics Education* 3 (1&2): 1–41.

Lee, F. S. 2007. "Research Assessment Exercise, the State, and the Dominance of Mainstream Economics in British Universities." *Cambridge Journal of Economics* 31 (2): 309–325.

Lee, F. S. 2008a. "A Case for Ranking Heterodox Journals and Departments." *On the Horizon* 16 (4): 241–251.

Lee, F. S. 2008b. "A Note on the Pluralism Debate in Heterodox Economics." Unpublished working paper.

Lee, F. S. 2009. *A History of Heterodox Economics: Challenging the Mainstream in the Twentieth Century*. London: Routledge.

Lee, F. S. 2010. "Alfred Eichner's Missing 'Complete Model': A Heterodox Micro-Macro Model of a Monetary Production Economy." In *Money and Macrodynamics: Alfred Eichner and Post-Keynesian economics*, edited by M. Lavoie, L.-P. Rochon, and M. Seccareccia, 22–42. Armonk, NY: M. E. Sharpe.

Lee, F. S. 2011a. "Heterodox Microeconomics and the Foundation of Heterodox Macroeconomics." *Economia Informa* 367: 6–20.

Lee, F. S. 2011b. "Modeling the Economy as a Whole: An Integrative Approach." *American Journal of Economics and Sociology* 70 (5): 1282–1314.

Lee, F. S. 2011c. "Old Controversy Revisited: Pricing, Market Structure, and Competition." MPRA Working Paper 30490. Accessed February 12, 2015. http://mpra.ub.uni-muenchen.de/30490/.

Lee, F. S. 2012a. "Competition, Going Enterprise, and Economic Activity." In *Alternative Theories of Competition: Challenges to the Orthodoxy*, edited by J. K. Moudud, C. Bina, and P. L. Mason, 160–173. London: Routledge.

Lee, F. S. 2012b. "Critical Realism, Grounded Theory, and Theory Construction in Heterodox Economics." MPRA Working Paper 40341. Accessed February 12, 2015. http://mpra.ub.uni-muenchen.de/40341.

Lee, F. S. 2012c. "Heterodox Surplus Approach: Production, Prices, and Value Theory." *Bulletin of Political Economy* 6 (2): 65–105.

Lee, F. S. 2013a. "Heterodox Approach to Cartels and Market Competition." Paper presented at the Allied Social Science Associations Annual Meetings, San Diego, CA.

Lee, F. S. 2013b. "Heterodox Economics and its Critics." In *In Defense of Post-Keynesian and Heterodox Economics*, edited by F. S. Lee and M. Lavoie, 104–132. London: Routledge.

Lee, F. S. 2013c. "Post-Keynesian Price Theory: From Pricing to Market Governance to the Economy as a Whole." In *The Oxford Handbook of Post-Keynesian Economics, Vol. I: Theory and Origins*, edited by G. C. Harcourt and P. Kriesler, 467–484. Oxford: Oxford University Press.

Lee, F. S. 2013d. "Review of John E. King, 2012, *The Microfoundations Delusion: Metaphor and Dogma in the History of Macroeconomics*." *Economic and Labour Relations Review* 24 (2): 255–260.

Lee, F. S. 2014a. "Heterodox Theory of Production and the Mythology of Capital: A Critical Inquiry into the Circuit of Production." Unpublished working paper.

Lee, F. S. 2014b. *Microeconomic Theory: A Heterodox Approach*. Unpublished manuscript.

Lee, F. S. 2015a. "Critical Realism, Method of Grounded Theory, and Theory Construction." In *Handbook of Research Methods and Applications in Heterodox Economics*, edited by F. S. Lee and B. C. Cronin. Cheltenham: Edward Elgar.

Lee, F. S. 2015b. "Modeling as a Research Method in Heterodox Economics." In *Handbook of Research Methods and Applications in Heterodox Economics*, edited by F. S. Lee and B. C. Cronin. Cheltenham: Edward Elgar.

Lee, F. S. and J. Bekken. 2009. "Introduction: Radical Economics and the Labor Movement." In *Radical Economics and Labor: Essays Inspired by the IWW Centennial*, edited by F. S. Lee and J. Bekken. London: Routledge.

Lee, F. S. and B. C. Cronin. 2010. "Research Quality Rankings of Heterodox Economic Journals in a Contested Discipline." *American Journal of Economics and Sociology* 69 (5): 1409–1452.

Lee, F. S., T. C. Grijalva, and C. Nowell. 2010. "Ranking Economics Departments in a Contested Discipline: A Bibliometric Approach to Quality Equality Between Theoretically Distinct Subdisciplines." *American Journal of Economics and Sociology* 69 (5): 1345–1375.

Lee, F. S. and S. Harley. 1998. "Peer Review, the Research Assessment Exercise and the Demise of Non-Mainstream Economics." *Capital and Class* 22 (66): 23–51.

Lee, F. S. and T.-H. Jo. 2010. "Heterodox Production and Cost Theory of the Business Enterprise." MPRA working paper 27635. Accessed February 12, 2015. http://mpra.ub.uni-muenchen.de/27635.

Lee, F. S. and T.-H. Jo. 2011. "Social Surplus Approach and Heterodox Economics." *Journal of Economic Issues* 45 (4): 857–875.

Lee, F. S. and T.-H. Jo. 2013. "Post Keynesian Macroeconomics and Microfoundations Debate: A Suggested Resolution." Paper presented at the Association for Heterodox Economics Annual Conference, London, UK.

Lee, F. S., X. Pham, and G. Gu. 2013. "The UK Research Assessment Exercise and the Narrowing of UK Economics." *Cambridge Journal of Economics* 37 (4): 693–717.

Wood, A. 1975. *A Theory of Profits*. Cambridge: Cambridge University Press.

# Part I

# Making history and identity of heterodox economics by developing theory and institutions

# 1 Heterodox economics and the history of economic thought

*Carlo D'Ippoliti and Alessandro Roncaglia*

> This is probably all one can ask of history, and of the history of ideas in particular: not to resolve issues, but to raise the level of the debate.
>
> (Hirschman 1977, 135)

The declining role of the history of economic thought (HET) in university research and teaching has been increasingly under debate. Many historians often recall the relationship between HET and heterodox economics (HEC), considering it as a strength of HET and/or one of the reasons for its damnation among mainstream economists. In this contribution we reconsider the reasons for such connection focusing on the converse and less debated side of the issue—that is, the role of HET for and within HEC.

Such a topic seems a fitting theme for a tribute to Frederic Lee, who shares with us both heterodoxy and an active interest in HET. He even combined these elements in his research on the history of heterodox streams of economics (see Lee 2009). It is also a way of recalling the first meeting of both authors with Fred: with Alessandro Roncaglia, the lecture hall of a course in HET in the Fall semester 1978, when Alessandro was a visiting professor at Rutgers University and Fred was a research student; and with Carlo D'Ippoliti, at a conference on the impact of journal and department rankings on heterodox economics, organized by Fred and Wolfram Elsner at the University of Bremen.

In the following section we consider the main reasons that HET and HEC are often practiced together. We then proceed to delineate why, in our view, they should mutually reinforce each other, by briefly reviewing the debate on the existence of different streams of heterodox economics. We suggest in this section that the history of economic thought can play a crucial role in precisely defining a program of research and thus in defining the scope and limits of heterodox economics. In what follows we highlight our own perspective on how HET should play such a role, by shortly recalling the paradigmatic contrast in price and value theory between the marginalist and the Classical-Keynesian approaches. Our 'mundane' conclusions will instead recall a number of more 'tactical' reasons for forging pluralist alliances between historians of economic thought and heterodox economists.

## A longstanding liaison: history of economic thought and heterodox economics

The close connection between heterodox economics and the history of economic thought is a literary *topos* among scholars in the latter field. For example, Blaug (2001) claims that there are two types of like-minded economists: those origin-ally attracted by the mathematical mastery of social phenomena, and those inclined to philosophical research on these phenomena. In his view heterodox economists and historians of economics share the latter approach. They thus work on similar topics, meet each other at the conferences, and often happen to be the same people. Weintraub (2002b) adds that

> the traditions of heterodox economics utilize historical argumentation in ways quite different from the practices of neoclassical economists ... in the way that game theorists would not appeal to a point of interpretation in *The Theory of Games and Economic Behavior* in order to assess the merits of a particular form of an auction.
>
> (8)

At the same time, he notes, the history of economics community has been a "big tent" and even a "welcoming tent" for heterodox economists (Weintraub 2002b, 8). But while the expedience and relevance for HET to include heterodox per-spectives has been frequently discussed (including in the essays contained in Weintraub 2002a), the importance of HET for heterodox economics has mostly been taken for granted, often without adequate reflection. In fact, in the passage quoted above Weintraub might be read as suggesting that heterodox economists make use of HET in order to "appeal to authority," while orthodox economists are content with theoretical argumentations. This would involve a subtle sugges-tion that heterodox economists cannot find sufficient support in open scientific confrontation. It hardly needs reminding that such interpretation would be gratu-itous—suffice here to recall the theoretical import of the Sraffian critiques to Marshallian U-shaped cost curves, which are notwithstanding still utilized by mainstream economists in many applied fields, or the results of the Cambridge-Cambridge debates of the 1960s–1970s on capital theory, whose results should have implied the abandonment of most of mainstream (one-commodity) macroeconomics.

Indeed, it is undeniable that some scholars—both mainstream but more often heterodox—make direct or indirect use of the principle of authority on rhetorical grounds (even if, of course, such an approach cannot be recognized as a decisive scientific argument). Thus, for instance it is commonplace to recall the historical analyses and discussions by several founders or pioneers of various heterodox schools of economics, from Thorstein Veblen to Piero Sraffa and back to Karl Marx, encompassing John Maynard Keynes as well as Joseph Schumpeter.[1] These economists who significantly departed from the mainstream of their contemporar-ies felt compelled—probably because of their 'heresy'—to trace a heritage line of their ideas with some prior tradition or great thinker. In turn, they have then inspired fellows and followers to engage an economic argument historically and often to actively work in the history of thought.

However, several historians—not only mainstream ones—have complained that this tendency appears to be related to a 'whiggish' approach to HET. One could say that as much as for mainstream-inclined historians of economics the risk is to see the history of the discipline as a smooth process of error removal, for heterodox-friendly ones the risk is to only see the past as a goldmine of promising untaken roads. These sources of bias may in some cases even produce misrepresentation and/or misinterpretation of economic ideas. Marcuzzo and Rosselli (2002) aptly characterize these approaches to HET respectively as the "quest for ascendancy" vs. the "quest for alternative." Thus, narrating whiggish histories is not a heterodox-specific risk, and scientific practices such as good faith interpretation of the texts and proper textual exegesis enable doing history with an eye to the present without necessarily producing a bias, thus enabling good history and good economics.

However, such a larger role of historical argumentation within heterodoxy is not an unintended byproduct of the interests and needs of its founding fathers. Without accepting the appeal to authority as a ground for accepting or rejecting an economic argument, there are several reasons why heterodox economists develop an interest in or actively practice HET, and some such reasons show that they very appropriately do so. In the rest of this section we discuss the (descriptive) reasons for what we think they *do*, while in the following sections we set out our argument on why they *should* engage with HET.

A crucial explanation for the larger appeal of HET among heterodox economists rests, as it is well known, in the respective methods and contents of mainstream and heterodox economics. Mainstream economics, at least since the post-World War II period, has become almost exclusively interested in mathematical formalization and econometric estimation of evermore specific and narrow models.[2] Heterodox economics still regards history as a useful tool of analysis, rather than a specialist object of investigation. Some heterodox schools, by denying that a single all-encompassing mathematical model can explain everything that we are interested in (e.g., because they reject 'long causal chains' as Keynes did, or because they refuse mathematics altogether), necessarily require a comparison and integration of several pieces of theory as the only way to discuss economics and economic policy. For example, Dow (2002) considers the case of Post Keynesian economics. As she underlines, Post Keynesians, like other economists who believe the economy is best thought of as an open non-ergodic system, are bound to think that, to use Sylos Labini's (2005) term, economic theory is "historically conditioned." As social systems evolve, the appropriate theory to represent a certain phenomenon must evolve too. Therefore, plurality in methods including HET must be a deliberate choice. But for Post Keynesians and other heterodox economists who seriously consider the pervasiveness of uncertainty the reason is more specific. Uncertainty, as different from probabilistic risk, renders the tools of equilibrium analysis of little practical relevance, and conversely makes the recourse to history useful. This applies not only to economic history, but to the history of economics too:

> history of thought plays a constructive part by informing modern econo-mists of the choice of methods and theories made by their forebears in dif-ferent circumstances. The wider the knowledge of other contexts, the greater the capacity to develop the art of choosing methods and theories appropriate to the problem at hand.
>
> (Dow 2002, 330)

There are also sociological reasons for the longstanding liaison between HET and HEC. The strongest is possibly the academic marginalization and even the risk of survival suffered by the economists who practice any of the two fields. As Fred Lee documented for the cases of the USA and the UK (Lee 2009; Elsner and Lee 2010; Lee, Grijalva, and Nowell 2010; Lee, Cronin, *et al.* 2010; Lee, Pham and Gu 2013), the institutional pressures towards the eradication of every sort of economics deviating from mainstream model building or econometric estimation have considerably grown in the past decades. HEC and HET both suffer from the use of research assessment exercises and monodimensional rank-ings as 'theoretical police' devices. We have documented a similar, if not cruder, trend in Italy (see Pasinetti and Roncaglia 2006; Corsi *et al.* 2010), and the same has been done in Australia, France, and elsewhere, through such enforcement instruments as biased bibliometric-based research evaluation,[3] journal and uni-versity rankings, funding bodies policies, and even the attempt to place certain fields of inquiry out of the official classification of what constitutes 'economics' at all (Kates 2013).

A second sociological reason is the aim, especially strong among heterodox economists, to clarify the origins and foundations of a certain line of thought and sharpen the 'identity' of a certain school or approach. Indeed, this reason may underlie a minimum degree of interests for HET even among mainstream econo-mists. Gordon, Viner, and Schumpeter among others used to claim that any eco-nomist stands to profit from a certain knowledge of the past of its discipline, especially of what, following Schumpeter (1954), we may define the history of economic analysis. Not because, in their view, theories of some dead economists are still fecund today but, especially for students and younger scholars, to use Schumpeter's words, "in order to prevent a sense of *lacking direction and meaning*" (Schumpeter 1954, 4, italics in original). As we already noted for the pioneers of heterodox approaches, a sense of the 'big picture' is even more necessary for those who do not wish to follow the mainstream. In the current hostile environment it may indeed prove useful, again especially for students and younger scholars, for the psychological advantages of referring to a community identity.

Finally, it is worth mentioning a further trend. With the 2007–2008 economic crisis and the ensuing European crisis, a certain interest for the economic debate has grown in the public discourse, and this may have encouraged a stronger

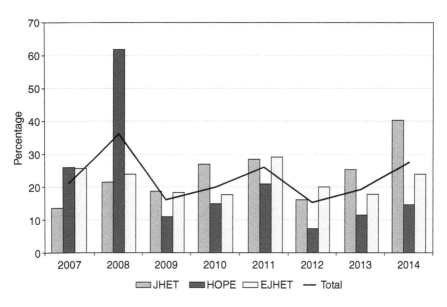

*Figure 1.1* Heterodox-related entries in the top three history of economic thought (HET) journals.

Note
Authors' calculation. Numbers are percents of HEC-related entries out of the total number of articles published in each journal. The journals included are *European Journal of the History of Economic Thought* (EJHET), *History of Political Economy* (HOPE), and *Journal of the History of Economic Thought* (JHET). Journal entries include research papers, replies, and book reviews.

emphasis on the analytical and predictive failures of mainstream economics, to be discussed both from a historical and a heterodox perspective (see, for instance, Roncaglia 2010; D'Ippoliti, 2011a; the debate still goes on by courtesy of the ongoing European crisis). However, a first look at rough bibliometric data does not seem to signal this debate as a reinforcement mechanism of the links between HET and HEC. For example, when considering the share of heterodox papers in the top three HET journals, no increasing trend emerges in the years since the crisis erupted (see Figure 1.1). Thus, the crisis does not seem to operate as an exogenous source of further integration between HET and HEC.

However, independently of considerations that belong to the sociology of the profession, we wish to highlight a major *theoretical* ground for the happy marriage of HET and HEC, whereby heterodox economists stand to profit from HET comparatively more than mainstream economists do. This ground is the instrumental use of HET in clarifying the conceptual foundations of different economic theories. However, to clarify this point it is necessary to briefly discuss some aspects of the debate on the definition of heterodox economics and its relation to the mainstream.

## The heterodox field is not a monolith

The previous discussion assumed a sufficiently clear (even if not rigidly defined) and a unanimously agreed idea of what heterodox economics is and where its borders are. So far, even after a few decades of debate, opinions are still divided on the subject (see Lee 2012; Elsner 2013). As we will show in this and the following sections, discussions and analyses in the history of economic thought may help define precisely what a certain author means by mainstream or heterodox economics, how they define both and their boundaries, and hence their relative standing.

Some non-mainstream economists, as diverse as Deirdre McCloskey, Robert Prasch, and Jan Kregel, prefer avoiding the term 'heterodox' altogether. In turn, many heterodox economists react by questioning how 'truly' these authors belong to the heterodox field. In our view, it is pointless to vet 'candidates' to a supposedly pure belief. Moreover, it cannot be doubted that several authors who cannot be labeled as mainstream consider it counter-productive to use a name that signals a minority status and possibly a lack of unity apart from the refusal of the mainstream. Such objection indubitably has some merits at least on the rhetorical and strategic ground that is irrespective of the truth of these accusations. Concerning the latter, it must also be noted that many economists, both sympathetic to heterodox approaches and not, denounce the political, theoretical, and methodological divisions between several heterodox schools and approaches.

Indeed, some heterodox economists consider several heterodox approaches as 'special cases' of their own, supposedly more general (e.g., Davidson 2004). Others consider only a few approaches among those often enlisted as 'heterodox' to be correct, the other approaches being as wrong as mainstream economics is (as it turns out, we might be included in this category, as discussed below). As Dobusch and Kapeller (2012) point out, bibliometric and citation patterns show how divided is the heterodox community in the scientific debate, with heterodox schools not "talking to each other" very much. According to their data, the typical engagement with extant literature by a typical heterodox economist is (in order of frequency): (1) cite your school, or yourself; (2) cite the mainstream, presumably to criticize it; and (3) only occasionally, cite other heterodox schools.

For these and other reasons, several economists consider 'heterodox economics' as a residual term: a collection of disparate, disconnected schools that only may be united by the common opposition to the economic mainstream. However, even such a definition of heterodox economics is imprecise, since different strands of heterodox economics criticize different aspects of mainstream economics and, most importantly, often some heterodox economists disagree with the criticisms of the mainstream raised by some other heterodox economists. For example, especially since the financial crisis erupted, some economists focus on the political/ideological role of mainstream economics in support of neo-liberal policies (we ourselves share this opinion: see the abovementioned

Roncaglia 2010 and D'Ippoliti 2011a). Against this claim, for example, Lawson (2013) strongly denies that mainstream economics serves any such political role, or that in any case this should be taken as its distinctive feature, because in his view "far from being a conspiracy or a uniformly misled project, mainstream economics lacks agreement even as to the project's purpose or direction" (10). On this point, while we recognize that mainstream economics often plays an important ideological role in support of very conservative political stances, we agree that it is not the political implications that should be the prime object of criticism, because these implications rather descend from erroneous theoretical premises.[4]

However, to highlight how heterodox economists disagree even in their criticisms of the mainstream, it may be worthwhile recalling that the same Lawson (2003) singles out the refusal of mathematics and of closed systems as, in his view, the necessary distinctive feature of heterodox economics and its prime critique against the mainstream. Evidently, this stance must be rejected by several other heterodox economists who would otherwise be relabeled as mainstream due to their adoption of closed systems and/or mathematical tools (e.g., some Sraffians and Post Keynesians). In our view Lawson's position confounds here the analytical tools with the use they are put to. In a sense, rejecting mathematics is equivalent to rejecting logic. A formal model that might be considered to represent a 'closed system' may in fact be part of an open one, when we carefully consider the assumptions on which it relies (e.g., see the fourth section and Roncaglia 2009, for the case of Sraffa's analysis of prices of production).

In the face of this confusion and, especially, of attacks on heterodox economics, as is well known to most heterodox economists of our time, Fred Lee has been very active in defending and building the community of heterodox economics, and in developing heterodox economic theory. He produced a very interesting work, *A History of Heterodox Economics* (2009), which focuses on American and British heterodox economics in the twentieth century. Fred's argument mostly deals with the institutional and sociological aspects of the profession—academic journals, associations, and departments that historically constituted avenues for exchange and gathering of economic dissenters—what Schumpeter (1954) referred to as a "history of economic thought" rather than a "history of economic analysis" (which mainly concerns the contents of economic theories). To use Fred's words, the importance of a "community study" (Lee 2009, 19) should not be overlooked: "what constitutes scientific knowledge has both a subjective and a 'community approval' component" (11, original emphasis). Thus, by demonstrating the past and current openness to mutual engagement in terms of professional, social, and scientific activities, Fred is able to show that even if its theoretical corpus is not yet finally defined heterodox economic theory as a shared body of knowledge already exists. Thence his tireless efforts to create and develop places and occasions for cross-approach engagements among heterodox economists of different orientations, efforts of which many of us bear testimony.

Moving from the sociological to the analytical level, Fred has developed and defended a definition of heterodox economics along the following lines:

> heterodox economics is a historical science of the social provisioning process.... The heterodox explanation involves human agency embedded in cultural context and social processes in historical time affecting resources, consumption patterns, production and reproduction, and the meaning (or ideology) of the market, state and non-market/state activities engaged in social provisioning.
>
> (Lee 2012, 340)

Indeed, if one was to delimit heterodox economics on the basis of this statement only (undoubtedly no definition can be self-contained and exhaustive, but we are playing the devil's advocate here), such a definition may appear, depending on the interpretation of the several concepts contained therein, either as very narrow or very wide. That is, it runs a concrete risk of encompassing too much, including the whole or part of mainstream economics. For example, Fred's view that "heterodox economics involves agency embedded in cultural context and social processes" is obviously meant to imply a criticism of methodological individualism and of the *homo oeconomicus* construction. However, as Hodgson (2011) notices, if mainstream economics is to be applied to the real world, it must not be interpreted as assuming a society composed of several atomistic and perfectly disconnected individuals, a situation that would be in fact impossible. Rather, the whole social structure that underlies individual behavior must be understood as contained in the explicit or implicit *coeteris paribus* clause of the *homo oeconomicus* model.[5] Thus, the real criticism of mainstream economics is not *if* it considers at all the influence of factors other than price movements on individual behavior, but rather if it does so *appropriately*. The problem with *homo oeconomicus* is not that it is not a conceptualization of "agency embedded in cultural context and social processes" (Lee 2012, 340), but rather that it is a wrong, misleading, and unsatisfactory conceptualization.

The same reasoning goes for the rest of the above definition. If we interpret all or most of the concepts therein in their wider sense, that is independently of extant literature or of the history of such concepts and analyses, Fred's definition does not appear to us to properly delimit heterodox economics from mainstream economics. Virtually, any open minded economist, be she mainstream or heterodox, may agree that Fred's definition reflects what she does. Thus, the importance of studying the development, meaning, and uses of a concept within certain communities of scientists—precisely the job the history of ideas does. Specifically, by 'precise' versus 'wider' sense of the terms involved we first mean the basic need to be precise in scientific terminology. For example, an economist should never talk of 'demand' for a commodity unless the meaning of the word is obvious from the context, because such a term may puzzlingly mean either the quantity demanded or the demand function. However, perhaps more significantly, concepts too may be employed in different, often conflicting ways. Thus, in our example it is obvious that when comparing, say, the complex conceptualization of human behavior adopted by J. S. Mill with the subjective utility theory à la Jevons, Fred's reference to "human agency embedded in cultural context and social processes" is obviously meant to include the former but not the latter. But such distinction can only be drawn after a thorough historical reconstruction of the two authors' conceptualizations of individual behavior.[6]

More to our point here, when applied to the conceptual foundations of an economic paradigm, the historical analysis of these foundational concepts serves to clarify a research program, such as 'mainstream economics,' and to distinguish it from other ones.

Thus, in the next section, we aim to show the relevance of the history of economics—especially the history of economic analysis, in Schumpeter's terms—in allowing us to better clarify the relation of heterodox schools to each other and vis-à-vis mainstream economics. To articulate our position, it is useful to turn to a second, narrower definition of the boundaries of mainstream vs. heterodox economics put forward by Lee (2009), this time with reference to economic theory. When considering economic analysis, Fred points out that the refusal of neoclassical price theory and its "core propositions, such as scarcity, preferences and utility functions, technology and production functions, rationality, equilibrium, methodological individualism, and positivist and deductivist methodology" is a defining characteristic of heterodox economics (7). In what follows we thus set out to explain why we agree with this second, more restrictive definition of heterodox economics, focusing on the centrality of price and value theory. In other words, we set out to explain why it is best to make reference to a definition of heterodox *economic analysis* (and we agree with Fred's) rather than a definition of the *field* of heterodox economics.

## The role of conceptualization in economic analysis

In chapter 4 of his *History of Economic Analysis*, Schumpeter (1954, 41–42) identifies distinct stages in economic research:

1   the "pre-analytic cognitive act" or "vision"—that is, a vague vision of the issue to be considered and some tentative hypotheses as to the direction of research;
2   conceptualization—that is, "to verbalize the vision or to conceptualize it in such a way that its elements take their places, with names attached to them that facilitate recognition and manipulation, in a more or less orderly schema or picture";
3   model building; and, finally,
4   the application of such models to the interpretation of economic reality.

What matters to us here is the second stage, which is quite often overlooked, though Schumpeter himself attributes great importance to it. The fact is that model building and applied analysis do not exhaust the economists' task: as

Schumpeter recalled, the very first stage of economic theorizing consists in building a conceptual framework for the analysis; and in this HET is a decisive tool (as one of us argued at length elsewhere; see Roncaglia 2005, chapter 1; 2014).

Quite commonly, mainstream economists overlook the role of this stage in economic research. This is clearly due to the fact that the underlying vision and the conceptualization of the economy is common to all of them (though with different nuances) and is considered as the only possible one. Supply and demand reasoning reigns supreme; differences between streams of mainstream economics are a matter of the framework to which supply and demand analysis is applied—for instance, markets are different in terms of competition and information (e.g., perfect competition, imperfect competition, asymmetric information), but still the same supply-demand analysis is the rule. Thus, it is only these latter aspects that are considered, when reflecting on the conceptual foundations for the activity of model building.

On the other hand, there are profound differences in the visions of the economy underlying, for example, Classical, Keynesian, and neoclassical-marginalist economics. In order to understand them, recourse to HET is necessary: it is only when seeking through HET a direct understanding of the visions of the world of a Smith, a Ricardo, a Keynes, a Jevons, or a Walras that we can perceive these differences, and the true content of the different concepts referred to in formal analyses of the economy.

Conceptualization, thus, becomes an essential aspect of the economist's work when the vision that the researcher is trying to develop differs from the visions adopted/developed by other theoreticians—as it is the case for heterodox economists. It is in this stage of work that the theoretician can clarify the distinct character of her/his own representation of the world: not only the relative importance attributed to different aspects of the real world, but also and especially the perspective from which each aspect is viewed. Conceptualization is a complex activity, where for instance the requirement of consistency (which of course still holds) has a different, broader meaning as compared with the formal coherence required by mathematically framed theories; in any case, conceptualization represents the explicit or implicit foundation for clarifying the connection between such mathematically framed theories and the real world. For example, a formal model of functional income distribution relies on a class representation of society; the analysis of financial managers' incentives relies on the conceptualization of a managerial (or large corporate) economy, rather than an economy based on small competitive firms.

Underlying the mainstream view on the limited usefulness of HET is a clear (though usually not explicitly stated) assumption, namely that there is but one correct approach to economics. We may label this a 'cumulative view' in that economics does change over time, but with steady progress in the understanding of economic reality, piling up new theories and new facts. As mentioned above, the toolbox of an economic theorist may change (for instance, from Marshallian U-shaped cost curves to axiomatic Arrow–Debreu general equilibrium theory), but the underlying pillar—in short, the notion of market equilibrium between supply and demand—remains the same (see next section). From this viewpoint, the provisional point of arrival of contemporary economics incorporates all previous contributions in an improved way.

The methodological background (often implicit and occasionally unconscious) of the 'cumulative view' is a positivist view of science: economic theories based on deduction from first principles (scarcity of resources, agents' preferences, demand and supply equilibrium) are either logically consistent and hence true, or logically contradictory and hence false; factual statements are once again either empirically confirmed or contradicted. Science progresses as theories and knowledge of facts cumulate. This viewpoint has been supported by mainstream historians of economic thought (e.g., from Jacob Hollander [1904, 1910] to Samuel Hollander [1973, 1979]) through an interpretation of classical economists aligning them with the supply-and-demand-equilibrium view, so that they can be considered as perceptive but defective precursors of later views.

By contrast, heterodox economists commonly embrace a 'competitive view' of the development of economic ideas—that is, different paradigms coexist; some come to dominate for a period and then perish, others recurrently reappear; they are subject to a different conceptualization and an update to the spirit of the time. This explains for example the importance of Piero Sraffa's (1951) reinterpretation of Ricardo (and with him of the whole Classical economists' approach) as embedded in a different paradigm, which can be succinctly expressed as the "picture of the system of production and consumption as a circular process" (Sraffa 1960, 93). As a consequence, in the 1960s and 1970s the debate between the contending paradigms proceeded along two parallel paths: the "Cambridge controversies" in the theory of capital and distribution (as illustrated for instance in Harcourt 1972) and debates in the history of economic thought concerning, for instance, the role of supply and demand in the Classical (Smith's or Ricardo's in particular) theory of value and distribution. This historical stream of the controversy is not less important than that in capital theory and was not perceived to be so by most of those involved in both controversies at the time.

### The price system: the Classical and the marginalist conceptual frameworks

As mentioned earlier, we agree with Fred Lee on the centrality of price theory for economic *analysis*. As indicated above, price theory (or the theory of value) expresses in a nutshell the conceptualization of an economy. By price theory, of course, we mean here what both marginalist and Classical economists designated as the theory of value, once what most economists (including us) consider to be the metaphysical element—i.e., the quest for the 'nature' or the 'ultimate cause' of value—is left aside. Price theory is central in an economic paradigm because it embodies the vision and conceptualization of the working of the whole economy at its most abstract level. In previous work one of us has proposed the distinction of two paradigms in particular, in the field of price theory (see, especially, Roncaglia 2005).

On the one hand we have an archetypical idea of an economic region or nation, possibly divided between land and city, and with different productive activities taking place simultaneously in different places (e.g., in Cantillon's and Quesnay's analysis, the geographical city-land divide corresponds to the economic distinction between agriculture and industry), and different activities are carried out by different classes of people. This imprecise, rough vision may be said to underlie the conceptualization of the economy proper of Classical economists (and Sraffa). They posited an economy grounded on the division of labor, where the connection between the different sectors is provided by a necessary web of market exchanges, whereby each sector obtains the necessary means of production for continuing its activity in exchange for (at least part of) its own physical surplus product. Prices here must determine the distribution of the surplus in such a way that production activities can go on indefinitely.

This vision is alternative and in contrast to the other archetypical vision common to many economists: that of the medieval fair or, in modern times, the exchange. This idea corresponds to the conceptualization of the economy as the place in which all producers and all consumers simultaneously meet. Everyone arrives at the marketplace endowed with his or her resources, which s/he wishes to exchange for. Central to this vision are not production activities, but the acts of exchange. As a consequence, if the marketplace functions well, prices here must 'clear' the market—that is, they must ensure the equality between supply and demand and all resources must be fully utilized, so that the established equilibrium thus is considered as an optimal one.

Accordingly, we have two different visions of how the whole economy (should) works—that is, two ideas of 'equilibrium' in a general loose sense. On the one hand, we have the Classical representation of the economy as 'a circular flow of production and consumption,' where prices of production express the relative difficulty of production of the different commodities. In a society based on the division of labor and where the connection between different production activities is mediated through the market, each sector must continuously receive from the other sectors its means of production (and the means of consumption for its workers) giving in exchange its own products; the exchange ratios that allow for the continuance of production in all sectors imply that each sector obtains a rate of profits not inferior to that prevailing in other sectors.

On the other hand we have the marginalist representation of an economy as a 'one-way avenue,' where agents are motivated by maximization of their satisfaction and constrained by the amounts of available resources. In this case, prices are indexes of relative scarcity, mediating (and realizing an equilibrium) between the preferences of economic agents and the availability of resources.[7] As a consequence, the notion of equilibrium between supply and demand is central to the marginalist approach, while in the Classical approach equilibrium simply refers to the assumption of a uniform rate of profits prevailing in all sectors of the economy, and the reproduction of the economy can be obtained even under the assumption of a set of sectorial profit differentials (which is, for example, determined by the size of the barriers to entry into each sector, under oligopolistic conditions).

When economic agents are connected in such a way as to constitute an economic system (an interconnected whole), the mainstream notion of equilibrium between scarce resources and the agents' preferences is of necessity an all-embracing one. Thus, any economic issue must be tackled as a problem of equilibrium between supply and demand. Also, any 'partial' analysis (whereby a specific issue, such as the analysis of an individual market or the behavior of a single agent under given assumptions concerning preferences and constraints, is considered) is bound to be of limited validity, since all sorts of 'aggregation fallacies' may arise when such analyses are applied to the interpretation of the economy as an emergent whole.

On the contrary, the problem of value in the Classical tradition is tackled in such a way as to allow for separate consideration of other issues: technological choice and technological change, income distribution, levels of production and employment (with no necessity whatsoever for such levels to imply full utilization of resources and hence full employment), and so on. The analysis of such issues may involve abstract models specific to the issue at hand or historical-institutional analyses, with the possibility of separate use of the different analytical tools but leading to complementarity of the results obtained for the interpretation of the real-world economy.

The 'separation of issues' is a necessary aspect for the integration of Classical, Keynesian, institutional, and evolutionary approaches. Such integration should not take the form of the construction of an all-embracing model of the economy, but an openness to consider how the different viewpoints can be integrated in tackling specific issues. Thus, there are no general rules on how such an integration may be pursued (an illustration of how it took place in a variety of ways is provided by Lee (2009, 201); on the Classical-Keynesian integration, see Roncaglia and Tonveronachi (2014).

It should be clear, however, that the possibility of integration does not cover all kind of theories. In fact, as we hinted at, when accepting the distinction sketched here between the two competing visions and conceptualizations of the economy, it is the recourse to analysis based on supply-demand equilibrium which constitutes the boundary of non-inclusiveness. This points to a demarcation between 'fully' heterodox theories and 'apparent' heterodox theories relying on demand-supply equilibrium analysis and deviating from the mainstream only for the attempt to consider specific aspects of economic life previously neglected (such as bounded rationality, asymmetric information, increasing returns, but also institutions, the environment, uncertainty, non-ergodicity).[8]

These two very different visions and conceptualization of the whole economy, which necessarily lie (albeit implicitly) beneath any formal analysis, constitute in our view the crucial determinant in distinguishing mainstream economics from heterodox approaches. From what was said above, we hope it is clear that reference to price theory as the crucial milestone of economic analysis does not imply the centrality of the theory of exchange: in the Classical view price theory is a theory of *production and* exchange.

However, we are aware that by adopting this criterion we may in fact delimit the field of what is 'heterodox' in a different way from Fred Lee's (2009, 2012) definition of heterodox economics (not that of heterodox economic theory, though). For example, it is obvious that the Austrian reliance on marginalist price theory implies, in our understanding, its inclusion in the mainstream. More subtly, certain interpretations of Keynes's and some Post Keynesians' (such as Minsky) analysis may inappropriately place them in the mainstream field too. This is why it is so important to highlight that Keynes represented the demand for investments as dependent on the entrepreneurs' expectations, not on some demand function (Roncaglia 2005).

We do not wish, however, to convince every reader of the goodness of our proposed criterion, but rather to demonstrate how the history of economic thought is a major battlefield in which such discussion should take place. Clarifying the concepts of equilibrium, market, price, value, etc. is precisely the way in which one can study other authors' conceptualization of the economy, and perhaps even try to infer their pre-analytical vision. This is the most interesting job of HET, and precisely the history of economic analysis, for heterodox economists.

## Conclusions

Coming back to Fred Lee, we noted above his two definitions of heterodox economics. We discussed the second, more restrictive definition of heterodox economic analysis, noting that it may be less inclusive and pluralist than the definition of heterodox economics, shared by several heterodox associations and groups (Fred Lee himself has always been aware of this tension between the two definitions). In our proposal, we place the Austrian approach, many evolutionist models, most behavioral analyses, among others, outside the domain of heterodox economic analysis. However, if from the theoretical viewpoint this is in our view the inevitable price of coherence, there is another level at which occasions of academic alliances can and should be as broad and inclusive as possible. This is the 'tactical level,' that concerns the profession and role of economists in a world especially challenging many of them (including heterodox economists and historians of economic thought). As is well known, Fred Lee has been very active also on this front and thus it will suffice here to briefly recall the position of HET, by considering the recent experience of the Italian case.

The menace to a downgrading of HET both in teaching and research evaluation arises on two sides. First we have the hostility of mainstream economists towards a research field which stresses the existence of alternative approaches to economics: whether because these are considered irrelevant and/or overcome by most recent theorizing, or because they constitute a dangerous rival, especially after the financial crisis that showed how naked (and ugly) the Emperor of mainstream economics is, as heterodox economists would contend. Second, there is the preference on the side of some historians of economics with deservedly high repute in the profession for shifting economics out of the field of social sciences, into the field of the 'hard' sciences. In this situation, as Kates (2013) stresses, new attacks on HET are likely, and practitioners of this field must be prepared to resist.

One such new episode took place in Italy, when Anvur (the recently instituted national agency for the evaluation of research) adopted an undifferentiated bibliometric criterion for the assessment of research in the whole fields of economics, without considering the differences between subfields of research (in striking contrast to what for instance the physics panel had done, adopting a rigorous normalization between finely specified subfields). This gave a huge advantage to econometrics and a large one to applied macroeconomics compared to all other fields; the most disadvantaged subfield turned out to be the history of economic thought, with heterodox economics and general equilibrium theory following at a distance. This contradicts a basic principle of research assessment exercises that they should be neutral between research fields; but all protests (including those of SIE, the Italian Economists Association) were to no avail. In the Italian case, the usefulness or uselessness of HET was not at issue, at least not explicitly: other fields, such as general equilibrium theory or the study of the Italian fiscal system, were also damaged. An alliance between econometricians and mainstream macroeconomists discarded all attempts at argumentation over how research evaluation in the economics field should be conducted. If there is a teaching in this, it is that HET should look to other subfields of economics for alliances in support of a level playing field. All economists who do not feel or are not perceived to be mainstream (including those who do not fit our theoretical definition of heterodox) should come first in line.[9]

It is thus clear that research assessment exercises, rankings, and other biased 'merit-based' forms of research financing and personnel selection strongly impact both the kind of research that is undertaken and the quality of teaching. We thus believe that Fred Lee's conclusion, highlighting the relevance of developing (as he has long tried to do) alternative ways to compare research 'quality' across different scientific paradigms, can indeed be generalized to the need of a broad defense and counter-attack against the further institutionalization of the mainstream:

> [i]n a world where heterodox economists and their journals and departments are always on the defensive, advocating an alternative measure is not just a radical and emotionally needed step forward, but also a proclamation that heterodox economists are not second-class or invisible economists but are equal to but different from neoclassical economists. To do nothing is not an option.
>
> (Lee 2009, 226)

## Acknowledgments

We wish to thank Fred Lee, John Henry, Tae-Hee Jo, and Zdravka Todorova for their insightful comments on a first draft of this work.

## Notes

1 Of course, this is not to say that all these founding fathers adopted rigorous scientific standards in their HET investigations or were in some other sense 'good' historians of economics. For example, Sraffa was awarded the gold medal of the Swedish Academy of Science for his work on David Ricardo, while some historians blame Marx for his historical imprecisions (see, for example, Brewer 2002).

2 Moreover, since the ascent of Becker's approach to Chicago economics and the subsequent 'freakonomics,' an increasing number of these models are not even concerned with 'core' economic issues.

3 Apart from the inadequacy of bibliometric assessments in the case of individuals, there is the fact that the different size of specific research communities and different citation habits create a strongly uneven playing field (see the references in the main text and the conclusions below).

4 It may also be the case that Lawson focuses more on mainstream microeconomics, while mainstream macroeconomics retained a stronger interest in real-world policymaking.

5 As Fred Lee commented in private conversation with us, one may reject Hodgson's point replying that mainstream economics by construction cannot be applied to the real world. It is rather a set of implications or conclusions drawn from it that might be tested or applied.

6 See for example D'Ippoliti (2011b, chapter 4).

7 For a book-length illustration of this contrast in the history of economic thought, see Roncaglia (2005). The counter-position between the "circular flow" view and the "one-way avenue" view is suggested by Sraffa (1960, 93).

8 By the way, we may surmise as a general rule that such attempts are bound to fail because of aggregation fallacies of various kinds, when conducted on the basis of supply-demand analysis.

9 Besides academic survival, at risk is also the quality and mission of economics teaching (Roncaglia 2014).

## References

Blaug, M. 2001. "No History of Ideas, Please, We're Economists." *Journal of Economic Perspectives* 15: 145–164.

Brewer, A. 2002. "The Marxist Tradition in the History of Economics." In *The Future of the History of Economics*, edited by R. Weintraub. *History of Political Economy* 34: 361–377.

Corsi, M., C. D'Ippoliti, and F. Lucidi. 2010. "Pluralism at Risk? On the Evaluation of Economic Research in Italy." *American Journal of Economics and Sociology* 69 (5): 1495–1529.

Davidson, P. 2004. "A Response to King's Argument for Pluralism." *Post-Autistic Economics Review* 24.

D'Ippoliti, C. 2011a. "Introduction: The Crisis of Economies and Economics." *PSL Quarterly Review* 64 (257): 95–103.

D'Ippoliti, C. 2011b. *Economics and Diversity*. London and New York: Routledge.

Dobusch, L. and J. Kapeller. 2012. "A Guide To Paradigmatic Self-Marginalization: Lessons for Post-Keynesian Economists." *Review of Political Economy* 24 (3): 469–487.

Dow, S.C. 2002. "History of Economic Thought in the Post-Keynesian Tradition." In *The Future of the History of Economics*, edited by R. Weintraub. *History of Political Economy* 34: 319–336.

Elsner, W. 2013. "State and Future of the 'Citadel' and of the Heterodoxies in Economics: Challenges and Dangers, Convergences and Cooperation." *European Journal of Economics and Economic Policies: Intervention* 10 (3): 286–298.

Elsner, W. and F. S. Lee. 2010. "Editors' Introduction. Evaluating Economic Research in a Contested Discipline: Rankings, Pluralism, and the Future of Heterodox Economics." *American Journal of Economics and Sociology* 69(5): 1333–1344.

Harcourt, G. C. 1972. *Some Cambridge Controversies in the Theory of Capital.* Cambridge: Cambridge University Press.

Hirschman, A. O. 1977. *The Passions and the Interests: Political Arguments for Capitalism before Its Triumph.* Princeton, NJ: Princeton University Press.

Hodgson, G. M. 2011. "Sickonomics: Diagnoses and Remedies." *Review of Social Economy* 69 (3): 357–376.

Hollander, J. 1904. "The Development of Ricardo's Theory of Value." *Quarterly Journal of Economics* 18: 455–491.

Hollander, J. 1910. *David Ricardo: A Centenary Estimate.* Baltimore: Johns Hopkins University Press. Reprinted New York: McKelley, 1968.

Hollander, S. 1973. *The Economics of Adam Smith.* Toronto: University of Toronto Press.

Hollander, S. 1979. *The Economics of David Ricardo.* Toronto: University of Toronto Press.

Kates, S. 2013. *Defending the History of Economic Thought.* Cheltenham: Edward Elgar.

Lawson, T. 2003. *Reorienting Economics.* London and New York: Routledge.

Lawson, T. 2013. "Mathematical Modelling and Ideology in the Economics Academy: Competing Explanations of the Failings of the Modern Discipline?" *Economic Thought* 1: 3–22.

Lee, F. S. 2009. *A History of Heterodox Economics: Challenging the Mainstream in the Twentieth Century.* London and New York: Routledge.

Lee, F. S. 2012. "Heterodox Economics and Its Critics." *Review of Political Economy* 24 (2): 337–351.

Lee, F. S., B. C. Cronin, S. McConnell, and E. Dean. 2010. "Research Quality Rankings of Heterodox Economic Journals in a Contested Discipline." *American Journal of Economics and Sociology* 69 (5): 1409–1452.

Lee, F. S., T. C. Grijalva, and C. Nowell. 2010. "Ranking Economics Departments in a Contested Discipline: A Bibliometric Approach to Quality Equality Between Theoretically Distinct Subdisciplines." *American Journal of Economics and Sociology* 69 (5): 1345–1375.

Lee, F. S., X. Pham, and G. Gu. 2013. "The UK Research Assessment Exercise and the Narrowing of UK Economics." *Cambridge Journal of Economics* 37: 693–717.

Marcuzzo, M. C. and A. Rosselli. 2002. "Economics as History of Economics: The Italian Case in Retrospect." In *The Future of the History of Economics*, edited by R. Weintraub. *History of Political Economy* 34: 98–109.

Pasinetti, L. L. and A. Roncaglia. 2006. "Le scienze umane in Italia: il caso dell'economia politica." *Rivista Italiana degli Economisti* 11: 461–499.

Roncaglia, A. 2005. *The Wealth of Ideas.* Cambridge: Cambridge University Press.

Roncaglia, A. 2009. *Piero Sraffa.* Basingstoke: Palgrave Macmillan.

Roncaglia, A. 2010. *Why the Economists Got It Wrong: The Crisis and its Cultural Roots.* London: Anthem Press.

Roncaglia, A. 2014. "Should the History of Economic Thought be Included in Undergraduate Curricula?" *Economic Thought* 3 (1).

Roncaglia, A. and M. Tonveronachi. 2014. "Post-Keynesian Post-Sraffian Economics: An Outline." In *Contributions to Economic Theory, Policy, Development and Finance:*

*Essays in Honor of Jan A. Kregel*, edited by D. B. Papadimitriou. Basingstoke: Palgrave Macmillan.

Schumpeter, J. 1954. *History of Economic Analysis*, edited by E. Boody Schumpeter. New York: Oxford University Press.

Sraffa, P. 1951. "Introduction." In *The Works and Correspondence of David Ricardo*, Vol. 1., edited by P. Sraffa, xiii–lxii. Cambridge: Cambridge University Press.

Sraffa, P. 1960. *Production of Commodities by Means of Commodities*. Cambridge: Cambridge University Press.

Sylos Labini, P. 2005. *Torniamo ai classici. Produttività del lavoro, progresso tecnico e sviluppo economico*. Rome and Bari: Laterza.

Viner, J. 1991. *Essays on the Intellectual History of Economics*, edited by D. A. Irwin. Princeton: Princeton University Press.

Weintraub, R., ed. 2002a. *The Future of the History of Economics*. Annual Supplement, *History of Political Economy*, 34.

Weintraub, R. 2002b. "Will Economics Ever Have a Past Again?" In *The Future of the History of Economics*, edited by R. Weintraub. *History of Political Economy* 34: 1–14.

# 2 The Association for Heterodox Economics

## Past, present, and future

*Andrew Mearman and Bruce Philp*

## Introduction

Through various, often large, changes in economics it is usually the case that a dominant institutionalized 'mainstream' has been identifiable: first a classical, then neoclassical dominance; thereafter a Keynesian version; subsequently a synthesis of that with neoclassical economics; then, a restatement of neoclassical principles; finally, more recently, a methodological mainstream, within or around which there has been theoretical fracturing. In this last period there have emerged strong new strands in economics—such as behavioral, complexity, or experimental economics—which have the potential to change the mainstream fundamentally (although many are skeptical about that: e.g., Lee 2013, 112–116). However, throughout these periods, there has remained a largely marginalized set of economists and their ideas. The Association for Heterodox Economics (AHE) can be seen as another attempt by economists on the fringes of economics to gain recognition and exercise power in favor of a pluralist discipline. This chapter considers the history of the AHE in this regard.

There are several possible ways to write a history of the AHE. In this chapter we will examine the development of the AHE in three periods: from its beginnings, to its expansion in Ireland and the provinces of England, to recent years when the annual conference has twice visited France, while engaging with related organizations, such as l'Association Française d'Économie Politique (AFEP), the International Initiative for Promoting Political Economy (IIPPE) and, albeit to a lesser extent, with International Association for Feminist Economics (IAFFE) and European Association for Evolutionary Political Economy (EAEPE). In so doing several key themes will be stressed: the AHE's relations with the rest of the discipline; its position on pluralism; its impact on the profession, and specifically on young heterodox economists; and, its geographic spread and internationalization.

In the first part of the chapter we will offer some personal reflections concerning the state of heterodox economics at the end of the 1990s. Thereafter we will trace the development of the AHE through a historical analysis of documents (which are available on the AHE website: www.hetecon.net), reinforced with the reflections (gleaned through semi-structured interviews) of each of the AHE

*Table 2.1* AHE coordinators

| Years | Coordinator | Institution |
|---|---|---|
| 1999–2000 | Fred Lee | De Montfort University |
| 2000–2002 | Andrew Trigg | Open University |
| 2002–2005 | Gary Slater | Nottingham Trent University |
| 2005–2008 | Andrew Mearman | University of the West of England, Bristol |
| 2008–2010 | Alan Freeman | University of Greenwich |
| 2011–2013 | Bruce Philp | Nottingham Trent University |
| 2013–2015 | Jamie Morgan | Leeds Metropolitan University |

coordinators (see Table 2.1). Our intention is to locate heterodox economics in the context of UK academia in the late 1990s, before tracing the historical development of the AHE, both as an organization in itself, and as an organization in context.

## A young heterodox economist's guide to the discipline, *c.*1998

One of the purposes of this chapter is to consider the emergence of the AHE, and in particular its effect on the landscape facing a young economist. As already suggested, the discipline had undertaken considerable qualitative change in the post-war period. In this section we shall provide a very brief history, examining first the wider disciplinary context and, second, specific aspects of the heterodox landscape. In this second element it is clear that certain individuals and geographical centers of activity were highly important in the development of heterodox economics—and this theme continues through the subsequent narrative concerning the history of the AHE.

It was really in the post-World War II period that the clear and dominant mainstream we recognize today emerged in economics, albeit not a particularly coherent one. Arguably this emergent mainstream can be characterized thus: it adopted methodological individualism, with an associated search for microfoundations; it is mathematical in approach; it adopts equilibrium modeling; the principle of the margin underpins its microeconomics; it adopts competitive general equilibrium modeling; and, in so far as it was influenced by Keynes, this was assimilated into a neoclassical-Keynesian synthesis. In addition, the mainstream largely ignores issues such as money, banking and finance, and distribution; further, it has limited treatments of power, the environment, institutions, growth and change, and on the education of economists. By contrast, these areas provide the habitat for heterodox economists.

Our studies took us to institutions with solid heterodox credentials. Manchester (where Bruce Philp studied) had become an important center, and in the early years of the Conference of Socialist Economists (CSE), academics from Manchester such as Ian Steedman, Geoff Hodgson, Diane Elson, Pat Devine, David Purdy, Mike Walsh, and George Zis were prominent (Lee 2009, 130–133). In the 1980s and 1990s Manchester Polytechnic had a political economy strand on its program and, at the University in the early 1990s, Ian Steedman and Pat Devine remained, as well as Stanley Metcalfe, Terry Peach, and David Young. Another graduate of Manchester, Andrew Trigg, notes that the University of Manchester Students' Union was very political—the "heart of student politics"—especially during the miners' strike (1984–1985).

The University of Leeds, likewise, had attracted a number of heterodox economists, notably Hugo Radice (who had been influential in the creation of the CSE) and Malcolm Sawyer. Postgraduate students would also have been exposed to Paul Dunne, Man-Seop Park, Francis Green, Cathy O'Donnell, and Peter Nolan. Bill Gerard also made a contribution and, in 1996, the locus of the Post-Keynesian Economics Study Group (PKSG) was shifted to Leeds, where John Hillard was also based (Lee 2009, 145). It can be argued that Leeds and Manchester have helped to shape current UK heterodoxy with two coordinators being graduates from Leeds (Gary Slater and Andrew Mearman) and two from Manchester (Bruce Philp and Andrew Trigg). For a list of coordinators and the institutions at which they worked see Table 2.1. However, as will be noted in due course, the trend at these respective institutions has been dichotomous since the 1990s.

In addition to these universities, other institutions were also important in the 1970s, 1980s, and 1990s: South Bank, Thames (now the University of Greenwich), East London, Birkbeck, Stirling, Staffordshire, De Montfort, and Middlesex. All had vibrant economics departments with at least a flavor of heterodoxy, i.e., work sitting outside the mainstream. Many of the people in these institutions had connections to the contemporarily existing heterodox groups such as PKSG and CSE. In considering the history of heterodox economics in Great Britain, two things emerge: first, it seems necessary to have outposts or strongholds in order to develop a critical mass and a network for aspiring economists. Second, of those listed above, we must ask how many remain anything like strongholds? Arguably only Leeds and Greenwich qualify. After a small dip in the 2000s, once again Leeds has a strong heterodox strand to its offering: Malcolm Sawyer remains in place and has been joined by Giuseppe Fontana, David Spencer, Andrew Brown, and Gary Slater (all Leeds PhD graduates), Annina Kaltenbrunner (SOAS), Philip Hughes (Stirling), Stefan Kesting (Bremen), and Gary Dymski (UMass-Amherst). Greenwich has now arguably strengthened its heterodox provision with key professors Bruce Cronin and Ozlem Onaran, and a number of more junior heterodox faculty being appointed in recent years. In contrast it is hard to discern noteworthy heterodox research in the School of Economics at the University of Manchester (though in other departments economists like Wendy Olsen prosper). Indeed, the University has attracted notoriety recently because of its Post-Crash Economics Society, the organizers of which have criticized courses for doing little to explain why economists failed to warn about the global financial crisis, and for having too heavy a focus on training students for City jobs (Inman 2013). Other institutions have suffered too, partly because of closure of economics departments and provision. Meanwhile, new places have grown—particularly Kingston (Engelbert Stockhammer, Steve

Keen), Nottingham Trent (Bruce Philp, Dan Wheatley), SOAS (Jan Toporowski, Ben Fine, Costas Lapavitsas), and UWE (Andrew Mearman, Daniela Gabor)—each of which has actively recruited heterodox talent of late. Clearly, strongholds wax and wane.

As well as specific university structures, a young economist needs networks that extend beyond these. There were various outlets at which we could present and get feedback in the 1980s and early 1990s. Around this time there was an ESRC (Economic and Social Research Council)-funded Political Economy Study Group and, since 1988, there had been the ESRC-funded PKSG (Lee 2009, 143–145). The latter were very welcoming; however, it was not as broad a church as you would find, for example, at the Malvern conferences organized by John Pheby and *Review of Political Economy* (ROPE). The Malvern conferences were small, and not broadly publicized, and although there was one in 2014 this was the first to have occurred since 1995 (see Pressman 1996, for a discussion of early conferences). In the context of the emergence of the AHE there was a ROPE conference in Trier, Germany, in 1997. This, again, provided the forum for methodological debate, theoretical insight, and empirical analysis, from a plurality of perspectives, but given the now-sporadic nature of the conference, and relatively compact nature of it, there emerged a gap in UK academia.

Groups like the Cambridge Realist Workshop provided a nurturing environment (from 1994), but, like the PKSG, they did not have the range of interests that were to be accommodated at Malvern (and subsequently by the AHE). Leeds held postgraduate research conferences in the 1990s but these depended on there being a clear sympathetic cohort of PhD students in place. More widely afield, the summer schools at Trieste from 1981 to 1990 attempted to serve a similar function (see Lavoie 2011). Subsequently, summer schools have been held in various places, organized by various groups. For instance, several young UK heterodox economists were invited to attend a training event by the Association for Evolutionary Economics (AFEE), at Bard College, in 1999. Kingston University has become the latest to revive this practice, holding a summer school in Post Keynesian economics. The AHE would also respond in this way, by organizing research methods workshops (see the section '2000–2001: Like it or not, we are here!' below).

In this context we need to understand what the distinctive contribution of the AHE has been. We might consider a world without the AHE: it is possibly one in which things would have happened anyway—for instance, other groups hold conferences and training events. Other groups have engaged in advocacy, e.g., PKSG wrote to the *Guardian* in 2013, as did the AHE. However, we would maintain that the distinctiveness of the AHE should be found in the combination of methodological, theoretical, and empirical dialogue, to be conducted by, and *between*, different schools of economic thought. In this sense it had the 'broad church' of the Malvern Conferences, but on a larger scale, and with a more widely circulated call for papers.

## 1999: no such thing as a free lunch?

The first AHE event was as a fringe event organized at the Royal Economic Society (RES) Conference, at the University of Nottingham in 1999 (for a list of AHE Conferences, see Table 2.2). The prime mover for the AHE Fringe was Fred Lee. For a number of years the RES had become increasingly dominated by mainstream economics, with econometric analysis being seen as the only legitimate form of empirical investigation. Historically, the *Economic Journal* had published a diverse range of papers (one can think of a number of important papers in the Marxian tradition, for example, being published in the 1970s and early 1980s). However, by the late 1990s heterodox papers were only very rarely published in any of the 'leading' economics journals (including *American Economic Review, Quarterly Journal of Economics, Journal of Political Economy*, etc.). The *Economic Journal* was no exception. The ramifications for this in the context of the subsequent Research Assessment Exercise (RAE) period was likely to be reduced opportunities for non-mainstream economists in the UK, steadily eroding the plurality of perspectives which had previously been more pronounced.

Fred Lee's sense of indignation and injustice at this state of affairs caused him to act. He telephoned the University of Nottingham with the intention of booking some rooms and organizing a fringe event. When asked for the name of the organization in which the event was being booked he invented the name 'Association for Heterodox Economics.' This was an important moment inspiring a chain of events which led to the creation of the Association, with its annual conference, postgraduate training workshop, and website. Perhaps, suggests one

*Table 2.2* AHE conferences and themes

| Year | Venue (UK unless stated) | Title/theme |
|------|--------------------------|-------------|
| 1999 | Nottingham | Fringe Conference at the RES Conference |
| 2000 | Open, London | The Other Economics conference |
| 2001 | Open, London | Third Annual Conference |
| 2002 | Dublin City University, Ireland | Fourth Annual Conference |
| 2003 | Nottingham Trent | Fifth Annual Conference |
| 2004 | Leeds | Opening Up Economics |
| 2005 | City, London | Pluralism in Economics |
| 2006 | London School of Economics | Economics, Pluralism and the Social Sciences |
| 2007 | West of England, Bristol | Pluralism in Action |
| 2008 | Anglia Ruskin, Cambridge | Tenth Annual Conference |
| 2009 | Kingston, London | Heterodox Economics and Sustainable Development, 20 Years On |
| 2010 | Bordeaux, France | The Economy of Tomorrow |
| 2011 | Nottingham Trent | Economists of Tomorrow |
| 2012 | Paris, France | Political Economy and the Outlook for Capitalism (joint with IIPPE and AFEP) |
| 2013 | London Metropolitan | Economy and Organisation |
| 2014 | Greenwich, London | The Triple Crisis |

of the coordinators, Andrew Trigg, the moment was instrumental in the term 'heterodox' being used more broadly in the lexicon of the discipline.

The event itself attracted over 40 participants, overwhelmingly from the UK (see Figure 2.1), and it received sponsorship from a number of organizations, including the Conference for Socialist Economists (CSE, who publish *Capital and Class*), the PKSG, the Cambridge Realist Workshop, and the International Working Group on Value Theory (IWGVT). As Andrew Trigg noted the delegates were inspired by Fred Lee's injunction not to worry about the mainstream and just "go ahead and do economics differently—to do heterodox economics well." More generally, the emergence of the AHE signaled a willingness to engage with a plurality of perspectives. Although there are other conferences and associations that are important for non-mainstream research, the AHE provided the space for dialogue, with a broad base of theoretical perspectives, empirical approaches, and institutions represented.

Sessions at this fringe event were structured into core sub-disciplines, which we would associate with the economics discipline—e.g., macroeconomics, microeconomics, and industrial economics—as well as sessions on methodology that have been a feature of subsequent AHE Conferences. In the closing plenary panel Victoria Chick, Fred Lee, and Luigi Pasinetti reflected on the future of heterodox economics. Pasinetti's contribution was especially noteworthy since he also delivered the *Economic Issues* lecture at the RES conference, thereby offering a plenary presentation at each event. Bruce Philp recalled part of Pasinetti's exposition:

> He emphasised the history of economic thought as an area where heterodox economists could prosper. I wasn't sure about the emphasis, and took issue with it in the ensuring discussion. The history of economic thought has

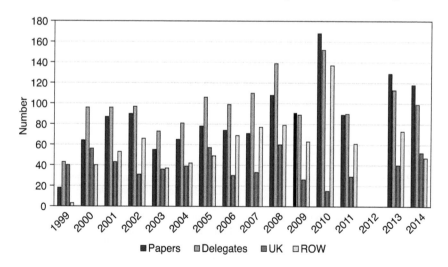

*Figure 2.1* AHE conference participation, 1999–2014.[1]

value, and helps us understand the past, as well as the here and now, but I was concerned that we would be further marginalized if we were *just* seen to just focus on Smith, Ricardo, Marx and Keynes, to the detriment of engaging with mainstream economists and policymakers on the terrain of contemporary theoretical, empirical and policy concerns.

Following discussion at the Fringe Fred Lee subsequently wrote to Anton Muscatelli, local organizer of the 2000 RES Conference, to be held at the University of St. Andrews. In a letter dated April 29th, 1999, Fred Lee reported a conversation with Manfredi La Manna (who was the local organizer at the University of Nottingham) who had suggested a number of members had objected to the AHE's presence at the University of Nottingham because it "portrayed the RES as a closed organization not willing to tolerate heterodox views." In subsequent correspondence Partha Dasgupta (the Chair of the RES) wrote to Fred Lee (May 7th, 1999) and stated there was no need to incorporate heterodox streams because "there is a general feeling that the academic standard [at the RES Conference] has been rising ... markedly." Invited sessions, Dasgupta went on, are also created where someone approaches the Chair with "a proposal having real intellectual merit" (for correspondence related to this see AHE 2014a). Since the response from the Chair of the RES did not make any attempt to explore potential avenues for heterodox sessions at the University of St. Andrews, we could infer that the proposals for heterodox sessions advanced by Fred Lee, on behalf of the Association, did not have, in Dasgupta's view, "real intellectual merit." So the heterodox sessions were not included. In addition, the University of St. Andrews also refused to permit room bookings, thereby preventing a repeat of a concurrent fringe event as had taken place in Nottingham. The RES, Dasgupta reported, were concerned about other associations holding events at the same time, at the same venue, "So I am instructing the Programme Chair and Chair of the Organizing Committee of the RES annual conference that this should not be allowed to happen." The door was thus shut. As Alan Freeman remarked, somewhat tongue-in-cheek: "They went to St. Andrews to get as far away from us as possible!" This closed one particular avenue: however, in so doing, the path for the Association became clear, as a dedicated conference was planned. This may have been a blessing in disguise, though it is impossible to know the counterfactual.

## 2000–2001: like it or not, we are here!

The first full AHE Conference was held at the Open University (OU) Conference Centre in London in July 2000, and it received 64 papers from 96 delegates (see Figure 2.1). Financial and administrative support had been provided by the OU, and Andrew Trigg acted as the Conference Organizer (with Fred Lee as the Coordinator). The Conference was branded *The Other Economics Conference*. This period, involving the two conferences at the Open University, was characterized by an evolution in our self-perception, as Alan Freeman notes: "The AHE went from being a fringe organization to being an organization." This was not the only change: whereas the 1999 event saw 3 non-UK delegates, there were 40 overseas delegates at the 2000 conference (see Figure 2.1).

Organizationally, this was where a committee proper was formed and Andrew Trigg, who was the Conference Organizer for the OU events, was elected Coordinator. The term 'coordinator' (rather than 'president') was chosen because it signaled a commitment on the part of the Association to being a committee-run democratic group. Also, as Andrew Trigg notes, the term signals that decision-making is non-hierarchical, encouraging all committee members to be active. The coordinator was there to facilitate decision-making, rather than make operational, strategic, or organizational decisions. A committee was elected, and by 2001 this comprised 13 members. Concerning this group, Andrew Trigg recalls: "We had a young, vibrant, organizing committee. This was a generation of left wing economists who came out of the Thatcher generation." Fred Lee had been a prime mover in the Fringe, and now encouraged many of this generation to take up the gauntlet: "Fred's point was that it's all going to die-off if we don't renew" (Andrew Trigg). By this time the Malvern conference had ceased (2014 notwithstanding), and Post Keynesian economics was engaged in a discussion about coherence (Walters and Young 1997; Arestis, Dunn, and Sawyer 1999), with an associated narrowing of the 'broad church' on which it had been founded. Furthermore, heterodox economics in the UK had begun to feel the pressure emanating from selectivity associated with the RAE. The issue was: Where could emerging economists from different scholarly traditions engage with one another? The AHE offered this, and grew in the early years accordingly. Indeed, "the AHE was established as a conference that was entirely open, a general conference" (Andrew Trigg).

This raises an issue as to what it was that organizers and participants were trying to achieve. Certainly many of the committee members had different goals. Some saw the AHE as occupying a space encompassing Post Keynesian and Marxian economics, both singularly and at their intersection. However, others saw it as important to retain a broad base, expanding the aforementioned groups to include feminist economics, old institutionalism, and those interested in Austrian economics. But, however broadly heterodox economics was conceived, things were mixed up at these early events. Andrew Trigg and Alan Freeman both observed that one of the goals at the OU Conferences was to provide a platform on which academics from different traditions evaluated a common theme, thereby fostering dialogue by design.

The 2001 conference was again held at the OU, and presenters included Tony Lawson, Ben Fine, Paul Ormerod, and Victoria Chick. New problems presented themselves, in particular it was felt that the capacity constraint associated with the North London venue might present difficulties for future events. Although the conference had the same number of delegates as the year before the number of international delegates now exceeded the number of UK delegates for the first time. Concurrently there was a movement to increase the scope of the Association's activity beyond just the conference. A proposal for a postgraduate advanced training workshop was turned into a reality through the hard work of Alfredo

*Table 2.3* AHE postgraduate workshops

| Year | Venue | Funding source |
| --- | --- | --- |
| 2001 | SOAS, London | ESRC |
| 2002 | Manchester | ESRC |
| 2004 | Manchester | ESRC |
| 2005 | Manchester | ESRC |
| 2007 | UWE, Bristol | CPEST/AHE |
| 2009 | Kingston | AHE |
| 2012 | London Metropolitan | CPEST/AHE/AJES |
| 2014 | Open, London | AHE/AJES |

Notes
CPEST: Cambridge Political Economy Society Trust; AJES: *American Journal of Economics and Sociology*

Saad-Filho and Wendy Olsen. They successfully sought funding (for an initial period of two years) from the Economic and Social Research Council (ESRC). This, of course, provided financial support, but it also lent some external weight to our credibility as an Association. The workshop first ran in 2001, and has run on seven occasions since (see Table 2.3 for a list of the workshops, and associated funding). It provided postgraduate researchers with an insight into the methods employed by a variety of heterodox economists. This was a valuable exercise since it signaled the AHE was not just an 'oppositional' organization: it was prepared to demonstrate what an 'alternative' economics, or varieties thereof, might look like. It also aided attempts to renew heterodox economics.

## 2002–2009: pluralist expansion

In geographical terms, the 2002 AHE conference marked a departure for the Association. That year the AHE conference went abroad for the first time, to Dublin City University (with Siobhain McGovern as the Conference Organizer). In some ways the conference merely continued the thrust of the previous three—of establishing the organization as a functioning body. Again, there was no conference theme. However, as well as the international move, this event marked a point of departure from the first three conferences. This was the first time when the Association began to consider its identity and role and thought began to turn to a constitution. Also, the move outside the UK led us to consider the AHE's purpose. The Dublin event attracted an almost identical number of delegates—including Peter Cain, Ian Steedman, and Joseph Halevi—as at the OU. As would have been expected there was some contraction in the number of delegates from the UK (to 31, or around one-third of the total). This raised questions because the initial purpose of the AHE had been to assist academics in the specific UK context; however, clearly, the challenges facing UK academics were replicated elsewhere. There was a logic in going international. However, the AHE persistently returns to the UK, and constitutionally is based there.

Internationalization was, perhaps, a factor in the decision to go to Dublin. The AHE had grown into a diverse association, and academics from all over the world had attended the two OU conferences, whereas as a 'fringe' to the UK RES conference it was distinctly UK-based in its constituency. The period 2000–2002 had seen it grow into an event that was increasingly international in character. The invitation to host the conference by Dublin City University was universally welcomed at the annual general meeting (AGM), though whether this was driven by a conscious attempt toward internationalization is less clear. For Alan Freeman, he saw the possibility for the AHE as a world-leading organization, an 'incubator' as it were. A possible example of this—or perhaps just a parallel initiative—was the formation in Australia of the Society for Heterodox Economists (SHE), and its inaugural conference was held at the University of New South Wales, in Sydney, in 2002.

At the Dublin conference AGM it was decided to host the next conference at Nottingham Trent University, and Gary Slater—a graduate of Leeds who was based there—was elected as the Coordinator. He saw his role as follows:

> I think my main goal as AHE Coordinator was to try to ensure that we maintained the momentum built-up by Fred and the committee under Andrew Trigg. The AHE was still young—I took over some three years after it began—and it was evolving as a grouping. I had come from Leeds where, with others, we had run PhD student conferences for a few years. This helped enormously since the annual conference was the focal activity back then and as well as experience in running conferences I had built-up a good set of connections with other young heterodox economists, many of whom had joined the committee and could be relied upon to help out.

The 2003 conference sessions featured a wide variety of areas of concern. As one might expect there was some criticism of mainstream approaches (specifically of new institutionalism), some methodology (reflecting the methodological turn in heterodoxy), and the history of economic thought (including a plenary address on Joan Robinson by Geoff Harcourt). There was a significant strand of papers on finance, and on development, again reflecting established heterodox themes and anticipating future conferences. Two other significant elements are worthy of mention. Tony Lawson offered an address on the definition of heterodox economics. This prefigured a great deal of discussion on this question as the decade progressed. Second, John Harvey spoke as the Executive Director of ICAPE (International Confederation of Associations for Pluralism in Economics), which had recently held their triennial conference in Kansas City, then emerging as a world center of heterodox thought (though recently dormant). His invitation arguably signaled the AHE's desire to be part of international alliance and also anticipated the subsequent focus on pluralism.

The 2004 conference, held at Leeds, arguably heralded a distinctive new phase in the approach of the AHE. Previous conferences had largely eschewed conference titles and themes, perhaps reflecting a need to establish the AHE, and gain confidence. However, the Leeds event had a specific theme, one that was to dominate until at least 2008: pluralism. This focus reflected the reality of economics at that time, and the personal experiences and interests of members of the AHE. As Alan Freeman reflected: "I was working with Andrew Kliman and we were doubly unorthodox: unorthodox as economists, and unorthodox among Marxists." As a consequence of exclusion Alan Freeman "drifted towards pluralism." A similar story might be told by a number of members and this has been one of the AHE's subsequent hallmarks.

Concurrently the discipline as a whole was confused: on the one hand it displayed fractures (as discussed above), but on the other hand it became institutionally increasingly monistic. The latter was evidenced both by state mechanisms such as the QAA Benchmark Statement for Economics (QAA BSE) and the RAE and REF (the latter being the Research Excellence Framework) (see Lee 2009). The QAA BSE is viewed by some as dogmatic: for example Freeman (2008) argues convincingly that the BSE is doctrinaire relative to other disciplines, citing theology that is reluctant even to define the discipline. Other readings are that the document itself is quite benign (Clarke and Mearman 2003) but does not compel any department to be more pluralistic, and that the consequence of the RAE and REF would be that no one would be interested or able to teach pluralistically anyway. Significantly, at time of writing the QAA BSE is being reviewed: we await its verdict and its implications for pluralism.

Within heterodox economics there had been an established belief that pluralism was necessary in teaching and research, (see, e.g., Dow 1985; Hamouda and Harcourt 1989), largely derived from the discussions within Post Keynesian economics in the 1980s and 1990s, and the rediscovery of Keynes's philosophical writings. Several authors in the AHE had argued for pluralism in teaching and there was a growing belief in the AHE that pluralism ought to be campaigned for. Indeed, this has happened, for instance via appeals to the RAE assessment panel (for example Andrew Mearman petitioned the then RAE Chair David Greenaway). In addition the AHE petitioned the Economics Network on pluralism, the result being a special issue on pluralism in the *International Review of Economics Education*. Unfortunately, despite attempts to engage with the mainstream, e.g., through the Committee of Heads of University Departments in Economics (CHUDE), little was forthcoming. The AHE continues to campaign along these lines, e.g., in a letter to the *Guardian* in 2013, plus a series of pieces in the *RES Newsletter* (2014).

The Leeds conference program displayed a very wide range of topics, including many of the ones listed above, in addition to the main theme: thus, the AHE conference remains a 'general conference.' Amongst the sessions were those on industrial economics, economics and religion, a set of critical perspectives on globalization, institutions, labor markets and development; and sessions relating to specific approaches within heterodoxy, such as Post Keynesianism and Marxism. Other significant elements were special sessions on teaching, and on the environment, both of which gained in prominence throughout the decade. A plenary session on econometrics was another feature, and a session on care showed engagement with ethics and feminist approaches, both of which would re-emerge, e.g., at the 2011 conference.

The 2005 conference at City University marked a return to London (which would be repeated), but arguably as a very different organization to that extant at the OU gatherings. The conference formally heralded a concern with pluralism, both within heterodoxy and more broadly in the discipline. The conference call for papers also made explicit reference to teaching. This was now clearly seen as an important battleground and, moreover, one on which heterodox, pluralist economists had superior weaponry. The conference program has a much more definite structure than the Leeds event. An entire conference stream of sessions focused on the topic of pluralism. One plenary was a discussion of Edward Full-brook's (2004) *What's Wrong with Economics*. Another featured Gary Mongio-vi's evaluation of Modigliani's work: this exemplified the desire to offer critique but also engage with mainstream topics and thinkers. The conference was the first to feature explicit discussion of banking (as opposed to the well-established theme of money and finance). This was both appropriate given the location of the conference, and also prescient.

Another significant element of the 2005 conference was that it was the site of the first AGM of the AHE (Business Meeting notes). Andrew Mearman, as the new Coordinator, had made it a specific goal to establish firmer institutional structures for the AHE, "to place the AHE on a surer footing," as a sign of a maturing body. Building on work started under Gary Slater, a membership system was being established. Also a draft constitution was discussed (published the following year as a set of Principles of Unity). Discussion also continued about setting up a heterodox journal. This journal never did materialize, although it was superseded by other developments, most notably the online establishment of the *Post-Autistic Economics Review* (subsequently *Real World Economic Review*) and the World Economics Association. Also noted at this meeting was the ceasing of funding of the Postgraduate training workshops by the ESRC. This was a significant blow but was gradually overcome by self-funding out of surplus and by sponsorship by the Cambridge Political Economy Society Trust (CPEST) and others (see Table 2.3).

The 2006 conference was based at the LSE and UCL. It developed some of the earlier themes such as pluralism and interdisciplinarity, the latter being stressed strongly here. One plenary—involving Sheila Dow and Riccardo Bel-lofiore—debated pluralism. Teaching was also restated as a key area, building on an event earlier in the year on 'teaching heterodox economics' (AGM minutes 2006). At the 2006 conference the TSSI (Temporal Single-System Interpreta-tion) debate also continued unabated. Many papers embraced the conference call and examined the potential influence of cybernetics, systems thinking, psycho-analysis, law, sociology, and ecology. The ethic of care was again discussed. There were also strong contributions on financial instability vis-à-vis Minsky. It is especially important to recognize this since, within a year or so, the financial crisis had flung Minsky into popular discourse, despite his absence from main-stream economic thought.

Significantly, partly reflecting Andrew Mearman's agenda to focus the AHE on practical impact, there was specific reference to policy areas. Consequently a second plenary reflected a policy focus, looking at the role of the economic adviser. In it there was recognition that government economists have power, and also may not be beholden to the academic mainstream. Heterodox economists may consider policy relevance as a comparative advantage, particularly in light of recent economic policy failures. At this conference the Principles of Unity were approved, and a membership scheme was adopted.

The 2007 conference was held at UWE, Bristol. The conference organizer (and then Coordinator), Andrew Mearman, retained frustration at the abstract nature of the discussion on pluralism and wanted some more concrete outcomes. A plenary on the future of pluralism in research and teaching featured discussion by Paul Dunne and Alan Freeman respectively. The conference had a stream of panels on 'the economics of the modern world'; however, relatively few papers were given about the impending economic crisis. Indeed, in many ways the conference was a return to traditional theoretical themes with the culmination of a stream on a Whig history of economics.

As Coordinator, Mearman made several moves to broaden out the AHE, as it had been reported to him that some viewed it as the preserve of Post Keynesians and Marxists. He wrote to key figures in feminist, evolutionary, Austrian, and behavioral economics, and others to encourage attendance at AHE conferences (see the Business Meeting 2006 conference at the LSE). Significantly, also reflecting personal interest, he also contacted ecological economists and encouraged them to attend. Ali Douai answered this call, which eventually partly led to a series of sessions at the 2008 conference, the 2010 Bordeaux conference, and a special issue of the *Cambridge Journal of Economics* on heterodox economics and the environment (see Douai, Mearman, and Negru 2012). These moves reflected a generally greater engagement with environmental and sustainability issues within heterodox economics, as partly evidenced by the theme of the 2009 Kingston conference.

The 2008 conference at Anglia Ruskin had no named theme but its foci can be divined. Building on 2007 and previewing 2009, a plenary on sustainable development brought to the conference leading figures in ecological and green economics, and a set of sessions on that theme reinforced its importance. In addition to this theme, there was further reflection on pluralism and heterodoxy, with a return to that question in a plenary by Tony Lawson, plus forward-looking contributions from Ha-Joon Chang, Victoria Chick, and Geoff Harcourt. The conference made its best attempt to draw on the (waning) power of Cambridge. The conference also saw a greater focus on the ongoing crisis and witnessed the emergence of a stream on the ethics of economists. This theme reached its acme at the 2011 conference.

In 2009 the conference continued an increased focus on sustainability: for the first time it was the named theme of the conference. This was a natural move by the AHE given the organization's desire to focus on the real world. Also, as the 2009 call for papers expressed, sustainable development necessitates pluralist, interdisciplinary study, and thus builds on the foci of several preceding conferences. The engagement with ecological economics also continued, as Clive Spash was a plenary speaker. In addition, though, as one might expect, engagement with the ongoing economic crisis again increased. Another plenary speaker was Ann Pettifor, a journalist-economist who has been prominent in the critique of austerity, and also a signatory of the Green New Deal (Elliot *et al.* 2008). Her presence is significant by its rarity. Indeed, Andrew Trigg has suggested the AHE be more political, citing Pettifor as an unusual case of engagement with political groups.

Special sessions once more on the financial crisis and on Minskyian perspectives are also noteworthy in this aspect. However, despite these apparent changes in focus, staple themes in AHE conferences remained in place. Sessions on history of economic thought, pedagogy, and several Marxian themes are evidence of this. And 'pluralism in economics' was now a clearly established theme.

It is also worth noting the presence of a specific strand of sessions organized by the PKSG. A consistent feature of AHE conferences has been openness to single group strands of this type. This type of session does present some philosophical problems for the Association, however, if they seem closed to other groups. To guard against this, as established in the very first AHE conference, special sessions, which deliberately bring together commentators from different heterodox perspectives, are intentionally created. An example from the 2009 conference was a special session on Marx, Keynes, and the crisis, which brought together Radhika Desai, Andrew Kliman, and Geoff Tily. These sessions give AHE conferences a distinctive flavor and are crucial to their continued relevance.

## 2010–2014: a new era?

The conference in Bordeaux was a highpoint for the AHE. Aside from excellent presenters—such as Diane Elson, Richard Wolff, and Arild Vatn—it was well attended (with 152 delegates and 168 papers). As Bruce Philp noted: "There were some excellent sessions. The conference dinner was hosted in a Chateau, which the Marxists just about coped with having been anesthetized by the local wines." After a meeting in Lille in 2010, the AHE conference also provided a forum for members of l'Association Française d'Économie Politique (AFEP) to continue their engagement. As Alan Freeman noted: "A great achievement of the AHE was helping in the development of AFEP."

The Bordeaux conference was likely to be a difficult conference to follow, as Bruce Philp noted:

> The plenaries [at Bordeaux] were great, the papers were fantastic, the sun shone. I hadn't intended to, but I found myself offering to host the 2011 conference in Nottingham, forgetting that I live in a provincial English town whose only claim to fame is it once harbored a famous criminal.

Indeed, as occurred in the case of the 2002 Dublin Conference, the number of UK delegates dropped markedly at the Bordeaux conference to 15 (see Figure 2.1). Although there were many French delegates there were also many from other parts of the world, including South America, North America, and Australia. The fear had to be that the momentum from the 2010 conference would not carry over to the subsequent conference and, indeed, only four delegates from France attended the 2011 Nottingham conference. Delegate numbers fell to 90, with 29 UK delegates. A total of 89 papers were delivered on a variety of topics, including methodology, financialization, and the nature of work. The 2011 Nottingham Trent Conference featured talks from Irene van Staveren and George DeMartino, with the ethical void in mainstream economics being a key theme. The opening plenary involved talks from Ioana Negru (AHE), Dimitris Milonakis (IIPPE), and Dany Lang (AFEP), on the future for heterodoxy, and plans were already progressing for a large multi-association conference in 2012, to be held at Paris I, together with AFEP and IIPPE.

The planning for the 2012 conference was, according to Bruce Philp, "complicated." The event attracted far more papers than was manageable and this created fears as respective associations tried to minimize the impact on their own constituencies, while also trying to act in a spirit of cooperation. The plenaries were not a particular problem, and there were inspiring presentations from the likes of Ben Fine, Tony Lawson, Fred Lee, Molly Scott Cato, and Jack Reardon. However, the panel and individual session negotiations were more protracted, but an amicable outcome was reached (partly as a result of Simon Mohun and Bruno Tinel, from IIPPE and AFEP respectively, being able to lift the capacity constraint somewhat). Nevertheless, the AHE found itself in a position where previous presenters at our conferences had papers rejected and there was a genuine fear that there would be a 'dead cat bounce' at the 2013 conference, to be held at London Metropolitan University. One thing that did become apparent, however, is that French organizers have a proclivity for organizing excellent conference dinners—at the Paris conference the event was held at a venue which had working fairground rides from the nineteenth and early twentieth centuries, and people of all generations regressed to their childhoods.

For 2013 and 2014 the AHE returned to London. London remains an important hub, not only reflecting UK economic and political geography, but in addition is an attractive and accessible destination for overseas delegates. The 2013 event at London Metropolitan was reasonably well attended (113 delegates, 129 papers, 40 UK). The named theme of the conference was 'Economics and Organizations' reflecting local research interests. Plenary sessions demonstrated pluralist outreach, with a high point being the panel on gender budgeting organized by members from IAFFE. This reflected renewed efforts to engage with that group. Another was on inequality—again reflecting a desire to engage with issues of societal concern—and this presentation from Tony Atkinson also touched on themes such as the unwillingness of highly ranked journals to consider the nature and sources of data. This plenary created some controversy because some regarded Atkinson as too mainstream; alternatively, it could be viewed as an act of pluralist engagement. However, the flavor of the conference was, as usual, diverse. Indeed, the program displayed a huge variety—perhaps greater than ever before. A notable addition, linking to a plenary address in 2008 by Nicholas Garnham, was a stream on the creative industries, with a succession of connected papers on this topic. There were also streams on heterodox micro-economics, organized by Tae-Hee Jo and Fred Lee, this having also emerged as a mainstay of the AHE conference (since the beginning). Finally, there were a dozen papers on the economics of Luigi Pasinetti, convened by Andrew Trigg, which was noteworthy, especially given that Pasinetti offered one of the first keynote talks to the AHE.

The 2014 conference was held at Greenwich, one of the new beacons of heterodoxy in the UK, its position reinforced by recent appointments, and centrally by the construction of a genuinely pluralist degree program. The conference itself had as its theme the Triple Crisis. Emblematic of this was the plenary by Molly Scott Cato, an established AHE participant and newly elected Member of the European Parliament. Fred Lee's plenary was notable, not least for its poignancy, but also because of his attempt to lay out the role of microeconomics in heterodox economics. Specifically, Lee said that in writing microeconomics he first thought about the macroeconomic implications. More specifically he argued that heterodox microeconomics is the study of the sub-systems and their interdependencies, which constitute the social provisioning process as a whole. This of course is not to be confused with mainstream macroeconomic aggregation. Lee would also have been pleased to see the increased representation of Post Keynesian economists. This may simply reflect the presence of Ozlem Oznaran, at Greenwich, and her links to PKSG. But, it may also be a result of increasing cooperation, for instance discussion over the CORE (Curriculum Open-Access Resources in Economics) initiative (see AHE 2014b). The Conference program reflected strongly the Conference theme, with contributions on ecology, macroeconomics, and money. A session on money featured Molly Scott Cato, Tony Greenham from the New Economics Foundation, and a speaker from a City think-tank. This was a good example of both the conference theme, and the potential for conversation between diverse presenters. This, after all, may be the manifestation of the distinctive contribution of the AHE.

## What next for heterodoxy?

The AHE follows, but also to a degree anticipates, the wider heterodox movement. Debates within the AHE about its identity mirror broader discussions about the definition of heterodoxy. It is clear that heterodoxy is a complex object, possibly comprising all of the following: a set of theories, methods, and key principles; a set of social networks and institutional structures; a set of attitudes and outlooks; a position of relative powerlessness in relation to those structures which maintain a mainstream. In turn, as the above narrative clarifies, the AHE has those facets. The social aspect to the AHE is also noted: for example the most recent coordinator, Jamie Morgan, stated that he drifted into the AHE and found the people with whom he engaged were pleasant ("nice people"). This notwithstanding, the discussion so far suggests some historical patterns, which may indicate the immediate and longer-term future for the AHE. Hence, they suggest a possible future for heterodoxy.

One clear strand within the AHE has been attitudinal. The AHE was borne out of frustration that sets of ideas and people were being systematically marginalized. It was a demand to be heard; but also to be allowed to exist. It was a safe haven. It continues to act as such, in part by campaigning on issues important to it (see below). It also maintains a strong skepticism about the mainstream, in terms of its theoretical framework(s), methodologies, approach to economic education, inter alia, and of its attitude toward non-mainstream work. There are grounds for this skepticism but also room for viewing the mainstream differently. This is not unique to the AHE: strands within PKSG have consistently adopted a strategy of engagement with the mainstream. What might make the AHE unique is its commitment towards pluralism. Arguably this has emerged from the long methodological discussions of the 1980s.

A defining mark of the AHE, and increasingly of heterodox economics more generally, is that of pluralism, at various levels. Bruce Philp sees pluralism as dialectical, addressing different theses, in order to advance science, perhaps utilizing different units of analysis and levels of investigation. Indeed, at one point, a proposal was made to change the name of the AHE to incorporate the word 'pluralism/pluralist.' While 'Association for Pluralist Economics'—with the unfortunate APE acronym—did not happen, pluralism has taken root. Further, though pluralism has strategic advantages—including perhaps better research and teaching, and popularity amongst students (see below)—our view is that the AHE practices a genuine pluralism, and is not merely engaged in strategic pluralism (Garnett 2009). Further, the AHE needs to continue to practice pluralism and function pluralistically. Pluralism needs to be in action at the conference, for example with sessions within which different perspectives engage.

This line of argument points to the greatest outstanding conundrum facing the AHE, i.e., whether or not to engage with the mainstream. One argument is that mainstream economics evolves and in many ways the mainstream moves closer to heterodox positions. In areas such as economics teaching, mixed research methods, monetary economics, the environment, and labor markets, mainstream thought might engage with the heterodox. However, Gary Slater is less optimistic:

> Sadly, I think that lines have, if anything, hardened between mainstream and heterodoxy. The AHE is a great forum for engagement within the heterodox community but I don't think that the relationship is really any different to what it was in 1999 when AHE held its fringe conference to the RES meeting. Despite the challenges wrought by the financial crisis, mainstream economics remains dominant and where it is innovating at the margins it tends to imperialistically annex heterodox ideas without engaging with heterodox thinking.

This notwithstanding, our view is that pluralism is key and there is a need to build pluralist departments—rather than heterodox and mainstream ones—with students being introduced to alternative research and policy strategies. However, Andrew Trigg implores heterodox economists not to sacrifice the discipline to the mainstream: heterodoxy must do it better. This relates to one of Andrew Mearman's aims, which was to improve the quality of papers at the AHE conference, through stricter scrutiny of proposals, thereby trying to deal with perception (from the mainstream) of low quality.

However, the mainstream moves in mysterious ways. Mainstream economics dominates regulatory mechanisms such as the QAA, REF and still does not like to admit heterodox economics or acknowledge that it needs to be admitted. Jamie Morgan warns that:

> Mainstream departments are simply engaged in a form of self-cannibalizing auto-destruct by neo-Darwinian non-survival of the least-fit—they will die out, [so] if we spend our time trying to colonize their spaces we may ironically be revitalizing them but not fundamentally changing them and so we may be extending their life cycle...

His response is that heterodox economists should continue to operate in other, more interdisciplinary, departments.

Whether or not heterodox economics does engage with the mainstream, recent history suggests that work will continue in a range of key areas. Core theoretical work attached to canonical traditions will continue; and, indeed, from various perspectives, including a pluralist one, it is important that this does happen. In addition, it would seem likely that heterodox work will continue in areas in which there is a comparative advantage, such as in methodology and economics of the environment. Recent developments in macroeconomic modeling and in monetary theory suggest potential for progress in that crucial policy arena. Heterodox economists have been able to address the nature of finance and its links to crisis in a way far more powerful than mainstream commentators have done. Andrew Trigg, in particular, sees macroeconomics as an area of promise for heterodoxy, pointing to a lost British tradition of macroeconomics which needs revitalizing.

Other areas of strength for heterodox economics are in history of economic thought (HET), and this has been a consistent source of presentations at AHE conferences. These are areas of strategic importance as they can remind economists that economics other than that currently extant has existed. It also allows for older theories to be preserved for future use. When the crisis hit, Federal Reserve Chairman Bernanke was perhaps the right person for the job because of his knowledge of economic history (see also Caldwell 2013). The CORE initiative has stressed the importance of historical knowledge, partly in response to employers who complained that students knew too little of the past. That said this, too, presents problems: it may be a Whig history, as discussed at the Bristol Conference (2007).

Pedagogy has featured heavily in many AHE conferences and has been a defining element of recent heterodoxy. This partly reflects heterodoxy's pluralist focus: a key argument is that pluralism leads to better teaching and learning. Moreover, throughout the history of the AHE, a series of student-led movements have made demands that curricula are delivered based on more pluralist principles and with more attention paid to the real world. Student protests about curricula are not new—witness the active disobedience against a mainstream curriculum at Sydney in the early 1970s (see Stilwell 2006). But, since 2000, these movements have grown more frequent, possibly bolstered by higher student fees and concerns that abstract, formalistic curricula may not boost graduate job prospects in a difficult economic context. These modern student movements—beginning with the Post-Autistic Movement in France, and present now in Rethinking Economics and the International Student Initiative for Pluralism in Economics—have made fundamental criticisms about the method of mainstream economics. The AHE must continue to support these groups. If the student campaigns are successful it might be that more space is available for heterodox material within economics curricula and departments.

Thus far this discussion of heterodoxy has been largely intellectual but, as stated, a crucial facet of heterodoxy is its social structure. It will remain necessary to form and maintain coalitions with other groups with shared visions: this is already evident in the history of the AHE. It will be strategically necessary to pay attention to the extant social networks of heterodoxy—inside and outside economics—specifically in maintaining current heterodox centers of excellence, developing new ones, and creating networks between them. The latter is clearly an important feature of the AHE. Networking is achieved through the AHE conference, but also increasingly virtually, for example through the *Heterodox Economics Newsletter* and the Economics Network TRUE materials. A type of entrepreneurial flexibility will be necessary here—not opportunism but open to exploit opportunities. For example, the leading heterodox journal, the *Cambridge Journal of Economics*, was set up because the *Economic Journal* was moving to the (relatively mainstream) Oxford. These flexible adaptive institutional structures will be crucial because it is inevitable that the context, created by mechanisms such as the RAE and the REF, and state-sanctioned curriculum monitoring, are unlikely to disappear. Indeed, one of the features of the AHE has been its internationalization. This is positive: networks are expanding and heterodox economists are talking more than before. However, it also reflects the crisis facing UK heterodox economists, who struggle to get jobs and/or research support because their core journals are low on various lists of 'quality.' It is crucial to remember that strongholds can be fragile: Cambridge University is the best example of this.

An important part of this story must be renewal: in short, heterodoxy needs new people. The AHE Postgraduate Workshop is crucial in this regard. The history of the AHE reveals several people who have drifted away after taking up significant positions. Others have come in from the fringes or from nowhere.

This is fine. Indeed, Andrew Mearman talked about the AHE as a voluntary organization in which burn-out is a critical problem. Indeed, Alan Freeman used Andrew Mearman as an example! It is crucial to allow people to move in and out of the AHE, but also to keep them animated with political activity. As before, the AHE must continue to be active within the discipline: for example arguing against instruments of mainstream dominance, and supporting progressive student movements. But the Association should also be more active in policy debates and other political fora. For Andrew Trigg this is a crucial element of activity for heterodox economists.

The final element to note in the history of the AHE is the role of key individuals. In the case of the AHE, the key individual is the Coordinator. One must not overplay the role and importance of the Coordinator. Often they are just administering, keeping the show on the road. The AHE is a collective organization after all, and cannot function without the Committee. On the other hand, tasks tend to fall on key people. Some of these individuals have been hugely influential, and have been recognized as such: note honorary life memberships for Victoria Chick and Alan Freeman. Above all, we must stress the contribution of Fred Lee. Without him, the AHE may not have existed, and heterodoxy may have looked very different.

## Conclusion

Our perception of the AHE is framed by our understanding of the term 'heterodox economics.' Fred Lee, for example, sees the emergence of a coherent alternative to mainstream economics as manifest and desirable (Lee 2009, 2013). Others argue that heterodox economics represents "diverse groups of non-mainstream economists" (Stockhammer and Ramskogler 2013). Although we would endorse the latter perspective, one common theme among heterodox economists is a commitment to dialogue and pluralism. While other associations, such as IIPPE, or the PKSG, may be tolerant and open, they nevertheless coalesce around a particular mode of economic thought. Although IIPPE recognizes a plurality of perspectives they are constitutionally bound to a Marxist approach. Likewise the PKSG will elevate Post Keynesian economics above other heterodox approaches. Of course, the AHE provides a platform for Post Keynesian and Marxian economists. But, constitutionally and practically, it comprises a much broader church than is the case with other heterodox associations (with the exception of SHE, which is likewise composed).

In establishing the AHE Fred Lee may have had the intention of creating a coherent alternative to mainstream economics. Even if this comes to naught, his contribution has been to create a space for dialogue between alternative (and sometimes complementary) approaches to economics, which are committed to a progressive understanding of the social forces which underpin economic interactions, using a plurality of methodological approaches. For this heterodox economists, young and old, should be grateful.

## Note

1 The data for this table was taken from AHE (2014c) using the programme and delegate list. Although delegate numbers were provided for the 2001 conference (see the Conference Report on the AHE website) no delegate list was available and the breakdown of UK and 'Rest of the World' (ROW) delegates was proxied using the ratio of presenters. A delegate list was unavailable for 2006 and so the programme (comprising presenters, chairs, and discussants) was used to estimate the number and breakdown. Using this approach the 2006 figures were broadly similar to 2007. Data for 2012 and 2013 was not available online.

## References

AHE. 2014a. "Early History of the Association for Heterodox Economics." Accessed September 8, 2014. www.hetecon.net/division.php?page=about&side=early_history_of_the_ahe.

AHE. 2014b. "Pluralism, Heterodoxy, and the Prospects for a New Economics Curriculum: Assessing the Potential of INET, What's the Use of Economics, and the CORE Project." Accessed September 8, 2014. www.hetecon.net/documents/The_prospects_for_a_new_economic_curriculum.pdf.

AHE. 2014c. "Conference Archives." Accessed March 21, 2015. http://hetecon.net/division.php?page=ahe_conferences&side=conference_archives&sub=conference_2014.

Arestis, P., S. Dunn, and M. Sawyer. 1999. "On the Coherence of Post-Keynesian Economics: A Comment upon Walters and Young." *Scottish Journal of Political Economy* 46 (3): 527–550.

Caldwell, B. 2013. "Of Positivism and the History of Economic Thought." *Southern Economic Journal* 79 (4): 753–767.

Clarke, P. and A. Mearman. 2003. "Why Marxist Economics Should be Taught; But Probably Won't Be!" *Capital and Class* 27 (1): 55–80.

Douai, A., A. Mearman, and I. Negru. 2012. "Prospects for a Heterodox Economics of the Environment and Sustainability." *Cambridge Journal of Economics* 36: 1019–1032.

Dow, S. 1985. *Macroeconomic Thought: A Methodological Approach*. Oxford: Blackwell.

Elliott, L., R. Murphy, T. Juniper, J. Legget, C. Hines, C. Secrett, C. Lucas, A. Simms, and A. Pettifor. 2008. *A Green New Deal*. London: New Economics Foundation.

Freeman, A. 2008. "Submission from the Association for Heterodox Economics to the International Benchmarking Review on Research Assessment." *On the Horizon* 16 (4): 279–285.

Fullbrook, E., ed. 2004. *A Guide to What's Wrong with Economics*. London: Anthem.

Garnett, R. 2009. "Rethinking the Pluralist Debate in Economics Education." *International Review of Economics Education* 8 (2): 58–71.

Hamouda, O. and G. Harcourt. 1989. "Post-Keynesianism: From Criticism to Coherence?" In *New Directions in Economics*, edited by J. Pheby. Aldershot: Edward Elgar.

Inman, P. 2013. "Economics Students Aim to Tear Up Free-market Syllabus." *Guardian*, October 24. Accessed March 13, 2014. www.theguardian.com/business/2013/oct/24/students-post-crash-economics.

Lavoie, M. 2011. "History and Methods of Post-Keynesian Economics." In *A Modern Guide to Keynesian Macroeconomics and Economic Policies*, edited by E. Hein and E. Stockhammer. Cheltenham: Edward Elgar.

Lee, F. 2009. *A History of Heterodox Economics: Challenging the Mainstream on the Twentieth Century*. London: Routledge.

Lee, F. 2013. "Heterodox Economics and Its Critics." In *In Defense of Post-Keynesian and Heterodox Economics*, edited by F. Lee and M. Lavoie. London: Routledge.

Pressman, S. 1996. *Interactions in Political Economy: Malvern After Ten Years*. London: Routledge.

Stilwell, F. 2006. "The Struggle for Political Economy at the University of Sydney." *Review of Radical Political Economics* 38 (4): 538–550.

Stockhammer, E. and P. Ramskogler. 2013. "Post Keynesian Economics: How to Move Forward." In *In Defense of Post-Keynesian and Heterodox Economics*, edited by F. Lee and M. Lavoie. London: Routledge.

Walters, B. and D. Young. 1997. "On the Coherence of Post-Keynesian Economics." *Scottish Journal of Political Economy* 44 (3): 329–349.

# 3 Heterodox economics, distribution, and the class struggle

*Bruce Philp and Andrew Trigg*

## Introduction

Our understanding of contemporary economies is contested: indeed, economics is a discipline in 'schism.' In post-war Western capitalist economies one approach—mainstream economics—has tended to predominate in university departments and policy formulation, with profound consequences. This 'neoclassical' approach emphasizes the efficiency of markets (except in isolated cases of market failure, e.g., public goods), rarely challenges the ethics of capitalist distribution (and initial endowments), adopts an instrumental view of rationality, and utilizes a narrow 'positive' methodology. Recent history exposes the problem this creates. Although in the wake of the Global Financial Crisis (GFC) a critical economist, or healthy discipline, might have subjected such fundamentals to introspective evaluation, this has only really happened on the periphery of this approach, in its heterodox fringe.

Perhaps a clue to why this might be can be found in the Postface to the Second Edition of the first volume of *Capital*, where Marx indicated a historical trend in the early nineteenth century which resonates with, and explains, the contemporary power of mainstream economics. He observed that the subject of class antagonisms, manifest in Smith and Ricardo, was forced into the background from 1830, with the emergence of an uncritical political economy:

> It sounded the knell of scientific bourgeois economy. It was thenceforth no longer a question, whether this theorem or that was true, but whether it was useful to capital or harmful, expedient or inexpedient, politically dangerous or not. In place of disinterested inquirers, there were hired prize fighters; in place of genuine scientific research, the bad conscience and the evil intent of apologetics.
>
> (Marx [1867] 1976, 97)

The social nature of political economy, with class antagonisms, the evolution of property rights, and its explicit consideration of issues of moral philosophy, was eroded such that by the 1870s we witnessed what might now be considered mainstream economics, with its focus on marginal principles, individual decision-making, the efficiency of markets, and general multi-market equilibrium. Thus John Henry (1990, 2009) argues that neoclassical economics (in particular with its 'utility' theory of value) emerged as an antithesis to classical and Marxian political economy. And, we would argue, one thing that distinguishes mainstream from heterodox approaches is the latter's emphasis on social rather than purely economic relationships. Since the 1870s mainstream economics has essentially ignored class analysis and, instead, adopted a methodological individualist approach, basing its analysis on individual optimizing agents with given preferences. Although the likes of Gary Becker have sought to examine social phenomena, this particular manifestation of economic imperialism retains the calculus of optimization and its individualist approach. Game theory, of course, emphasizes interaction between agents but, again, it is principally individualistic in its methodological formulation. In macroeconomics, methodological individualism manifests as the 'microfoundations' agenda, which has sought to explain macroeconomic phenomena in terms of the agency of individual agents.

This asocial approach of mainstream economics runs counter to social reality, as noted by Lee and Jo (2011):

> People have social lives; they have families, parents, children, and a history; they need to be fed, housed, clothed, married and schooled. And, the needed and desired 'surplus' goods and services are produced to sustain their socially constructed, meaningful lifestyle. Thus the social provisioning process is a continuous, non-accidental series of production-based, production-derived economic activities through historical time that provide needy individuals and families the goods and services necessary to carry out their sequential reoccurring and changing social activities through time.
>
> (859)

These are mediated through societal institutions, cultural values, norms and beliefs, and in the environmental context within which social and economic activities take place; there are "both social structures and social agency" (859).

Among these social forces are the structure of production, the role of the capitalist state, and socio-economic classes. The latter is a familiar element in the analyses of classical political economy, as well as Marxian economics. Moreover, in the twentieth century many heterodox approaches (including Post Keynesian, Marxian, Sraffian, and Kaleckian economics) made income distribution associated with socio-economic classes a cornerstone of their economic analyses. Of course, reference is made in the literature to 'social class' and to 'socio-economic class' (for example Lee and Jo (2011) use the latter). However, first and foremost, classes are defined in classical and Marxian political economy in terms of the category of income members of that class receive: wages in the case of workers, profits in the case of capitalists, and rents for the landlords. It is this economic definition of class, driven by processes which are part-and-parcel of the social provisioning process, which the present chapter will consider.[1]

The aim of this chapter is to demonstrate that class conflict is a *core* theme of heterodox economics, manifest as it is in the work of classical and Marxian political economy, as well as the major stands of contemporary heterodox economics. In order to demonstrate this point the chapter is structured as follows. In the next section we shall begin by considering the class-based distribution of income—the basis for class conflict—from three progenitors of heterodox economics, namely Smith, Ricardo, and Marx. Thereafter we will consider the distributive approach of Sraffa, evaluating it as a heterodox approach to a class-based analysis of the distribution of income. Finally, we shall consider some complicating factors with regard to class-based distribution of income, in particular in relation to contemporary fracturing of the clearly delineated categories of these economists. In concluding we argue that although we would concede that class-based conflict over distribution is somewhat obscured by the nature of contemporary capitalism, class and class struggle remain essential, defining, characteristics of various heterodox analyses of capitalism.

## Classical and Marxian political economy

According to Lee and Jo (2011), "[t]he classical surplus approach delineates the determination of the proportion between capitalists' profits and workers' wage income, given (1) the production technology, (2) the level and composition of the social product, and (3) real wage rates" (860). This classical surplus approach is identified with Smith and Ricardo and, albeit differently, with Marx. An understanding of the surplus approach in these political economy traditions is thus a necessary step in locating contemporary heterodox approaches to distribution, the class struggle, and social provisioning. In this section we shall therefore outline these three perspectives on the class-based distribution of income, beginning with Smith and Ricardo, followed by the contribution of Marx.

Smith's theory of distribution was connected to his theories of price and growth, representing a radical departure from the mercantilist doctrines that preceded them. He constructed his theory of income distribution from a primitive society (the 'rude state of society') to a more developed one. The first phase in this is the accumulation of stock, which represents a deduction from output prior to determining the wages of labor. Effectively, if $Y$ is national output (or income), aggregate wages are $W$, and aggregate profits $\Pi$, we may write:

$$Y = W + \Pi \tag{1}$$

Once land has been appropriated, rent forms a second deduction from output prior to the wages of labor being paid, and once this advanced state of society has been reached there emerge three component parts which prices resolve into: wages, profits, and rents. Thus, price is intimately bound up with income and, in macroeconomic terms, national income will resolve itself into the distribution between the social and economic classes—laborers (workers), masters (capitalists), and landlords—with the associated aggregate income streams of wages, profits, and rents ($R$). Thus:

$$Y = W + \Pi + R \tag{2}$$

For a given level of national income this suggests a conflict over distribution of income, and Smith elaborated on this, in particular in relation to the level of wages and profits. For Smith:

> [i]t is not ... difficult to foresee which of the two parties must, upon all ordinary occasions, have the advantage in the dispute.... The masters, being fewer in number, can combine much more easily: and the law, besides, authorises, or at least does not prohibit, their combinations, while it prohibits those of the workmen.
>
> ([1776] 1981, 83–84)

Monopoly power of labor was illegal, but monopsony power of capital was not. Smith also observed that, in any dispute, the accumulated wealth of capitalists implies they can live for a period of time without their factories working, whereas workers do not have accumulated reserves which can be used for short-run consumption purposes. As Smith notes: "In the long run, the workman may be as necessary to his master as his master is to him; but the necessity is not so immediate" (84).

The power of the capitalists to collude tacitly is noted by Smith:

> We rarely hear ... of the combinations of masters, though frequently of those of workmen.... Masters are always and everywhere in a sort of tacit, but constant and uniform, combination, not to raise the wages of labour above their actual rate.
>
> (Smith [1776] 1981, 84)

Of course, workers too sought to collude in order to raise their wages (or resist their reduction), but "whether their combinations be offensive or defensive, they are always abundantly heard of" as the capitalists would seek to use the power of the law to support their position: they "never cease to call aloud for the assistance of the civil magistrate, and the rigorous execution of those laws which have been enacted with so much severity against the combination of servants, labourers, and journeymen" (84–85).[2]

It is therefore apparent from this textual exegesis that: (i) Smith identified a class conflict over distribution; (ii) the combination of capitalists (which we might think of as an abuse of monopsony power) did occur; and (iii) workers were not as successful in combining to raise the wages of labor. One of the reasons that Smith believed that capitalists had greater power than workers in this conflict was owing to the power of the law on combination, and the fact that capitalists have greater capacity (in terms of wealth) to outlast workers in any dispute. This 'positive' aspect (in a methodological sense) notwithstanding, some reflection on Smith's normative view of wages is interesting, especially with the association between Smith's contemporary interpretation and supply-side policies. In particular, Smith was an advocate of high wages:

> Is this improvement in the circumstances of the lower ranks of the people to be regarded as an advantage, or as an inconveniency, to the society?... Servants, labourers, and workmen of different kinds, make up the far greater part of every great political society. But what improves the circumstances of the greater part, can never be regarded as any inconveniency to the whole.... It is but equity ... that they who feed, clothe, and lodge the whole body of the people, should have such a share of the produce of their own labour as to be themselves tolerably well fed, clothed, and lodged.
>
> (Smith [1776] 1981, 96)

The class-based conflict over the distribution of income was important, too, in Ricardo's analysis. As Ricardo noted in the preface to his *Principles*:

> The produce of the earth—all that is derived from its surface by the untied application of labour, machinery and capital, is divided among three classes of the community; namely, the proprietor of the land, the owner of the stock or capital necessary for its cultivation, and the labourers by whose industry it is cultivated.... To determine the laws which regulate this distribution, is the principal problem in Political Economy...
>
> ([1821] 1951, 5)

And, this appears to resonate with Smith's treatment of the distribution of income encapsulated in equations (1) and (2). However, there are crucial differences with regard to rents, with differences in land quality determining the rents which can be achieved on that land. Because of diminishing returns, which is manifest in Ricardo's rent theory, rents are eradicated at the margin, and the subsistence wage is deducted from the marginal product, thereby determining the rate of profit, or 'surplus' (Lee and Jo 2011, 860). Thus Kaldor (1955–56) advances a corn model interpretation of Ricardo—in common with Sraffa (1951)—in which the rate of profit in agriculture determines the rate of profit in industry and the iron law of wages holds. As capital accumulates, the labor force will grow, eradicating any increase in the wage rate.

The notion of surplus which underpins this interpretation of Ricardo is one in which wages are measured in corn (a particular form of the real wage) and spent on corn. If this were not the case then any change in the relative prices of agricultural and industrial goods would influence the real wage (if it includes industrial goods) so that we would no longer be able to derive the corn rate of profit in terms of "the relationship between the product of labour and the cost of labour working on marginal land" (Kaldor 1955–56, 86). Any increase in the wage rate would diminish the rate of profit (i.e., there is a class conflict) and any taxes, other than property taxes levied on the land, would fall on the capitalist, thereby driving down profits and the rate of accumulation. This notwithstanding, in the absence of technical change there will be a tendency for the rate of profit to fall as more labor is employed, ultimately leading to the motivation for accumulation ceasing altogether (Ricardo [1821] 1951, 122). And, this falling rate of profit hypothesis was developed by Marx, albeit driven by a different mechanic.

Whether this corn model—which some consider to be a reasonable interpretation of Ricardo (1815)—can be applied to the *Principles* is, of course, contested in the history of economic thought (for a critique of the Sraffian interpretation, see Peach 1993). However, this notwithstanding, the dynamic of class conflict is different in Ricardo in comparison to Marx. Whereas Marx saw the principal conflict between the capitalist and the workers, in Ricardo the main tension was between the capitalists (manufacturers) and the landlords (as can be illustrated using the corn model). As inputs increase and we move onto the marginal lands so profits have a tendency to fall while aggregate rents increase. In contrast Marx followed Smith in locating his economic theory in a broader social setting. Moreover, contra Ricardo, Marx did not believe in the law of diminishing returns (Marx 1969, 144–149, approvingly cites Anderson's critique of Ricardo). Concerning wages, Marx did adopt a subsistence wage approach, but this was not a biologically determined subsistence level. Rather, a historically determined level prevailed:

> In contrast, therefore, with the case of other commodities, the determination of the value of labour-power contains a historical and moral element. Nevertheless, in a given country at a given period, the average amount of the means of subsistence necessary for the worker is a known *datum*.
>
> (Marx [1867] 1976, 275)

One of the factors which governs the surplus in Marx is the size of the reserve army of the unemployed and it is this which prevents wages from rising above this historically determined level (Lee and Jo 2011).

The notion of class conflict and distribution which is embodied in Marx's account of capitalism is represented in the model of surplus-value, or exploitation. This is analyzed in terms of the working day, taken to be a representative unit of time in the capitalist labor process. During part of the working day the worker produces the equivalent of what they (and their family) consume. This period of time (termed 'necessary labor') represents the time necessary for the worker to produce their wage. *Contra* Ricardo this real wage is comprised of agricultural and industrial goods. The surplus is derived from 'surplus labor' (the difference between the length of the working day and the time required to produce the wage) and the surplus-value is manifest as profits, interest, and rent. The ratio of surplus-value to wages, or the rate of surplus-value, can be measured in aggregate as the ratio $\Pi / W$, which gives a measure of the degree of exploitation of the workers by the capitalists.[3]

There are various factors which can influence this ratio. If there is a large and expanding body of the unemployed it may be possible to reduce the real wage;

likewise, there may be occasions when workers gain through effective action. Of more significance, for Marx, was the effect of conflict over the length of the working day (the process of absolute surplus-value production) and the effect of productivity increase emanating from an increased division of labor, the growth in the modern factory, and increased application of machinery (relative surplus-value production). As the length of the working day increased, so more could be produced for a given quantity of wage or, equivalently, the same could be produced with less wages, leading to a rise in $\Pi/W$. In reality, by the middle of the nineteenth century working hours were restricted in Great Britain and hence a second method of influencing the class-based distribution of income came to the fore: the process of relative surplus-value production. New technologies implied labor could once again be saved, raising the rate of surplus-value.

In Marx's *Capital* this process is underpinned by capitalist production relations, an element which is essential in the social provisioning process. Property relations lie at the heart of the distributive struggle in Marx's economics, and these represent an essential societal institution for the capitalist socio-economic system. Coupled with technology and direct capitalist-worker relations these comprise the economic base. However, as noted above in the context of Marx's subsistence wage, with its historical and moral element, there is far more to the socio-economic system than this. Capitalism, like other socio-economic systems, is mediated through societal institutions, cultural values, norms and beliefs, and there are social structures and is social agency. This superstructure thus reinforces the economic base thereby creating a capitalist totality. The economic, social, and legal basis of capitalism frames the contemporary social provisioning process, which is an essential element in heterodox approaches to capitalism. Reinforcing the Marxian approach with the insight derived from institutionalist economics can serve to enhance these insights as capitalism evolves. Capitalism imposes values, beliefs, and constraints on people. But, capitalism remains a product of human agency and it is the relationship between social, historical, and individual process which heterodox economists, of whatever persuasion, should continue to strive to understand.

## Sraffa, Marx, and the wage-profit frontier

The purpose of the theoretical core in Sraffian economics is to "illuminate the structural and persistent forces underlying the capitalist system" (Lee and Jo 2011, 860). In Sraffa's (1960) system he initially investigates production for subsistence using a simultaneous equation approach in which sufficient commodities are produced to reproduce those consumed in the production process. He uses the examples of wheat, iron, and pigs to illustrate a simple society which produces enough to maintain itself, and no more. These commodities are used as both the means of production (seed corn and tools for example) and as sustenance for workers. The latter implies that the subsistence of workers enters into the production process in much the same way as feed for cattle, or energy for production (Sraffa 1960, 9). This subsistence economy is extended to incorporate production with a surplus, which is conceived of as a physical surplus. This surplus, rather than being all appropriated by the capitalist class, is apportioned between wages and profits. Thus Sraffian production entails a notion that the overall social surplus is the difference between the total social product and the total amount of intermediate inputs, to be distributed between capitalist and workers. With an appropriate numéraire, the requirement of a viable self-replacing economy, an equal-profit-rate, and given technological coefficients, there emerges a vector of prices and an associated wage-profit trade-off characteristic of the Sraffian approach to class conflict.

One of the elements of Ricardo's ([1821] 1951, 43) analysis was his search for an "invariable standard measure of value, which should itself be subject to none of the fluctuations to which other commodities are exposed." Although Ricardo's search for an invariable measure of value was unsuccessful, Sraffa's standard commodity—which is essentially a composite measure—has been argued to fulfill the requirements of an invariable measure (Bellino 2004).[4] On the basis of the standard commodity (as numéraire) the relationship between wages and profits becomes independent of prices. The implication is that, at a point in time, with given technology, there is a linear inverse relationship between wages and profits, and a class-based notion of distribution emerges, not dissimilar to that of Smith and Ricardo. Given input-output coefficients, the only way to increase the profit rate is to diminish the wages of labor, and vice-versa. Thus, there is an inherent class-based conflict over the distribution of income.

The link between this and Marx's approach to class struggle is more problematic, not least because of the controversial value controversy which impacted Marxian and Sraffian heterodox economics in the 1970s (Howard and King 1992, 245–290; Lee 2009, 126–152). While the central focus of the present chapter is on the distribution of income, it is important to note that some saw Sraffa's work as complementary with that of Marx, in particular with regard to exploitation and class conflict. As Roncaglia notes:

> Marx's exploitation is considered as a matter of fact, since the surplus generated in the productive process is at least partly appropriated, as profits and rents, by social classes other than the workers. Besides, the antagonistic relation between wages and profits—expressing on the ground of income distribution the class conflict opposing capitalists and workers—is highlighted with exceptional clarity by means of an analytical tool developed by Sraffa, namely the standard commodity. Indeed, when the standard commodity is used as numéraire for measuring the wage rate, we get a negative linear relationship between the wage rate and the rate of profits.
>
> (2009, 149)

A key problem in examining the interface with Sraffa is that Marx assumed, throughout the three volumes of *Capital*, that labor is remunerated at a social subsistence level. With wages anchored in this way, it is difficult to model an inverse relationship between wages and profits. As argued in a recent treatment of this issue by Polak:

Sraffa investigates how prices vary as the labour portion of the surplus changes from zero to 100 per cent; but since for Marx, the wage is treated as a subsistence-level bundle, this investigation cannot even begin. To put it simply, from the Sraffian point of view Marx is stuck at zero.

(Polak 2013, 158)

This is not an argument which we would concur with because it ignores the role of class struggle in Marx's wider economic analysis, beyond the confines of the first three volumes of *Capital*. As argued by Lebowitz (1992), in *Capital* Marx makes an assumption that wages are given, as a basis for capturing the origins of capital in surplus-value. This assumption is required when Marx is considering the political economy of capital, but relaxed when he considers the political economy of wage labor.[5]

To find an explicit summary of Marx's ideas on wage labor an important source is his pamphlet, *Wages, Prices and Profit*. Marx wrote this as a submission to the meeting of the First International in 1865, in response to the Owenite John Weston. It is pointless, argued Weston, for workers to struggle for wage increases, since these will only be passed on by capitalists in the form of price increases. Marx used the labor theory of value to argue against Weston's position, and in defense of the nascent trade union movement.

As shown in the second section above, the key point for Marx is that workers contribute unpaid labor to the production process. Total value consists of an unpaid part (surplus-value) and a paid part (value of labor power). Marx (1965, 35) writes: "You must, however, be aware that the reward for labour, and quantity of labour, are quite disparate things." So, if wages increase, under class struggle this does not alter the value of commodities produced. Thus prices, when determined by value, are unaffected by an increase in wages. Why is this? The answer is that when wages increase the distribution between paid and unpaid labor changes. In his argument with Weston, Marx did not assume that the paid part of wages, based on social subsistence, is given: it varies under conditions of class struggle, between workers and capitalists.

The challenge, then, for workers and their trade unions, is to increase their wages at the expense of profits: without, that is, workers being blamed for price inflation. "A general rise in the rate of wages would result in a fall in the general rate of profit, but, broadly speaking not affect the prices of commodities" (Marx 1965, 78). On this ground, Marx's analysis of wage labor is much in tune with Sraffa's wage-profit frontier, which is also independent of prices.

This, too, provides a theoretical foundation for challenging the assumptions of mainstream economics (as indicated by Sraffa's subtitle to *Production of Commodities*). As shown in Trigg (2013), an orthodox position has developed in central banking and mainstream economics that interest rate policy should be geared towards the targeting of inflation. The logical consequence of the orthodox position is that the key problem that needs to be addressed is the continual, pointless, and damaging efforts of trade unions to seek higher wages. Only by ensuring an appropriate rate of unemployment, as underpinned by the vertical Phillips curve, can wage inflation (and hence price inflation) be control-led. In this mainstream narrative unemployment is a price worth paying to secure stable prices (generating, as Marxists would maintain, a reserve army of labor).

To illustrate the problems with this approach consider, for example, the widely used New Keynesian textbook by Carlin and Soskice (2006), which develops a model of inflation targeting that incorporates class struggle, with an explicit role for wage bargaining by workers. However, two key assumptions of this influential model can be brought into question from a Marx-Sraffa per-spective. First, a fixed mark-up on wages is used by firms to set prices. So, when wages increase, firms increase prices according to this mark-up. Of course, this device is not new to political economy; Marx (1965, 29) observed: "all the superannuated writers on political economy who propounded the dogma that wages regulate prices, have tried to prove it by treating profit ... as mere addi-tional percentages upon wages." Thus, for Marx, the mark-up is far from being the fixed parameter of mainstream economics: it is, rather, an arena for class conflict. And, as also shown by Steedman (1992), from a Sraffian perspective, mark-ups in different industries are interdependent, governed by the structure of production and distribution—they are far from being exogenous parameters.

Second, the inflation-targeting approach assumes that wages are determined by marginal productivity. Workers are paid according to how much they produce under diminishing returns, so any increase in wages must involve higher mar-ginal productivity and hence higher prices. As we have seen under Marx's labor theory of value, a part of the productive activity of workers is unpaid surplus-value. Indeed, this is the very basis and origin of capital. By attacking the theor-etical underpinnings of marginal productivity, and establishing a wage-profit frontier, the Sraffian capital critique also allies itself with Marx's defense of wage labor.

These arguments are as relevant now as they were when Marx helped form the First International. Depressed wages, as experienced now under con-temporary capitalism, are not a new phenomenon. In combatting the arguments of the mainstream, heterodox economics can draw on the rich seams of both Sraffian and Marxian perspectives on class struggle.

## Contemporary capitalism and extensions in the heterodox tradition

There are arguably some complexities in contemporary capitalism which imply that the historic forms predominantly analyzed in Smith, Ricardo, and Marx, differ markedly from those in developed capitalist economies in the twenty-first century. Financialization has been a process involving a rapid growth in the (largely unregulated) financial sector, including banks and institutional investors, coupled with fluctuations in asset markets and rising household debt (Onaran, Stockhammer, and Grafl 2011). And, although Marx foresaw many aspects of this (Fine 2010), the extent of the development of financial capital is a hallmark of capitalism in the later years of the twentieth century. Although writers in a

Ricardian or Sraffian tradition have analyzed financialization (see Panico, Pinto, and Anyul 2012), in modern heterodox economics the nature of capitalism investigated by Smith, Ricardo, and Sraffa, is more recognizable in terms of tangible outputs. That is not to say that the class conflict approach of the aforementioned authors is incongruent with analysis of the financial sector. Indeed, we would argue that class-based conflict over the distribution of income should be the starting point of heterodox analyses. However, more refined analyses which recognize the fractured and contradictory nature of classes are, and should be, provided by heterodox economists.

Intermediate classes are also recognized in the analytical Marxist work of Roemer (1982, 1994), although some may challenge the contention that analytical Marxism represents a heterodox approach (in conversation Fred Lee, for example, argued that analytical Marxian economic theory was neoclassical in its makeup). Returning to Roemer and the class struggle, he argued that in a subsistence economy, with a labor market, where each agent has an initial endowment of assets, they can hire, sell or work their own capital with the aim of minimizing their labor input to obtain a given subsistence level. In such circumstances those with the greatest capital endowment will be able to hire labor thereby not having to work themselves (big capitalists), whereas those with no capital endowment will need to sell their labor power in order to subsist (proletarians). However, a series of intermediate classes will emerge, each of which involves some self-employment. Small capitalists will employ others while also engaging in some self-employment. The petty bourgeoisie will be entirely self-employed, working their own capital. Finally, semi-proletarians would have some capital endowment but it would be insufficient to provide a subsistence income so they would be compelled to sell some of their labor power on the labor market. Thus, five classes emerge and Roemer derives the class exploitation correspondence principle (CECP) whereby every producer who must hire labor power in order to optimize is classified as an exploiter (in a Marxian sense) and every producer who must sell their labor power in order to optimize is classified as exploited (1982, 78–82).

In developing this work Roemer (1994) sought, using a microfoundations approach, to identify the source of exploitation. Using abstract, formal models, he demonstrated that, in principle, exploitation could be mediated though a number of institutional environments, for example in a setting solely comprising initial endowments and a credit market. In this environment the wealthy lend other agents money and receive interest in recompense. A five-class structure emerges and the significance of this model is that it has no labor market. This hypothetical example convinces Roemer that it is not the exploitation of labor per se which is the central injustice of capitalism, but rather the unequal distribution of endowments, or differential ownership of productive assets (DOPA) which underpins this.

The rise of managerial capitalism (involving unproductive labor in an orthodox Marxist sense) implies wages and profits can be further decomposed from the Smithian formulation in equation (1), as well as in the Ricardian and

Sraffian formulations. Linked to the Cambridge theory of income distribution, Palley (2005) treats managers as an intermediate group. Thus, if we let $W^K$ be the wages for the supervisory labor of manager capitalists, and if $W^W$ are the wages of workers, the following adding-up constraint is derived: $W = W^W + W^K$. Likewise, aggregate profits ($\Pi$) can be decomposed into those which are retained by the company (*Ret*), those which accrue to workers ($\Pi^W$), and those which accrue to manager capitalists, i.e., $\Pi = \Pi^W + \Pi^K + Ret$. The consequences of this for aggregate demand are significant in that it is not just the distribution of income between profits and wages which matters. Labor market conflict over the distribution of wages also impacts on aggregate demand. The distribution of wage income ($W^W/W^K$) depends on the state of technology (à la Marx), as well as the labor market and policy setting, including bargaining power derived from union density, workers' militancy, employment legislation, and benefit levels for the unemployed (Palley 2005). One of the outcomes of this model is that by 'improving' the distribution of the wage bill (i.e., raising the ratio $W^W/W^K$) we generate expansion in the economy because it positively contributes to consumption because workers have a lower propensity to save. Finally, distribution can also be linked to ownership—as implied by Roemer and suggested by Palley, with two possible drivers being considered. On the one hand it may be possible for aggregate demand to be brought in line with output via a redistribution of income between profits and wages; on the other it may be that by changing the ownership structure between workers and capitalists the same end can be accomplished.

Another heterodox approach which discusses the nature of class struggle in capitalism has been articulated by Lee and Jo (2011). They maintain a view of heterodox economics as an emerging school in its own right, challenging the notion that it comprises an eclectic mix of theories that resist integration (863). In common with the Sraffian approach their ("the") heterodox surplus approach begins with a given technology, a class structure, and the assumption that the economy is viable. They also assume the existence of the capitalist state. However, they do not assume that the composition and level of the social product (in terms of produced commodities) is given, nor that a "self-replacing with a surplus economy" is assumed. They replace the latter with emphasis upon individual or collective agency (in keeping with Lee's heterodox microeconomics approach) embedded in the social structure. Agency and social structure combine to direct the nature of commodities produced, and their distribution. Thus: "the social product is not given and the surplus is not a residual" (863). It is, rather, the outcome of a social provisioning process.

Lee and Jo's model is formulated in terms of the total social product which is divided between basics and non-basic goods. And (social) surplus goods are resolved into household consumption (of capitalists and workers), investment, and government expenditure, which in total is analogous to the Keynesian-Kaleckian principle of effective demand. The factors which determine the social surplus include the output-employment multiplier, the level and composition of the total social product, and the total amount of employment (864). Thus the social product is not allocated via production prices; rather "the decisions to produce the social surplus 'coordinates' economic activity" (864) with four theoretical consequences:

1  Consumption, investment, and government expenditure are independent.
2  Profits are produced in the form of fixed investment, and wages are produced in the form of consumption goods (as are government goods and services). The consequence of this is that the volume of profits and wages are unrelated, each being dependent on the decisions associated with the amount of surplus to be produced.
3  Government goods and services are prior to, and thus independent of, taxation.
4  Other traditional determinants break down: "prices do not allocate the social product, money wage rates do not allocate labor, profit mark ups do not allocate fixed investment goods or profits among the various industries" (865).

These views are plainly discordant with Sraffian and Marxian approaches in some sense. Although Lee and Jo recognize the power of the business community and ruling elite to determine the output level, and we would argue that in moving from a low-output to a high-output economy it is possible for profits and wages to rise simultaneously, this does not invalidate the fact that for a given output level there is an inherent conflict between workers and capitalists over the distribution of income. And, in this context, absolute surplus-value is important too, as workers frequently exhibit a preference for reduced hours even if it means lower wages. Lee and Jo are quite correct to point to the role of the business community and ruling elite in controlling decisions concerning the social surplus ('production relations' as it were) but by reframing the social provisioning process in the way they do they diminish the central conceptual role of the wage-profit conflict which can be traced from Smith to Marx, also being manifest (albeit in a different form) in Sraffa.[6] In this sense Lee and Jo's approach makes a central theme—class conflict over the distribution of income—secondary to conflict over the volume, nature, and recipients of consumption goods produced.

## Conclusion

This chapter has sought to demonstrate that there are commonalities in a variety of heterodox approaches to conflict over the distribution of income. Classes, and associated conflicts over distribution, are neglected in mainstream economics since the methodological individualist approach they espouse prevents the meaningful study of the socio-economy as a holistic entity. Micro-processes are important in determining outcomes, but so are irreducible social entities. Classes, as such, are an essential element of heterodox economics and meaningful social science more generally.

One common element in political economy and heterodox economics is that classes are defined economically by category of income. However, there are also social bonds which connect classes—e.g., class consciousness and class histories—and these indicate why micro-reductionism offers an unsatisfactory explanation of factor, or class-based incomes, both at the level of the individual agent and in aggregate. Although heterodox economists must be mindful of micro-processes (to do otherwise would expose one to the criticism of teleology) these are insufficient to capture the nature of capitalism and the social individual therein.

While mainstream historians of thought would seek to reinterpret Smith, Ricardo, and Marx in terms of their contribution to mainstream economics, there is a common element in the work of these great thinkers which is central: the economics of class conflict. Workers combine to raise wages, capitalists combine to lower them. As Smith noted capitalists are advantaged in this conflict by their being fewer of them, and by their ability to endure struggles over distribution for longer. At any given moment the incomes of capitalists and workers are in opposition, as noted in the work of Smith, Ricardo, and Marx, and latterly in the economics of more recent contributions such as Sraffian and contemporary Marxian economics. While there remain differences in the 'protective belt' there should be, at its core, a clear and general focus on class conflict over the distribution of income by heterodox economists. The focus on this, rather than the machinations of individual agents, is what singles heterodox economics out in this regard.

## Notes

1  It is for this reason that, in their quantitative Marxist approach, Cuestas and Philp (2012) use the term 'economic class' rather than 'social class' to categorize and analyze conflict over the distribution of income. In institutional economics the notion of class is not economically reductionist as in Marx's *Capital*. With respect to Marxian approaches, Todorova (2013) observes two broad classes: those who own the means of production and those without access to the means of production who must sell their labor power. In contrast, according to Todorova, Veblen's class categorization—which focuses on 'the kept classes' and the 'common man'—is subtly different. The kept classes are

> capitalists, rentier/leisure class, elite professionals, and political elite, who constitute the ruling class which actively seeks preserving their social power through collectively engaging in various economic, political, and social activities. They exercise agency through the institutions of the business enterprise, non-governmental organizations, the media, and state, schools, think-tanks, foundations, and international organizations.... This is not only through the decisions about production and distribution of the social surplus, but also by the cultural influence of the 'kept classes.' This includes the evolution of consumption patterns, standards, norms, symbols, conventional wisdom, expert discourse, and rhetorical constructs.
>
> (2013, 7)

Although the exercise of agency identified resonates somewhat with the Marxian analysis of the capitalist superstructure, the latter 'institutions' are investigated more elaborately in the institutional tradition.

2  Interestingly the Combination Acts of 1799 and 1800 and the Combinations of Workmen Act (1825) only came in a number of years after the publication of the

*Wealth of Nations* (for a discussion of these see Orth 1991). However, the Ordinance of Labourers 1349 and Statute of Labourers of 1351 had (with limited success) tried to fix wages at pre-Black Death levels, and outlawed trade unions and collective bargaining.

3 We abstract here from the productive-unproductive labour distinction as, to all intents and purposes, Marx did in the published volumes of *Capital*.

4 Sraffa defines the prefect composite commodity as

> one which consists of the same commodities (combined in the same proportions) as does the aggregate of its own means of production—in other words, such that both product and its means of production are quantities of the self-same composite commodity.
>
> (1960, 19)

5 Of course, Marx only published the first volume of *Capital*, and did not even get around to drafting his one-time planned book on wage labor. However, for some, such as Rosdolsky (1977), the book on wage labor is not missing—Marx's planned material on wage labor is incorporated into *Capital*. Lebowitz (1992) contests this, arguing that Rosdolsky interprets material that is only implicit in Marx's writings.

6 In spite of their discussion of agency and heterodox microeconomics there are also occasions when Lee and Jo (2011) lapse into statements which may be considered teleological, whereby there is a presumed trajectory in society which is exhibited independently of the goals and aspirations of human agents. Consider the following: "Also evident is that the social provisioning process must ensure, broadly speaking, that the social activities reoccur over time. Consequently, the composition and magnitude of the social surplus is based on productive capabilities and agency decisions" (859). It's not clear how the latter follows from the former. Consider, too, this: "To be a viable economy, the economic system as a whole organizes economic activities and structures such that productive capacity is physically reproduced ..." (866). This is fetishistic with regard to the economic system, which is assumed to have a will of its own.

## References

Bellino, E. 2004. "On Sraffa's Standard Commodity." *Cambridge Journal of Economics* 28 (1): 121–132.

Carlin, W. and D. Soskice. 2006. *Macroeconomics: Imperfections, Institutions and Policies*. Oxford: Oxford University Press.

Cuestas, J. and B. Philp. 2012. "Economic Class and the Distribution of Income: A Time-Series Analysis of the UK Economy, 1955–2010." *International Review of Applied Economics* 26 (5): 565–578.

Fine, B. 2010. "Locating Financialisation." *Historical Materialism* 18: 97–116.

Henry, J. F. 1990. *The Making of Neoclassical Economics*. Boston: Unwin Hyman.

Henry, J. F. 2009. "The Illusion of the Epoch: Neoclassical Economics as a Case Study." *Studi e Note di Economia* 14 (1): 27–44.

Howard, M. and J. E. King. 1992. *A History of Marxian Economics: Volume II, 1929–1990*. London: Macmillan.

Kaldor, N. 1955–56. "Alternative Theories of Distribution." *Review of Economic Studies* 23 (2): 83–100.

Lee, F. S. 2009. *A History of Heterodox Economics: Challenging the Mainstream in the Twentieth Century*. London: Routledge.

Lee, F. S. and T.-H. Jo. 2011. "Social Surplus Approach and Heterodox Economics." *Journal of Economic Issues* 45 (4): 857–875.

Lebowitz, M. 1992. *Beyond Capital: Marx's Political Economy of the Working Class*. London: Macmillan.

Marx, K. 1965. *Wages, Prices and Profit*. Peking: Foreign Languages Press.

Marx, K. 1969. *Theories of Surplus Value Part 2*. London: Lawrence and Wishart.

Marx, K. [1867] 1976. *Capital, Volume 1*, Harmondsworth: Penguin.

Onaran, O., E. Stockhammer, and L. Grafl. 2011. "Financialisation, Income Distribution and Aggregate Demand in the USA." *Cambridge Journal of Economics* 35 (4): 637–661.

Orth, J. 1991. *Combination and Conspiracy: A Legal History of Trade Unionism, 1721–1906*. Oxford: Oxford University Press.

Palley, T. 2005. "Class Conflict and the Cambridge Theory of Distribution." In *Joan Robinson's Economics: A Centennial Celebration*, edited by B. Gibson. Cheltenham: Elgar.

Panico, C., A. Pinto, and M. Anyul. 2012. "Income Distribution and the Size of the Financial Sector: A Sraffian Analysis." *Cambridge Journal of Economics* 36 (6): 1455–1477.

Peach, T. 1993. *Interpreting Ricardo*. Cambridge: Cambridge University Press.

Polak, M. 2013. *Class, Surplus and the Division of Labour: A Post-Marxian Explanation*. Basingstoke: Palgrave Macmillan.

Ricardo, D. 1815. *An Essay on the Influence of a Low Price of Corn on the Profits of Stock*. London: John Murray. Accessed December 19, 2015. http://la.utexas.edu/users/hcleaver/368/368RicardoOnCornLaws.html.

Ricardo, D. [1821] 1951. *On the Principles of Political Economy and Taxation*. In *The Works and Correspondence of David Ricardo*, Volume I, edited by P. Sraffa. Cambridge: Cambridge University Press.

Roemer, J. 1982. *A General Theory of Exploitation and Class*. Cambridge, MA: Harvard University Press.

Roemer, J. 1994. *Egalitarian Perspectives: Essays in Philosophical Economics*. Cambridge: Cambridge University Press.

Roncaglia, A. 2009. *Piero Sraffa*. Basingstoke: Palgrave Macmillan.

Rosdolsky, R. 1977. *The Making of Marx's Capital*. London: Pluto Press.

Smith, A. [1776] 1981. *An Inquiry into the Nature and Causes of the Wealth of Nations, Volume 1*. Indianapolis: Liberty Fund.

Sraffa, P. 1951. "Introduction." In *The Works and Correspondence of David Ricardo*, Volume I, *On the Principles of Political Economy and Taxation*, xiii–lxii, edited by P. Sraffa. Cambridge: Cambridge University Press.

Sraffa, P. 1960. *Production of Commodities by Means of Commodities: Prelude to a Critique of Economic Theory*. Cambridge: Cambridge University Press.

Steedman, I. 1992. "Questions for Kaleckians." *Review of Political Economy* 4 (2): 125–151.

Todorova, Z. 2013. "Consumption as a Social Process within Social Provisioning and Capitalism: Implications for Heterodox Economics." MPRA Working Paper 51516. Accessed February 16, 2015. http://mpra.ub.uni-muenchen.de/51516.

Trigg, A. B. 2013. "Towards a Marxian Critique of Inflation Targeting." *International Journal of Pluralism and Economics Education* 4 (3): 274–281.

# 4 Qualitative data and grounded theory in heterodox economic research

## Insights from three Australian studies

*Therese Jefferson*

## Introduction

In early 2004 I was fortunate enough to attend a postgraduate workshop on advanced research methods organized by the Association for Heterodox Economics and coordinated by Paul Downward. The workshop was funded by the United Kingdom's Economic and Social Research Council and held in Manchester. It was scheduled to be held when I was a doctoral candidate about one-third of the way through my studies. The workshop included sessions run by Tony Lawson, Paul Omerod, Andrew Mearman, Paul Downward, Wendy Olsen, Stephen Gorard, Peter Davies, and, of course, Fred Lee. My recollection is that all the sessions were excellent and highly informative for a doctoral student interested in heterodox economics and research methods. It was, however, Fred Lee's session that I anticipated most keenly.[1]

Fred Lee's session was on the application of grounded theory research methods to a study on pricing. At that stage I had participated as a research assistant in a study using grounded theory (Austen, Jefferson, and Thein 2003) and decided to apply it to a study of the retirement savings strategies of Australian women. With the support of my supervisors I had managed to have my project proposal approved as part of the candidacy process at Curtin University. I was pleased to have achieved these initial goals but was left in a situation of undertaking a study that applied grounded theory to the very 'economic' topic of decisions to save. While there are many published studies using grounded theory, its application and discussion within the context of economic research was relatively rare in the early 2000s. The method had been applied to studies of firms and behavioral organization (Finch 2002), Post Keynesian research on pricing (Lee 1998; Lee and Downward 1999), and feminist research on gendered social indicators (Austen *et al.* 2003). In this context, one of the few economists who had critically discussed and analyzed the methodological basis of grounded theory and its potential use in economic research was Fred Lee (Lee 2002).

As discussed below, grounded theory was originally developed by sociologists as an approach for systematically constructing theory from data and its analysis. The approach is, therefore, a significant departure from the deductive approaches to theorizing traditionally used within economics. In this chapter I would like to consider Lee's (2002, 2005, 2012) discussions of the relevance of grounded theory for economic research as well as some of the practical issues of implementation that I have encountered in three different economic research projects that have since been undertaken within Australia. In doing so the aim of this chapter is to identify and discuss specific advantages, disadvantages, and lessons learned from utilizing a grounded theory approach in specific empirical studies. To this end five particular aspects of each project are considered, including the: (i) background; (ii) rationale for utilizing grounded theory; (iii) project design; (iv) data and analytical approach; and (v) project findings and limitations.

The aim of the chapter is to argue and demonstrate that grounded theory can produce important empirical and theoretical insights in contexts that constrain the development of theory in the manner described by Lee (2002, 2005, 2012). The key conclusion from this exercise is that while the application of grounded theory may not generate 'new theory' in all contexts, it does provide a productive approach to generating important economic insights. This is particularly important in contexts where a lack of data or previous economic research mean there is a limited understanding of the causal processes underlying specific economic events. Prior to considering these issues, a first step is to consider the arguments put forward by Lee (2002, 2005, 2012) and the links between grounded theory and the qualitative research described later in this chapter.

## Lee's arguments for the application of grounded theory to economic research

Grounded theory was originally developed by Glaser and Strauss (1967) and further developed in varying iterations by Strauss (1987), Strauss and Corbin (1990, 1994), and Glaser (1992, 1998). In simple terms, grounded theory is a research method designed to systematically allow the development of theory from data. In more formal terms it has been defined as

> a set of fully integrated and practical steps aimed at guiding the research process to completion, the end product of which is the generation of theoretical statements about the data. The chief mark is that this theory is grounded in data and built up from the bottom.
>
> (Gibson 2003, 133)

While grounded theory is a research method that is relatively well known among many social researchers, there was little written on the method and its intersections with key debates on economic research methodology prior to the publication of Lee's contribution to the *Cambridge Journal of Economics* (2002). In his article, Lee presents an accessible and coherent argument for the use of grounded theory and outlines key features of the method that make it relevant for economists wishing to develop theory which is "historical in structure, content and explanation" (Lee 2002, 790). Lee links grounded theory with debates about the ontological and epistemological foundations of economics but, in keeping with the development and purpose of grounded theory, he focuses closely on its role as a basis for creating theory. He develops a schema (see Figure 4.1) to represent the key elements of grounded theory method: data collection, theoretical analysis, and theory development.

The process utilized by grounded theorists and described by Lee is one in which data are collected, compared, analyzed, and categorized so that individual pieces of data develop a "collective significance" (Lee 2002, 794). Through this process, data categories are formulated that contain individual pieces of data collected from multiple sources. The basis for determining possible sources of data is theoretical sampling, which involves the purposeful collection of data that is expected to increase the density of specific categories. In his discussion Lee identifies the important concept of 'theoretical saturation' which occurs when "no new data regarding a category and the relationships between the category continue to emerge" (795).

Theory building continues by exploring relationships between data categories. To facilitate this, different categories might be grouped conceptually as representing key elements of the field of inquiry, for example, economic structures, human motivation, actions, or outcomes. Possible causal links between the categories or groups of categories are then investigated and causal mechanisms theorized. Ideally, this process will assist the identification of a central causal mechanism that provides an explanation of the events relevant to the field of inquiry and captured in data. To use Lee's words, the "grounded economic

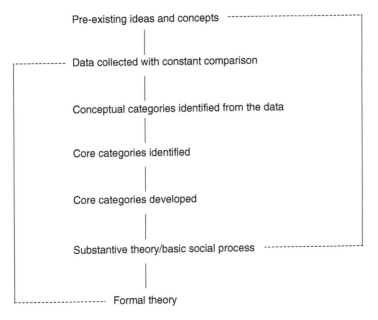

*Figure 4.1* Lee's (2002) schema of the grounded theory method.

theory that eventually emerges is a complex analytical explanation or interpretation of actual economic events represented in the data" (Lee 2002, 796). The flexibility of grounded theory is demonstrated by the fact that it can accommodate analyses focused on very specific events, such as discussed in this chapter, but has also been applied to modeling the economy as a whole (Lee 2011).

A key issue identified by Lee is that a grounded theory is "only as good as the categories which make it up" (Lee 2002, 797). This is an important issue for grounded theorists and Lee notes that category development that is inadequately grounded in data is likely to be criticized as "poor, ill developed ... and unable to provide a comprehensive and convincing explanation of actual economic events" (797–798). The adequate grounding of categories with data is closely associated with the concept of "saturation." Grounded theory requires that researchers continue with data collection and analysis until further collection of data reveals no new insights into the relationship between the codes, categories, and the core category. At this point the categories, codes, and emergent theory are said to have reached theoretical saturation.

## Extending Lee's arguments beyond Post Keynesian theory formation

Lee's (2002) arguments were a contribution to discussions about the appropriate research methods for use in Post Keynesian economics. He based his arguments in favor of grounded theory on relevance to Post Keynesian approaches to ontology and a relativist approach to epistemology. However, there was an important point in Lee's argument that was not made explicit: grounded theory is an appropriate method for any school of thought characterized by similar philosophical underpinnings of realism. For example, feminist economists who accept similar philosophical approaches to those that Lee identifies as relevant to Post Keynesians, may find that his arguments have similar force and relevance (Austen and Jefferson 2006). Thus, Lee's arguments have potential relevance to economic researchers who have interests outside of the traditional Post Keynesian agenda that focuses mainly on issues of uncertainty, money, and unemployment (King 2012, xvi; see also Lee 2012).

Lee's arguments are also framed within a discussion focused on the development of new theory, often referred to as "theory creation." In doing so he stresses the need for theoretical saturation and the development of relatively complete accounts of specific economic events. Saturation is a key issue for grounded theorists. It can, however potentially act as a deterrent to utilizing grounded research methods, due to constraints of time and funding that can impede the likelihood of sufficient data collection to ensure saturation. Given that the development of new theory is the key goal of grounded theory, this can be viewed as a major limitation.

However, Finch suggests that the iterative process of data collection and hypothesis formation that forms the basis of grounded theory, allows the emergence of "novel contributions to knowledge." These contributions can extend existing theory and be incorporated into future research projects (Finch 2002). Finch's argument is consistent with the view that theory construction is part of an ongoing process (Glaser and Strauss 1967). That is, while the goal of research projects using grounded theory is to construct new theory, it is unlikely that a single project with specified time and resources constraints will generate an all-encompassing theory of a specific economic event.

Whitely (2005) suggests that the term 'grounded research' should be used to describe the use of grounded theory in a constrained context that requires modification of either its application or goals. In such circumstances, grounded research projects tend to use the data analysis process of forming categories and concepts through the comparison of data to develop specific insights into economic events, without necessarily contributing to the development of new theory. Her arguments suggest that Lee's discussions are relevant to contexts where constraints may mean that grounded research is a realistic goal for exploring specific economic events.

The following discussion of three empirical studies of economic events is undertaken to provide critical and practical examples of utilizing grounded theory in projects that extend beyond the context of Lee's (2002) arguments and differ from his (2011) analysis of a whole economy.

## Extending grounded research to three empirical economic research projects

The following discussion summarizes three specific research projects undertaken within contexts that constrained the full implementation of grounded theory. The projects are used as examples to support an argument that grounded research based on qualitative data collection can provide useful additions to empirical economic studies, even if there is limited capacity for new theory development. Each of the studies has been the focus of previously published papers. However, the aim of the following discussion is to develop insights from the context which informed the design of each project. The discussion also considers the advantages and disadvantages that arose from the various project designs. Reflection on these aspects provides a basis from which to discuss and assess methodological issues that often receive relatively little attention in published findings from empirical research. With this aim in mind, the background to each study is considered and this is linked with each project's design, which all involved constraints of funding and timing.

While each project was undertaken separately, there are some key elements in common. Each study was designed in response to specific economic policy debates and, in the case of the first two studies, changes in economic regulation. Second, each study was characterized by research questions in which gender was a key issue for consideration but had been relatively neglected in mainstream economic theorizing. Third, each study was undertaken in a context of very limited data from which to gain insights into gendered aspects of specific economic theories. Fourth, all three studies utilized qualitative data as either the main source of data (studies one and two) or a key source of data in a mixed methods project. Grounded theory does not require that qualitative data be used as the basis for analysis although this is a relatively common occurrence (Lee 2002, 799). Further, each study was informed by the research team members' understandings of the ontological and epistemological characteristics of each project

The summaries below give a brief description of each project and focus on four particular aspects of each project, including: (i) the rationale for utilizing grounded theory; (ii) project design; (iii) data and analytical approach; and (iv) project findings.

## Study one: women's patterns of retirement saving

### Background

This study arose in response to changes in Australia's retirement income framework that occurred throughout the 1990s (Jefferson 2007a, 2007b). In common with other western, developed countries, population ageing was associated with concerns about future fiscal stresses. In Australia these policy concerns contributed to the introduction of compulsory occupational superannuation (a form of private contributory, pension scheme) as the national government's preferred system for the provision of income in retirement. Published research spanning two decades had highlighted gender biases inherent in a retirement income system based on occupational superannuation (Jefferson 2005b). Not surprisingly forecasts of highly gendered patterns of adverse retirement outcomes became a key concern for women's groups and government departments charged with framing social policy. Contributors to the debate felt that equity considerations of retirement incomes policy warranted further attention.

### Rationale for collecting qualitative data

Discussions of retirement income systems are strongly informed by economic literature on savings decisions. Mainstream economic analyses are typically based on the life cycle hypothesis of consumption and saving and models of intertemporal choice (Deaton 1992). However, many of the underlying assumptions for these models are either based on tenuous empirical evidence or neglect important aspects of many women's decision-making contexts. Intertemporal models of consumption and saving usually neglect the potentially important roles played by uncertainty, non-monetary household income, patterns of asset accumulation, social institutions, motivations, attitudes, and decision-making processes.

In 2002 the Office for Women's Policy in Western Australia had made a decision to undertake a study in partnership with researchers from Curtin University to undertake an exploratory study to investigate women's approaches to retirement savings. The project was ultimately funded by the Australian Research

Council under the Linkage Project scheme (project number LP0347060). Given the lack of existing economic theory that appeared directly relevant to women's retirement savings decisions in Western Australia, it was decided to use a research approach that put women's experiences and decisions at the center of the data collection and analysis process. From the perspective of the research team at Curtin University the potential to make an innovative contribution to theory was an important consideration. The rationale for utilizing grounded theory was therefore twofold: it was perceived as facilitating data collection and analysis that was directly relevant to policy and it involved a systematic approach to theory development on savings decisions.

### Project design

The aim of this project was to extend current understanding of Australian women's decisions about saving and retirement within the broad context of the experiences and institutions that inform and constrain those decisions. Information about household financial arrangements has been recognized as particularly sensitive and confidential within Australian society and in previous studies this has resulted in reluctance by participants to openly discuss such issues (Olsberg 1997; Singh 1997). For this reason, individual interviewing, with an emphasis on confidentiality, was adopted as the specific data collection method used in this study.

### Data collection and analysis

Recruitment of interview participants was designed to facilitate the collection of data from a heterogeneous sample of participants from Western Australia. Participants were recruited via invitations distributed through primary schools, playgroups, community-based groups, and workplaces. Funding constraints allowed for 30 interviews to be conducted. With the participants' consent, interviews were audio taped for subsequent analysis and transcription. Data analysis was undertaken to identify common themes and categories from the transcripts.

### Findings and limitations

Data were categorized in a manner consistent with the methods outlined by Lee (2002). Three key themes emerged as particularly relevant to women's discussions of retirement savings. The first was that interview participants' own definitions of savings often differed from formal definitions commonly used in economic analysis. Some forms of debt were perceived as types of savings and family 'traditions' or lessons learned from parents appeared to be highly influential in how savings were defined. A second theme was the importance of changing institutional context to women's patterns of savings. Several interview participants had been required to leave their employment when they married and had no method for participating in occupationally based savings schemes. Others had been actively discouraged from participating in early superannuation schemes that operated in the public sector on the basis that their husband's savings would provide for them in retirement. This theme might be considered to be closely aligned with the "economic structures" referred to by Lee as an emergent component of grounded theory development (Lee 2002, 795). A third key theme was the practice of establishing processes which reduced the need for ongoing active decision-making about savings. Routines or contractual obligations that facilitated regular savings were important in this area of data. This theme also aligns with Lee's discussion of human actions (795).

Despite the purposeful design of the study to contribute new theory, the capacity of the study to contribute an innovative and comprehensive approach to the analysis of saving decisions was limited. The number of interviews restricted the capacity for data categories to be saturated and there is little doubt that it would have been beneficial to undertake both more interviews and another form of data collection, possibly a survey (Jefferson 2005a, 259). However, the involvement of government offices and the Australian Research Council in the funding process required, to a significant extent, that the team comply with established processes of complying with research processes outlined in the original funding agreement. These processes included both the scope and type of data collection and analysis to be undertaken. A key lesson from this project was that relatively ambitious projects, including the development of new theory, are more likely to be successful if they are part of a coordinated range of projects undertaken by a community of scholars rather than a modest single study.

## Study two: decentralization of labor market regulatory framework

### Background

This study was linked closely to major changes in Australian legislation relevant to the regulation of wages and conditions of employment. The 2006 legislation was designed to decentralize wage determination and facilitate individual negotiations between employers and employees (Jefferson and Preston 2010). Existing research suggested that gender pay gaps are greater in jurisdictions where wage setting processes are relatively decentralized (Gregory and Ho 1985; Gregory and Daly 1990, 1994; Blau and Kahn 1992, 2003; Gregory 1999). This finding had been reinforced in Australia through the experience of decentralized employment contracts in the jurisdiction of Western Australia (Jefferson and Preston 2007; Preston and Jefferson 2007).

In 2006 Australia's Human Rights and Equal Opportunity Commission (HREOC) commissioned a report identifying sources of official data that might be used for monitoring the effects of the legislation on men's and women's conditions of employment (Preston, Jefferson, and Seymour 2006). The report documented inconsistencies, fragmentation, and gaps in data collections that otherwise might have been useful for this purpose.

*Rationale for collecting qualitative data*

In the absence of adequate official data collections for monitoring the possible effects of the legislation, many researchers and policy makers were seeking to employ research methods that could provide timely insights into relatively short-term outcomes from the legislation. Regular surveys undertaken at the University of Sydney partially met this need (van Wanrooy *et al.* 2007, 2009). A second option, utilized by an informal network of researchers throughout different states within Australia, was to utilize qualitative research methods to provide early indications of labor market developments (Elton *et al.* 2007).

The rationale for the collection of qualitative data was, from the outset, a response to a perceived need for relatively rapid data collection and analysis within a context of constrained resources (both funding and time). In this project there was a low expectation that the data collection and analysis would be part of a larger agenda of developing new theory. The project's aims were not focused strongly on theory creation but adhered closely to the processes of data analysis associated with grounded research.

*Project design*

The project was designed as a series of individual interviews. This design was selected as a flexible and rapid response to the need for initial research that might contribute to an important policy debate. The experiences of workers in relatively vulnerable labor market positions were identified as a potential indicator of possible outcomes from the new legislation. In the Australian context, workers in potentially vulnerable labor market positions have traditionally had their minimum levels of pay and conditions defined in documents known as 'industrial awards.' Based on levels of earnings, feminization, and casualization, the hospitality industry and retail trade were identified as areas that might be particularly affected by the legislative changes. Data collection focused on individual interviews with employees from these sectors.

*Data collection and analysis*

Invitations to participate in the project were distributed through personal contacts, unions, and a large employer group and 22 interview participants were selected from volunteers to reflect a diversity of ages, household type, marital status, and cultural backgrounds. A single interview instrument was developed with both structured questions and semi-structured interview prompts. The structured questions gave some areas of data collection that were common to all participations, while the semi-structured prompts allowed participants to explain their experiences, perceptions, and expectations of the negotiating of employment conditions. Open coding was used to facilitate the identification of themes and grouping of data.

## Findings and limitations

The project generated insights into specific instances of changes to employees' wage rates or, more commonly, working hours. However, few of the interview participants related these changes specifically to recent changes in the legislative framework. Several interview participants told stories of unhappy labor market experiences extending to time frames well before the new national legislation. This was in contrast with similar studies in other Australian states and may have been related to the particular context of decentralized employment regulation in Western Australia (Elton *et al.* 2007).

A key finding from the project, however, related to the role played by poor or limited information about wage rates and employment conditions. In many respects, the interview participants were working within a context with characteristics closely aligned with a competitive market, including a large number of small employers, a large pool of labor, and low barriers to entry and exit. The interviews revealed, however, that information about wages was severely restricted. Interview participants had little knowledge of, or access to, key areas of information that are required for efficient markets—that is, prevailing prices. This was further hampered by new confidentiality provisions under the new regulatory framework. In this context, interview participants demonstrated a preparedness to rely on employers to define appropriate employment standards and to adjust wage rates.

Participants' experiences also suggested that some employers were relatively uninformed about appropriate employment standards. Without an acknowledged community standard and perceptions that award minimum wages were no longer mandatory, there appeared to be an incentive for employers to avoid any risk of paying wages that were above those of a competitor. In addition, payment of wages in cash appeared to be a relatively common practice and timely and reliable information about wage practices were difficult to obtain. There appeared to be underpayment of wages among some interviewees.

Although the sample of interview participants was small, it was sufficient to suggest that the 'free-market' rhetoric used to support the decentralization of labor market regulation had been implemented in a less than comprehensive fashion. If the purpose of the legislation was to bring the operation of labor markets closer to mainstream economic models of highly competitive and efficient markets then the role of accessible information about wages was of high importance. In this particular study, a small sample of participants providing rich descriptions of their lack of access to information about wages provided a reasonable basis for assessing the extent to which the new legislation was consistent with its stated aims of efficient, competitive labor markets.

A disadvantage of the project design and sample, however, was that the small sample provided a convenient excuse for the research to be dismissed by key policy makers. Commenting on the small-scale studies that were carried out independently across Australia (Elton *et al.* 2007) the Workplace Relations

Minister, Joe Hockey, claimed that the research was "flawed" and carried out by "left-wing" academics (ABC News 2007). While the minister accused other, larger-scale projects in even stronger terms (Gittens 2007; Shaw 2007) the purposeful nature of the sample provided the basis for a particular type of criticism that could not be leveled at research based on a large, representative sample. It is perhaps noteworthy that in the longer term, the findings from large-scale analyses were consistent with the early findings from small qualitative projects (van Wanrooy *et al.* 2007, 2009). To this extent the project may be assessed as being somewhat successful in providing a lead indicator of subsequent labor market events.

## Study three: employment decisions of mature age women working in aged care

### Background

Internationally, it has been recognized that mature age women are a rapidly growing demographic group with potential for higher rates of workforce participation and improved retention (OECD 2006). Removing barriers to the employment of mature age women has been identified as important to achieving labor supply growth in the context of an ageing labor force (Australian Government, Productivity Commission 2005; Australian Government, The Treasury 2010).

At the time of designing this study, the importance of understanding mature aged women's labor supply was particularly high in the aged care sector where women comprised more than 90 percent of the workforce and the median age of workers was over 45 years. The sector was also characterized by a strong growth in labor demand and ongoing problems with the retention of workers. The number of full-time equivalent direct care workers needed for aged care accommodation has been projected to rise by 325 percent between 2003 and 2031 (Hugo 2007).

### Rationale for collecting qualitative data

Qualitative data were collected as part of a mixed methods research project to assist with interpreting survey data and to provide an opportunity to identify emergent issues which may have been neglected in the survey instrument. The potential role for theory development was not, therefore, the main priority for inclusion of qualitative data analysis in the project. While thematic analysis of the data was planned as an integral part of the project, this was to be done to inform the identification of causal processes relevant to correlations in a relatively large survey data set. It was also planned that the two forms of data collection and analysis would facilitate triangulation whereby similarities and differences in the findings from the different analyses could be identified (Austen *et al.* 2014; Jefferson *et al.* 2014).

*Project design*

This project was relatively well funded by the Australian Research Council under the Discovery Grant program. The research was designed and conducted by a team of six researchers and compared with the previous two projects it had considerably greater resources in terms of funding, staffing, and time. The study was designed as a sequential, explanatory mixed methods project (Creswell and Plano-Clark 2007). Two waves of survey panel data totaling over 6,000 responses were complemented by a program of 43 individual interviews conducted with a subset of survey participants.

*Data collection and analysis*

Forty-three semi-structured interviews were conducted to collect detailed case descriptions of mature age women's descriptions of experiences and plans for remaining in paid care work. Recruitment of interview participants was achieved by asking participants in the initial survey whether they were prepared to participate in an interview to further discuss their experiences of working in aged care. In response, 1,568 survey participants indicated their willingness to participate in this part of the project. Potential interview participants were selected to ensure a diversity of carers in terms of occupation, residential and community care roles, intentions to stay or leave aged care, and geographic location. The interviews were held between the two waves of survey data collection.

The analytical approach applied to interview transcripts was twofold. First all transcripts were analyzed using a constant comparison approach to open coding. This allowed key concepts and constructs relevant to mature age women's employment decisions to emerge from the experiences of interview participants. This part of the analysis is largely consistent with Lee's (2002, 2005, 2012) discussions of theory development. Second, the transcripts were analyzed for key developments and changes during the study period. This allows for the development of insights into the dynamics of employment decision-making and for the identification of key variables that may be important over time.

*Findings and limitations*

Preliminary findings suggest that the combination of data and analysis will generate insights that are rarely considered in mainstream economic analysis. One key example relates to links between low wages and 'misrecognition' (Fraser and Honneth 2003), which has emerged through the range of data and analytical methods that have been utilized in our project.

By comparing insights from the various data collections (particularly the interviews and surveys) it is likely that we will be able to contribute convincing analyses that will allow the outcomes from our project to be integrated with important areas of debate and critique from other areas of social science (Fraser and Honneth 2003). This will, we expect, be an important theme in the findings published from our project.

## Summary and lessons learned from three studies

Table 4.1 provides a brief summary of the key points discussed above and shows that while there are some similarities between the studies, each study demonstrates very different contexts, rationales, project designs, findings, and limitations. By comparing the three studies we can gain some insights into the advantages and disadvantages of grounded research that are more generalized than those that can be identified by considering the individual projects.

The first lesson is that the theoretical importance of the findings from each project did not necessarily match the rationale for engaging with grounded research methods and qualitative data collection and analysis. While the first study was designed purposefully to contribute to theory building this goal was constrained by the lack of theoretical saturation. This is not to say that the study did not produce insights. The emergent categories appeared linked with significant and important areas of economic literature, particularly in the areas of habits and rules of thumb in some areas of economic decision-making (Hodgson 1997). However, the capacity to develop an adequate theoretical contribution with comprehensive account of the causal mechanisms that contribute to women's low retirement savings was limited.

In contrast with the aims of the first study, the second study which had a smaller sample and had more modest theoretical aims generated important theoretical insights. The theoretical insights were specifically relevant to the role that access to information played in specific labor market sectors in Western Australia in 2006. This was an outcome not purposefully targeted nor expected by the research team but, as an emergent finding, was in keeping with the nature of data analysis in grounded research. While the finding was relatively restricted in nature, it gained importance from the rationale in which the reforms to labor market regulations had been embedded. The rhetoric and assumptions of traditional competitive market theory was being used to justify major public policy changes. However, the findings from the study demonstrated that information about wages and employment conditions was often difficult for workers to access. Thus a key assumption of the institutional framework underpinning efficient markets was missing from the policy context and it was questionable whether the stated legislative aims could be achieved.

Theoretical contributions are likely to be most substantial in the case of the third study on mature age women working in aged care, which is a work in progress at the time of writing this chapter. The study was explicitly designed as a mixed methods project in which the qualitative data collection and analysis would play a subsidiary role in the context of a project which utilized large-scale survey data collection (Jefferson *et al.* 2014). However, the relative flexibility of grounded theory and its capacity to utilize both quantitative and qualitative data in the analysis process (Lee 2002, 799) have provided ample opportunity to

Table 4.1 A summary of three Australian economic studies using grounded research methods

| | Study one: women's retirement incomes | Study two: labor market decentralization | Study three: mature women working in aged care |
|---|---|---|---|
| **Background** | A policy concern with the gendered implications of retirement income policy changes. | A response to policy changes decentralizing the processes which determine wages and conditions of employment. | An investigation of the employment decisions of mature age women working in aged care to gain insights into mature age women's labor participation. |
| **Rationale for qualitative data collection** | To develop a contribution to economic theory development to reflect gendered aspects of retirement savings decisions. | To address the need for rapid data collection and analysis in a context of constrained resources (funding). | Insights into possible causal relationships between correlated variables identified in survey data. |
| **Project design** | Based on grounded theory method. | Qualitative data analysis using coding processes associated with grounded research. | Explanatory, sequential mixed methods project design. |
| **Qualitative data collection and analysis** | Thirty individual, semi-structured interviews. Open coding and triangulation of key themes with existing literature. | Twenty-two individual, semi-structured interviews. Open coding followed by comparison of theoretical constructs with market rhetoric used to justify policy changes. | Forty-three semi-structured interviews with participants who had previously participated in a survey. Open coding and purposeful coding linked with emergent themes from survey data analysis. |
| **Key findings** | Three key themes relating to social structures and human actions that inform the outcome of women's relatively low retirement savings. | Insights into the lack of information about wages and employment conditions that constrained the operation of competitive labor markets portrayed in policy rhetoric. | Emergent themes relevant to recognition which are relatively undertheorized in economic research. Despite being a mixed methods project, the qualitative data appear likely to support new theoretical contributions. |
| **Key limitations** | Small sample and lack of theoretical saturation in categories impeded new theory development. | Small sample provided an excuse for the study to be dismissed as 'flawed.' | Work in progress and limitations yet to be explored. |

develop new theoretical insights which are currently being explored. In addition, the combination of data forms have provided an opportunity to develop and test links between the data in the study and theoretical discussion on the issue of recognition which have largely taken place outside of economic research.

A second key lesson was the flexibility provided by utilizing a grounded research approach in these projects. This was particularly relevant to the second study (on labor market regulation) where the use of grounded research allowed the timely collection and analysis of data within a context of limited resources. However, it has also been a key advantage of utilizing a grounded research approach in the third study. In this case, the capacity to analyze data for emergent themes provided an opportunity to develop categories and further investigate the relevance and causal processes suggested by these categories in later rounds of data collection. This has facilitated an iterative approach between data collection and theory development which provides an enhanced capacity for category saturation and theory development.

A third lesson is the extent to which category saturation is closely linked with the confidence with which causal processes can be theorized (Lee 2002, 795). This is noticeable by its absence in the first study and its presence in the third study. The combination of rich qualitative data with relatively large-scale survey data, at the time of writing this chapter, facilitates the development of theoretical links that have been relatively lacking in previous economic literature, particularly in the area of recognition as an important issue in employment decision-making.

A final lesson has been the relatively low value put on findings from qualitative research methods among some areas of the policy-making community. This might reflect some degree of expedience on the part of political or policy commentators if the findings from small qualitative studies do not suit their purposes. More generally, however, it might be linked with a lack of knowledge about the appropriate purposes and uses of qualitative research and grounded research methods.

## Conclusions

With reference to three specific projects conducted in Australia, this chapter has demonstrated grounded theory as method for theory creation can be utilized in projects and contexts that extend beyond those specifically discussed by Lee in his papers on grounded theory (2002, 2005, 2012). The present chapter particularly draws attention to the role that Lee's insights can provide as part of an engagement with empirical research, pluralistic research methods, and theory engagement. Key findings from each study demonstrate specific insights that could not be achieved from mainstream methods of deductive modeling or applied regression analysis. There is ample scope for future engagement with Lee's identification of grounded theory as an appropriate method for heterodox economic research. If Lee's project is actively pursued by heterodox economists, it could have significant and long-term implications for the design of economic research projects and theory development that are grounded in the social reality in which economic events take place.

## Note

1 My attendance at the conference was facilitated by one of my co-supervisors, Siobhan Austen. Siobhan arranged funding of my attendance at the workshop by gaining permission from her Head of School to use her own funding allocation to support my education in research methods. As I was to be traveling from Perth, Australia to Manchester, England this represented a significant proportion of Siobhan's conference funding. It was a generous act and it was only in later years that I fully appreciated how lucky I was to have a supervisor who would actively address the required administrative hurdles involved in supporting a student's research program in this manner.

## References

ABC News. 2007. "Work Choices Hitting Women Hardest." Accessed May 7, 2014. www.abc.net.au/news/2007-08-13/workchoices-hitting-women-hardest-study/638070.

Austen, S. and T. Jefferson. 2006. "Comparing Responses to Critical Realism." *Journal of Economic Methodology* 13 (2): 257–282.

Austen, S., T. Jefferson, R. Sharp, V. Adams, R. Ong, and G. Lewin. 2014. "Mixed Methods Research: What's in it for Economists?" *Economic and Labour Relations Review* 25 (2): 290–305.

Austen, S., T. Jefferson, and V. Thein. 2003. "Gendered Social Indicators and Grounded Theory." *Feminist Economics* 9 (1): 1–18.

Australian Government, Productivity Commission. 2005. *Economic Implications of an Ageing Australia, Research Report.* Canberra Productivity Commission.

Australian Government, The Treasury. 2010. *Intergenerational Report 2010.* Canberra: Australian Government. Accessed May 6, 2014. http://archive.treasury.gov.au/igr/igr2010/report/pdf/IGR_2010.pdf.

Blau, F. D. and L. M. Kahn. 1992. "The Gender Earnings Gap: Learnings from International Comparisons." *American Economic Review* 82: 302–328.

Blau, F. D. and L. M. Kahn. 2003. "Understanding International Differences in the Gender Pay Gap." *Journal of Labor Economics* 21 (1): 106–144.

Creswell, J. W. and V. L. Plano-Clark. 2007. *Designing and Conducting Mixed Methods Research.* Thousand Oaks, CA: Sage.

Deaton, A. 1992. *Understanding Consumption.* Oxford: Clarendon Press.

Elton, J., J. Bailey, M. Baird, M. S. Charlesworth, R. Cooper, B. Ellem, T. Jefferson, F. McDonald, D. Oliver, B. Pocock, A. Preston, and G. Whitehouse. 2007. "Women and Workchoices: Impacts on the Low Pay Sector." University of South Australia: Centre for Work and Life, Hawke Research Institute for Sustainable Societies.

Finch, J. 2002. "The Role of Grounded Theory in Developing Economic Theory." *Journal of Economic Methodology* 9 (2): 213–234.

Fraser, N. and A. Honneth, eds. 2003. *Redistribution or Recognition? A Political-Philosophical Exchange.* London: Verso.

Gibson, B. 2003. "Grounded Theory." In *The A–Z of Social Research,* edited by R. L. Miller and J. D. Brewer. Thousand Oaks, CA: Sage.

Gittins, R. 2007. "Hockey Goes Over the Top in Work Choices Dogfight." *Sydney Morning Herald.* Accessed April 20, 2015. www.smh.com.au/articles/2007/10/07/1191 695737785.html?page=fullpage#contentSwap1.

Glaser, B. 1992. *Basics of Grounded Theory Analysis.* Mill Valley, CA: Sociology Press.

Glaser, B. 1998. *Doing Grounded Theory: Issues and Discussion.* Mill Valley, CA: Sociology Press.

Glaser, B. and A. Strauss. 1967. *The Discovery of Grounded Theory*. Chicago: Aldine.

Gregory, R. 1999. "Labour Market Institutions and the Gender Pay Ratio." *The Australian Economic Review* 32 (3): 273–278.

Gregory, R. and A. Daly. 1990. "Can Economic Theory Explain Why Australian Women Are So Well Paid Relative to Their US Counterparts?" Discussion Paper 26. Centre for Economic Policy, Australian National University.

Gregory, R. and A. Daly. 1994. "Who Gets What? Institutions, Human Capital, and Black Boxes as Determinants of Relative Wages in Australia and the United States." In *The Future of Industrial Relations: Global Change and Challenges*, edited by J. R. Niland, R. D. Lansbury, and C. Verevis. California: Sage.

Gregory, R. and V. Ho. 1985. "Equal Pay and Comparable Worth: What Can the US Learn from the Australian Experience?" Discussion Paper 123. Centre for Economic Policy Research, Australian National University.

Hodgson, G. M. 1997. "The Ubiquity of Habits and Rules." In *Recent Developments in Institutional Economics*, edited by G. M. Hodgson, 379–400. Cheltenham: Edward Elgar.

Hugo, G. 2007. "Contextualising the 'Crisis in Aged Care' in Australia: A Demographic Perspective." *Australian Journal of Social Issues* 42 (2): 169–182.

Jefferson, T. 2005a. "Australian Women's Financial Security in Later Life: The Effects of Social Structures and Decision Processes." PhD diss., Curtin University. http://adt. curtin.edu.au/theses/available/adt-WCU20060515.111648.

Jefferson, T. 2005b. "Women and Retirement Incomes in Australia: A Review." *Economic Record* 81 (254): 273–291.

Jefferson, T. 2007a. "Discussing Retirement: Insights from a Qualitative Research Project." *Australian Journal of Labour Economics* 10 (2): 75–91.

Jefferson, T. 2007b. "Two Studies of Women's Retirement Incomes in Australia: Assessing Some Outcomes of Pluralism in Economic Research." *Cambridge Journal of Economics* 31 (3): 363–378.

Jefferson, T., S. Austen, R. Sharp, V. Adams, R. Ong, and G. Lewin. 2014. "A Mixed Methods Approach to Investigating the Employment Decisions of Aged Care Workers in Australia." In *Handbook of Research Methods and Applications in Heterodox Economics*, edited by F. S. Lee and B. Cronin. Cheltenham: Edward Elgar.

Jefferson, T. and A. Preston. 2007. "Australian Wage Determination and Gender Equity: A View from the West." *Public Policy* 2 (2): 119–129.

Jefferson, T. and A. Preston. 2010. "Negotiating Fair Pay and Conditions: Low Paid Women's Experience and Perceptions of Labour Market Deregulation and Individual Wage Bargaining." *Industrial Relations Journal* 41 (4): 351–366.

King, J. E., ed. 2012. *The Elgar Companion to Post Keynesian Economics*. 2nd ed. Cheltenham: Edward Elgar.

Lee, F. S. 1998. *Post Keynesian Price Theory*. Cambridge: Cambridge University Press.

Lee, F. S. 2002. "Theory Creation and the Methodological Foundation of Post Keynesian Economics." *Cambridge Journal of Economics* 26 (6): 789–804.

Lee, F. S. 2005. "Grounded Theory and Heterodox Economics." *The Grounded Theory Review* 4 (2): 95–116.

Lee, F. S. 2011. "Modeling the Economy as a Whole: An Integrative Approach." *American Journal of Economics and Sociology* 70 (5): 1282–1314.

Lee, F. S. 2012. "Critical Realism, Grounded Theory, and Theory Construction in Heterodox Economics." MPRA Working Paper 40341. Accessed May 7, 2014. http://mpra. ub.uni-muenchen.de/40341.

Lee, F. S. and P. Downward. 1999. "Re-testing Gardiner Means's Evidence on Administered Prices." *Journal of Economic Issues* 33 (4): 861–886.

Organisation for Economic Co-operation and Development (OECD). 2006. *Live Longer, Work Longer*. Paris: OECD. Accessed April 20, 2015. www.oecd.org/employment/emp/36218997.pdf.

Olsberg, D. 1997. *Ageing and Money: Australia's Retirement Revolution*. St. Leonards, New South Wales: Allen and Unwin.

Preston, A. and T. Jefferson. 2007. "Trends in Australia's Gender Wage Ratio." *Labour and Industry* 18 (2): 97–112.

Preston, A., T. Jefferson, and R. Seymour. 2006. "Women's Pay and Conditions in an Era of Changing Workplace Regulations: Towards a 'Women's Employment Status Key Indicators' (WESKI) Database." Sydney, Human Rights and Equal Opportunity Commission, National Foundation for Australian Women and the Women's Electoral Lobby.

Shaw, M. 2007. "Women Are Hardest Hit by Workplace Laws." *Sydney Morning Herald*. Accessed May 7, 2014. www.smh.com.au/news/national/women-are-hardest-hit-by-workplace-laws/2007/02/13/1171128973785.html.

Singh, S. 1997. *Marriage Money*. Sydney: Allen and Unwin.

Strauss, A. 1987. *Qualitative Analysis for Social Scientists*. Cambridge: Cambridge University Press.

Strauss, A. and J. Corbin. 1990. "Grounded Theory Research: Procedures, Canons, and Evaluative Criteria." *Qualitative Sociology* 13 (1): 3–21.

Strauss, A. and J. Corbin. 1994. *Basics of Qualitative Research: Techniques and Procedures for Developing Grounded Theory*. Thousand Oaks, CA: Sage.

Van Wanrooy, B., S. Oxenbridge, J. Buchanan, and M. Jakubauskas. 2007. "Australia at Work: The Benchmark Report." Workplace Research Centre, Sydney.

Van Wanrooy, B., S. Wright, J. Buchanan, S. Baldwin, and S. Wilson. 2009. "Australia at Work in a Changing World." Workplace Research Centre, Sydney.

Whitely, A. 2005. "Grounded Research: A Modified Grounded Theory for the Business Setting." *Qualitative Research Journal* 4 (1/2): 27–46.

## Part II

# Heterodox microeconomics and the foundations of heterodox macroeconomics

# 5 Heterodox microeconomics and heterodox microfoundations

*Tae-Hee Jo*

## Introduction

Frederic S. Lee is the most important heterodox microeconomist in our time to whom one must refer in doing a micro analysis that is alternative to neoclassical microeconomics and its variants. His primary contribution to heterodox microeconomic theory lies in the areas of pricing, price, production, costs, market competition, market governance, and modeling the economy as a whole (or heterodox microfoundations of macroeconomics).

One might be puzzled why a microeconomist deals with the economy as a whole, since virtually all economists are taught that an analysis of a whole economy falls into the domain of macroeconomics. This is indeed a puzzle if one clings to neoclassical economics. In fact, some heterodox economists are not free of the neoclassical economics of which they are critical. Others also seem to believe that some aspects (in theory, policy, or method) of neoclassical economics are compatible with and, thereby, can be incorporated into heterodox economics. Such a dogmatic, self-contradictory, or apologetic attitude was never accepted by Fred Lee. In developing heterodox microeconomic theories, Lee long argued in a rigorous manner that the micro-macro dichotomy or the notion that micro- and macro-levels of economy are unrelated is fallacious. For example, pricing, production, and employment decisions by the business enterprise can only be understood and analyzed if one has a clear macro vision—that is, the "economy as a differentiated disaggregated [emergent] whole" (Lee 2011a, 16).

From Lee's viewpoint, macro-structural analysis without micro-behavioral analysis, or vice versa, does not rest on solid methodological and empirical grounds. If one's vision is confined to changes in aggregate data, a resulting analysis is blind of underlying agency and its reciprocal relationship with structures that give rise to macroeconomic outcomes. Hence, a macro analysis without human agency embedded in a historical context is incapable of challenging the status quo in theory and in practice. In other words, root causes or hidden driving forces remain unseen in macro-only analysis. In this respect, Lee's heterodox microeconomic framework offers important insights into the progress of heterodox economics. The starting point of heterodox analysis should be the vision of the system as a whole or the social provisioning process. But such a vision should be explained through the interactions between agency and structure. Agency represents actual decisions and actions taking place in a particular historical and social context. Therefore heterodox microeconomics is not simply about "individual" behaviors. Rather it "involves working with the sub-systems and interdependencies to develop analytical narratives qua theoretical explanations that contribute to understanding the social provisioning process" (Lee 2011a, 18). Such a concept of heterodox microeconomics is more comprehensive, realistic, relevant, and radical than most heterodox macroeconomic theories.

Many heterodox economists, however, assume that either there is no heterodox microeconomics or heterodox microeconomics is all about individual behaviors. Consequently, they believe that if heterodox macroeconomics needs a microfoundation, it is the mainstream kind—optimizing behaviors given scarce resources; or, there is no need to develop heterodox microfoundations. In this chapter I argue that such a misunderstanding of heterodox microeconomics is inimical to the development of heterodox economics. Drawing upon Fred Lee's contributions to heterodox microeconomics, I discuss what heterodox microeconomics is, how it is different from neoclassical microeconomics as well as heterodox macroeconomics, and why heterodox microeconomics is essential in analyzing the social provisioning process. The elaboration of Lee's theoretical framework, and hopefully advancing his theoretical tradition, is the objective of this chapter.

## Microeconomics in heterodox economics

There are different perceptions of heterodox economics. One conventional view of heterodox economics is that it is a body of critical theories in opposition to the core propositions of current mainstream economics, such as ubiquitous individual rationality, constrained optimizing behavior, stable equilibrium, and the law of supply and demand. Such critical theories are certainly part of heterodox economics since they are likely to lead to alternative theories and policies. But the mere objection to mainstream economics is not a sufficient condition for doing heterodox economics. There must be a shared vision of reality that is represented by particular methodology and methods used by a group of economists (Lawson 1997, 2003, 2006). Methodological individualism, for example, represents the mainstream-neoclassical vision of the world in which isolated individuals make rational-optimal decisions given scarce resources. The reliance on deductive logic and the use of mathematical-quantitative models are thus the most appropriate method of doing neoclassical economics. Indeed, methodological individualism has been the defining characteristic of neoclassical economics since the beginning of its history. However, methodological individualism is not the only way to understand and analyze the real world. There are distinctive and long traditions of methodologies in science, such as holism, systemism, structuralism, (critical) realism, among others, which result in alternative, often opposing, narratives of the subject in question.

Yet the emphasis on ontology and methodology is still not sufficient to define heterodox economics. A more comprehensive and historical understanding of heterodox economics is that it is a body of theory or a system of works that is built and shared by the community of heterodox economists. This multi-layered definition of heterodox economics is never fixed but emergent and open, since it is created by economists qua acting persons embedded in a social-historical context. Nor does the name, heterodox economics, imply that it is a single school of thought. Rather, heterodox economics is an umbrella term that refers to various approaches to economics and communities of economists, such as Marxian-radical political, Post Keynesian (including Sraffian and Kaleckian), institutional-evolutionary, social, feminist, ecological economics (Lee 2009, 6–7). Indeed, this is a view generally taken by those who identify themselves as heterodox economists (see Mearman 2011).

Heterodox economics thus bears a specific meaning in particular time and space. In its process of emergence along with the establishment of regional or international communities, such as the Association for Heterodox Economics, the Society of Heterodox Economists, and *Heterodox Economics Newsletter*, the term heterodox economics as we understand now has been widely used among dissent economists since the early 1990s. A notable trend over the past two decades is that various strands in heterodox economics have increasingly engaged with each other more than they did before the 1990s (Lee 2009, 2012a; see also Chapters 1 and 2 of this book).

Given the wide spectrum of heterodox economics, I find that the most appropriate—in the sense of comprehensive and constructive—definition is the following:

> Heterodox economic theory is an empirically grounded theoretical explanation of the historical process of social provisioning within the context of a capitalist economy. Therefore it is concerned with explaining those factors that are part of the process of social provisioning, including the structure and use of resources, the structure and change of social wants, structure of production and the reproduction of the business enterprise, family, state, and other relevant institutions and organizations, and distribution.
>
> (Lee 2009, 8–9)

The way Lee defines heterodox economics is pluralistic, comprehensive, and historical. It is pluralistic in that we admit the concomitant existence of contending ideas of economic activities. Mainstream-neoclassical economics is one that advocates self-interested, individualistic, and asocial explanations of economic activities, whereas heterodox economics explains economy as a system of instituted process or the social provisioning process with an emphasis on different aspects of economic activities (Polanyi 1968; Gruchy 1987; Dugger 1996; Power 2004; Jo 2011b; Lee 2011b; Todorova 2013).

Heterodox economics is comprehensive since it deals with both the economy as a whole as well as its sub-systems—structures, agency, and organizations, whose interactions in a particular institutional setting generate changes in the economy. This characteristic indicates that a macro theory ignoring agency or a micro theory without a view of the whole system adds little to the understanding of the real world (the micro-macro dichotomy in heterodox economics is discussed later while discussing heterodox microfoundations). Comprehensive heterodox economics also implies that a model of the economy must include the essential components of the actual economy. For instance, if a model of capitalist economy is free of a capitalist state (and state money) or the financial sector (and credit-debt relations), it does not represent the real economy. Likewise, it is hard to find useful implications from a model of production without natural resources and produced means of production (Lee 2014).

Lastly, heterodox economics is historical in its nature in that theories and policies are concerned about actual workings of the emergent system over historical time. While general theories, such as Marx's labor theory of value, Keynes's principle of effective demand, Sraffa's theory of social process of production, value, and distribution, have merits as "tools of thought" that accentuate "the essence of the causal forces or determining principles that are *probably* at work in specific spheres of the socioeconomic world" (Bortis 1997, 82, italics added). However, if a general theory stops short of explaining historical phenomena, its function as a tool of thought is greatly dismissed. The importance of an empirically and historically grounded theory is that it takes "the form of a complex analytical explanation based on the data's core concepts. An essential property of the [grounded qua historical] theory is that it explains why and how the sequence of economic events represented in the data took place" (Lee 2002, 794). That is to say, causal mechanisms are explained in a particular historical context which is represented by both quantitative and qualitative data. It thus follows from such a view that

> grounded economic theories are also historical theories in that they are historical narratives that explain the internal workings of historical economic processes and events in the context of relatively stable causal mechanisms (whose actions and outcomes can be temporally different) and structures.
>
> (Lee 2005, 108; see also Jefferson's chapter in this book)

Lee's definition further implies that heterodox economics is the emergent qua open-ended paradigm that lends support to cross-fertilization among theoretically compatible schools of thought in economics. It should be noted that such a pluralistic position does not mean to include all the existing and contending approaches to economics since some approaches are incompatible with each other—for example, Post Keynesian economics with historical time and fundamental uncertainty and neoclassical economics with logical time and market-clearing equilibrium. Ad hoc pluralism (or eclecticism which assumes the compatibility between mainstream and heterodox economics) should be differentiated from intellectual-scientific pluralism (which assumes that economics is a contested discipline). The latter position thus implies that it is virtually impossible to integrate incompatible theories or paradigms in any meaningful manner, although contending approaches should be taught in academia for the purpose of education (Henry and Lee 2009; Lee 2009, 2010b, 2011a, 2012a; Lee and Lavoie 2012). However, as discussed later with regard to various positions on the relationship between micro and macro, it is not difficult to find some heterodox economists who support ad hoc pluralism that does not help advance heterodox economics.

Lee's approach to heterodox microeconomics follows his vision of heterodox economics. In brief,

> [h]eterodox microeconomic theory ... involves working with the sub-systems and interdependencies to develop analytical narratives qua theoretical explanations that contribute to understanding the social provisioning process.
>
> (Lee 2011a, 18)

Essentially, heterodox microeconomics is the study of the sub-systems of the economy, which include markets, industries, institutions (non-market, legal, political, and social), and the five forms of agency—that is, the business enterprise, the state, households, market governance organizations (cartels, trade associations, etc.), and trade unions. Since the economy is conceived of as a differentiated, disaggregated, and emergent system, sub-systems therein cannot be separated from the economy. Sub-systems are embedded in the larger system. The latter is emergent—that is, its dynamics is open-ended—due to agency taking place in a particular sub-system with a vision of the whole system. Social agency or the 'socialized individual,' as opposed to an isolated individual decision maker, is confined by existing socio-economic structures (including class structure). But more importantly social agency deliberately makes structures following its social, political, ethical values so as to maintain, reproduce, or transcend its social status. Furthermore, sub-systems are connected through various structures of economy, such as the productive structure, monetary structure, employment structure, and income structure (Lee 2010a, 2011a, 2011b).

The following two sections showcase the extent and relevance of heterodox microeconomics vis-à-vis heterodox macroeconomics focusing on the theory of investment and the principle of effective demand.

### Investment: micro and macro explanations

Investment is a flow of demand for fixed investment goods. An investment decision is made by the business enterprise for the sake of remaining as a going concern over time. Conceivably, there must exist the capacity of producing an array of fixed investment goods as well as money capital to finance investment before an investment decision is made. The existence of the former, on the one hand, requires that an economy is composed of at least two productive sectors—that is, an intermediate or "basic" goods sector and a surplus or "non-basic" goods sector—in addition to household and government sectors purchasing consumption goods and services. Investment financing, on the other hand, requires the banking sector (to finance investment externally or to save enterprises' retained earnings in bank accounts) and an array of financial assets. Financing also implies that there must exist credit-debt relationships that are denominated in state money. Thus the existence of the state is a precondition for any economic activities. Households require the banking sector to purchase goods and services above their incomes or to save part of incomes. Governments run deficits in the form of financial liabilities that are owned by private business enterprises and households. With all the sub-systems and agency in place, the business enterprise is able to generate a flow of profits and retained earnings (that is, gross profits less tax payments, dividends, debt payments, etc.) through the production process and market exchanges. Insofar as enterprise investment is concerned in the context of monetary production economy, therefore, any of the agency and sub-systems delineated above cannot be omitted, if one attempts to explain real world investment.

Heterodox economists, especially in the Marxian, Post Keynesian, and Institutionalist traditions, theorize the capitalist economy as a monetary production economy. Central to the analysis of the monetary production economy is the view that it is the decision to produce surplus goods and services made by the business enterprise and the state that drives the production of intermediate capital goods and, hence, of the total social product. More specifically, the effective demand for fixed investment goods generates the flow of the production of intermediate inputs, the flow of the production of fixed investment goods, and the flow of funds to finance the demand for fixed investment goods. This is the principle of effective demand coupled with the surplus approach, which provides a context for investment decisions (this point is discussed further below). With this theoretical view of the economy as a whole, a micro explanation of investment is that *it is a strategic decision under fundamental uncertainty to purchase investment goods in order to survive and expand over time by way of generating internal cash flows or borrowing from banking institutions* (with a greater weight on the former—see below on this). As a corollary, investment decisions are also closely linked to pricing, production, and employment decisions. This implies that business enterprises do not passively take prices, but actively make prices, individually and collectively, so as to achieve their long-term goals, such as survival and growth. It is evident that the heterodox microeconomic account of investment is alternative to and incompatible with the mainstream explanation that investment is determined in efficient loanable funds markets by way of interest rate adjustments (Eichner 1976, 1987; Lee 2010a, 2011b, 2013b; Lee and Jo 2011; Jo 2015).

How is then a heterodox microeconomic account of investment different from a heterodox macroeconomic theory of investment? Keynes and Post Keynesian macroeconomists, for example, argue that the level of aggregate investment is determined by the supply and demand prices of capital goods, which represent lenders' and borrowers' risks, respectively (Keynes 1936, 248; Minsky 1986, ch. 8). Underlying this financial theory of investment is the assumption that either internal funds are constant or aggregate external funds are proportional to aggregate investment (Lavoie and Seccareccia 2001). Apart from unrealistic assumptions on financing, two serious problems present themselves. First, this macroeconomic view of investment presumes the Marshallian supply-demand framework that is based upon the concepts of scarce financial resources and marginal productivity to which most Post Keynesians object. Not to mention, the law of supply-demand is both theoretically incoherent and empirically invalid (Lee and Keen 2004). Second, empirical data show that private enterprises rely chiefly on internally generated funds rather than external funds in financing their investment; and that any functional relationship between external financing and fixed investment is hardly found (see, for example, Corbett and Jenkinson 1997; Jo 2015; Kliman and Williams 2015). Other empirical studies also find that enterprise financing behavior is both institutionally and historically contingent, rather than dependent upon the size of the business enterprise (see, for example, Mina, Lahr, and Hughes 2013). In short, Keynes's and Post Keynesian aggregate investment theory is limited to the extent that, as Kalecki remarks in his review of Keynes's *General Theory*, strategic financing-investment decision-making mechanisms are absent (Targetti and Kinda-Hass 1982, 251). The absence of 'real' decision-making mechanisms amounts to the absence of agency, which, from a heterodox microeconomic perspective, plays an essential role in explaining the real world.

It is clear from the comparison between heterodox micro and macro approaches to investment that the former is not only empirically grounded but also, in contrast to the conventional view of micro, more comprehensive than the latter. In other words, while heterodox macroeconomists deal with the "tip of an iceberg" (Jespersen 2009, 97), heterodox microeconomists dive into the sea to actually explain the hidden part of the iceberg. Why do heterodox macro-economists stop short of explaining the hidden 90 percent of the iceberg? Jespersen (2009) explains that

> only 10 per cent of the macroeconomic system can be directly observed. In this case, it is largely the underlying structures, which cannot be observed, that determine the appearance of the tip of the iceberg, as well as how it changes through time.
>
> (97)

Admittedly, this is a common view shared by heterodox macroeconomists, which indicates a sorry state of heterodox macroeconomics. As long as macro-economists stay with "aggregate statistical entities," they will find it impossible to fully explain underlying structures, which are formed and altered by social agency through causal mechanisms. Instead of analyzing actual and deeper reality, heterodox macroeconomists create fictitious "macro-actors," such as "macro-households, macro-firms, macro-wage-earners and macro-consumers" that are "not to be found in the world" (see Jespersen 2009, 103).

Another important implication derived from the heterodox micro approach to investment is that if a monetary production economy is inherently unstable (as many heterodox macroeconomists argue), business enterprises should make strategic decisions about internal cash flows to contain the vulnerability in their business activities (that is, micro instability) as well as the instability in the economy as a whole (that is, macro instability). Financing investment internally as part of strategic investment decisions, rather than assuming that the financial market decides how much to invest, is the necessary condition for the business enterprise to remain ongoing (Jo 2011a, 2015).

### Effective demand: beyond Keynes's and Post Keynesian macro analysis

In the previous section it is argued that the principle of effective demand coupled with the surplus approach is a theoretical framework in which strategic investment decisions are explained from the heterodox microeconomic perspective. Effective demand in this context means that it is a decision made by the business enterprise, households, and the state to purchase surplus goods and services (investment, consumption, and government goods and services, respectively). Hence effective demand drives the production of the investment and intermediate goods, the flow of investment funds, employment, and incomes. In radical contrast to the neoclassical argument that economic activities are primarily coordinated by market prices, heterodox microeconomists argue that effective demand is the organizing principle of the entire social provisioning process (Jo 2007). Let us consider a disaggregated output-employment model of the economy, which is derived from the principle of effective demand embedded in the surplus approach framework (see Lee and Jo 2011; Lee 2012b, for a detailed description of the model):

| | |
|---|---|
| Basic goods sector | $Q_1 = [I - A_{11}^T]^{-1} A_{21}^T S$ |
| Surplus goods sector | $S = Q_2 = Q_{21} + Q_{2C} + Q_{2G}$ |
| Total social product | $Q = Q_1 + Q_2$ |
| Total employment | $L = l_1^T [I - A_{11}^T]^{-1} A_{21}^T S + l_2^T S + L_{31}$ |

where $S$ or $Q_2$ is a $(m-n) \times 1$ column vector of the social surplus (first $n$ rows are zeros and the next $m - n$ rows semi-positive) composed of fixed investment goods ($Q_{21}$), consumption goods ($Q_{2C}$), and government goods/services ($Q_{2G}$); $Q_1$ is a strictly positive $n \times 1$ column vector of the total amount of intermediate inputs used in production; $Q$ is a strictly positive $m \times 1$ column vector of the total social product; $A_{11}$ is a $n \times n$ technology matrix comprised of material production coefficients used in the production $Q_1$; $A_{21}$ is a $(m-n) \times n$ technology matrix comprised of material production coefficients used in the production $Q_2$; $[I-A_{11}^T]^{-1} > 0$ is the $n \times n$ Leontief inverse matrix; $[I-A_{11}^T]^{-1} A_{21}^T > 0$ is a $n \times (n-m)$ matrix of the output-employment multiplier; $L$ is a $z \times 1$ column vector of the total amount of labor employed in the economy; $l_1$ is a strictly positive $n \times z$ matrix of labor production coefficients used in the production $\mathbf{Q}_1$; $\mathbf{l}_2$ is a strictly positive $(m-n) \times z$ matrix of labor production coefficients used in the production $\mathbf{Q}_2$; and $\mathbf{L}_{31}$ is a $z \times 1$ column vector of the total amount of government employees.

The above output-employment model of the economy demonstrates that the decision to produce surplus goods and services (**S**) determines the composition and level of the basic goods and services ($\mathbf{Q}_1$) and, hence, the total social product (**Q**) and the total employment (**L**), through the output-employment multiplier (see Trigg and Lee 2005, for the discussion of a matrix multiplier vis-à-vis a scalar multiplier as in Keynes's original framework). In the first place it is the ruling-capitalist class agency that determines the social surplus—capitalist investment and consumption, government demand. Thus the surplus is not a residual; its composition and magnitude are strategically determined by the business enterprise and the state, since the production of the surplus (and, hence, of the total social product and of profits) is essential for the capitalist class agents to reproduce sub-systems as well as the whole economic system. In this class-based, surplus-based quantity model of effective demand, employment and resulting wage income accruing to the working class are residual, although being necessary for a viable economy, to the extent that production decisions must be made prior to employment-wage decisions, and that wages are produced in the form of consumption goods. Indicative of this model is a theoretical argument that productive economic activities can be delineated independently of production prices, wage rates, and profit mark-ups. That is to say, prices do not coordinate economic activities; nor do they allocate the social product, labor, and investment goods. Production prices are altered if the business enterprise and the state change nominal wage rates and/ or profit mark-ups (or if there occurs a change in production technology that alters the labor and material input coefficients). In short, contra to the price mechanism in mainstream economics, the principle of effective demand is the organizing principle of the economy from the heterodox economic perspective (Lee 2010a; Lee and Jo 2011).

Apparently, this is not the conventional interpretation of the principle of effective demand. Keynes defines the level of effective demand as "the point of intersection between the aggregate demand function and the aggregate supply function" (Keynes 1936, 25). At this point of effective demand, aggregate employment is determined and in turn consumption demand is determined accordingly. Investment demand is determined in the capital market when the supply price of capital meets the demand price of capital—more specifically, when the marginal efficiency of capital is equalized to the money rate of interest, and the latter is the function of liquidity preference (136–137). The gist of the principle from the macroeconomic perspective is that profit-maximizing entrepreneurs' aggregate expenditure decisions drive overall economic activities—income, output, and employment at the aggregate level. As a corollary, investment demand is not constrained by saving and there is no reason to assume that the equilibrium employment is at the full employment level.

To illustrate the schema of effective demand:

$$Y^e \rightarrow E \rightarrow N \rightarrow D = C + I \rightarrow \text{multiplier} \rightarrow Y \rightarrow C \rightarrow S$$

Capital market $\left\{ \begin{array}{l} f(w, r) \rightarrow p_k^s \\ f(MEC, i); f(LP, M) \rightarrow p_k^d \end{array} \right\} \rightarrow I$

Investment multipler $\dfrac{dY}{dI} = \dfrac{1}{1 - \alpha}$

Aggregate economy $\left\{ \begin{array}{c} Y = C + I + G \\ C = \alpha Y \\ I = S \\ Z = D \end{array} \right\}$

where $Y^e$, $E$, $N$ are entrepreneurs' expected proceeds, the point of effective demand, and employment; $D$ is aggregate demand composed of consumption demand ($C$) and investment demand ($I$); $Y$ aggregate income; $S$ saving; $p_k^s$ and $p_k^d$ are the supply and demand price of capital goods, respectively; $w$ is wage rates; $r$ is an average profit mark-up; $MEC$ is the marginal efficiency of capital; $i$ is the money rate of interest; $LP$ is liquidity preference; $M$ is the quantity of money; $\alpha$ is the marginal propensity to consume. When $p_k^s < p_k^d$, new investment is induced. At the ex-post equilibrium, $MEC = i$, $I = S$, and $D = Z$.

In light of both micro and macro explanations, the principle of effective demand illuminates that a monetary production economy is organized by effective demand—that is, *decisions* to produce goods and services drive entire economic activities. Resource scarcity plays no role. The principle thus raises questions as to how resources are created, how investment is financed, and how incomes are generated and distributed (see Minsky 1983). In addition, the heterodox microeconomic approach goes deeper and broader than macroeconomic effective demand theory. First, it explains how social agency embedded in a class society plays an essential role in the social provisioning process. Social agency is, however, ignored by macro theories that assume fictitious macro actors. Second, it is entirely independent of neoclassical frameworks—e.g., equilibrium, marginal analysis, the structural relationship between supply and demand through the price mechanism, and optimizing behaviors. Moreover, the heterodox micro approach to effective demand in a matrix form (that is, monetary input-output matrix) delineates an economy as a differentiated, disaggregate emergent whole in which sub-systems are interrelated with each other, rather than reducing it to either the sum of isolated individuals or the aggregated statistical entity. Thus, the fallacy of composition is not a concern in heterodox microeconomics. The following section discusses these issues in the context of microfoundations.

## Heterodox microfoundation is a project of linking micro and macro

What is the microeconomic foundation of the Keynes's and Post Keynesian principle of effective demand? In other words, is it necessary for them to include sub-systems and agency in the principle of effective demand? Being attentive to the fallacy of composition, Keynes himself made this point clear that he did not need any microfoundations. Consequently, Keynes's *General Theory* is devoted to macro analysis:

> I have called my theory a *general* theory. I mean by that I am chiefly concerned with the behaviour of the economic system as a whole.... And I argue that important mistakes have been made through extending to the system as a whole conclusions which have been correctly arrived at in respect of a part of it taken in isolation.
>
> (Keynes 1973, xxxii, original italics)

However, Keynes de facto based his macro theory on neoclassical microeconomic theory. In particular, it is profit maximizing entrepreneurs qua firms that are represented by aggregate functions (Keynes 1936, 24; King 2002, 238; Harcourt 2004). Moreover, such concepts as equilibrium and the marginal efficiency of capital are largely influenced by Alfred Marshall and other neoclassical economists. It is not a surprise that neoclassical economists re-interpreted (and trivialized) Keynes's effective demand in the form of IS-LM curves. It is thus fair to argue that Keynes's macroeconomics has a microeconomic foundation and it is a neoclassical kind. Later Post Keynesians have followed suit (Weintraub 1979; Reynolds 1987, ch. 8; King 2002, ch. 5; Jespersen 2009, ch. 8). What is implied is that many Post Keynesian macroeconomists believe that heterodox-Post Keynesian microeconomics is nothing but neoclassical microeconomics. To argue that this belief is false, let us discuss how Post Keynesian macroeconomists actually approach microeconomic issues in their macroeconomic theories—this is part of the ongoing debate on microfoundations.

Post Keynesian and other heterodox macroeconomists take one of the following three positions on the relationship between micro and macro. First, like Keynes who was concerned with the fallacy of composition Post Keynesians opt for the analysis of the economy as a whole qua aggregate data without recourse to sub-systems and agency. This position is *macro-autonomy* or *anti-foundations* in the sense that macroeconomics is a "relatively autonomous discipline, a 'special science', in its own right" (King 2012, 234, original emphasis) and, therefore, "[t]he obvious aims of such a reconstruction [i.e., the separation of macro from micro in the post graduate curriculum] is to protect macroeconomics from the encroachment of the methods and habits of thought of microeconomics" (Skidelsky 2009, 190). From this view, aggregate variables, macro actors, macro institutions are autonomous and self-sustaining. It follows that macroeconomics is independent of microeconomics and, thereby, micro and macro are analytically separate domains that may be, in principle, 'bridged' to each other, rather than one domain is 'founded' upon the other (Kriesler 1996; King 2009, 2012).

A second position supports *macrofoundations* of microeconomics. Macro-foundationists argue that the primary concern is to identify structural properties of capitalist economy since actual qua micro decisions and actions are constrained by surrounding structures (Weintraub 1979; Crotty 1980; Tarshis 1980; Harcourt 2004; Smithin 2004; Pasinetti 2005). The third position concerns the development of heterodox macroeconomics by incorporating recent development in mainstream microeconomics. They support the neoclassical microfoundations of heterodox macroeconomics (although they do not say it explicitly), insofar as the former is compatible with the latter. For example, Dymski (1992, 1993), Fazzari and Variato (1994), and Fazzari (2012) argue that banking behavior or enterprise investment can be more comprehensively explained by asymmetric information along with fundamental uncertainty prevailing in the market. Some may go further to argue that optimizing behavior and equilibrium concepts are compatible with and thus could be used by heterodox macroeconomics (Fazzari 2012).

Heterodox microeconomists are critical of the above positions on the relationship between micro and macro on the following grounds. All three positions in varying degrees presume that there exist only neoclassical microeconomics and its variants following Marshall's economics. However, the core of Marshallian microeconomics is the relative scarcity of resources, which leads all the scarce goods and services to be traded in the market in which the price mechanism rules; marginal utility/productivity and the average/representative consumer/producer on which the law of demand and supply at the micro as well as macro level are based. If fundamental uncertainty is the basis of the theory of money, employment, and output, market equilibrium analysis in logical time cannot be part of macroeconomic analysis (Davidson 1982–1983; Crotty 1996). Since most heterodox theories reject scarce factor inputs and marginal productivity, neoclassical production theory and the law of supply is to be rejected as well—for example, since financial resources or savings are not scarce but created by the demand for funds, the financial market cannot be adequately analyzed through the law of supply and demand (or the functional relationship between price and quantity) that assumes the scarcity of funds and the price of funds as a scarcity index.

Furthermore, since the principle of effective demand demonstrates that expenditure decisions create resources and reproduce the economy as a whole, market clearing equilibrium has no meaning and "the main propositions of static price theory—the existence of coherence and the efficiency of outcome—do not carry through (Minsky 1983, 44). It goes without saying that the surplus approach in the traditions of classical political economy, Sraffian economics, and Veblenian institutionalist economics also runs counter to the Marshallian microeconomics since the former posits that the distribution of surplus depends upon socio-economic structures rather than marginal productivity (see Nuno Ornelas Martins' chapter in this book). Insofar as the theoretical core of heterodox economics is consisting of the theory of monetary production, the principle of effective demand, the surplus approach, and the evolutionary-institutional analysis, "production is not an activity to overcome scarcity, exchange does not arise from scarcity, and prices are not scarcity indexes" (Lee 2011b, 1287). In short, not only is mainstream micro incompatible with both heterodox macro and micro, but also Marshallian-neoclassical micro cannot be the foundation of heterodox-Post Keynesian macro (Lee 2011a, 2013c; Lee and Jo 2013).

At this point it should be clear that heterodox microeconomics is not merely the rejection of mainstream microeconomics. The former is a radical and constructive alternative to the latter. More importantly, heterodox microeconomics is not confined to the explanations of 'individual' behaviors. It explores not only specific agents, organizations and institutions that constitute an economy as a whole, but also the interactions and interrelationships between sub-systems which are inextricably entangled with each other. Being consistent with this conception of heterodox microeconomics, a heterodox microfoundation is a project of linking micro and macro. Hence, there is no micro-macro dichotomy.

It should be noted that the rejection of the micro-macro dichotomy is not in conflict with heterodox microfoundations, since the latter are based upon the view of the social provisioning process where its parts (micro) and the economy as an emergent whole (macro) interact with each other.

> Heterodox microfoundations is about putting together the components of the economy into a whole; and then examining how various components work will have impacts across the economy and looking at these interdependent effects is doing macro. So when doing micro one is also doing macro and vice versa.
>
> (Lee 2013a)

Following this viewpoint, the fallacy of composition legitimizing the micro-macro dichotomy can be avoided. Not to mention, heterodox microfoundations are not concerned about reducing macro to micro as in neoclassical microfoundations. Moreover, there have been a series of efforts aiming at constructing microfoundations from a heterodox economic perspective. For further discussions and applications of heterodox microfoundations, see Eichner (1976, 1987), Jo (2007, 2011a, 2015), Todorova (2009), Lee (2011a, 2011b, 2012b), and Lee and Jo (2011).

## Conclusion

No doubt that heterodox economics is in the process of development and its future depends upon contemporary heterodox economists' contributions including, in particular, advancing heterodox theories in a more pluralistic, comprehensive, and historical manner as well as building active communities and networks of heterodox economists, such as academic programs, associations, journals, discussion groups, newsletters, conferences, workshops, and the like. The present chapter concerns the theoretical development of heterodox economics with a focus on the relationship between microeconomics and macroeconomics.

One of the problems that hinders the advancement of heterodox economics is the reliance on mainstream microeconomics in doing a heterodox macro analysis, in spite of well-articulated heterodox micro theories that are completely distinctive from mainstream microeconomics. The mismatch between heterodox macro and mainstream micro is due largely to the misunderstandings of heterodox microeconomics. For example, many heterodox economists assume that heterodox micro is all about individual behaviors, and that there is only mainstream micro. Hence if heterodox macro needs a microfoundation, it is the mainstream kind—optimizing behaviors given scarce resources. Another related position is that there is no need to develop heterodox microfoundations. Such misunderstandings indicate that heterodox microeconomics is not widely taught in academia (instead, many heterodox programs still heavily teach mainstream micro theories without reference to heterodox micro theories). Those positions together indicate that many heterodox economists are reluctant in dealing with real driving forces (that is, social agency) and underlying social relationships of the economic system; rather, they prefer to stay with the observable 'tip of an iceberg' qua aggregate statistical data.

For sure, almost all heterodox economists understand that a capitalist economy cannot be represented by a self-adjusting market system. In radical contrast to mainstream microeconomic narratives, heterodox microeconomics posits that the economy as a whole is an emergent and historical process that is driven by an array of interdependent sub-systems, organizations, and agency. If one wishes to explain real economic activities in historical context, it is necessary to deal with the components embedded in the whole system. Its scope thus ranges from socialized individuals undertaking actual decisions and actions, emergent entities such as markets, industries, and other governance organizations, to the economy as a whole that is conceptualized as the social provisioning process. These are the core properties and scope of heterodox microeconomic theory developed by Fred Lee.

Is it conceivable that heterodox macroeconomics will continue to advance without fully incorporating heterodox microeconomics? My answer is negative. There is no reason to believe that macro is the only legitimate analysis of capitalist economy. The next question would be how can we move forward? It seems to me that in the strange world of heterodox economics, we must outrun mainstream economists if we are concerned with the survival and reproduction of heterodox economics. Fred Lee always places the following quote in his heterodox microeconomics course syllabus.

"Well, in our country," said Alice, still panting a little, "you'd generally get somewhere else—if you ran very fast for a long time." "A slow sort of country!" said the Queen. "Now here, you see, it takes all the running you can do to keep in the same place. If you want to get somewhere else, you must run at least twice as fast as that!"

(Lewis Carroll, *Through the Looking-Glass*)

Many heterodox economists know that Fred Lee has been running at least twice as fast as the rest of economists in order to build heterodox microeconomic theory as well as the community of heterodox economists. I hope that many young heterodox economists follow his footsteps and, eventually, make heterodox economics keep moving forward.

## Acknowledgments

I am grateful to Fred Lee, John Henry, and Zdravka Todorova for their valuable comments. This particular work as well as my approach to heterodox economics are greatly influenced and inspired by Fred Lee, my mentor and dissertation advisor. Fred once said that the "discovery of Alfred Eichner" was "the most important in my entire academic career." To me it's my discovery of Fred Lee in 2003 that completely changed the way I do economics. Because of Fred, I have become a heterodox microeconomist. Because of Fred Lee's life-long contributions to the development of heterodox microeconomic theory, we were/are/will be able to go beyond the straightjacket of neoclassical economics. The legacy started with Alfred Eichner and continued by Fred Lee will grow in the work of younger heterodox economists (including myself).

## References

Bortis, H. 1997. *Institutions, Behaviour and Economic Theory*. Cambridge: Cambridge University Press.

Corbett, J. and T. Jenkinson. 1997. "How is Investment Financed? A Study of Germany, Japan, the United Kingdom and the United States." *The Manchester School of Economic and Social Studies* 65 (Supplement 1): 69–93.

Crotty, J. R. 1980. "Post-Keynesian Economic Theory: An Overview and Evaluation." *American Economic Review* 70 (2): 20–25.

Crotty, J. R. 1996. "Is New Keynesian Investment Theory Really 'Keynesian'?" *Journal of Post Keynesian Economics* 18 (3): 333–358.

Davidson, P. 1982–3. "Rational Expectations: A Fallacious Foundation for Studying Crucial Decision-Making Processes." *Journal of Post Keynesian Economics* 5: 182–197.

Dugger, W. M. 1996. "Redefining Economics: From Market Allocation to Social Provisioning." In *Political Economy for the 21st Century*, edited by C. J. Whalen, 31–43. Armonk, NY: M. E. Sharpe.

Dymski, G. A. 1992. "A 'New View' of the Role of Banking Firms in Keynesian Monetary Theory." *Journal of Post Keynesian Economics* 14 (3): 311–320.

Dymski, G. A. 1993. "Keynesian Uncertainty and Asymmetric Information: Complementary or Contradictory?" *Journal of Post Keynesian Economics* 16 (1): 49–54.

Eichner, A. S. 1976. *The Megacorp and Oligopoly: Micro Foundations of Macro Dynamics*. Cambridge: Cambridge University Press.

Eichner, A. S. 1987. *The Macrodynamics of Advanced Market Economies*. New York: M. E. Sharpe.

Fazzari, S. 2012. "Microfoundations." In *Elgar Companion to Post Keynesian Economics*, 2nd ed., edited by J. E. King, 392–396. Cheltenham: Edward Elgar.

Fazzari, S. and A. M. Variato. 1994. "Asymmetric Information and Keynesian Theories of Investment." *Journal of Post Keynesian Economics* 16 (3): 351–370.

Gruchy, A. G. 1987. *The Reconstruction of Economics: An Analysis of the Fundamentals of Institutional Economics*. New York: Greenwood Press.

Harcourt, G. C. 2004. "The Economics of Keynes and Its Theoretical and Political Importance: Or, What Would Marx and Keynes Have Made of the Happenings of the Past 30 Years and More?" *Post-Autistic Economics Review* 27.

Henry, J. F. and F. S. Lee. 2009. "John Davis and the Recent Turn in Economics." Paper presented at the Association for Institutional Thought Annual Conference, Albuquerque, NM.

Jespersen, J. 2009. *Macroeconomic Methodology: A Post-Keynesian Perspective*. Cheltenham: Edward Elgar.

Jo, T.-H. 2007. "Microfoundations of Effective Demand." PhD diss., University of Missouri–Kansas City.

Jo, T-H. 2011a. "A Heterodox Microfoundation of Business Cycles." In *Heterodox Analysis of Financial Crisis and Reform*, edited by J. Leclaire, T.-H. Jo, and J. Knodell, 111–123. Cheltenham: Edward Elgar.

Jo, T.-H. 2011b. "Social Provisioning Process and Socio-Economic Modeling." *American Journal of Economics and Sociology* 70 (5): 1094–1116.

Jo, T.-H. 2015. "Financing Investment under Fundamental Uncertainty and Instability: A Heterodox Microeconomic View." *Bulletin of Political Economy* 9 (1): forthcoming.

Keynes, J. M. 1936. *The General Theory of Employment, Interest and Money*. London: Macmillan.

Keynes, J. M. 1973. *The Collected Writings of John Maynard Keynes*. Vol. VII. London: Macmillan.

King, J. E. 2002. *A History of Post Keynesian Economics since 1936*. Northampton: Edward Elgar.

King, J. E. 2009. "Microfoundations?" In *Macroeconomic Policies on Shaky Foundations: Whither Mainstream Economics*, edited by E. Hein, T. Niechoj, and E. Stockhammer. Marburg: Metropolis.

King, J. E. 2012. *The Microfoundations Delusion: Metaphor and Dogma in the History of Macroeconomics*. Cheltenham: Edward Elgar.

Kliman, A. and S. D. Williams. 2015. "Why 'Financialization' Hasn't Depressed US Productive Investment." *Cambridge Journal of Economics* 39 (1): 67–92.

Kriesler, P. 1996. "Microfoundations: A Kaleckian Perspective." In *An Alternative Macroeconomic Theory: The Kaleckian Model and Post Keynesian Economics*, edited by J. E. King, 55–72. Boston: Kluwer.

Lavoie, M. and M. Seccareccia. 2001. "Minsky's Financial Fragility Hypothesis: A Missing Macroeconomic Link?" In *Financial Fragility and Investment in the Capitalist Economy: The Economic Legacy of Hyman Minsky*, Vol. II, edited by R. Bellofiore and P. Ferri, 76–96. Cheltenham: Edward Elgar.

Lawson, T. 1997. *Economics and Reality*. London: Routledge.

Lawson, T. 2003. *Reorienting Economics*. London: Routledge.

Lawson, T. 2006. "The Nature of Heterodox Economics." *Cambridge Journal of Economics* 30 (4): 483–505.

Lee, F. S. 2002. "Theory Creation and the Methodological Foundation of Post Keynesian Economics." *Cambridge Journal of Economics* 26 (6): 789–804.

Lee, F. S. 2005. "Grounded Theory and Heterodox Economics." *Grounded Theory Review* 4 (2): 95–116.

Lee, F. S. 2009. *A History of Heterodox Economics: Challenging the Mainstream in the Twentieth Century*. London: Routledge.

Lee, F. S. 2010a. Alfred Eichner's Missing 'Complete Model': A Heterodox Micro-Macro Model of a Monetary Production Economy. In *Money and Macrodynamics: Alfred Eichner and Post-Keynesian Economics*, edited by M. Lavoie, L.-P. Rochon, and Mario Seccareccia, 22–42. Armonk, NY: M. E. Sharpe.

Lee, F. S. 2010b. "A Heterodox Teaching of Neoclassical Microeconomic Theory." *International Journal of Pluralism and Economic Education* 1 (3): 203–235.

Lee, F. S. 2011a. "Heterodox Microeconomics and the Foundation of Heterodox Macroeconomics." *Economia Informa* 367: 6–20.

Lee, F. S. 2011b. "Modeling the Economy as a Whole: An Integrative Approach." *American Journal of Economics and Sociology* 70 (5): 1282–1314.

Lee, F. S. 2012a. "Heterodox Economics and its Critics." *Review of Political Economy* 24 (2): 337–351.

Lee, F. S. 2012b. "Heterodox Surplus Approach: Production, Prices, and Value Theory." *Bulletin of Political Economy* 6 (2): 65–105.

Lee, F. S. 2013a. "Personal correspondence." Email, November 26.

Lee, F. S. 2013b. "Post-Keynesian Price Theory: From Pricing to Market Governance to the Economy as a Whole." In *The Oxford Handbook of Post-Keynesian Economics*, edited by G. C. Harcourt and P. Kriesler, 467–484. Oxford: Oxford University Press.

Lee, F. S. 2013c. "Review of John E. King, 2012, *The Microfoundations Delusion: Metaphor and Dogma in the History of Macroeconomics*." *Economic and Labour Relations Review* 24 (2): 255–260.

Lee, F. S. 2014. "Heterodox Theory of Production and the Mythology of Capital: A Critical Inquiry into the Circuit of Production." Unpublished working paper.

Lee, F. S. and S. Keen. 2004. "The Incoherent Emperor: A Heterodox Critique of Neoclassical Microeconomic Theory." *Review of Social Economy* 62 (2): 169–199.

Lee, F. S. and T.-H. Jo. 2011. "Social Surplus Approach and Heterodox Economics." *Journal of Economic Issues* 45 (4): 857–875.

Lee, F. S. and T.-H. Jo. 2013. "Post Keynesian Macroeconomics and Microfoundations Debate: A Suggested Resolution." Paper presented at the Association for Heterodox Economics Annual Conference, London, UK.

Lee, F. S. and M. Lavoie, eds. 2012. *In Defense of Post-Keynesian and Heterodox Economics*. London: Routledge.

Mearman, A. 2011. "What Do Heterodox Economists Think They Are?" *American Journal of Economics and Sociology* 70 (2): 480–507.

Mina, A., H. Lahr, and A. Hughes. 2013. "The Demand and Supply of External Finance for Innovative Firms." *Industrial and Corporate Change* 22 (4): 869–901.

Minsky, H. P. 1983. "Notes on Effective Demand: Comment on Bharadwaj." In *Distribution, Effective Demand and International Economic Relations*, edited by J. A. Kregel. New York: St. Martin's Press.

Minsky, H. P. 1986. *Stabilizing an Unstable Economy*. New Haven, CT: Yale University Press.

Pasinetti, L. L. 2005. "From Pure Theory to Full Economic Analysis—A Place for the Economic Agent." *Cahiers d'économie Politique* 2 (49): 211–216.

Polanyi, K. 1968. "The Economy as Instituted Process." In *Primitive, Archaic and Modern Economies: Essays of Karl Polanyi*, edited by G. Dalton, 139–174. Garden City, NY: A Doubleday Anchor Original.

Power, M. 2004. "Social Provisioning as a Starting Point for Feminist Economics." *Feminist Economics* 10 (3): 3–19.

Reynolds, P. J. 1987. *Political Economy: A Synthesis of Kaleckian and Post Keynesian Economics*. Sussex: Wheatsheaf Books.

Skidelsky, R. 2009. *Keynes: The Return of the Master*. New York: Public Affairs.

Smithin, J. 2004. "Macroeconomic Theory, (Critical) Realism and Capitalism." In *Transforming Economics: Perspectives on the Critical Realist Project*, edited by P. Lewis, 55–75. London: Routledge.

Targetti, F. and B. Kinda-Hass. 1982. "Kalecki's Review of Keynes' *General Theory*." *Australian Economic Papers* 21 (39): 245–260.

Tarshis, L. 1980. "Post-Keynesian Economics: A Promise that Bounced?" *American Economic Review* 70 (2): 10–14.

Todorova, Z. 2009. *Money and Households in a Capitalist Economy: A Gendered Post Keynesian–Institutional Analysis*. Cheltenham: Edward Elgar.

Todorova, Z. 2013. "Connecting Social Provisioning and Functional Finance in a Post-Keynesian–Institutional Analysis of the Public Sector." *European Journal of Economics and Economic Policies: Intervention* 10 (1): 61–75.

Trigg, A. B. and F. S. Lee. 2005. "Pasinetti, Keynes and the Multiplier." *Review of Political Economy* 17 (1): 29–43.

Weintraub, S. 1979. "Generalising Kalecki and Simplifying Macroeconomics." *Journal of Post Keynesian Economics* 1 (3): 101–106.

# 6 Beyond foundations

## Systemism in economic thinking

*Jakob Kapeller*

## Introduction

Economics abounds in problems of aggregation. Just think of the classic question asking how the process of market allocation emerges from a series of distinctive individual actions. The basic issue of aggregation affects all economic theories, since the latter inherently deal with either aggregate states (i.e., macroeconomic variables such as GDP, inflation, the interest rate, etc.) or the relation of individual actions to aggregate outcomes (e.g., the influence of entrepreneurial decisions on technological development). However, its role is specifically peculiar in current mainstream economic thought, since methodological individualism strictly demands that all social and economic analysis be based on theories of individual actions.

In this context, this chapter not only aims at illuminating the 'microfoundational approach' currently prevailing in mainstream economics, but also provides a coherent alternative framework for conceptually organizing different layers of economic analysis. This alternative framework comes under the label of 'systemism' and addresses ontological aspects relating to the relevance and constitution of different economic entities as well as methodological questions carrying implications for the development of adequate theoretical arguments in economics.

In addressing these main questions, this chapter draws not only on arguments occurring in economic contexts, but also imports some ideas from other disciplines. Specifically, it points to an existing concept for organizing and conceptualizing different layers of analysis labeled *systemism*. This approach goes back to a series of contributions made by an eminent philosopher Mario Bunge (see Bunge 1996, [1998] 1999, 2000, 2004, among others), who developed the concept of systemism to denote research practices sharing similar features not compatible to traditional conceptions of either individualism or holism.[1] Hence, a systemist viewpoint is applicable to the whole breadth of the social sciences and I think there are several reasons for economists to adopt Bunge's stance on this question. First, the systemist framework provided by Bunge is suitable for analyzing and comparing a wide range of economic theories, since it is equipped with a rich descriptive apparatus, including clear-cut concepts and a well-developed terminology. Second, being grounded in a general philosophy of science, Bunge's systemist approach can also be applied outside the social sciences. Third, systemism benefits from a broad philosophical background allowing for addressing and differentiating ontological, methodological, and normative aspects. Fourth, systemism combines clarity with flexibility by emphasizing that relevant layers as well as their respective ordering depend on a specific research question at hand, and, hence, it transgresses any simple micro-macro duality. Finally and most importantly, since systemism eschews any kind of *a priori* hierarchical arguments (as it is evident in both neoclassical methodological individualism and naïve/collectivist forms of Marxian holism), it leads to a dynamic perspective on social systems inherently related to questions of social (i.e., 'aggregate') change as well as active (i.e., 'individual') agency. Especially this final point also attains a prominent role in Frederic S. Lee's approach to the "micro-macro distinction in heterodox economics" (Lee 2011a, 19). Following Lee, the micro-macro distinction as commonly envisaged is a chimera, since it implicitly suggests a strict demarcation of micro- and macro-related phenomena, whereas viewing the very same phenomena as intrinsically linked and part of the very same social realm provides a much more promising starting point for social analysis. In this respect Fred Lee's take on the micro-macro link in economics is in complete agreement with the systemist approach advanced by Bunge. Systemism in this context can be understood as a well-suited conceptual apparatus that is tacitly underlying Fred Lee's more specific arguments and attempts to model "the economy as whole," without neglecting the aspect of individual agency (e.g., Lee 2011a, 2011b, 2013).

This chapter proceeds as follows. The next section delivers a comprehensive perspective on different problems arising in the treatment of aggregates and aggregation and how these problems may turn into fallacies of composition. In turn, I will introduce the main building blocks of a systemic approach to social science in the third section and review some parallels or possible complementarities between a systemist approach and heterodox economics in the section after that. The last section offers some concluding thoughts.

## Fallacies of composition and emergent properties: assessing the microfoundational view

It has already been emphasized that economics abounds in problems of aggregation. These problems are especially prevalent in mainstream economics due to its reliance on methodological individualism as a basic prerequisite of scientific analysis. To illustrate this claim, consider the following examples of problems and their typical solutions: the aggregation of individual decisions to aggregate market outcomes (Walrasian *tâtonnement*), the aggregation of individual preferences to consistent democratic decision-making (Arrow's Impossibility Theorem), the aggregation of individual states of welfare to social welfare (aggregate welfare functions), the aggregation of individual trading behavior to aggregate bubbles (herding), the aggregation of individual demand curves to aggregate demand curves (the Sonnenschein–Mantel–Debreu Theorem), the aggregation of a diverse set of durable material and immaterial goods used for productive purposes into one economic category (capital), and the assembly of different inputs into a common output (gross-substitutability of inputs). These examples signify that traditional mainstream economics is indeed confronted with aggregation problems in various contexts.

In what follows I will argue that such aggregation problems give rise to four different types of possible fallacies of composition, which may arise from either a wrong treatment of aggregation or a wrong treatment of aggregates. While the microfoundational approach encounters problems on both ends, the differentiation between aggregation and aggregates is often helpful, especially since in the more careful applications of the microfoundational view a wrong treatment of aggregates is more common than that of aggregation.

### The simplistic fallacy

Let us examine the example of Thomas C. Schelling, who, in the introduction to his *Micromotives and Macrobehavior*, posits that "there are easy cases ... in which the aggregate is merely an extrapolation of the individual" (Schelling 1978, 13). According to Schelling these "easy cases" are marked by the fact that the underlying decisions are made completely autonomously—that is, they are completely *unrelated* to the decisions and actions of other agents. Conversely, if decisions are somehow interrelated the resulting situations "usually don't permit any simple summation or extrapolation to the aggregates," since they constitute a "system of interactions" (14). Hence, Schelling uncovers a specific aspect of the aggregation problem, namely that any aggregate consists not only of individuals, but also of the relations between these individuals. Ignoring these relations is to commit a *simplistic fallacy of composition* by underestimating the complexity of correct aggregation. This fallacy is prevalent in most of current mainstream macroeconomics (including real business cycles theory as well as dynamic stochastic general equilibrium models) and may lead to an overly simplistic and, hence, deficient understanding of aggregates. In sharp contrast, Schelling is able to anticipate and avoid the *simplistic fallacy* by taking into account the relatedness of agents.

We can translate Schelling's argument into usual philosophical terms by positing that any aggregate might exhibit so-called "emergent properties" that arise in either wholes or parts if some whole is constituted. For Bunge (1996, 19–23) these emergent properties are essentially ontological novelties occurring in (social) systems. Thereby, emergent properties may fall into two main groups: first, there are *global* properties of aggregate systems (e.g., a nation's culture or language, a firm's success or failure), which emerge at the level of the system exactly because individual components constitute the latter. Second, individual parts within a system may acquire *relational* properties (e.g., being a daughter or an employee), because they are part of a social system. Since these ontological novelties are properties or features of concrete things, they can carry mechanisms and have real effects. Hence, such emergent properties stand in stark contrast to mere statistical or arithmetic extrapolations, like calculating the mean of a certain variable. Such *aggregate* statistical or arithmetic properties may be useful for describing a certain system, but do not necessarily illuminate the actual processes induced by or occurring within a given system.[2]

The *simplistic fallacy* and the importance of relations are well-known in the logical and physical sciences. A typical illustration for the simplistic fallacy is that the difference between the words 'dog' and 'god' does not reside in their micro-components (the letters d, o, and g) but in the way these components are ordered, that is in their relations or structure.[3] The emergent property in this context is commonly called 'meaning.' Similarly, it is obvious that if two particles hit a third with equal intensity the aggregate effect is not necessarily attainable by extrapolation. Instead the relative direction of the two former particles has to be analyzed to make a valid statement about the aggregate effect. Obvious examples also stem from chemistry. For example, if a sodium ion $Na^+$ shares an electron with a $Cl^-$ anion the resulting $NaCl$ molecule has a series of emergent properties with electric neutrality and a specific taste counting among them (see Anderson 1972 or Bunge 2004 for a series of related examples).

So does Schelling solve the problem of aggregation and master the fallacy of composition? The answer to this question is: yes and no. In contrast to much of mainstream economic thought, Schelling indeed resolves the "crucial ambivalence" of methodological individualism (Hodgson 2007, 220) by explicitly employing a relational approach and thereby masters *the simplistic fallacy of composition*. However, Schelling nonetheless overlooks that aggregate patterns eventually constitute "ontological novelties." While this stance is possibly grounded in Schelling's strong commitment to methodological individualism, it is harmful in various ways, since it invites other, more subtle fallacies with respect to the treatment of aggregates and aggregation. Let us analyze these fallacies in turn.

### The static fallacy

Schelling notes that the difference between the "easy cases," in which aggregate behavior is a simple summation of individual actions, and the converse cases is simply that the latter "are not easily guessed" (Schelling 1978, 14). In doing so Schelling presents a case for "weak emergence" implying that aggregates lead to unexpected, but deducible results. "Weak emergence" is thus only "an observer-relative property" (Chalmers 2006, 251). So, any failure to account for aggregate results by analyzing individual action must stem simply from deficiencies in human understanding, e.g., observer-bias or a lack of deductive efforts. What is thus absent from the microfoundational approach is that reduction might be either principally *or* practically infeasible, even when adequately modeling individuals and their relations. Principal infeasibility is often directly associated with 'strongly emergent properties,' i.e., *global* properties, which cannot be explained by resorting to individuals and their relative setup. The scope of this argument is very general and it is heavily contested, at least in the natural sciences. Practical infeasibility is sometimes also subsumed under the label of 'strong emergence' in the sense that initial data (facts, conditions, laws, etc.) is never fully available, and even if data is available no definite calculations could be made. This argument is hardly contested, at least in the social sciences and has already been expressed clearly in the alleged heyday of methodological individualism in the first half of the twentieth century. Back then even decidedly reductionist researchers were aware of the argument of practical infeasibility and, hence, recognized a greater spectrum of compositional fallacies.

> Clearly psychology is fundamental to political economy and all the social sciences in general. Perhaps a day will come when the laws of social science can be deduced from the principles of psychology, just as some day perhaps the principles of the composition of matters will give us all the laws of physics and chemistry by deduction, but we are still very far from that state of affairs, and we must take a different approach.
>
> (Pareto [1927] 1971, 29)

To overlook the possibility of practical infeasibility systematically—as preached by the microfoundational approach to aggregation—is to commit *the static fallacy*, i.e., to assume that reducibility is always possible and feasible. Such a stance holds that no unexplainable properties can emerge in any given system and, thus, any unexpected aggregate outcome is to be attributed to the deficiencies of the observer.

### *The dogmatic fallacy*

Following this microfoundational perspective there exist only two routes to deal with emergent properties: Either we know some individual characteristics allowing us to directly deduce these properties, or we may spot some pattern in an aggregate system, which is in turn to be explained by assuming appropriate individual characteristics.[4] The methodological imperative inherent in this dualism complements the idea that reduction is always feasible with the postulate that reduction is a necessary prerequisite for understanding. This imperative, that 'only to reduce is to understand,' is also explicitly espoused by Schelling.

> If we see pattern and order and regularity, we should withhold judgment about whether it is the pattern and order of a jungle, a slave system, or a community infested by parasitic diseases, and inquire first of all what it is that the individuals who comprise the system seem to be doing and how it is that their actions, in the large, produce the patterns we see.
>
> (Schelling 1978, 22)

The 'microfoundational approach' prevalent in current mainstream economics mainly rests on understanding reduction as the sole and best way to achieve understanding about aggregate patterns and constellations. And indeed, the history of the natural sciences is full of examples for the success of micro-reduction in enhancing our scientific understanding. However, a *purely* micro-foundational approach amounts to ignoring that emergent properties are ontological novelties and, thus, may carry real effects. Since the latter aspect is the most important characteristic of an emergent property, a microfoundational approach eventually leads to ignoring emergent properties at all. In other words, the microfoundational approach espoused in current mainstream economic thought commits *the dogmatic fallacy*, i.e., to willfully abstain from studying mechanisms at the level on which they are located. Since science is interested in mechanisms of all kinds there is no point in consciously abstaining from studying higher-level mechanisms by enforcing reduction as the prime and only approach to social analysis. Quite on the contrary, any mechanism can and should be studied in its own right no matter on which level it operates. Abstaining from such an analysis eventually constitutes a "serious omission because mechanisms—such as those of diffusion, clumping, negative feedback, metabo-lism, cooperation, competition, mediation, and debate—happen to be processes in material complex things, *not in their individual constituents*" (Bunge 2004, 183, emphasis added). By forcing a reductionist view on these phenomena we therefore inherently limit our understanding.

Taking into account the *dogmatic fallacy* when studying social mechanisms is of vital importance if situations are complex, that is, when "it is not a trivial matter to infer the properties of the whole" even when "the properties of the parts and the laws of their interaction" (Simon 1962, 468) are given. In this context, Herbert Simon emphasized that complex arrangements often require flexible and versatile approaches, while a sole focus reduction would lead to overly narrow research strategies. Hence, Simon's argument that "[i]n the face of complexity, an in-principle reductionist may be at the same time a pragmatic holist" (468) implies that studying mechanisms at the level where they are located is a well-suited antidote to reductionist parochialism.

### The hierarchical fallacy

The final flaw of the microfoundational approach is to neglect that emergent properties as ontological novelties carry mechanisms and, thus, bear the possib-ility of downward causation—that is, macro-phenomena influencing individual action. Ignoring this possibility of downward causation is to commit *the hierar-chical fallacy* by *a priori* assuming that mechanisms only work bottom up. This assumption strongly restricts the scope of the microfoundational approach and is the reason why aspects of downward causation are completely missing in Schell-ing's famous "checkerboard model" (Schelling 1969, 1978; Sugden 2000), which explains spatial racial segregation simply in terms of individual prefer-ences. This focus implies that racial segregation is to be seen as a matter of indi-vidual preferences and not as "the result of active racial discrimination," i.e., as part of a top-down process (Bunge 2004, 194). This viewpoint, contrary to Schelling, would emphasize the importance of social prejudice and structural discrimination. Such an argument alludes to a form of downward causation, where social structures influence individual agency without determining the latter. In economics such an argument takes the form of "macro-foundations," which are deemed relevant for fully understanding micro-level behavior (King 2012, 42–45). From such a viewpoint

> there can be no hierarchical stipulation that macro-theories require a micro-economic foundation to obtain full validity. One could just as well demand a macroeconomic foundation for microeconomics, when the latter finds it difficult to fit macroeconomic realities into its own framework.
>
> (Rothschild 1988, 14)

And indeed such 'macro-foundational' assumptions, like the assumptions of full employment and general equilibrium in the context of partial market analysis, are often made in mainstream microeconomic theory.

It should be noted that downward causation is a commonplace in the natural sciences and can often be explained by recourse to micro-level arguments (Andersen *et al.* 2000). For instance, the weight of the sun is simply the sum of weights of individual particles (mostly hydrogen). However, this cumulative weight in turn produces strong downwardly causal effects, since it triggers a process of nuclear fusion, when individual hydrogen atoms are fused into helium. Thereby, the process of fusion differs with respect to the exact weight of the aggregate compositum, i.e., the respective star.[5]

### Taking stock

Let us return to Schelling's checkerboard model. Even in its most basic variant Schelling explicitly introduces an argument about who is related to whom (there are two types of agents and any agent has relations to her neighbors) as well as the effect of relations in his model (if some proportion of neighbors is of the other type the agent tries to change his position). This consideration of relations is exactly why he is able to go beyond mere summation or, in other words, why he is able to avoid *the simplistic fallacy*. Similar things could be said about related examples such as Akerlof's (1970) 'market for lemons,' where relations are specified as asymmetric informational endowments, or Fehr and Schmidt's (1999) 'inequality aversion,' where concern for others prominently enters agents' utility functions. This observation is decisive. If aggregation does not account for the relations of individual agents, but only sums up their individual characteristics, the resulting *aggregate* property is by definition unsuitable to capture any emergent properties.

We find approaches to aggregation problems similar to Schelling's in diverse areas of mainstream microeconomics: one of the most important is the Sonnenschein-Mantel-Debreu condition that explicitly addresses that while we can access the sum of individual demands at a given point in time by simply summing up individual demands, the very same argument does not hold for individual demand curves (Kirman 1992). Here, the logic is similar to Schelling's basic case: while individual demands at a given time are independent from each other, an individual's reaction to a change in price indeed depends on the reaction of other individuals and, thus, the aggregation of individual demand curves is possible only under very restrictive conditions, which require the assumption that all individuals have homothetic and identical utility functions. Consequently, this assumption also pervades neoclassical macroeconomics and is one main reason for assuming a single representative agent (Kirman 1992; Gun 2004)— that is, this assumption resorts to extrapolation in order to avoid any variant of emergent properties in mainstream macroeconomics.

In alignment with the microfoundational approach, the possibility of 'strong emergence'—that is, currently or principally unexplainable emergent properties like unforeseeable shifts in the evolution of preferences induced by the interplay between product innovation on the supply-side and learning-effects on the demand-side (Witt 2001)—is excluded *a priori*. The same holds for downwardly causal effects, i.e., the possibility that some mechanisms located at the level of the system, like the social mediation of preferences (Veblen [1899] 1994, 43–62), might influence individual demand.

In sum we have identified four different constellations or cases, which might give rise to different 'fallacies of composition' resulting from a microfoundational view. Table 6.1 provides a summary of these four constellations.

Our examples suggest that, ironically, current mainstream microeconomics seems to exhibits greater awareness for problems of aggregation and fallacies of composition than current mainstream macroeconomics. In the latter, all of the above fallacies are prevalent, since the macroeconomic system is interpreted as a mere extrapolation of a single, "representative" individual (Kirman 1992; Gun 2004; King 2012, 118–122), while in mainstream microeconomics at least the *simplistic fallacy* is partially addressed.

In order to cope with the full scope of possible fallacies of aggregation I suggest to adopt a systemist approach to provide a suitable methodological and ontological framework for detecting and avoiding these fallacies.

## Systemism: main features

While the concept of systemism might seem new, one can be assured that the practice from systemism is far from something completely novel. In his diverse assessments on systemism, Mario Bunge cites a variety of examples for what he conceives as a "systemist" social research. Interestingly, Bunge makes reference to some eminent heterodox economists—in particular, John Maynard Keynes and Wassily Leontief (Bunge 2004, 187), Max Weber,[6] Joseph A. Schumpeter, Thorstein B. Veblen, and K. William Kapp (Bunge [1998] 1999, 92–93). Bunge's observation implies that from a philosopher's viewpoint heterodox economics, unlike mainstream economics and most other social sciences, offers significant insights into the economy and society as a system. Therefore, although there is a notion of *ad auctoritatem* in this observation, it suggests that heterodox economic approaches could serve as natural candidates for illustrating

Table 6.1 A typology of aggregation problems and corresponding fallacies of composition

| | Linear aggregation | Weak emergence | Strong emergence | Downward causation |
|---|---|---|---|---|
| The 'aggregation problem' | Aggregate properties can be derived by a linear extrapolation or summation of individual properties. | Aggregate properties are novel: they differ from the individual's, but can be derived from the latter. | Aggregate properties are novel: they differ from the individual's and cannot be derived from the latter. | Aggregate properties influence the behavior of individual elements. |
| Economic example: product markets | Aggregation of individual demands. | Aggregation of individual demand curves. | Innovation in market environments. | Social mediation of preferences. |
| The microfoundational view | Treatment of aggregation: 'the whole is nothing more than the sum of its parts.' | Treatment of aggregation: 'the whole is nothing more than the sum of its parts.' | Treatment of aggregates: 'wholes cannot be explanatory—they do not carry mechanisms.' | |
| Resulting 'fallacy of composition' | The simplistic fallacy: underestimating the complexity of aggregation, i.e., ignoring relations. | The static fallacy: ignoring the possibility of arising novelties not explainable with (current) micro-knowledge . | The dogmatic fallacy: ignoring that complex higher-level mechanisms can be studied on their own. | The hierarchical fallacy: ignoring the possibility of downward causation. |

a systemist approach to social and economic issues. However, before fully exploring this possibility I will give a short introduction to 'systemism.'

For Bunge every item or entity is either

> a system or a part of one ... a *system* is a complex object every part or component of which is connected with other parts of the same object in such a manner that the whole possesses some features that its components lack—that is, emergent properties.
>
> (Bunge 1996, 20, original emphasis)

Thus, he conceptually ties the concept of a system to the idea of related nodes forming an aggregate with some emergent properties. These emergent properties carry mechanisms, whose effects lead to continuous changes and stabilization of a given system,[7] which is why we conceive of them "as a process (or sequence of states, or pathway) in a concrete system, natural or social" (Bunge 2004, 186). Thereby, these mechanisms are mostly "concealed" and, thus, "have to be conjectured" (186). Some mechanisms are "essential" in that they are unique to a given system (193) and that they potentially carry "specific" functions that may be used to achieve specific goals. Bunge emphasizes that mechanisms and functions are decidedly different from each other, as the former answer how things work, while the latter show how to achieve a given aim. However, functions and mechanisms can be mapped on each other. In this context the function-mechanism relation is principally a one-to-many one, since different mechanisms can be used to achieve a specific aim. Success on markets, for instance, is determined by different mechanisms and, hence, "markets can be conquered" in different ways, e.g., "by force, dumping, free-trade agreements or even honest competition" (194).

Additionally, any system is characterized by a specific *composition* (the set of nodes), an *environment* and a certain *structure or organization* (the collection of relations between the nodes as well as between the nodes and the environment). The latter is a novel and necessary element of any system as well as the source of emergent properties and, hence, mechanisms. While this basic concept of a system can be applied to a variety of concrete or even conceptual items, we can for the matter at hand explicitly apply it to social systems, like a family, a firm, or a nation. Thereby, novel properties emerge at the level of the whole system (global properties, like a firm's success or failure) or at the level of its individual components (relational properties, like the role assigned to a given employee).

The main contribution of systemism from a practical perspective is its capacity of putting the most interesting aspect of any system and structures therein—e.g., the organization of relations—at the center stage. By focusing on the relations between individuals it aims to transgress the traditional dichotomy of an individualist and a holist approach and thereby to preserve "the grains of truth" involved in these approaches. In doing so, systemism "handles wholes without being holistic and studies their individual components without being individualistic" (Bunge 1996, 281). Following this argument Bunge juxtaposes systemism to individualism and holism by referring to three different layers: ontology, methodology, and morals (Bunge 1996, 2000). Table 6.2 gives a stylized representation of the differences between these three distinctive approaches with respect to three different layers. This illustration indicates that systemism indeed comes as a rather full-fledged concept.

According to the systemist view social science is the study of social systems as well as their components. In this respect, systemism is compatible with a broad range of heterodox approaches trying to include both, social structure as well as individual agency. Recent examples for such approaches are supplied by an understanding of economics as the study of the social provisioning process (Lee 2011a) or the postulate of evolutionary economists to focus on the meso-level of economic activity (e.g., Dopfer, Foster, and Potts 2004).

Thereby systemism explicitly rejects the *dogmatic fallacy* that 'only to reduce is to understand' by emphasizing that "every system must be studied on its own level as well as analyzed into its interacting components" (Bunge 1996, 266). Moreover, since it takes into account relations between individual nodes, it is also well equipped to deal with the *simplistic fallacy*. Finally, since emergent properties are conceived as ontological novelties, which in turn may carry mechanisms, systemism also anticipates the *static* as well as the *hierarchical fallacy*. To sustain the coherence of the approaches collected in Table 6.2 ontological and methodological arguments have to be closely intertwined in all three cases, while the normative part on morals is to be seen as less obliging. Nonetheless, the moral aspect provides an interesting juxtaposition of a systemist viewpoint to the more common variants of a moralist interpretation of individualism and holism.

Given that some systems may be necessary to constitute others (e.g., "subsystems" such as firms and families that might constitute a "supersystem" such as a market for consumption goods), there is a natural hierarchy of levels within the realm of human activity. Therefore, what is conceived as either the 'micro' or the 'macro' strongly depends on the question at stake. From a bird's eye's view, it makes a lot of sense to schematically structure levels in social analysis not in a dichotomic micro-vs.-macro perspective, but instead as a gradual movement from a pico- or nano-level (with a single individual person as central reference point) to the mega- or giga-level (e.g., transnational corporations and organizations, international relations, globalization). While this arrangement is far from fully original, it is suitable for conceptually organizing and comparing different research settings (Bunge 1996, 278–279; [1998] 1999, 73).

Finally we arrive at a consistent vision of micro-macro interaction in social science. First, it assumes that the "social sciences study social systems and their subsystems and supersystems" (Bunge 1996, 273). Second, it recognizes that any system carries emergent properties as ontological novelties, which may come in two forms—either the system possesses some properties that its parts do not possess (*global* properties), or the parts possess some properties exactly because they are part of a given system (*relational* properties). Thereby, the approach to understand emergent properties as ontological novelties is rather a

Table 6.2 Individualism, holism, and systemism in comparison

| | Individualism | Holism | Systemism |
|---|---|---|---|
| **Ontology** | A society is an aggregate of persons—any super-individual totalities are fictitious. | A society is whole transcending its members due to emergent and non-reducible collective properties. | A society is a system composed of changing subsystems and has global properties, both reducible and non-reducible. |
| **Methodology** | Social science is the study of the individual and to explain a social fact amounts to explaining individual action. | Social science is the study of social wholes, since only they may constitute social facts, which in turn determine individual behavior. | Social science is the study of social systems; their changing composition, environment, and structure as well as the mechanisms they bring forth. |
| **Morals** | Only individuals can be morally valuable and, hence, should have the liberty to pursue their self-interest. | Social wholes, like nations or families, are maximally morally valuable. Individuals are valuable to the extent that they contribute to social wholes. | Whereas all individuals are morally valuable, those who render useful services to others are more valuable than those who harm others. |

Note
Author's tabulation based on Bunge (1996, 243–268).

universal take on the question whether "more is different." It summarizes one basic answer to this question, namely the idea that "at each new level of complexity entirely new properties appear" (Anderson 1972, 393), which takes the form of ontological novelties. Third, systemism posits that different ontological levels in social research—no matter where these levels are exactly located in a given application—are bridged by mechanisms (additionally to within-level mechanisms), which replace those simple aggregation rules that are exemplified by typical formal procedures (e.g., summing up, calculating a mean, classifying, etc.). The question of 'aggregation' is thereby explicitly tackled as a potentially interesting theoretical problem and not primarily as a technical difficulty. The very same argument holds when analyzing top-down effects. Hence these 'bridging' mechanisms can take the form of agency-structure relations (i.e., a bottom-up mechanism or upward causation) or structure-agency relations (i.e., top-down mechanisms or downward causation).

Based on this conceptual groundwork, Bunge develops a series of examples to illustrate the practical implication of a systemist approach. I will reproduce two of them here and, in turn, apply the very same logic to typical economic examples.

Figure 6.1 is basically a stylized representation of a simple hypothesis for explaining the often observed correlation that higher economic growth leads to a decline in fertility and, hence, to a slowdown or even a stagnation of demographic growth. Three main mechanisms are involved in this argument. First, it assumes that higher economic growth allows for (privately or publicly) insuring one's old-age security at the micro-level (a structure-agency relation). Second, it posits that these forms of welfare provision for the elderly reduce the individual incentive to bear and raise children (a within-level mechanism). Third, it asks for the effects of individual fertility decisions on demography—for example, a decline in fertility might lead to a reduction in demographic growth (an agency-structure relation). Taken together, these three mechanisms provide a specific rationale for a fourth one, which depicts the overall argument regarding the observed macro-level development that an increase in economic prosperity leads, quite contrary to what Malthus predicted, to a corresponding decrease in demographic growth.

Our next example (Figure 6.2) relates to nineteenth century France, which has been extensively analyzed by the contemporary historian Alexander de Toqueville. One of Toqueville's ([1856] 1998) arguments presupposes that the high political and economic concentration in nineteenth century France caused rural nobility to disregard their landholdings in favor of conducting businesses (or intrigues) at the royal court. This 'landlord absenteeism' in turn led to relative economic stagnation, especially in the agricultural sector, where technical and

*Figure 6.1* From economic growth to population stagnation (source: Bunge 1996, 281).

*Figure 6.2* Toqueville's analysis of the Ancien Régime (source: Bunge 2000, 151).

organizational improvements strongly depended on the individual capabilities of landlords. For Toqueville this dysfunctional state of affairs is not only a main reason for widespread poverty found especially in rural areas, but also partly explains the comparatively better economic development in the UK at the same time.

Such arguments on micro-macro-interactions also allow for the introduction of positive feedback effects working in one way or the other. With respect to the example of nineteenth century France, one might argue that the relative decrease in agricultural productivity made court-related business even more attractive for rural landlords, which in turn intensified economic and technological retardation within the agricultural sector. Similarly, Bunge argues a decrease in political honesty at the aggregate level might deter ambitious and honest young women and men from entering the political sphere, which in turn contributes to a further deterioration of the moral standards prevailing in political discourse and decision-making (he labels this alleged process as "Gresham's Law of Political Apathy," see Bunge 2004, 192).

These examples show that what Bunge's concept of systemism offers is far away from a methodological straight-jacket. Quite on the contrary, the schematic approach utilized in these examples provides some simple tools for expressing and conceptualizing theoretical relationships with special attention dedicated to micro-macro interactions. In what follows I will apply this basic logic to some examples related to heterodox economic arguments and theories.

## Systemism and heterodoxy

As we have already seen, there is some affinity between a systemist approach to science in general and heterodox economics. This affinity is partially related to the evaluation of past theorists (heterodox economists often turn out to be systemists from a methodological perspective). However, the very same affinity also relates to conceptual issues like the possibility of downward causation (in the form of structure-agency relations), the emphasis on complexity or the basic idea that an individual constitutes "the ensemble of social relations" (Marx and Engels [1845] 1962).

Therefore, it comes as no surprise that we can use similar theoretical sketches as used in the preceding chapter to illustrate well-known heterodox economic arguments from a systemist perspective. Our first example is the 'paradox of thrift.' This paradox postulates that the collective aim to increase savings will be unsuccessful, exactly because it is a collective aim. The intuition behind the paradox of thrift is as follows: If agents collectively try to increase their savings, they will reduce spending and thereby also decrease their aggregate income. This decrease in income might in turn render any individual ambition to increase savings obsolete.[8]

Figures 6.3 and 6.4 present the paradox of thrift in two variants. In the first variant the paradox of thrift is conceptualized as a self-fulfilling prophecy where uncertain prospects lead to an increase in precautionary savings, which reduces expenditures, lowers income, and, hence, renders economic prospects even more uncertain or even gloomy.

In the second variant the paradox of thrift is presented as a self-defeating prophecy. In this scenario increased savings are not the result of rising pessimism, but are rather induced by experts' or politicians' advice for economic consolidation of households and firms by means of increased private saving. In both cases self-reinforcing effects obviously play a crucial role.

Another classic heterodox line of argument that can be illustrated in such a simple, interactive micro-macro framework is Hyman P. Minsky's financial instability hypothesis (Figure 6.5) stating, in short, that "stability breeds instability," or more specifically:

> A period of successful functioning of the economy leads to a decrease in the value of liquidity and to an acceptance of more aggressive financing practices. Banks, nonbank financial institutions, and money-market organizations can experiment with new liabilities and increase their asset-equity ratio without their liabilities losing any significant credence.
>
> (Minsky 1986, 249)

This kind of financial expansion anchoring in economic stability can again be expressed in a schematic form including macro-to-micro (or structure-agency) as

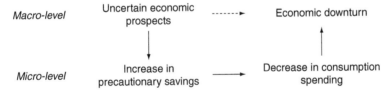

*Figure 6.3* The paradox of thrift as a self-fulfilling prophecy.

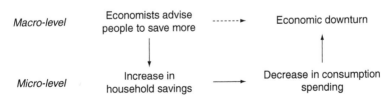

*Figure 6.4* The paradox of thrift as a self-defeating prophecy.

*Figure 6.5* The financial instability hypothesis in a systemist framework.

well as micro-macro (or agency-structure) relations accompanied by within-level mechanisms. It thereby employs both upward and downward causation in expressing a global macro-mechanism.

The use of such approaches for a conceptual work in designing and evaluating theories is thereby not limited to classical arguments relating only to two levels of interaction but can also be applied to more current research and thus be extended to include additional ontological layers. An example for the first feature—the applicability to more current research—can be provided with reference to Bowles and Park (2005), which suggests a positive relationship between income inequality and aggregate working hours (a global macro-mechanism) based on theoretical and empirical arguments. Specifically, they use the Veblenian concept of social emulation by arguing that consumption preferences are transmitted via social relations and, hence, increase with increasing income inequality, since the consumption of top income groups grows faster than average consumption. Bowles and Park argue that one way to actually live up to the increased consumption aspirations induced by the increase in inequality is to aim at an increase in hours worked to afford additional consumption expenditures. Hence, they provide a global macro-mechanism, with a more specific and detailed explanation, which also incorporates an argument operating at the micro-level. Note that this approach is far from being microfoundational from a conceptual point of view, since we find that a macro-level mechanism (from aggregate inequality to individual hours worked) proceeds within social systems (in this case nation states) by inducing processes among individual parts of the very same system via downward causation and social relations. Figure 6.6 summarizes this argument in a graphical form.

My final example relates to the possibility of extending such a systemic framework to include additional layers (see Kapeller and Schütz 2013). Specifically, we

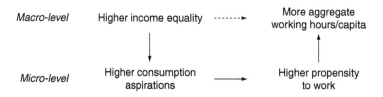

*Figure 6.6* Thorstein Veblen and working hours according to Bowles and Park (2005) in a systemist framework.

developed a dynamic and stock-flow consistent Post Keynesian economic model (Kapeller and Schütz 2014), where inequality within the working class increases. As a reaction to increasing inequality, those workers who fall back in terms of income are affected by Veblenian conspicuous consumption motives and, hence, try to compensate these losses by incurring additional debt. As a consequence demand for credit is increasing. This setup is complemented by the introduction of a Minskyian banking sector roughly conforming to the mechanism depicted in Figure 6.5: stable economic conditions decrease risk-management standards in the banking sector and contribute to the creation of financial innovation, both of which lead to an increase in credit supply matching the increased credit demand by households. If households eventually incur debt to afford additional consumption, the economy will experience a boom-phase due to increased aggregate demand, which ceases only if either inequality decreases or credit requirements are again increased in the face of rising systemic risk. In the corresponding model only the second option is implemented, which leads to a decrease in economic activity due to more restricted lending conditions and bankrupts within the household sector, which further reinforce lending restrictions. This self-propagating spiral finally leads to recession in the economy, which forces households to repair their balance sheets. In a full-fledged framework such a model delivers an economy exhibiting a constant cyclical behavior labeled as 'Minsky–Veblen Cycles.' However, as is illustrated in Figure 6.7 the main aspects of the model can still be relatively easily

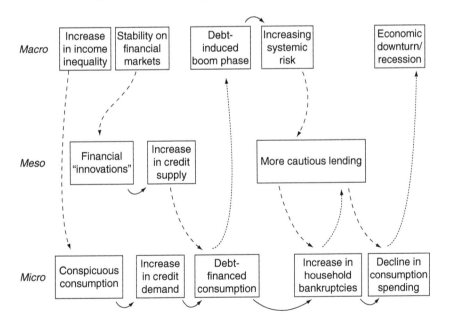

*Figure 6.7* Minsky–Veblen cycles in a systemist framework (source: Kapeller and Schütz 2013, 521).

expressed in a systemist fashion by representing the model's main mechanisms as well as their chronology and relative impact. In a second step we can graphically illustrate these relationships by referring to three different layers: that is, households at the micro-level, the banking sector at the meso-level, and the aggregate economic behavior at the macro-level.

## Conclusions

The main and obvious aim of this chapter is to provide a constructive and philosophically sound perspective on the question of reductionism in economics. In this respect this chapter makes two main contributions. First, by distinguishing different forms of aggregation problems as well as their corresponding fallacies of compositions it gives a precise and specific account of the rather general notion that 'the whole is something more than the sum of its parts.' This analysis in turn points to a series of fundamental weaknesses associated with the microfoundational approach prevailing in current mainstream economics. Second, it provides a specific suggestion on how to think about handling different layers of analysis in social research by referring to systemism as a conceptual anchor for heterodox economic practice. It is shown that a systemist approach is not only highly compatible with arguments to be found in heterodox economics, but also provides heterodox economics with a solid and highly consistent ontological and methodological foundation.

## Acknowledgments

I have to thank Leonhard Dobusch, Volker Gadenne, Claudius Gräbner, Tae-Hee Jo, Bernhard Schütz, and Zdravka Todorova for their comments on an earlier draft of this chapter.

## Notes

1 As such systemism bears no direct relation to systems theory as advanced by Niklas Luhmann (see Wan 2011 for a treatment of this relationship). Instead Bunge rather points to the works of Raymond Boudon or James Coleman as archetypical for a systemist approach. The fact that these two authors self-identify with methodological individualism is not decisive here, since they "practice the systemic approach even while preaching an individualistic one" (Bunge 1996, 148).

2 Descriptive results stemming from statistical or arithmetic extrapolations are explicitly labeled as "aggregate properties" in Bunge's approach.

3 Nagel (1952) suggests a classic and more elaborate example based on comparing the ordered class of all natural numbers K with another class K*, which is equal to the conjoined set of the ordered classes of all even (Ke) and odd numbers (Ko) so that K* = {Ke, Ko}. As in the example given above the microelements of the classes K and K* are equal, while their relations differ.

4 The strategy to spot a specific aggregate pattern and in turn explain this pattern by assuming an appropriate micro-setup, can be found in many famous models, e.g., Schelling's checkerboard model of racial segregation (Schelling 1969), Akerlof's 'market for lemons' (1970) or Fehr and Schmidt's 'inequality aversion' (1999). One of

the first examples from modern economics is Adam Smith's *Theory of Moral Sentiments* (Smith [1759] 2009). Smith develops assumptions on individual dispositions (like sympathy and the impartial spectator) to explain the allegedly rather harmonious social order, which served as Smith's main intellectual puzzle.

5 While in the sun and similar heavy stars helium is produced via the successive fusion of hydrogen atoms, in heavier stars (with more than 1.3 times the mass of the sun) carbon, nitrogen, and oxygen also play a role in the creation of helium through nuclear fusion.

6 With regard to Max Weber, Bunge notes that while Weber did preach individualism, he practiced systemism (Bunge 2000, 149; see also Albert 2005 for a similar argument).

7 In this very Schumpeterian notion Bunge not only analyzes the market as a volatile system and identifies "innovation" as its "essential" mechanism, but also gives due credit to Schumpeter for pinning down this mechanism "in a single magisterial page" making him stand in sharp contrast to "neoclassical economists, obsessed like shop-keepers with price competition" (Bunge 2004, 189).

8 To illustrate this argument one can assume a simple model where aggregate income is equal to aggregate expenditure, which is the sum of consumption spending and investment, i.e., $Y = C + I$, where $C = c_1 Y$ and investment spending is autonomous. If, we now take $c_1 = 0.9$ and $I = 100$, aggregate income $Y$ is equal to 1000 and aggregate savings are equal to 100. Now, assume that households want to double their savings by doubling their savings rate $(1-c_1)$ from 10 to 20 per cent, which decreases $c_1$ to 0.8. In turn aggregate income is reduced to 500, where one-fifth of this income is saved. Hence, aggregate savings stay constant at 100, since there has been an economic downturn due to the decrease in consumption spending.

# References

Akerlof, G. A. 1970. "The Market for 'Lemons': Quality Uncertainty and the Market Mechanism." *Quarterly Journal of Economics* 84 (3): 488–500.

Albert, G. 2005. "Moderater Methodologischer Individualismus: Eine Weberianische Interpretation des Makro-Mikro-Makro-Modells." *Kölner Zeitschrift für Soziologie und Sozialpsychologie* 57 (3): 387–413.

Andersen, P. B., C. Emmeche, N. O. Finnemann, and P. V. Christiansen, eds. 2000. *Downward Causation.* Aarhus: Aarhus University Press.

Anderson, P. W. 1972. "More is Different." *Science* 177: 393–396.

Bowles, S. and Y. Park. 2005. "Emulation, Inequality, and Work Hours: Was Thorsten Veblen Right?" *The Economic Journal* 115: F397–F412.

Bunge, M. A. 1996. *Finding Philosophy in Social Science.* New Haven, CT: Yale University Press.

Bunge, M. A. [1998] 1999. *Social Science under Debate.* Toronto: University of Toronto Press.

Bunge, M. A. 2000. "Systemism: The Alternative to Individualism and Holism." *Journal of Socio-Economics* 29: 147–157.

Bunge, M. A. 2004. "How Does It Work: The Search for Explanatory Mechanisms." *Philosophy of the Social Sciences* 34 (2): 182–210.

Chalmers, D. J. 2006. "Strong and Weak Emergence." In *The Re-emergence of Emergence,* edited by Philip Clayton and Paul Davies, 244–254. Cambridge: Cambridge University Press.

Dopfer, K., J. Foster, and J. Potts. 2004. "Micro-Meso-Macro." *Journal of Evolutionary Economics* 14 (3): 263–279.

Fehr, E. and K. M. Schmidt. 1999. "A Theory of Fairness, Competition and Cooperation." *Quarterly Journal of Economics* 114 (3): 817–868.

Gun, O. 2004. "Why Do We Have Separate Courses in 'Micro' and 'Macro' Economics?" In *A Guide to What's Wrong in Economics*, edited by E. Fullbrook, 115–125. London: Anthem.

Hodgson, G. M. 2007. "Meanings of Methodological Individualism." *Journal of Economic Methodology* 14 (2): 211–226.

Kapeller, J. and B. Schütz. 2013. "Exploring Pluralist Economics: The Case of Minsky-Veblen Cycles." *Journal of Economic Issues* 47 (2): 515–524.

Kapeller, J. and B. Schütz. 2014. "Debt, Boom, Bust: A Theory of Minsky–Veblen Cycles." *Journal of Post-Keynesian Economics* 36 (4): 781–813.

King, J. E. 2012. *The Microfoundations Delusion: Metaphor and Dogma in the History of Macroeconomics*. Cheltenham, UK: Edward Elgar.

Kirman, A. P. 1992. "Whom or What Does the Representative Individual Represent?" *Journal of Economic Perspectives* 6 (2): 117–136.

Lee, F. S. 2011a. "Heterodox Microeconomics and the Foundation of Heterodox Macroeconomics." *Economia Informa* 367: 6–20.

Lee, F. S. 2011b. "Modeling the Economy as a Whole: An Integrative Approach." *American Journal of Economics and Sociology* 70 (5): 1282–1314.

Lee, F. S. 2013. "Book Review of John E. King's *The Microfoundations Delusion*." *The Economic and Labor Relations Review* 24 (2): 255–260.

Marx, K. and F. Engels. [1845] 1962. "Critique of Feuerbach." In *The German Ideology*. Moscow: Progress Publishers.

Minsky, H. P. 1986. *Stabilizing an Unstable Economy*. New Haven, CT: Yale University Press.

Nagel, E. 1952. "Wholes, Sums and Organic Unities." In *Philosophical Studies, Volume III*, edited by H. Feigl, 17–26. Minneapolis: University of Minnesota Press.

Pareto, V. [1927] 1971. *Manual of Political Economy*. London: Macmillan.

Rothschild, K. W. 1988. "Micro-Foundations, Ad Hocery, and Keynesian Theory." *Atlantic Economic Journal* 16 (2): 12–21.

Schelling, T. C. 1969. "Models of Segregation." *American Economic Review* 59 (2): 488–493.

Schelling, T. C. 1978. *Micromotives and Macrobehavior*. New York: Norton & Company.

Simon, H. A. 1962. "The Architecture of Complexity." *Proceedings of the American Philosophical Society* 106 (6): 467–482.

Smith, A. [1759] 2009. *The Theory of Moral Sentiments*. New York: Penguin Books.

Sugden, R. 2000. "Credible Worlds: The Status of Theoretical Models in Economics." *Journal of Economic Methodology* 7 (1): 1–31.

Toqueville, Alexander de. [1856] 1998. *The Old Regime and the French Revolution*. Chicago: University of Chicago Press.

Veblen, T. B. [1899] 1994. *The Theory of the Leisure Class*. New York: Dover.

Wan, P. Yu-ze. 2011. "Emergence à la Systems Theory: Epistemological Totalausschluss or Ontological Novelty?" *Philosophy of the Social Sciences* 41 (2): 178–210.

Witt, U. 2001. "Learning to Consume: A Theory of Wants and the Growth of Demand." *Journal of Evolutionary Economics* 11 (1): 23–36.

# 7 Post Keynesian investment and pricing theory
## Contributions of Alfred S. Eichner and Frederic S. Lee

*Ruslan Dzarasov*

## Introduction

Capital formation is the major driving force of capitalist development. That is why the theory of investment lies at the heart of any comprehensive theory of capitalism. Post Keynesian economics challenges the neoclassical theory of capital formation and offers a viable and coherent alternative to it. One of the main features of Post Keynesian economics is its way of treating growth and distribution together. That is why pricing and investment are linked to each other in this school of thought. Alfred S. Eichner and Frederic S. Lee, among others, have made most important contributions to Post Keynesian investment and pricing theory. Their rich legacy in this area is the prime focus of the present chapter.

The first section looks into the historical and theoretical background of Eichner's and Lee's thinking. The second examines the Eichner's model of investment and pricing. The third expounds Lee's grounded theory approach to investment and pricing. The fourth introduces the paper profit concept and suggests some modifications to the original Eichnerian model. The last section concludes the chapter by highlighting Eichner's and Lee's contributions.

## Historical and theoretical background

The Eichner-Lee tradition of investment and pricing theory appeared in the course of emerging American heterodox thinking in the 1970s. The origin of this tradition goes back to the debates on the nature of capitalism rampant in the 1930s. The Great Depression challenged orthodox neoclassical thinking, while giving rise to Keynesianism and invigorating Marxism. At the heart of the debates was the question of the factors determining investment and, hence, economic growth as a whole in the long run (Rosenof 1997). One of the prominent contributors to the controversy was Gardiner C. Means whose legacy later significantly influenced both Eichner and Lee.

Means (1962; Berle and Means 1932) argued that the rise of the modern corporation along with the concentration of production in a modern industry led not only to the corporate revolution, but to profound changes in the market mechanism and, particularly, in pricing procedures. Big corporations became price setters, instead of being Marshallian type price takers. In a modern industry, maintained Means, prices do not change in response to variations in demand. Administrative prices are set by corporate management and remain stable for a certain period of time and series of transactions. Corporations react to the oscillations of market demand by contracting or expanding production rather than by changing price. Being associated with institutional arrangements, this price rigidity was not the prime cause of the Great Depression (Means discussed a number of such causes), but the reason of its continuation. Treating the Great Depression as a structural problem, Means suggested a structural solution. He argued that structural planning, based on a multi-industrial model of economy, is a key to resuming growth. This structural approach was, however, confronted by mainstream Keynesianism.

The latter was represented by Alvin H. Hansen, a major American proponent of Keynes. Following Keynes, Hansen suggested a fiscal approach to inducing economic growth through financing public works (see Rosenof 1997, 62–63). State investments in long-term public goods like infrastructure, were expected to create favorable external conditions for private investments. In the late 1930s the (mainstream) Keynesian approach succeeded over the structural planning policy. With the start of the post-war boom Means's emphasis on institutional deficiencies of capitalism was increasingly received as out of date, and short-term 'fine tuning' endorsed by the neoclassical synthesis utterly triumphed.

Meanwhile the 'administrative pricing' model was reformulated and treated in a wider economic context by Michal Kalecki (1971), a Polish economist who stayed in Oxford in the 1930s. Kalecki reconsidered the problem of pricing and investment in the corporate economy in his famous 'degree of monopoly' theory. The latter term denotes a synthetic institutional characteristic of a modern corporation, allowing it to control markets, including, but not limited to, the level of concentration in a given industry, promotion, and the level of indirect costs. The degree of labor organization is a factor limiting the corporate power. Thus, the degree of monopoly reflects the relative power of capital and labor.

The degree of monopoly is reflected in the size of a mark-up over unit prime costs. This mark-up determines the share of profit in national income created by a firm. The distribution of unit mark-ups across industries determines the price structure of the national economy. Hence, prices in a corporate economy directly reflect the relative power of industrial oligopolies. Moreover, the aggregate mark-up in a modern capitalist society determines the distribution of national income among its social classes. This is the gist of the Kaleckian degree of monopoly theory of distribution, which is contrasted to the neoclassical marginal productivity theory of distribution.

According to Kalecki the size of mark-up on unit costs determines the scale of accumulation of capital by a firm, since it is financed primarily from its profit. However, there is a powerful factor limiting the size of investment. Unlike the neoclassical theory it has nothing to do with diseconomies of scale or imperfect product markets. It is the 'principle of increasing risk' (Kalecki 1971, ch. 9), which relates the size of investment to the size of the firm's own capital. The principle fixes the obvious fact that with the growth of new investment relative to accumulated capital, the damage inflicted to a firm in case of a failure of the business enterprise increases. In contrast to the work of Keynes, investment in Kalecki's theory contains the endogenous character to the extent that investment depends on the nature of the oligopolistic capitalist firm, rather than on external business environment.

This tradition was continued by Josef Steindl, an Austrian-born Post Keynesian economist, working in Oxford with Kalecki. In his masterpiece *Maturity and Stagnation in American Capitalism* ([1952] 1976), Steindl further developed the Kaleckian theory of oligopoly. He argued that maturing of capitalist economies entailed increased degrees of concentration of production. Here he applied the Kaleckian degree of monopoly thesis. Increased mark-ups allowed big American corporations to raise their profit margins simultaneously reducing the degree of capacity utilization. This discouraged investment in fixed assets, which diminished employment and aggregate demand, and which, in turn, put further downward pressure on investment. Only vast state expenditures on social security and the arms race, Steindl argued, could help the American economy to avoid depression in the postwar period. Thus, unlike Keynes, Steindl linked depression to imperfect competition preserving, and at the same time, Marxian 'underconsumption' idea. At the same time, in contrast to Hansen, he developed an endogenous approach to depression that is inherent to modern capitalism. One should note that Steindl articulated the tendency of American capitalism toward stagnation in the light of the Kaleckian degree of monopoly thesis, which differs from the Meansian 'price rigidity' approach.

The oligopolistic perspective on modern capitalism was further developed by Paul Sweezy, who wedded Marxian and Keynesian strands of economic thought. In his *Theory of Capitalist Development* ([1942] 1970) he agrees with Steindl that oligopolies exercise depressing effects on investment. Expanding production, argued Sweezy, big corporations undermine monopolistic prices. That is why they tend to invest less than their rival corporations. This leads to insufficient aggregate demand and underemployment equilibrium. These ideas were further elaborated by Sweezy in coauthorship with Paul Baran in their *Monopoly Capital* (Baran and Sweezy 1966). Massive military spending was necessary to absorb the rising surplus and prevent the Great Depression from happening again.

In sum, the endogenous approach to the causes and effects of the Great Depression links the deficiencies in capital accumulation to the market power of big business and its domination over labor. After temporal factors favoring the 'Golden Age of Capitalism' exhausted and stagflation of the early 1970s ushered in the 'age of diminished expectations' (Krugman 1994), the interest in secular stagnation theories revived again. Short-term Keynesianism was compromised and lost its appeal. Left Keynesians in the UK and the US, basing on the pioneering ideas of Kalecki, Robinson, Harrod, Kaldor, and others, consolidated their positions and Post Keynesian economics was born (see Lee 2009). They focused on long-term processes in the capitalist economy and formed a powerful and intellectually appealing alternative to neoclassical orthodoxy (King 2002). Just recently debates on secular stagnation once again were put to the forefront of the main strands of the world economic thought,[1] which make the Post Keynesian legacy quite modern.

In particular, Post-Keynesians were deeply concerned with the interplay between capital accumulation and income distribution. This involves the question of the nature of profit. In a neoclassical framework profit margins are determined by marginal productivity of capital. An intensive production function postulates that every variant of distribution of the national income is uniquely related to technological factors (capital–labor ratio). This view was sharply criticized by Post Keynesians in the course of the famous Cambridge controversies in the theory of capital (Harcourt 1972). On this Post Keynesians were influenced by Marx particularly through the Kaleckian connection. For Marx, profit margins are determined through the scale of exploitation allowed by unemployment on the labor market (reserve army of labor effect) and through redistribution of surplus value between the different groups of capitalists according to capital-labor ratio (organic composition of capital). In other words, income is redistributed under capitalism according to the power of capital. For Kalecki, as was already mentioned, profit margins depend on the "degree of monopoly"— that is, the institutional factor reflecting the market power of a firm (Kalecki 1971, 45). Although Kalecki, to the best of my knowledge, nowhere openly appeals to the notion of surplus value, but his 'degree of monopoly' looks like a surplus product approach to corporate economy. He speaks about the surplus product, which is distributed between social classes without impairing society's ability to reproduce the system. Indeed, on the one hand the group of industrial mark-ups on unit costs (which reflect industrial 'degrees of monopoly') is a factor of distribution between wage and profit funds, on the other the relative sizes of industrial mark-ups determine the distribution of profit among industrial oligopolies. It is very much like Marxian production of surplus value and its redistribution between industries with different capital–labor ratios; or like the second function of the relative prices in the Sraffian model which distributes surplus among social classes and sectors of economy. Some Post Keynesians use this framework to explain inflation in the corporate economy as a result of conflict of social classes over the distribution of the national income (Rowthorn 1977; Lavoie 2002). An increase in profit mark-ups by the corporations leads to a decrease in real wages, and therefore to prompt workers to demand higher compensation.

In this context Post Keynesians investigated the link between investment and pricing. In her theory of growth Joan Robinson (1962) suggested a synthesis of Keynesian and Kaleckian approach to the determinants of investment decisions. In Robinson's synthesis the most important for our present discussion is Kalecki's emphasis on *the two-way relationship between investments and profits,* which means that not only the level of expected profits induces investment, but the latter in turn enhances the former (Kalecki 1971, ch. 7). Joan Robinson further elaborated this idea. Her famous "banana diagram" illustrates that desired accumulation determines the rate of investment, which in turn determines net saving, which determines the rate of profit, which along with wages forms the normal prices (Robinson 1962, 47).

Harcourt and Kenyon (1976) also mixed investment and pricing in a comprehensive theory of firms' behavior. They arrived at a conclusion that "[w]hen all aspects of the investment decision are considered—the *amount* of extra capacity to be laid down each period, the choice of technique and the method and cost of finance" a unique solution can be found for the size of the mark-up on 'normal' prime costs (Harcourt and Kenyon 1976, 473, original emphasis). The link between investment and pricing is vital for Adrian Wood's *Theory of Profit* (1975) as well. According to Wood, the firm's profit margin, and, hence, its mark-up on unit costs, should generate funds that are sufficient to cover investment in productive capacities which cannot be financed entirely from external sources (1975, chs. 2–3).

## The Eichner model of pricing and investment

At the center of the consolidation process in the 1970s and 1980s was Alfred Eichner (1937–1988) who played a foundational role in the making of Post Keynesian economics in the US (Lee 2009, ch. 5). He undertook a great endeavor to develop a theory of the firm, which aimed at providing microeconomic foundations for Post Keynesian macroeconomics. His major contribution in this field is the 'megacorp' model. It refers to the representative (in the sense of possessing typical properties) big corporation of the US manufacturing sector of the Golden Age of capitalism (the late 1940s–early 1970s). Eichner's model has some distinctive features.

First, the separation of management from ownership is seen as a major precondition of the megacorp maximizing its long-term growth rather than short-term profits as in neoclassical thinking. A wider spreading of equities among the shareholders of the US and UK corporations in the twentieth century has led to the separation of ownership from control with the latter residing with the managers (Berle and Means 1932; Lee 1998, 22).[2] Prosperity of the managerial staff is based not on short-run profits but rather on the position of the firm in the industry. The bigger the market share of the given organization is, the more power it exercises over the market and the greater the salaries and privileges that management will receive. Thus, the organizational structure of the megacorp "dictates maximum growth as the goal of the firm" (Eichner 1991, 361). Second, the megacorp's production is organized within multiple plants and plant segments with fixed short-run technical coefficients due to enduring technological and institutional structures (Eichner 1976, 28). This leads to the assumption of constant prime unit costs of production.[3] Third, the megacorp is a price leader. Usually a fellow-oligopolist with the largest market share and/or with the lowest costs emerges as the leader announcing changes in the industry price (Eichner 1991, 364).

Since the imperative of growth becomes the prime objective of the megacorp, an investment decision becomes the core of its long-term strategy. The "corporate levy" (*CL*), which is defined "as the amount of funds available to the megacorp from internal sources to finance investment expenditure" (Eichner 1976, 61), determines the discretionary power of the firm over the resources that it needs to maintain growth maximization. It crucially depends on the size of the mark-up on prime unit costs set by the megacorp. It is the change in the size of a mark-up ($\Delta m$) that is the focus of Eichner's model. This is seen as the essence of the megacorp's pricing policy.

When considering a price increase, the megacorp compares the growth of internally generated funds to the long-term losses inflicted by the decrease in sales. The price increase is constrained by two powerful effects: (a) the growth of internally generated funds; (b) long-term losses inflicted by decreases in sales. The latter is comprised of three powerful constraints, namely, (i) the substitution effect, when customers move to other products/substitutes (Eichner 1991, 377); (ii) entry factors, when rivals join the industry attracted by increases in expected profits (379); and (iii) the probability of meaningful government intervention, when authorities react to what they consider to be a price increase unacceptable for social stability (77).

In the first period, following a price increase, two effects mentioned above are insignificant, while in the following periods these effects present themselves increasingly. The megacorp sums up additional funds accumulated due to a price increase and the corresponding reductions in profit, appropriately discounts the results, and divides the latter value by the former. As a result the costs of accumulating a unit of additional investment funds, or the *implicit interest rate (R)* are obtained. Let us consider Figure 7.1 drawn from Reynolds (1987, 70) with some minor modifications.

The figure represents a simplified version of Eichner's model of megacorps' pricing and investment (Eichner 1991, 375–393). The supply of investment funds is depicted as the relationship between the value of the implicit interest rate, $R$, the explicit interest rate, $i$, and the amount of additional internally generated and externally borrowed investment funds per planning period, $\Delta F/p$. The increase in the size of the mark-up, $\Delta m$, is associated with the growing value of the implicit interest rate, $R$. Increases in the mark-up lead to the growth of additional investment funds, $\Delta F/p$. The relation between $\Delta m$ and $R$ is reflected by the supply of internally generated investment funds curve, $S_I'$. One can see that every incremental portion of additional investment funds corresponds to a higher value of the implicit interest rate, which becomes prohibitively high starting from a certain point. This happens because all the effects of a price increase described above grow over time. Apart from internal accumulation, a firm can borrow some funds externally. Unlike Eichner, we depict the supply of external funds not as a horizontal, but rather as an increasing curve. This reflects the Kaleckian 'principle of increasing risk' (Kalecki 1971, ch. 9) discussed earlier. It is expedient to generate funds internally only when the implicit interest rate is lower than its external counterpart. Thus, the total supply of additional investment funds consists of two parts: internally and externally generated funds.

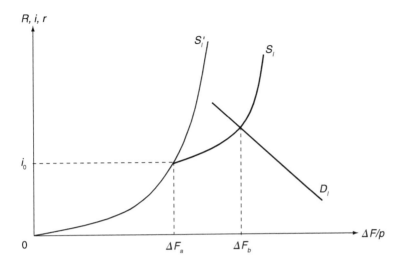

*Figure 7.1* The supply of and the demand for internally and externally generated funds.

Note
The vertical axis measures the implicit ($R$) and the external ($i$) interest rates and the rate of profit ($r$) expected from investment in question. The horizontal axis measures the additional investment funds generated in the pricing period ($\Delta F/p$).

The demand for investment funds in the model in question is based on the expected rate of return on investment, $r$. Eichner defines $r$ as the marginal efficiency of investment (Eichner 1991, 430). If we array the potential investment projects under consideration by the megacorp according to their descending prospective rates of return, we obtain the investment demand curve, $D_I$. The intersection of the demand for and the supply of investment funds curves determines the actual amount of investment undertaken by a megacorp at the level of $\Delta F_b$. It can be seen from Figure 7.1 that up to $\Delta F_a$ investment is financed internally, while between $\Delta F_a$ and $\Delta F_b$ investment is financed externally. The change in the mark-up, corresponding to the implicit interest rate $R$ exactly equal to $i_0$, determines the price change for the pricing period.

Here we can point out a theoretical limitation of the Eichnerian model. Although his model offers a realistic explanation of investment and financing behavior of big corporations that debunks the Modigliani-Miller theorem in particular and the neoclassical theory of the firm in general, Eichner makes a concession to the neoclassical supply and demand framework in his model. In his demand for funds function, Eichner lacks the double-sided relation between profit and investment, which was stressed by Robinson (1962), Wood (1975), and Harcourt and Kenyon (1976).

From the foregoing discussion one can draw a conclusion that in Eichner's model *pricing, finance, and investment decisions are made by the megacorp simultaneously*. Taking into account that unit costs to which a mark-up is added largely depend on wages, one can say that the accumulation of capital and the distribution of the firm's income are inseparable. Others' discussion and critique of Eichner's model clarify its important properties. The most important property is that Eichner's model reflects the conditions of advanced market economies with steady growth of demand off-setting the income-decreasing effect of mark-up increases.[4] Individual firms' rate of investment should be kept in pace with industry's growth rate of sales, which is in turn determined by national income dynamics. Thus, the investment process can be considered as the means to adjust the megacorp's growth to the macrodynamic context of advanced market economies.

Developing the macrodynamic model Eichner (1991, 338–359) suggests the *value condition of growth*, which is a set of prices covering both current costs of production and costs of expansion of economy (that is, investment) at the level of full employment. These prices are determined by technological conditions reflected in Leontief's matrix of technical input coefficients and by the distribution of national income between wages and profits. In a corporate economy the distribution of profits between industries depends on the distribution of mark-ups on unit costs (Eichner 1991, ch. 6). Since mark-ups represent firms' power over the market (that is, the Kaleckian degree of monopoly factor), it is clear that their distribution between industries is quite arbitrary and can coincide with the value condition of growth only at random. This means that stagflation is a result of institutional and distributional factors. It is another theory of endogenous tendency to secular stagnation. Eichner's remedy for stagnation restates another aspect of Means's legacy as well—that is, his concept of structural planning. The Eichnerian system of indicative planning is based on his megacorp model, assuming that decisions on the distribution of firms' income, investment, and pricing are made simultaneously (Eichner 1976, 278–288). The key to this system is an industrial committee, where representatives of the state, managers, shareholders, and trade unions seek a compromise on the level of wages, investments, and prices in the planning period.

Thus, for Eichner—but also Wood—in contrast to the abovementioned Post Keynesians, profit margins are determined by the necessity to finance investment. At the same time, although Eichner did not refer to labor values, he used a surplus product approach.[5] This can be drawn from the fact that, as was demonstrated, the megacorp makes decisions on investment and distribution of the firm's income simultaneously. In his value condition of growth Eichner, departing from the Sraffian approach mixed with the von Neumann model, postulates that the level of wages depends on corporate profit decisions (Eichner 1991, 260–342).

As argued by Rosenof (1997), Eichner synthesized Meansian and Keynesian approaches. Indeed, the megacorp model reformulates Means's administrative pricing theory along Kaleckian lines and incorporates investment as the core of its strategy. However, unlike Keynes, Eichner 'internalized investment' by making it a function of the megacorp, rather than of the external business environment[6] as a result of the influence of Marxian type Kalecki-Steindl-Sweezy thinking. However,

Lee's model attempts to synthesize mark-up, normal cost, and the target rate of return pricing procedures. It provides an insight into the mechanism as to how the corporate administrators set prices which are designed to cover costs and to produce profits which permit an enterprise to continue its existence as a going concern. Lee's model resembles the Eichnerian 'value condition of growth,' which, as was explained above, means a set of industrial prices covering both the costs of current production and the costs of expansion at the level of full employment. Lee's model also tries to provide a bridge between enterprise activities to its growth. However, Lee's model differs from Eichner's model in two crucial aspects.[8] First, it puts an emphasis on the role of intermediate (basic) products, which is essential not only to comprehend the mechanism of circular production but also to refute neoclassical market-clearing prices. Second, Lee's model assumes away the full employment equilibrium, which is seen as an utterly unrealistic hypothesis. This emphasis on non-market-clearing prices and on the absence of full employment indicates that Lee's approach to capitalism depicts an actual capitalist system that is intrinsically based in conflict. In other respects Lee's vision of pricing and investment is quite close to Eichner's approach.

## Paper profit and the modernization of the Eichnerian model

According to Lee, investment is renovation and expansion of enterprises' productive capacities. However, he recently analyzed the impact of growing financialization on the accumulation of capital.[9] The representative American firm of the 'Golden Age of Capitalism,' as it is reflected in Alfred Eichner's megacorp model, was characterized by the separation of ownership and control and long-term growth maximization. In the age of 'Money Manager Capitalism' corporate governance shifted to the domination of shareholders over managers. As a result, shareholder value maximization supplanted the long-term growth as the prime corporate objective (Lazonick and O'Sullivan 2000; Jo and Henry 2015). According to Milberg (2010), mark-ups increased in the first decade of the twenty-first century in the US due largely to various cost-cutting measures introduced by firms in the course of globalization. He observes that high value-added production processes are retained by large oligopolies in advanced countries, while low value-added value chains prevail across many poor countries of the world periphery. A global shift of the labor-intensive chains of production to low-wage countries helped increase profits with curtailed investments in productive capacities (Milberg and Winkler 2010), while the share of financial assets surpassed the share of productive capacities in the total amount of assets (Orhangazi 2008). Sawyer and Shapiro (2010) examine the notable changes in managerial behavior of the megacorp: while megacorps increased their ability to extract a corporate levy, they started financing dividends and executive pay to a greater extent than investment in productive capacity. Moreover, stock buybacks have been greater than dividend payouts in volume since 1997 in the US non-financial corporate sector of economy (Lazonick 2013,

882). Thus, the change in corporate governance as a result of the 'shareholder revolution' led to fundamental changes both in the sources and in the uses of profit, which undermined investments of modern big businesses.

Lee's theory of investment and pricing is not only germane to the changing corporate environment but also consistent with Kalecki's concept of 'paper profit.' Kalecki argues that real gross profits in a given time period are conditioned by capitalists' investment and consumption decisions in the past (Kalecki 1991, 240). Departing from this, Kalecki arrives at a conclusion that profits are equal to investment plus the export surplus plus the budget deficit plus capitalist consumption, assuming that workers do not save (245). This means that, *ceteris paribus*, an increase in export over import (the foreign trade surplus) will boost corporate profits not only in the export sector but also in the economy as a whole. This increase in profit happens through the Keynesian multiplier effect. Profits in the domestic sector supplying wage goods will grow in proportion to the increase in wage incomes in the export sector. As a result, total profits will exceed the level of profits set by corporate investment and capitalist consumption. "It is from this point of view," notes Kalecki, "that the fight for foreign markets may be viewed" (245).

Budget deficits affect the national economy in the same way as a trade surplus does. Essentially deficit financing of state expenditures is nothing else than a tax allowance. This means that government expenditures (or deficits) generate corporate profits. It is very similar to having more gains from exporting goods and services than paying for import. Budget deficits increase corporate profits to a greater level than suggested by investment and capitalist consumption due to the mechanism of the trade surplus described above.

> The counterpart of the export surplus is an increase in the indebtedness of the foreign countries towards the country considered. The counterpart of the budget deficit is an increase in the indebtedness of the government towards the private sector. Both of these surpluses or receipts over payments generate profit in the same way.
>
> (Kalecki 1991, 245–246)

The most important, essential feature of these profits is that they are extracted from markets in addition to those created by capitalists' investment and consumption. Lee borrowed the term "paper profits," meaning private incomes generated by a trade surplus and a budget deficit, from P. Erdös and F. Molnár (1990, 96–99), who contrasted it to "material profit" generated by capitalist production. Let us elaborate on the nature and sources of these types of capitalist incomes.

In fact profits extracted from these 'external' markets (created by the trade surplus and the budget deficit) come from sources other than created by the domestic labor power: "It is the export surplus and the budget deficit which enable the capitalists to make profits over and above their own purchases of goods and services" (Kalecki 1991, 246). Indeed, the trade surplus is appropriated at the expense of capitalists in trade deficit countries. The sources of profits created by budget deficits are even more disguised from a direct observation. Eventually, at least in principle, budget deficits should be covered by future taxes. (It is by no means an immediate necessity. Until it destabilizes the financial sphere, budget deficits can be tolerated.) Part of them will come from capitalist profits, but mostly from workers' wage incomes. Capitalists always have an opportunity to offset additional taxes through a price increase, which means that workers' real wage declines. To pay additional taxes workers should further decrease their consumption or go into debt. Hence, in the final account balance profits from budget deficits are financed from incomes of hired labor. Thus, paper profits, although unrelated to production activities of domestic corporations, give corporate capital command over real goods and services. These material values are obtained through the redistribution of the surplus value produced abroad and of wage incomes of domestic labor in favor of domestic corporations. Thus, imposing debts on workers is one of the means of 'accumulation by dispossession.' The opportunity to materialize paper profits thus arises from coercive power of capital.

In the case of the modern globalized and financialized US capitalism we can see a deep interplay between two Kaleckian factors of paper profits. At first glance, one may think that foreign trade subtracts from paper profits of US corporations that are generated by government deficits, since the US has both growing budget deficits and growing trade deficits. However, such a view is misleading, because it is US trade deficits that largely finance US budget deficits and the needs of US corporations. This happens because countries with large trade surpluses—and these are mainly such suppliers as China—invest the bulk of their earnings in US financial markets (Li 2008, 79).

The shareholder revolution implies that the Eichnerian megacorp model no longer stands in its original form. The concept of paper profits demands a significant modification. In fact, corresponding changes of this model were suggested in the 1970s in the discussion of Eichner's original paper, in which he first described the megacorp (1973). One of objections concerned the usage of internally generated funds. According to our earlier discussions, the prime determinant of the mark-up is the marginal efficiency of investment schedule. But critics argue that investment is not a single outlet for a megacorp to use obtained funds—lending money to other borrowers seems a reasonable alternative. Hazeldine (1974) refers to data showing that "typically, capital formation is a rather small fraction of margins" (968).

Hazeldine's main argument is that in both cases "there is *no direct link* between changes in price-cost margins and investment" (1974, 968, emphasis in original). Eichner (1974, 976–977) observes that a firm usually earns more from investing, because it does not have the same skills and knowledge as financial institutions. According to Eichner's data, the interest rate on external funds for American corporations was (in 1974, at the time of publication) about 15 percent, and the gain from lending out to other firms only about 5 per cent. With the overaccumulation of capital[10] (in the postwar era) and the shareholder revolution and financialization (since the 1970s), Hazeldine's (1974) argument seems reasonable if we consider firms' lending as financial investment. Let us consider Figure 7.2.

This figure depicts the demand for funds to be invested in financial assets ($D_{IF}$), that is distinct from the demand for funds to be invested in productive capacities ($D_I$). Both variables add up to the total demand for funds ($D_F$). The actual mark-up change, just as in the original Eichnerian model, is determined by the intersection of the demand for funds ($D_F$) and the supply of funds ($S_F$) curves. However, in contrast to the Eichnerian megacorp, a financialized corporation will use only $F_I$ part of accumulated funds for investments in productive capacities, investing the other $F_{IF}$ part in financial assets.

This does not necessarily mean that financialized corporations require productive capacities less than they did in earlier times. On the contrary, growing consumption at a global scale demands increases in production and, hence, more of productive capacities. However, with the development of a global commodity chain modern corporations rely on business partners from lower levels of the same chain to expand and modernize fixed assets. In a sense, financialized corporations have largely shifted the burden of production to others. That is, investments in productive capacities undertaken by business partners in less-developed countries are substituted for investments of corporations in core-advanced economies. Consequently, the latter is able to indulge in financial investments and speculations.

A modification of the Eichnerian model reflects the fundamental contradictions in capitalism, which are captured by the Kalecki-Lee paper profit

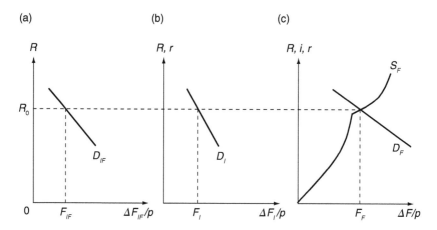

*Figure 7.2* Supply of and demand for funds of a financialized corporation.

Note

The vertical axis measures the implicit interest rate ($R$), the external interest rate ($i$), and the expected rate of return of investment projects ($r$). The horizontal axis at the figure (a) and (b) measures investment in financial assets ($\Delta F_{IF}/p$) and investment in productive capacities ($\Delta F_I/p$), while at figure (c)—the total value of funds ($\Delta F/p$). The figure (a) depicts the demand for funds for investments in financial assets ($D_{IF}$); while figure (b)—demand for investment funds ($D_I$); and the figure (c)—the total value of the demand for funds ($D_F$) and of the supply of funds ($S_F$).

concept. In contemporary capitalism this concept finds its powerful expression in the form of financialization that is institutionalized by Wall Street, and that reshapes the structure and behavior of megacorps through the shareholder revolution.

## Conclusion

The Eichner-Lee tradition of investment theory is rooted in the debates on the nature of the Great Depression of the 1930s and contributed to the development of Post Keynesian economics. It synthesizes institutional, Keynesian, and Marxian strands of heterodox analysis of capitalism. The first approach finds its most salient expression in Gardiner Means's theory of the modern corporation, which explains the phenomenon of administered prices resulting from the separation of ownership and control in modern corporations. Alfred Eichner wedded Means's theory with Keynes's theory of investment. While the latter emphasizes the importance of external environment of the business enterprise in the course of capital accumulation, Eichner 'internalizes' the capital accumulation process by linking investment to corporate governance and pricing. The Marxian influence figures in the treatment of capital accumulation as a part of distribution of the firm's income. Frederic Lee has continued the Eichnerian tradition providing an empirically grounded theory of pricing and investment. He relates the causal mechanisms of investment and pricing to a circular production model, which elucidates the reproduction conditions of a capitalist enterprise as a going concern. In the neoliberal era, the link between investment, pricing, and reproduction is undermined by financialization, which is reflected by the concept of paper profits. A modified approach suggested in this chapter puts more explicit emphasis on the conflict within the capitalist economy than is implied in Eichner's original model.

## Notes

1 See the recent debate on the topic between Larry Summers, Paul Krugman, Bob Gordon, Olivier Blanchard, Richard Koo, Barry Eichengreen, Ricardo Caballero, Ed Glaeser, and others in Teulings and Baldwin (2014).
2 By no means were Berle and Means the first to raise the question of separation of corporate ownership and control. J. M. Keynes in his *The End of Laissez-Faire* as early as in 1926 and W. Z. Ripley in his *Main Street and Wall Street* as early as in 1927 raised the same question, to mention only a couple of examples. However, Berle and Means articulated the doctrine in such a form and at such a moment that it attracted the wide attention of the public.
3 This assumption is certainly true for a single plant. Eichner was aware that costs of plants belonging to different vintages would differ. However, he believed that the difference in productivity between different plants or plant segments was not very significant, and management tended to assume it away and thought in terms of average costs (Eichner 1976, 28–31). Lee argues that the shape of average direct costs can take any form; constant, decreasing, or increasing. This is a critique of Eichner's assumption of constant prime unit costs (see, Lee 1986; Lee and Jo 2010; and Eichner's response in Eichner 1986).

4  See critiques in Hazeldine (1974, 967) and Robinson (1974, 972–973) and Eichner's response to critiques in Eichner (1974).

5  Lee's approach to the surplus approach in the tradition of Eichner (and Kalecki) differs from the classical Marxian-Sraffian surplus approach. Lee argues that while classicals believe that the level and composition of the social product (distributed between classes and industries) are given, there is no reason to take them as given if heterodox economists consider the effective demand is the organizing principle of capitalist economy. Instead of 'givens,' socially embedded agency determines the level and composition of the social product in the course of producing the surplus (Lee and Jo 2011).

6  Both marginal efficiency of capital—that is, the rate of discount which equates the price of a fixed capital asset with its present discounted value of expected income—and so-called 'animal spirits' of entrepreneurs play an important role in Keynes's investment theory. 'State of confidence,' in turn, is related to 'fundamental uncertainty,' which underlays all Keynesian thinking (Carabelli 1988). However, by increasing state expenditures the government is able to cause upward shift of effective demand closer to full employment equilibrium. In this sense Keynesian 'animal spirits' depends on external business environment. Maybe this was the reason why Joan Robinson, while accepting the famous idea of the 'animal spirits,' mentions that Keynes himself "did not take his formalism seriously" (1962, 37).

7  See Dzarasov (2010) for more details on the comparison between critical realism and Marxian methodology of core and derived notions in economics.

8

> With regard to the theory of investment, my position on Al's [Eichner's] argument is twofold: first I agree with him that investment decisions is [*sic*] a partial function of lagged sales—Robert Eisner also makes the same argument. Whether that notion can be generalized to all enterprises for all time is another matter. So I think that Al's argument needs to be broadened to include other variables—and this involves a lot of empirical work on how enterprises actually make their investment decisions. However, both Al and I agree that interest rates play an insignificant role in affecting business investment decisions. The second issue involves the adjustment of the profit mark up on products to fund investment decisions that are made specific to that product (or even to the enterprise in general). The empirical support for this is quite sparse. My ever changing views on this are that demand for investment goods has a weak impact on profit mark ups. But to establish this, more detailed research into the actual determination of the profit mark up per product across the range of products an enterprise produces is needed. I can easily produce models in which the profit mark up is determined/driven by the demand for investment goods. But these models need support from actual evidence of how actual enterprises make these decisions.
>
> (An email from Frederic Lee to Ruslan Dzarasov on February 7, 2013)

9  To the best of my knowledge Frederic Lee has not published his thoughts on this subject. In this section I am expounding his views according to my notes taken at our several discussions on paper profits during my visit to University of Missouri-Kansas City from October 2011 to May 2012. I am here referring to the literature suggested by Lee.

10  I use the term 'overaccumulation' in the Marxian sense, which means that it is relative, not absolute. Working class people need goods and services that could be produced, but they do not have enough money to pay for them. That is, accumulation is excessive relative to the low purchasing power of the working class population.

# References

Baran, P. and P. Sweezy. 1966. *Monopoly Capital*. New York: Monthly Review Press.

Berle, A. and G. C. Means. 1932. *The Modern Corporation and Private Property*. New York: Macmillan.

Bhaskar, R. 1993. *Dialectic: The Pulse of Freedom*. London: Verso.

Carabelli, A. 1988. *On Keynes's Method*. London: Macmillan.

Charmaz, K. 1983. "The Grounded Theory Method: An Explication and Interpretation." In *Contemporary Field Research: A Collection of Readings*, edited by R. M. Emerson, 109–126. Boston: Little, Brown.

Commons, J. R. [1924] 1974. *Legal Foundations of Capitalism*. New York: Augustus M. Kelley.

Dzarasov, S. 2010. "Critical Realism and Russian Economics." *Cambridge Journal of Economics* 34 (6): 1041–1056.

Eichner, A. S. 1973. "A Theory of the Determination of the Mark-up Under Oligopoly." *Economic Journal* 83 (332): 1185–1244.

Eichner, A. S. 1974. "Determination of the Mark-up Under Oligopoly: A Reply." *Economic Journal* 84 (336): 974–980.

Eichner, A. S. 1976. *The Megacorp and Oligopoly: Micro Foundations of Macro Dynamics*. Cambridge: Cambridge University Press.

Eichner, A. S. 1986. "A Comment on 'Post Keynesian View of Average Direct Costs'." *Journal of Post-Keynesian Economics* 8 (3): 425–426.

Eichner, A. S. 1991. *The Macrodynamics of Advanced Market Economies*. Armonk, NY: M. E. Sharpe.

Erdös, P. and F. Molnár. 1990. *Inflation and Recession in the U.S. Economy in the 1970s: Price, Profit, and Business Cycles in Theory and Practice*. Budapest: Akadémiai Kiadó.

Glaser, B. G. 1978. *Theoretical Sensitivity*. Mill Valley, CA: The Sociology Press.

Harcourt, G. C. 1972. *Some Cambridge Controversies in the Theory of Capital*. Cambridge: Cambridge University Press.

Harcourt, G. C. and P. Kenyon. 1976. "Pricing and the Investment Decision." *Kyklos* 29: 449–477.

Hazeldine, T. 1974. "Determination of the Mark-up Under Oligopoly: A Comment." *Economic Journal* 84: 967–970.

Jo, T.-H. and J. F. Henry. 2015. "The Business Enterprise in the Age of Money Manager Capitalism." *Journal of Economic Issues* 41 (1): 23–46.

Kalecki, M. 1971. *Selected Essays on the Dynamics of the Capitalist Economy, 1933–1970*. Cambridge: Cambridge University Press.

Kalecki, M. 1991. "Determinants of Profits." In *Capitalism: Economic Dynamics*, Collected Works of Michal Kalecki, Vol. II, 239–246. Oxford: Clarendon Press.

King, J. E. 2002. *A History of Post Keynesian Economics Since 1936*. Cheltenham: Edward Elgar.

Krugman, P. 1994. *Peddling Prosperity: Economic Sense and Nonsense in an Age of Diminished Expectations*. New York: W. W. Norton.

Lavoie, M. 2002. "The Kaleckian Growth Model with Target Return Pricing and Conflict Inflation." In *The Economics of Demand-Led Growth*, edited by M. Setterfield, 172–188. Cheltenham, UK: Edward Elgar.

Lazonick, W. 2013. "The Financialization of the U.S. Corporation: What Has Been Lost, and How It Can Be Regained." *Seattle University Law Review* 36: 857–909.

Lazonick, W. and M. O'Sullivan. 2000. "Maximizing Shareholder Value: A New Ideology for Corporate Governance." *Economy and Society* 29 (1): 13–35.

Lee, F. S. 1986. "Post Keynesian View of Average Direct Costs: A Critical Evaluation of the Theory and the Empirical Evidence." *Journal of Post Keynesian Economics* 8 (3): 400–424.

Lee, F. S. 1998. *Post Keynesian Price Theory*. Cambridge: Cambridge University Press.

Lee, F. S. 2002. "Theory Creation and the Methodological Foundation of Post Keynesian Economics." *Cambridge Journal of Economics* 26: 789–804.

Lee, F. S. 2005. "Grounded Theory and Heterodox Economics." *Grounded Theory Review* 4 (2): 95–116.

Lee, F. S. 2009. *A History of Heterodox Economics: Challenging the Mainstream in the Twentieth Century*. London: Routledge.

Lee, F. S. 2012. "Competition, Going Enterprise, and Economic Activity." In *Alternative Theories of Competition: Challenges to the Orthodoxy*, edited by J. K. Moudud, C. Bina, and P. L. Mason, 160–173. London: Routledge.

Lee, F. S. and T.-H. Jo. 2010. "Heterodox Production and Cost Theory of the Business Enterprise." MPRA Working Paper 27635. Accessed November 28, 2014. http://mpra. ub.uni-muenchen.de/27635/.

Lee, F. S. and T.-H. Jo. 2011. "Social Surplus Approach and Heterodox Economics." *Journal of Economic Issues* 45 (4): 857–875.

Li, M. 2008. *The Rise of China and the Demise of the Capitalist World Economy*. New York: Monthly Review Press.

Means, G. C. 1962. *The Corporate Revolution in America: Economic Reality vs. Economic Theory*. New York: Crowell Collier Press.

Milberg, W. 2010. "Pricing and Profits Under Globalised Production: A Post-Keynesian Perspective on U.S. Economic Hegemony." In *Money and Macrodynamics: Alfred Eichner and Post-Keynesian Economics*, edited by M. Lavoie, L.-P. Rochon, and M. Seccareccia, 116–137. New York: M. E. Sharpe.

Milberg, W. and D. Winkler. 2010. "Financialisation and the Dynamics of Offshoring in the USA." *Cambridge Journal of Economics* 34 (2): 275–293.

Orhangazi, O. 2008. "Financialisation and Capital Accumulation in the Non-financial Corporate Sector: A Theoretical and Empirical Investigation on the US Economy: 1973–2003." *Cambridge Journal of Economics* 32: 863–886.

Reynolds, P. 1987. *Political Economy: A Synthesis of Kaleckian and Post-Keynesian Economics*. Sussex: Wheatsheaf Books.

Robinson, J. 1962. *Essays in the Theory of Economic Growth*. London: Macmillan.

Robinson, R. 1974. "Determination of the Mark-up Under Oligopoly: A Comment." *Economic Journal* 84: 971–974.

Rosenof, T. 1997. *Economics in the Long Run: New Deal Theorists and their Legacies, 1933–1993*. Chapel Hill: University of North Carolina Press.

Rowthorn, R. E. 1977. "Conflict, Inflation and Money." *Cambridge Journal of Economics* 1: 215–239.

Sawyer, M. and N. Shapiro. 2010. "The Macroeconomics of Competition: Stability and Growth Questions." In *Money and Macrodynamics: Alfred Eichner and Post-Keynesian Economics*, edited by M. Lavoie, L.-P. Rochon, and M. Seccareccia, 83–95. New York: M. E. Sharpe.

Steindl, J. [1952] 1976. *Maturity and Stagnation in American Capitalism*. Oxford: Blackwell.

Strauss, A. 1987. *Qualitative Analysis for Social Scientists*. Cambridge: Cambridge University Press.

Strauss, A. and J. Corbin. 1990. *Basics of Qualitative Research: Grounded Theory Procedures and Techniques*. London: Sage.

Sweezy, P. [1942] 1970. *Theory of Capitalist Development*. New York: Monthly Review Press.

Teulings, C. and R. Baldwin. 2014. *Secular Stagnation: Facts, Causes and Cures*. London: SEPR Press. Accessed October 19, 2014. www.voxeu.org/sites/default/files/Vox_secular_stagnation.pdf.

Veblen, T. B. [1904] 1975. *The Theory of Business Enterprise*. New York: Augustus M. Kelley.

Wood, A. 1975. *A Theory of Profits*. Cambridge: Cambridge University Press.

# 8 Effects of competition on profit margins from a Post Keynesian perspective

*Jordan Melmiès*

## Introduction

The interdependence of competition and profit margins is one of the most important features of industrial economics. According to mainstream economics, intense market competition results in smaller profit margins. Long-term profits are contingent on competition and market imperfections; perfect competition presumably reduces profits to zero in the long run (excluding normal profits allocated to managerial compensation).

This relationship between competition and profit margins is also an important theme in Post Keynesian economics. From Joan Robinson's *Economics of Imperfect Competition* to Kalecki's analyses of the degree of monopoly, Post Keynesian economists have long been interested in this aspect of economic theory. There is however no unified Post Keynesian view of competition and its effect on profit margins, and we can, from a historical perspective, identify two main strands of Post Keynesian thought, each relying on a specific theory to determine profit margins. Based on the 'imperfect competition and degree of monopoly principle,' the first branch considers that profit margins are the result of market structure (market imperfections). In this view, as in the theory of monopoly capitalism (see Moudud, Bina, and Mason 2013), profit margins thus positively correlate with competition imperfections and degree of monopoly. Rooted in the 'investment financing tradition,' including the works of Alfred Eichner and Adrian Wood, the second branch makes a direct connection between profit margins and internal financing requirements for investment. We consider this second view to clearly represent Fred Lee's economic thinking (see, for example, Lee 2013b). A comparison of the two Post Keynesian branches shows that the first position closely resembles what later became the mainstream view on the relation between competition and profit margins (notably with the emergence of the so-called structure-conduct-paradigm in the 1960s and 1970s, which remains an influential theoretical framework for industry-competition policies). Stated succinctly, in this theory, the tougher the competition, the smaller the profit margins.

Nevertheless, empirical testing of this theory poses certain difficulties. In fact, many empirical studies fail to validate the direct link between the degree of competition (regardless of the chosen criterion) and profit margins. Such studies often report weak or even paradoxical results, be it at the sectoral or macro-economic level. These unexpected results can, however, be explained from the 'investment-financing' theory of profit margins. Based on the theories of Alfred Eichner (1973, 1976) and Adrian Wood (1975), this second branch offers an explanation for why profit margins are independent of the degree of competition in the market. In conjunction with his two-curve diagram, Adrian Wood's analysis (developed in his 1975 book, *A Theory of Profits*) enables us to show why competition does not affect the determination of profit margins. Therefore, the second strand's main contribution is its emphasis on the fundamental role of internal financing in capitalist economies, which is the missing link in industrial economics.

## Post Keynesian theories of the link between competition and profit margins

### The 'degree of competition' theory

Historically, the first branch of Post Keynesian theory that considers the link between competition and profit margins has its origin in the theories of Robinson and Kalecki. Both economists established price theories incorporating a theoretical determination of profit margins. Although Robinson and Kalecki developed distinct theories of price determination, we emphasize that, apart from a few details, both theories are based on a profit margin that depends on the intensity of competition, or what can be called the 'degree of competition' theory.

Robinson's theory, developed in her 1933 book, *Economics of Imperfect Competition*, reviews several market structures that depart from perfect competition and details price determination in all cases. The case most commonly retained in textbooks uses the extreme example of a monopolist, equating marginal cost not to price but to marginal revenue. In this case, firms earn a profit margin because prices exceed marginal and average costs in the long run. Evidently, compared with a perfectly competitive market scenario (in which price equals marginal cost in the short run and average cost in the long run), monopolists charge higher prices and hence extract positive profit margins from the market, because of competition imperfections. In essence, Robinson's theory states that the weaker the competition, the higher the profit margins.

Kalecki's theory of the degree of monopoly relies on similar reasoning. In his writings, Kalecki assumes that firms act in an oligopoly, duopoly, or monopoly world. Instead of concentrating on the profit margin, Kalecki sought to anchor his theory of the business cycle in the structure of the market. The theory nevertheless integrates a precise determination of profit based on the 'degree of monopoly' of an economy. He supposes that the degree of monopoly determines the level of individual profit margins and, at the aggregate level, the share of profit in national income. Although Kalecki's view has evolved, his concept of degree of monopoly establishes a direct link between competition and profit margins. Kalecki's pricing equations are consistently formulated as mark-up pricing over costs, in which the level of mark-up depends on several factors (e.g., the price elasticity of demand and the price of competitors) in what Kalecki called the "state of imperfection of the market" (Kalecki 1939). His theory thus remains consistent with Joan Robinson's imperfect competition theory and the first branch of Post Keynesian approach of profit margins.

## The 'investment financing' theory

### History of the hypothesis

The second branch of Post Keynesian profit margin theory connecting profit margins to the need for internal financing goes back to Gardiner Means, whose work was extensively examined by Lee and Samuels (1992) and Lee (1998). Means (1938) suggested that managers choose a profit margin that takes market competition into account *but also* yields a targeted profit rate needed to finance the growth of the firm:

> Means stated that management selected a target rate of return on equity capital invested in producing the output to determine a total amount of profit needed to be raised during the current pricing period for growth purposes. In deciding upon the specific rate of return, Means argued that management took into account the degree of market competition and the prices of competitors, and thus arrived at a rate of return that would not undermine the corporation's position in the market. Hence the rate of return decided upon by management was designed to maintain a healthy financial condition for the corporate enterprise and to generate enough funds to permit a continued expansion of capacity so as to maintain its desired growth rate.... Thus, since the corporation desires to generate its investment funds internally, it is possible to argue that the target rate of return (and, hence, the mark-up for profit) is largely a function of the desire for investment funds. However, when faced with the argument Means demurred, arguing that while the need for investment funds could play a role in pricing, it was only one of several factors.
>
> (Lee 1998, 56–57, fn. 8)

Thereafter, other Post Keynesian economists have repeatedly referenced this 'investment financing' theory. For example, Joan Robinson (1952) postulated a link between profit margins and the financing of investment (see Lee 1998, 174). She failed, however, to clearly link profit margins to investment and continued to rely on her theory of normal prices. Kaldor then expanded on this theory by assuming that profit margins depend on investment requirements and propensities to save (i.e., retained earnings) (Kaldor 1957; see also Lee 1998, 175). Ball (1964), Kregel (1971), and Harcourt and Kenyon (1976) further contributed to this theory. Finally, Robinson (1970) argued that the practice of integrating the needs for internal financing in the mark-up calculus was equivalent to considering that "[f]irms are, so to say, taxing the consumers to pay for their investment" (736).

Alfred Eichner offered perhaps the most complete theory of investment financing in his 1973 article and subsequent 1976 book, *The Megacorp and Oligopoly*. He noticed the importance of internal finance in modern capitalism:

> Between the fourth quarter, 1948, and the third quarter, 1960, only a little more than 10 percent of all investment in the manufacturing sector was financed through long-term external debt, with slightly more than half of that being accounted for by new fixed interest obligations and the rest by equity issues.
>
> (Eichner 1976, 289)

Eichner stresses the importance of financing in the pricing policy of a firm. He sees profit margins (what he called "average corporate levy") as dependent on a trade-off between the costs of internal and external financing. Managers seek to increase sales and to maintain a sufficient level of profit to be able to finance investment expenses, which are necessary to increase sales. Eichner formalized his theory in four-part diagrams (see Eichner 1976, ch. 3). Eichner's innovative theory considers demand management for a firm's product as a long-run activity; managers thus focus on the long-term growth rate rather than on short-term profit maximization. Therefore, the primary aim of a firm is to maximize growth *and* financing investment (see Dzarasov's chapter in this volume for further details on Eichner's theory of investment and pricing).

### Adrian Wood's two-curve diagram

Adrian Wood's theory developed in his 1975 book, *A Theory of Profits*, can be considered as one of the last contributions in the tradition of investment financing theory. In contrast to Eichner's diagram, which is quite complex and difficult to 'use,' Wood's theory benefits from incorporating the main features of this theoretical tradition into a relatively simple and manageable two-curve diagram. This two-curve diagram makes it possible to analyze various situations and challenge mainstream views. In spite of its simplicity, Wood's model provides a very comprehensible model of investment financing, which is a key feature in the Post Keynesian theory of the firm.

Wood begins with the hypothesis that managers aim to increase sales. His diagram is based on two curves symbolizing frontiers. The first curve represents what Wood calls the 'opportunity frontier.' This curve links profit margins to the growth of sales proceeds—a trade-off between profits and demand in the medium to long run (defined by Wood as a three- to five-year period). This trade-off is easily understood: all things being equal, managers have to choose between a high profit margin and a high sales growth rate. The underlying idea is that to stimulate the growth of sales, managers must reduce prices, and hence profit margins. With the goal of sales growth in mind, a firm stipulates its sales policy in terms of product, price, and advertisement. This trade-off occurs because Wood assumes that although demand for products increases over time, it remains limited for any individual firm (a particular firm does not experience an unlimited demand for its product). Firms thus have to compete to gain a greater share of this limited but growing demand. This opportunity frontier is represented by a concave, downward sloping curve (see Figure 8.1).

The opportunity frontier (*OF*) should be read as follows: In order for a firm to achieve a higher rate of sales growth (*g*) for a given type of product traded in the market, managers must charge a lower price and thus accept a lower profit margin ($\pi$). The opportunity frontier curve is concave because it assumes that higher growth rates when the initial rate is low can be attained through minimal reductions in mark-up, whereas significant reductions in mark-up are required to increase sales growth rates when the initial rate was already high. The opportunity frontier is thus a functional relation that exists in the mind of managers.

The second curve represents a relationship between sales growth and profit margins that is based on the reverse causality—the influence of growth rates on profit margins. Wood calls this the 'finance frontier' (*FF*), assuming that, in the long run, firms either seek to or are forced to internally finance part of their investment expenses for various reasons—for example, because of insufficient lines of bank credit, or a reluctance of managers to increase leverage ratios, such as in Kalecki's increasing risk principle (Kalecki 1937); or because of uncertain and unstable financial market conditions firms are facing (see Jo 2015). Profit margins are thus necessary to ensure a firm's continued existence. When a firm expects a higher sales growth rate, profit margins must also be increased. The finance frontier is thus an upward sloping curve (assumed linear by Wood); it is based on the idea that managers must acquire new plants and/or equipment to

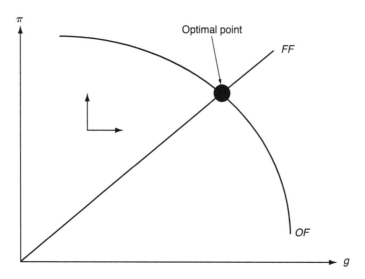

*Figure 8.1* Optimal point of the firm in Wood (1975).

attain a certain level of sales growth. For a given capital-output ratio, they must choose a profit margin in accordance with this level of growth (see Figure 8.1).

Managers will choose to operate at the intersection of these two curves because it is the point that permits the maximum financially viable sales growth rate under prevailing financial conditions. Firms will not operate below the opportunity frontier or above the finance frontier because they seek to achieve higher sales growth rates without financial risk. From a heterodox perspective, this concept presents certain limitations, particularly with respect to its conception of a maximizing behavior. In Wood's model, firms do not maximize profits under technological constraints; they maximize growth under financing constraints. Although this analysis is still based on an optimizing behavior (which was not favored by Fred Lee), it stresses the importance of 'required' internal financing. Thus, profit margins are not a result of market imperfections; they are a *necessity* for all businesses, independent of the market situation. This position is a clear departure from neoclassical theory.

## Mainstream approach to competition and profit margins

### Competition, profit margins, and industrial economics

It is important to remember that economists have always been interested in how competition influences profits—from classical political economists to current mainstream and heterodox economists. In *The Wealth of Nations*, Adam Smith assumes that competition among producers reduces their profits. Neoclassical economists have also attempted to answer this question. For Walras, competition—that is, free mobility of factors of production, especially capital and freedom of entry—allows profits to converge to a zero state in the long run. If some producers are making positive profits, other producers will enter into the industry, increase supply, and reduce the market price until it equals average cost. According to Walras, this progression eventually results in an equilibrium in which producers are making neither profit nor loss. This inverse relationship between competition and profit is also present in Cournot's and Bertrand's writings, although neither of them considers perfectly competitive markets. In Cournot's ([1838] 1897) model profits tend to decline as soon as the number of producers rises because the market power of each producer diminishes. Cournot's duopoly model thus tends toward a zero-profit equilibrium in the long run when the number of producers is high. Similarly, Bertrand's (1883) duopoly model does not require an increasingly large number of producers to arrive at a zero-profit result: it is sufficient that producers have the capacity to satisfy the entire market demand (and thus the ability to push other competitors out of the market). This relationship between competition and profit is also found in the Arrow-Debreu (1954) model of general equilibrium, which assumes constant returns to scale, unicity of price, and no out-of-equilibrium exchanges (Debreu 1959). Later, Debreu and Scarf (1963) show that the equilibrium in a decentralized economy with a large number of actors is similar to that of a competitive economy. Atomicity thus ensures a convergence to a long-run competitive equilibrium in which profit is zero.

In mainstream economics, an inverse relationship thus exists between competition intensity and profit, regardless of the definition of competition (be it atomicity, free entry, or free mobility of capital). This assumption is a fundamental component of neoclassical economics, which led to the emergence of industrial economics in the 1960s.

### *Emergence of industrial economics and the structure-conduct-performance paradigm*

Industrial economics emerged from a specific theoretical tradition that connects the degree of competitiveness of a market to its efficiency—the so-called structure-conduct-performance (SCP) paradigm. The SCP's basic idea is that the more competitive a market is, the more efficient this market will become. The paradigm originated from the works of Mason (1939), Bain (1951), and also Modigliani (1958).[1] Taking into account certain basic conditions of a market (e.g., substitutability), market structure (e.g., the number of sellers and buyers, barriers to entry and to exit, product differentiation) determines the behavior of firms in this market (i.e., the intensity of its market power) and thus the efficiency of this market including its profit margins (because profit margins are often taken as a proxy for efficiency in the allocative sense).

In his 1951 study of 42 American industries (335 firms in total), Bain focused on the link between CR8 ratios (the market share of the eight biggest firms in the industry) and the rate of return on capital over a four-year period (1936–1940). He showed that profit rates tend to be higher in industries with a CR8 ratio greater than 70 percent than in industries with a ratio of less than 70 percent. Later Bain (1956), focusing on barriers to entry rather than on concentration, showed more conclusive results. Mann (1966) was able to confirm the link between profits and barriers to entry for 30 industries (among which 17 also appeared in Bain's 1951 study) as well as establish the link between concentrations (CR8 greater than 70 percent). Collins and Preston (1969) also found a link between concentration and price-cost margin that is defined as a measure of profits over direct costs (not capital) for the period of 1958–1963. In the following years, numerous empirical studies established a similar link between concentration and profit, for example, Weiss (1974), and Jenny and Weber (1976) in France.

### *Similarities between the mainstream view of competition and the Post Keynesian 'degree of competition' theory*

In conclusion of the previous historical review, we deem it important to highlight the similarities between the mainstream view of the link between competition and profit margins and Post Keynesian 'degree of competition' theory. Lee (2013a) underlines that Post Keynesians as well as mainstream economists struggle with the idea of monopolies or cartels, which are assumed to reduce economic activity while fixing their prices at a higher level:

> On the other hand, if the degree of monopoly declines, hence the profit mark-up and prices decline, the wage share will increase and so will income and employment.... *From either mainstream or heterodox perspectives,* monopoly or collective-cartel price fixing leads to market and system failure that can only be alleviated by introducing more competition.
>
> (Lee 2013a, 4, italics added)

In fact, it is easy to recognize that the mainstream view of the link between the degree of competition and profit margins has exactly the same theoretical framework as Robinson-style theory of imperfect competition. The same is true for the Kaleckian theory of the degree of monopoly. Although Robinson (1969) later dismissed her own theory of imperfect competition (in the preface to the second edition, see also Robinson [1953]), the mainstream view that a direct inverse relationship exists between the degree of competition and profit margins is thus similar to the Post Keynesian degree of competition concept—both ideas share the same conclusions on this point.

## An unstable empirical relationship between profit margins and competition

Accordingly, the relationship between competition and profit margins has been, in one form or another, an essentially structural question in economics since the beginning of classical political economy. Although this relationship is well established in theory, it has yet to be validated empirically. In fact, this inverse relationship between competition and profit is frequently confronted with a problem: the link is not as strong in reality as it is in theory. Empirical studies on the topic often return very mixed results. Based on findings reported in Schmalensee's (1988) extensive review of empirical studies (from which we have taken most of the studies mentioned hereafter), we can show that this problem has existed since the birth of industrial economics.

Empirical results have been repeatedly criticized concerning the structural relationship between profit margins and competition. Even the results by Bain (1951) and Collins and Preston (1969) mentioned above are empirically debatable. Bain admits that the link between profit rate and concentration is unclear in his data: "there is no conclusive indication of any closely observed linear relationship of industry concentration to profit rate" (Bain 1951, 313). His first regressions clearly show that some low-concentrated industries exhibit higher profit rates than more highly concentrated industries (see Table 8.1). Furthermore, Bain's final equation (based on CR8 rates of greater than 70 percent), although significant, appears to be quite weak ($R^2 = 0.33$).

Collins and Preston (1969) detect a significant CR4 (percent of product supplied by the four biggest firms of the industry) effect, for which a ten-point

*Table 8.1* Average of industry average profit rates within concentration deciles, 1936–1940, for 42 selected industries

| Concentration range (percent of value product supplied by eight firms) | Number of industries | Average of industry average profit rates |
|---|---|---|
| 90–100 | 8 | 12.7 |
| 80–89.9 | 11 | 10.5 |
| 70–79.9 | 3 | 16.3 |
| 60–69.9 | 5 | 5.8 |
| 50–59.9 | 4 | 5.8 |
| 40–49.9 | 2 | 3.8 |
| 30–39.9 | 5 | 6.3 |
| 20–29.9 | 2 | 10.4 |
| 10–19.9 | 1 | 17.0 |
| 0–9.9 | 1 | 9.1 |

Source: Bain (1951, 313).

difference in ratio causes a one-point change in the price-cost margin ratio, which is a relatively low value. Brozen (1971) also showed that Bain's data for a subsequent period (1953–1957) exhibits a rise in profit rates for less concentrated industries and a decline for concentrated industries. As a result, Brozen argues that Bain underestimated profit rates in less concentrated industries and overestimated those in concentrated industries. Brozen concluded his findings could completely offset the difference between industries that was initially found by Bain (1951).

Salinger (1984) also reported ambiguous results: concentration ratios (for the period 1971–1976) had no significant effect on profit rates; barriers to entry produced varying effects (depending on their combination with other variables). In one of his regressions, Salinger even found that concentration had a negative effect on profit rates. In addition, $R^2$ was quite weak (18–20 percent).

Extending the analysis to a longer period (1958–1981) for 284 US manufacturing industries, Domowitz, Hubbard, and Petersen (1986) showed that, although the link between concentration and price-cost margins exists, it declines sharply during the sub-periods 1958–1965 and 1974–1981. Applying Collins and Preston's (1969) equation to their own data, Domowitz *et al.* also showed an initially strengthened effect of CR4 on profit rates that eventually lessened toward the end of the period (from 0.1 to 0.17 and then to 0.047 in 1981), with $R^2$ following a similar development (18 percent in 1958, 20 percent in 1965, and 1 percent in 1981). The authors thus conclude: "The simple Collins and Preston model has virtually no explanatory power in the 1970s" (Domowitz, Hubbard, and Petersen, 1986, 5).

Other studies even produced counter-intuitive results. Grabowski and Mueller (1978), Connolly and Hirschey (1984), and Hirschey (1985) found a negative relationship between concentration and profit rates for US data, suggesting that higher concentrations lead to lower profit margins. After reviewing a number of empirical studies, Schmalensee (1988) summarized the connection between concentration and profit as follows: "The relation, if any, between seller concentration and profitability is weak statistically, and the estimated concentration effect is usually small. The estimated relation is unstable over time and space and vanishes in many multivariate studies" (976). Schmalensee notes, however, a slightly stronger relation between advertising expenses and profitability in the consumption goods industries. He also recognizes a frequently positive link between sales growth and profitability, and between capital requirements and profitability (these two facts are important aspects of Post Keynesian investment financing theory, as discussed below).

Other studies analyzing the link between profit and competition report similarly uncertain results. While Bellone *et al.* (2008) found that the European Single Market Program (SMP)[2] had a negative impact on profit margins in French manufacturing industries, Cook (2011) reports a rise in profit mark-ups following the Euro implementation, even though a single currency would be expected to promote competition.

Badinger (2007) analyzed the effect of the SMP for ten countries at the sectoral level (manufacturing, construction, and service sectors). He found a decline in profit mark-ups in the manufacturing industry (although some sub-sectors exhibited a rise in profit mark-ups during the 1980s); the SMP affected the construction sector to a lesser degree, and profit mark-ups in the service sector have risen since the mid-1990s.

In a study on manufacturing industries in European Union countries conducted over the period 1987–2000, Sauner-Leroy (2003) identified two subperiods that exhibit opposite effects: first, as a result of the competitive effect of the SMP, a decline in mark-ups occurred until 1993, then a general reduction in costs led to increased mark-ups. The two sub-periods therefore present opposing effects on profit margins.

Konings, Van Cayseele, and Warzynski (2001) compared the evolution of mark-ups in Belgium (2,205 firms) and in the Netherlands (2,471 firms) from 1992 to 1997 in order to examine the relative effect of a competitive regulation that was implemented in Belgium in 1993 (the Netherlands, seen as more favorable to cartels, did not implement such a regulation). For the studied period, the authors found a rise in mark-ups in Belgium, compared with stable (but higher) mark-ups in the Netherlands. They thus concluded that "[t]he competition law that was implemented in Belgium did not have an effect on price cost margins of Belgian firms" (Konings, Van Cayseele, and Warzynski 2001, 850). They also observed that the effect of import openness on profit margins in Belgium was negative but insignificant. In contrast, a positive and significant effect was observed in the Netherlands, where industries that are more exposed to imports had higher mark-ups.

Similarly, Christopoulou and Vermeulen (2008) considered profit mark-ups across 50 sectors in nine countries (eight European countries and the US) for the periods 1981–1992 and 1992–2004. Except for Austria, they did not find any change in mark-ups between the two sub-periods, although competition is generally considered to have increased between these two periods.

Boulhol (2005, 2006), who examined mark-up variations in 13 OECD countries between 1980 and 2000, found a slight rise in these mark-ups with a convergence (i.e., high mark-ups declined, low mark-ups increased). He showed that declining wage shares in those countries offset the expected pro-competitive effect. Studying 23 manufacturing sectors in 17 OECD countries between 1970 and 2003, Boulhol (2006) also showed that the pro-competitive effect of international trade openness is relatively small with a similarly weak product market deregulation (measured by the OECD product market regulation indicator *PMR*) because both factors are offset by a decrease in the bargaining power of unions and by the rise of financialization of these economies.

## Adrian Wood's alternative explanation of the relationship between profit margins and competition

On the surface, the rigidity of the various measures of profit margins presented above might seem paradoxical from a mainstream perspective. Adrian Wood's (1975) theory of the determination of profit margins clarifies this apparent paradox. Wood presents a doubly interesting theory for industrial economics. First, prices are not the adjusting variable between supply and demand (in the short term), and, hence, prices are replaced by the utilization of output capacity. Second, he pays particular attention to the crucial role of self-financing for firms. In the long run, managers seek to maximize the growth of the firm by generating sufficient internal funds to finance investment expenses. The firm is therefore at the center of two constraints: a competitive constraint (the opportunity frontier) and a financial constraint (the finance frontier).

### The opportunity frontier's independence of market structure

In Wood's (1975) two-curve diagram, competitive conditions affect neither the industry's opportunity frontier nor the finance frontier. The opportunity frontier is the link between profit margins and expected long-run sales growth. Competitive conditions therefore have no effect on the profit margins that firms *must* maintain to internally finance the growth of their sales (by internally financing part of their investment expenses). A single firm can improve its competitive position at the expense of other firms. The firm's individual opportunity frontier will thus move upward, but the opportunity frontier of other firms will move downward, because their relative position has deteriorated as a result of the competitive struggle for sales.

Supposing a firm is initially a monopolist and a new firm comes into the market, if this new entrant produces the same goods or services at the same cost and under the same financial conditions, then there will now be two identical and superimposed opportunity frontiers, albeit without a change in the initial monopolist's opportunity frontier in the long run. In that case, market sales, which will merely be shared, would be expected to be equally distributed (i.e., the new entrant has an effect on long-run market shares and short-run sales growth), but in the long run the sales growth rate for both firms remains unaffected. From then on, neither firm is required to change its self-financing rate nor its profit margins, although competition has apparently increased. In Figure 8.2, the opportunity frontiers of firm A (the initial monopolist) and that of firm B (the new entrant) are superimposed and thus identical. The finance frontier is not concerned by this entry. The intersection of the opportunity frontiers with the finance frontier remains unaffected.

If the new firm enters into the market under different production conditions (e.g., better quality, lower labor cost), there will be two distinct opportunity frontiers, but with no change in the industry's opportunity frontier (representing the average position in the market). The new firm's opportunity frontier is located above the old firm's frontier because it will be able to reach a higher rate of sales growth than the older firm (due to better quality or lower costs). The older firm, however, sees its own opportunity frontier move downward, as it experiences a fall in sales growth (see Figure 8.3). Nevertheless, the industry's opportunity frontier remains unchanged as long as financial conditions (i.e., the finance frontier) stay constant (we discuss why competition does not affect financial conditions in the following).

Consider then the following case: Two firms produce a good or service under the same market conditions. Suppose these goods are identical, but not interchangeable. Consumers choose either one or the other (for example, two software solutions that fulfill the same function but are designed for two distinct operating systems). Further suppose that a new law forces both firms to guarantee the perfect interchangeability of their goods, allowing consumers to switch

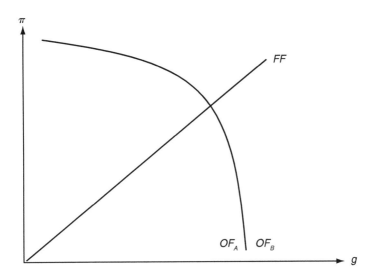

*Figure 8.2* Effect of a new entrant.

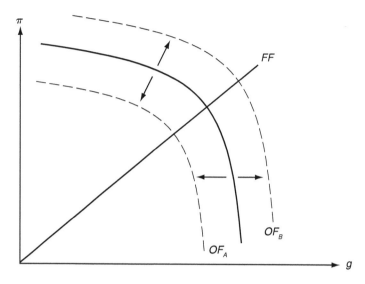

*Figure 8.3* Effect of a new entrant operating under different productive conditions.

from one producer to the other immediately and for free. *If both firms initially operate under the same conditions* (and therefore under the same financial conditions), then the new regulation does not change the intersection of the opportunity frontier with the finance frontier. However, the potential effect of an individual change in profit mark-up of one of the two firms is strengthened—that is, if one of the two firms raises its mark-up, the firm's sales will decline more severely than before, because consumers are now able to easily substitute one product for the other. Conversely, and for the same reason, if one of the two firms lowers its mark-up, this firm will experience higher sales growth than before. This means the opportunity frontier 'pivots' around its initial intersection with the finance frontier (see Figure 8.4). Starting from point $A$, a rise in the mark-up (of firm "A") from $\pi_A$ to $\pi'_A$ reduces the sales growth rate from $g_A$ to $g'_{A2}$; before the introduction of the competition law the new growth rate would have been $g'_{A1}$. Similarly, a reduction of profit margins from $\pi_A$ to $\pi''_A$ results in a sales growth rate of $g_A$ to $g''_{A2}$; without the new law, it would have merely reached $g''_{A1}$. These legal changes thus created a situation in which mark-up cuts (and thus price cuts) result in higher gains, and higher mark-ups result in higher losses. However, the new law has no effect on the intersection of frontiers and managers would have no reason to operate at a different point than $A$ (unless there are other changes in the finance frontier, which have no reason to occur in that case).

Changes in the degree of competition thus do not affect the intersection between the opportunity frontier and the finance frontier. We can therefore explain why competition (be it concentration, substitution, differentiation, or some other measure) leaves industry profit margins unaffected from the point of

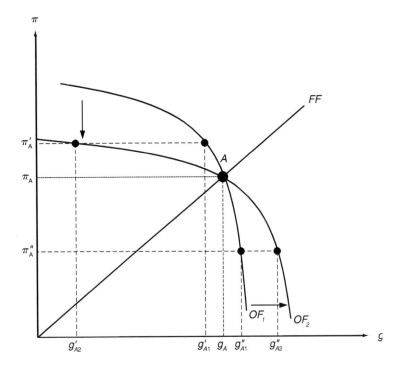

*Figure 8.4* Effects of a 'substitutability law.'

view of Wood's (1975) two-curve diagram, which provides a useful manageable tool in Post Keynesian profit margin theory.

### Competition and internal financing: Adrian Wood and Fred Lee

#### Self-financing: the missing link of industrial economics

Wood's (1975) non-mainstream explanations of profit margins not only provide a renewed understanding of the relationship between competition and profit, but also help explain why empirical studies on the topic may produce inconclusive results. In short, Wood's (1975) theory asserts that profit margins are not determined by the short-run degree of competition in the market, but are instead the outcome of two opposite forces:

1   The competitive constraint (the opportunity frontier), which results from long-run competition among firms in the market and competition among firms to conquer market shares of a growing but limited demand. This force drives prices and profit margins downward.
2   The financial constraint (the finance frontier), which links profit margins to the need to internally finance investment expenses that are necessary to meet

growing demands. This force drives profit margins upward, given that firms want to maintain their ability to finance their development on the market.

Consequently, profit margins are not a residual variable inherited from the firm's market power, but are a very important strategic variable that has to be secured in the long run, regardless of the degree of competition. This point was already noticed by Eichner (1976): "the cash flow is not simply a residue or balance figure but is in fact a quantity deliberately chosen to enable the megacorp to achieve its investment goals" (13).

An inverse relationship between competition and profit margins could only exist when increased competition changes the finance frontier (and shifts it downward)—for example, increased competition might induce external financing or decrease profit distribution in the long run. In any case, this case remains an exception. In fact, it is precisely for the reasons cited above that Wood himself doubted that competition policies could effectively reduce profit margins:

> It is an implication of the present theory that measures which attack monopolistic and collusive practices by companies will have little or no effect on the distribution of income … the size of the share of profits depends primarily on the growth rate of national income, the investment coefficient, the external finance ratio, the financial asset ratio, and the gross retention ratio, none of which is affected by anti-monopoly policies in any systematic way.
>
> (Wood 1975, 162–163)

It is even conceivable that a higher concentration could lead to a decline in profit margins (as reported in some studies mentioned previously), because a more secured market position (lower risk of losing sales) lessens the importance of defending profit margins. In our view, this argument can explain why several empirical studies struggle with a negative coefficient for the 'concentration' variables.

### Adrian Wood and Fred Lee

Several criticisms could be addressed to Wood's model, from a 'Fred Lee' perspective: first, it starts from an individual firm as a starting point, and thus does not take into account circular production, whereas Lee has always started from the economy as a whole in a circular production model (Lee 2013b, 162). Second, in Wood's analysis, firms are optimizing, whereas they are not in Lee's writings. Third, Wood's model postulates the existence of an opportunity frontier which is close to the concept of demand curve, whereas Lee always stressed the lack for a foundation of such a concept: "[T]he concept of the enterprise demand curve is highly problematical in mainstream theory, and there is no theoretical (and empirical) basis for such a demand curve in heterodox theory" (Lee 2011, 9).

However, there are strong similarities between Wood's analysis and Lee's writings. First, both Wood and Lee argue that competition is disconnected from or independent of the size of the mark-up. Lee notes that "it is unlikely that mark-up pricing and the profit mark-up are linked to an imperfectly competitive market structure via the price elasticity of demand" (2013b, 162; see also Lee 1990–91), and that "the degree of competition qua profit mark up does not affect the degree of economic activity in the economy" (2011, 4).

Lee (1998, 2011, 2013b) uses a two-sector production model and shows competition has no fundamental role in the making of profit mark-ups. Furthermore, in his circular production models, he found that the foundation for profit mark-ups comes from the capability of producing surplus machines, which constitutes

> a particular example (in the post-Keynesian 'structuralists' Wood (1975), Harcourt and Kenyon (1976) and Eichner (1976)) that the production of investment goods tied specifically to the business enterprise, brings into existence both profits and the profit mark-up.... This outcome supports the Wood–Harcourt–Eichner Post Keynesian view noted above that links investment to the profit mark up, but this has little to do with competition.
>
> (Lee 2013b, 164–165)

Finally, it is necessary to recall that further research is needed in the empirical validation of the investment financing theory, since it still lacks empirical testing. This fact was also noticed by Lee (1998, 212–213, 226–227; 2013b, 160). Indeed, there exists few empirical studies grounded on Eichner/Wood's theory of the firm (a recent one can be found in Sarich and Hecht 2013), so that future research should investigate the empirical validity of the 'investment financing' theory of the mark-up to make it stronger.

## Conclusion

Post Keynesians offer two distinct theories of mark-up determination—i.e., degree of competition theory and investment financing theory—that have completely different implications on several levels (theoretical, empirical, political) concerning the link between competition and profit. We have shown how the first branch (degree of competition theory) is connected to what later became a standard view in economics. This theory, however, continues to lack strong empirical support; studies on the subject often conclude that there is no structural relationship between profit mark-up and the degree of competition. It is only by considering the second branch of Post Keynesian mark-up determination theory—represented by Wood's (1975) two-curve diagram—that it is possible to explain this observed disconnection. Profit mark-up is not considered as a residual variable that firms can extract from competitive conditions in the market; instead it is a strategic variable that firms must maintain whatever the degree of competition because of the need for internal financing. This theory therefore encourages the reconsideration of several aspects of industrial economics.

## Notes

1　Compared with Bain's more empirical work, Modigliani's (1958) article is theoretical; it is therefore cited less frequently.
2　Implemented in 1992, the Single Market Program liberalized the movements of goods, services, people, and capital in the European Union.

## References

Arrow, K. J. and G. Debreu. 1954. "Existence of an Equilibrium for a Competitive Economy." *Econometrica* 22 (3): 265–290.

Badinger, H. 2007. "Has the EU's Single Market Programme Fostered Competition? Testing for a Decrease in Mark-up Ratios in EU Industries." *Oxford Bulletin of Economics and Statistics* 69 (4): 497–519.

Bain, J. S. 1951. "Relation of Profit Rate to Industry Concentration: American Manufacturing, 1936–1940." *The Quarterly Journal of Economics* 65 (3): 293–324.

Bain, J. S. 1956. *Barriers to New Competition*. Cambridge, MA: Harvard University Press.

Ball, R. J. 1964. *Inflation and the Theory of Money*. London: George Allen & Unwin.

Bellone, F., P. Musso, L. Nesta, and F. Warzynski. 2008. "L'effet pro-concurrentiel de l'intégration européenne: une analyse de l'évolution des taux de marge dans les industries manufacturières françaises." Document de travail de l'OFCE, n°2008–09, mars.

Bertrand, J. 1883. "Théorie des richesses." *Journal des savants*, Septembre: 499–508.

Boulhol, H. 2005. "The Convergence of Markups." *Cahiers de la MSE*, série blanche TEAM, 05–19.

Bouhlol, H. 2006. "Why Haven't Price-Cost Margins Decreased with Globalization?" *Cahiers de la MSE*, série blanche TEAM, 06–07.

Brozen, Y. 1971. "Bain's Concentration and Rates of Return Revisited." *Journal of Law and Economics* 14 (2): 351–369.

Christopoulou, R. and P. Vermeulen. 2008. "Markups in the Euro Area and the US over the Period 1981–2004: A Comparison of 50 Sectors." ECB Working Papers Series, No. 856. Accessed December 31, 2014. www.ecb.europa.eu/pub/pdf/scpwps/ecbwp856.pdf.

Collins, N. R. and L. E. Preston. 1969. "Price-Cost Margins and Industry Structure." *Review of Economics and Statistics* 51 (3): 271–286.

Connolly, R. A. and M. Hirschey. 1984. "R&D, Market Structure and Profits: A Value-Based Approach." *Review of Economics and Statistics* 66: 678–681.

Cook, D. 2011. "Markups and the Euro." *Review of Economics and Statistics* 93 (4): 1440–1452.

Cournot, A. [1838] 1897. *Researches on the Mathematical Principles of the Theory of Wealth*. London: Macmillan.

Debreu, G. 1959. *The Theory of Value: An Axiomatic Analysis of Economic Equilibrium*. New Haven, CT and London: Yale University Press.

Debreu, G. 1954. *Theory of Value: An Axiomatic Analysis of Economic Equilibrium*. Vol. 1. New York, John Wiley & Sons.

Debreu, G. and H. Scarf. 1963. "A Limit Theorem on the Core of an Economy." *International Economic Review* 4 (3): 235–246.

Domovitz, I., R. Hubbard, and B. C. Petersen. 1986.. "Business Cycles and the Relationship between Concentration and Price-Cost Margins." *The RAND Journal of Economics* 17 (1): 1–17.

Eichner, A. S. 1973. "A Theory of the Determination of the Mark-Up Under Oligopoly." *The Economic Journal* 83 (332): 1184–1200.

Eichner, A. S. 1976. *The Megacorp and Oligopoly: Micro Foundations of Macro Dynamics*. New York: Cambridge University Press.

Grabowski, H. G. and D. C. Mueller. 1978. "Industrial Research and Development, Intangible Capital Stocks, and Firm Profit Rates." *Bell Journal of Economics* 9: 328–343.

Harcourt, G. C. and P. Kenyon. 1976. "Pricing and the Investment Decision." *Kyklos* 29 (3): 449–477.

Hirschey, M. 1985. "Market Structure and Market Value." *Journal of Business* 58: 89–98.

Jenny, R. and A. P. Weber. 1976. "Profit Rates and Structural Variables in French Manufacturing Industries." *European Economic Review* 7: 187–206.

Jo, T.-H. 2015. "Financing Investment under Fundamental Uncertainty and Instability: A Heterodox Microeconomic View." *Bulletin of Political Economy* 9 (1): forthcoming.

Kaldor, N. 1957. "A Model of Economic Growth." In *Essays on Economic Stability and Growth*, edited by N. Kaldor, 259–300. London: Gerland Duckworth.

Kalecki, M. 1937. "The Principle of Increasing Risk." *Economica* 4 (16): 440–447.

Kalecki, M. 1939. *Essays in the Theory of Economic Fluctuations*. London: Allen and Unwin.

Konings, J., P. Van Cayseele, and F. Warzynski. 2001. "The Dynamics of Industrial Mark-ups in Two Small Open Economies: Does National Competition Policy Matter?" *International Journal of Industrial Organization* 19 (5): 841–859.

Kregel, J. A. 1971. *Rate of Profit, Distribution and Growth: Two Views*. Chicago: Aldine & Atherton.

Lee, F. S. 1990–91. "Marginalist Controversy and Post Keynesian Theory." *Journal of Post Keynesian Economics* 13 (2): 252–263.

Lee, F. S. 1998. *Post Keynesian Price Theory*. Cambridge: Cambridge University Press.

Lee, F. S. 2011. "Old Controversy Revisited: Pricing, Market Structure and Competition." MPRA Working Paper 30490. Accessed December 31, 2014. http://mpra.ub.uni-muenchen.de/30490/.

Lee, F. S. 2013a. "Heterodox Approach to Cartels and Market Competition." Paper presented at the annual URPE meeting at the ASSA Conference, San Diego, California.

Lee, F. S. 2013b. "Competition, Going Enterprise, and Economic Activity." In *Alternative Theories of Competition*, edited by J. Moudud, C. Bina, and P. L. Mason, 160–173. London: Routledge.

Lee, F. S. and W. Samuels. 1992. *The Heterodox Economics of Gardiner C. Means: A Collection*. Armonk, NY: M. E. Sharpe.

Mann, H. M. 1966. "Seller Concentration, Barriers to Entry, and Rates of Return in Thirty Industries, 1950–1960." *Review of Economics and Statistics* 48 (3): 296–307.

Mason, E. S. 1939. "Price and Production of Large Scale Enterprise." *American Economic Review* 29 (1): 61–74.

Means, G. C. 1938. "Incentives to Capital Creation." In *The Heterodox Economics of Gardiner C. Means: A Collection*, edited by F. S. Lee and W. Samuels, 110–112. Armonk, NY: M. E. Sharpe.

Modigliani, F. 1958. "New Developments on the Oligopoly Front." *Journal of Political Economy* 66 (3): 215–232.

Moudud, J. K., C. Bina, and P. L. Mason, eds. 2013. *Alternative Theories of Competition: Challenges to the Orthodoxy*. London: Routledge.

Robinson, J. V. 1933. *The Economics of Imperfect Competition*. London: Macmillan.

Robinson, J. 1952. *The Rate of Interest and Other Essays*. London: Macmillan.

Robinson, J. V. 1953. "Imperfect Competition Revisited." *Economic Journal* 63 (251): 579–593.

Robinson, J. V. 1969. *The Economics of Imperfect Competition*. 2nd ed. New York: Palgrave Macmillan.

Robinson, J. V. 1970. "Harrod after Twenty-one Years." *The Economic Journal* 80 (319): 741–742.

Salinger, M. A. 1984. "Tobin's *q*, Unionization, and the Concentration-Profits Relationship." *RAND Journal of Economics* 15 (2): 159–170.

Sarich, J. and J. Hecht. 2013. "Are Mega-corps Competitive? Some Empirical Test of Business Competition." In *Alternative Theories of Competition*, edited by J. Moudud, C. Bina, and P. L. Mason, 298–324. London: Routledge.

Sauner-Leroy, J.-B. 2003. "The Impact of the Implementation of the Single Market Programme on Productive Efficiency and on Mark-ups in the European Union Manufacturing Industry." European Commission, DG for Economic and Financial Affairs, Economic Papers, n° 192. Accessed December 31, 2014. www.banquefrance.fr/fileadmin/user_upload/banque_de_france/publications/publication845_en.pdf.

Schmalensee, R. 1988. "Inter-Industry Studies of Structure and Performance." In *Handbook of Industrial Organization*, edited by R. Schmalensee and R. D. Willig. Amsterdam: North Holland.

Weiss, L. W. 1974. "The Structure-Conduct-Performance Paradigm and Antitrust." *University of Pennsylvania Law Review* 127 (4): 1104–1140.

Wood, A. 1975. *A Theory of Profits*. London: Cambridge University Press.

This was in Bordeaux for the 2010 AHE Conference. We were having a cocktail in the beautiful 'Hôtel de ville.' When I asked him if we could take a picture together, Fred laughed and said "Pfff, the French are so sentimentalistic…"

# 9 Inter- and intra-firm governance in heterodox microeconomics

## The case of the US software industry

*Erik Dean*

## Introduction

This chapter will expand upon some of Frederic Lee's theoretical contributions to heterodox microeconomic theory, particularly as they have concerned the social construction of the modern business enterprise, its relation to the markets in which it operates, and ultimately to society as a whole. As Lee noted, "the theoretical significance of the going enterprise is that it is the organizational mechanism by which the capitalist class gains ongoing access to the state-monetized social provisioning process" (2013, 468). With this essential understanding of the business enterprise in mind, it will be argued that (1) certain technological and legal relationships can be identified as generic to the modern business enterprise, (2) the occupational hierarchy that results from these relationships creates conflicting methods of valuation, and (3) these conflicts are mitigated through the evolution of governance norms both within and between business enterprises.

The research behind this analysis, compiled in Dean (2013), was done in the spirit of Lee's methodological position of grounded theory, and includes an historical examination of the US software industry in the twentieth century. This method maintains the empirical relevance and realism of the model in addition to offering illustrative cases of the model's application (see Lee 2002). Hence, the following will present a theoretical narrative that synthesizes and augments previous theoretical work in heterodox economics while remaining grounded in the particular industry under study.

This chapter is organized as follows. First, a general discussion of Lee's social surplus approach is delineated, with connections drawn to additional ideas from the heterodox economics literature. This provides the foundation for the analysis of the business enterprise that follows. Next, the two essential components of the modern business enterprise—the going plant and the going business—are analyzed, along with illustrations drawn from the historical development of the US software industry. Reference to this industry is limited to the period beginning in the 1950s and ending in the 1990s for the sake of brevity, and because it is in this period that the institutions forming the business enterprise in software were initially constructed. The concluding section summarizes and draws the arguments herein back to the theoretical contributions of Frederic Lee.

## Social provisioning and the joint stock of knowledge

As the study of the social provisioning process,[1] heterodox economics involves the construction of historical narratives that describe and explain the processes by which society provides goods and services to its members within the context of capitalism (Lee 2009, 8–9). From this perspective it follows that "the economy is something akin to a going concern" (Lee 2013, 467). That is, the economy—and, following Veblen (1908, 1914), society generally—is a system of people and their interrelationships which perpetuates itself through time by organizing individuals toward a common purpose.

That economies typically operate as going concerns should not, however, be taken to suggest that the perpetuation of any group therein, or even society as a whole, is secured. Indeed, because communities are perpetually changing and struggling to adapt, they are generally discordant with the means and values that could constructively be put to use in their own service. That is to say, societies are characterized by power, conflict, and maladjustment (Dugger 1996). Hence, heterodox economists are tasked with uncovering the processes by which agency is exercised over others and over the economic system, as well as the implications of the same for the viability, adjustment, or lack thereof for individuals, groups, and society as a whole.

In this context of class and control Lee elaborated the social surplus approach that frames his key contributions to heterodox economics (Lee 2012b, 2013; Lee and Jo 2011). Though a complete review of this framework cannot be given here, a few essential points require mention. The 'structural core' of the social surplus approach "consists of technology, class, capitalist state, and a surplus producing economy qua social activities and the agency core consists of structure-altering decisions by the business enterprise and the state" (Lee and Jo 2011, 858). Through the exercise of agency, chiefly amongst the business elites through their control of business enterprises, the social surplus is generated. Hence, the magnitude and composition of the social product is determined by these elites, in conjunction with the political elites. In the interests of maintaining these business enterprises as going concerns, working rules including accounting and pricing procedures, are established. Prices, markups, and wages thus emerge as artifacts of the process by which the social surplus is created and by which rights of access to that surplus are apportioned.

At the most basic level the social surplus approach takes into account class, technology, the capitalist state, and a viable economy as a starting point (Lee and Jo 2011, 863; Lee 2012b). This leaves further work to be done in expanding the analysis into the construction and valuation of those institutions composing the evolving class structures, technologies, and laws in which the provisioning process is embedded. The present chapter argues that an important addition in this regard is the integration of Veblen's concept of the joint stock of knowledge and the various and complex ways in which business enterprises relate to that knowledge through technological, organizational, legal, and other manners in which social agency is effected. In particular, the (original) institutionalist approach to resources, technology, and capital adds analytical value to the structures which define that preeminent point of agency for the ruling class—that is, the business enterprise.

Resources are functions of institutional development, defined through technological change and social norms of 'appropriate' behavior, and allocated through social agency qua acting persons and organizations within the context of extant social norms (Zimmerman 1972; Tool 1979; De Gregori 1987; Dugger 1996; Lee 2012b). It follows from this that "knowledge is truly the mother of all other resources" (Zimmerman 1972, 11; see also Ayres 1967), and hence the structure of production on which the economy relies for its perpetuation derives originally from the community's knowledge, or more accurately its ways of knowing, doing, and valuing (Sturgeon 2009). In understanding society as a perpetually changing entity, then, it is necessary to distinguish instrumental characteristics of extant institutions—tending to efficaciously meet problems with solutions—from those which are ceremonial—restricting the realization of technologically feasible and constructive behavior and relationships (see, e.g., Samuels 1977). A dichotomy of the institutions that frame the social provisioning process, as opposed to a dualism of its components, can thus be constructed (De Gregori 1977; Todorova 2014).

On the instrumental side of this dichotomy lies "knowledge about how to do things, especially with respect to activity characterized by means-ends relationships appropriate to intended purposes" (Samuels 1977, 872; see also De Gregori 1977). This knowledge, furthermore, "is of the nature of a common stock, held and carried forward collectively by the community, which is in this relation to be conceived as a going concern" (Veblen 1914, 103). Reflecting that this distinction is a dichotomy of social processes and relations, a community's joint stock of (instrumental) knowledge is not separate from the power structure, which "govern[s] the distribution of technological opportunities" (Samuels 1997, 878). Hence, the joint stock of knowledge refers to the continuum of necessarily social behavior which affords the community its capacity to reproduce itself through serviceable and cooperative provisioning.

The task at hand, then, is to understand the modern business enterprise in its relationship to this joint stock of knowledge. This requires identification of dependencies and conflicts of knowledge and values vis-à-vis other groups as well as the requirements of the community as a going concern. As will be demonstrated in the following sections, the business enterprise constitutes a hierarchy of technological and property relations simultaneously defining both the structure of control to be exercised in determining the social surplus as well as the cannons of access to that surplus. Because this hierarchy necessarily creates norms of valuation at cross purposes with each other, it is fundamentally prone to conflict. In consequence, the business enterprise must develop governing norms, both internally and in relation to its environment, if it is to remain a going concern.

## The going plant

At its heart the business enterprise must stand in relation to some part of the community's joint stock of knowledge. This relationship bears most directly on the going plant, comprised of productive capabilities reflecting relationships between business enterprises and households in using, maintaining, and directing the future growth of that portion of the joint stock of knowledge within its purview (see Commons [1934] 1961, [1924] 1968; Lee 2013).

However, while the going plant might be treated as the 'productive' kernel of the business enterprise, it must be acknowledged that the structure of going plant relationships as organized under the ambit of the business enterprise is unlikely to be without systematic waste. Specifically, in order to maintain the profitable transactions on which its survival as a going concern depends, the business enterprise must organize its going plant such that it engrosses some portion of the joint stock knowledge to the exclusion of others—namely, its workers and its customers. For the latter, this typically means agency is limited to that which can be exercised through purchasing decisions. For the former, this means relegation to a position in which participation in the work to be done has been deemed necessary for the operation of the plant, but not for the direction of the joint stock of knowledge itself.

A familiar historical example is of the transition from what Veblen (1914) called the handicraft era to the machine era, marked by the mechanization of labor. With the factory system, beginning around 1840 in the US, workers became "subject to managerial administration as to the hours and the manner they worked" (Lee 1998, 49). Work that was once artisanal became routine toil (see Dewey 1922, 271; Mills 1951, 220). Skills once maintained through the education of workers were transferred to the machines they tended; and with those skills went also the discretion over the production process, from the workers to the interests for which the machines were designed. Hence, "more and more of the thought and will of the inventor, less and less of that of the immediate human agent or machine-tender is expressed in the product" (Hobson 1906, 70–71). In short, the worker became "an appendage of the machine" (Marx and Engels 1848; see also Braverman [1974] 1998), and this alienation of the machine tender is part and parcel to the going plant. It has, indeed, been argued that the machine and the factory system are to a significant extent a reflection of the extant hierarchical relationships prior to the development of the sophisticated production systems that would make artisanal production impracticable (Marglin 1996).

Concomitant to the going plant are institutions of property as the defining means of the business enterprise's participation in the industrial system (Veblen 1908; Gagnon 2007; Henry 2015). This property could be in physical machines, in patents, in the skills of employees, or otherwise, depending on the technological relationships of the going plant and the legal structures developed in sanction thereof. In any case, property reflects in law the relationships of the going plant vis-à-vis the joint stock of knowledge, allowing the business enterprise to engross, or 'corner' the usufruct of the commonplace knowledge of ways and means by taking over such of the requisite material as may be relatively scarce and relatively indispensable for procuring a livelihood under the current state of the industrial arts.

(Veblen 1908, 525)

The transfer of knowledge and values from artisan to machine means ultimately a transfer of discretion to the employer who owns the machine (Commons 1919, 16; see also Fisk 2009, 27). Investment in this property weds the business motives of profitable transactions between producer and consumer to the community's joint stock of knowledge, and in fact dictates the business enterprise's control over access to that knowledge, and thus the social surplus. Hence the 'original' site of conflict in the business enterprise is in the going plant itself: property holders control use and development of, as well as access to, the joint stock of knowledge, compelling in effect the unpropertied either to find alternative means of provisioning, or to come to an agreement with the propertied (Lee 2012b, 92; see also Henry 2015).

As indicated above, the going plant does not only impinge on the discretion exercised by the worker; it also relegates the discretion of users to only so much participation as can meet the requirements of that group's position as a purchaser. Because the generation of profitable transactions by the going plant is premised on the exclusive access to the joint stock of knowledge, it is likely that the user, like the worker qua machine tender, will be afforded only a limited interaction with the use, maintenance, and development of that knowledge. The development of going plant relationships in computer software will be discussed below to illustrate the essential features of this part of the theory.

### Establishing the going plant in computer software

Prior to the late 1970s, computer software was largely considered a non-product—i.e., not a distinct, salable good. For the large hardware vendors like IBM, who effectively controlled the computer industry, software was a marketing tool, a feature of the hardware which could make the latter more attractive (Haigh 2002; Campbell-Kelly 2003, 98; Campbell-Kelly and Garcia-Swartz 2009). However, these vendors generally lacked the capabilities to fully support their hardware with the software solutions each individual user would need (Dorn 2003). Under these conditions, user groups for different hardware platforms were common.[2] To give a case in point, IBM sales manager R. Blair Smith proposed in 1952 the association of IBM hardware users and IBM itself which would eventually become the SHARE user group.[3]

SHARE had two essential functions: first, to reduce redundant programming efforts among the users of IBM machines by facilitating free exchange of software between users of compatible hardware installations. Second, the user group acted as a technical intermediary between hardware users and IBM itself (Armer 1956; Akera 2007; Campbell-Kelly 2003). In this manner, SHARE "represented a viable organization, a going concern, around which computing specialists could assemble a broad range of new expertise" (Akera 2001, 716–717) in the management of the joint stock of knowledge of computer software.

The nature of SHARE suggests that these concerns differed from the going plant described above. A statement adopted February 1956 is indicative:

> The principal obligation of a member is to have a cooperative spirit. It is expected that each member approach each discussion with an open mind, and, having respect for the competence of other members, be willing to accept the opinions of others more frequently than he insists on his own.
>
> (quoted in Akera 2001, 719)

Likewise, though it is clear that both the users and IBM had a business interest in the software developed by the vendor as well as by users, the resulting software artifacts, embodied in both machine-readable *object* code and human-readable *source* code, were freely distributed without assertion of property rights.

The industry, however, gradually moved away from this early open-source model of software development, especially after IBM's pivotal 'unbundling'—that is, pricing software separate from hardware—in 1970 (see Grad 2002; Humphrey 2002). In the decade that followed, independent software vendors (ISVs) and the large hardware manufacturers would gradually develop what became, by the early 1980s, a full-fledged software products market. These products included large-scale enterprise software as well as mass-market 'shrink wrapped' products such as the VisiCalc spreadsheet software and the WordStar word processor (Campbell-Kelly 2003). Along with this market came the proprietary software conception of control—a novel form of inter- and intra-firm governance mechanism dealing with software as a salable technology.

These new relationships in effect organized and codified going plant structures engrossing software technologies as distinct from hardware. As indicated above, the development of a going plant capable of sustaining itself with profitable transactions through time requires that relationships to the enclosed knowledge be defined so as to limit access on the user side of the concern. This was accomplished among the ISVs by limiting the distribution of their products to only the object code of the software, which cannot be read and understood by humans without substantial efforts to reverse engineer the code into source code. Prior to the extension of copyright to software (see below), the legal mechanisms of trade secrecy and non-disclosure clauses further ensured that access remained limited. The major hardware vendors eventually followed suit. For instance, IBM announced in 1983 its 'object code only' (OCO) policy by which, over the next decade, most of its software would be distributed without the source code that had traditionally accompanied the object code (Goetz and Schneider 1988; Campbell-Kelly 2003; Campbell-Kelly and Garcia-Swartz 2009).

### Conflict within the nascent software going plant under the proprietary model

In the absence of source code, users of the software were made dependent on the software vendors for access to the industrial knowledge embodied in the object code. The discretion of the software user was thus relegated to purchasing decisions, with any additional technical interactions between producers and users being managed through the former's quality assurance and customer support capabilities for customization, trouble-shooting, upgrades, and user training (see Goetz and Schneider 1988 and Campbell-Kelly 2003, 6–8). In some cases, where the ability of the software vendor to maintain the software through time was in question, escrows were established ensuring the source code would be delivered to the user on, for instance, the vendor's bankruptcy (Maguire 1986; Mezrich 2001).

The reactions of various parties to this shift in the relationships concerned with the maintenance, use, and augmentation of the joint stock of knowledge embodied in computer software indicates key characteristics of the going plant within the modern business enterprise. Echoing what might have been the sentiments of the artisan-turned-machine-tender, Richard Stallman,[4] then a programmer at MIT's Artificial Intelligence Labs, described his first encounter with non-disclosure agreements as an apostasy from the open sharing norms of 'hacker culture' (Williams 2002, 6–7). "It immediately taught me" Stallman reflected, "that nondisclosure agreements have victims.... In this case I was the victim. My lab and I were victims" (11).

SHARE, along with the Guide user group and the Association of Data Processing Service Organizations (ADAPSO), protested IBM's OCO policy, arguing that it would hinder the maintenance of existing software and the development of new software. Though most users did not modify IBM's software, those that did make modifications found that without the source code, not only were improvements and customizations of IBM's software more onerous and potentially impractical, but finding the origin of problems in the code, whether IBM's or a third party's, was substantially more difficult. This was especially true among the users of IBM's VM operating systems (Gillin 1984; Gallant 1985a, 1985b).

A few months after the announcement of the OCO policy, IBM released the first OCO version of VM, VM/PC. VM/PC had a number of problems, including poor performance and incorrect or missing or incompatible functions. Without source [code], the users were unable to correct or compensate for these problems, so nobody was surprised when VM/PC fell flat.

(Varian 1991, 95)

In a *Computerworld* debate piece former ADAPSO president Martin Goetz argued that the OCO policy restricted innovation to within the framework IBM designed, necessarily limiting third-party developers where IBM had not anticipated the needs of their users (Goetz and Schneider 1988). IBM's response, by Peter Schneider, included commitments to work with developers in their established interface framework, but ultimately resolved to the business concerns of the company: "What IBM is not willing to do is turn over the results of its significant development investment to others to use for whatever purposes they may wish" (66).

The establishment of the software going plant under the proprietary model involved other constraints on the user as well. In particular, firms have been able to design and issue updates strategically in the interests of profitable transactions in ways that are clearly contrary to the interests of users:

> New software is often carefully calculated to reduce the value to consumers of the previous version. This is achieved by making programs upwardly compatible only; in other words, the new versions can read all the files of the old versions, but not the other way round.
>
> ("Idea" 2009; see also Forge 2006; Katz and Shapiro 1998)

Under this particular form of planned obsolescence users must continually choose between upgrading, and thereby devaluing existing components in their systems, or being left behind as other users upgrade (Katz and Shapiro 1998). This, again, is a manifestation of the conflict inherent in the structure of the going plant. Where users and producers of software are not separated by the rights and duties of property in the underlying technology, as for instance in open source software projects, the same results—lock-in and planned obsolescence—are typically absent (see Nyman *et al.* 2011).

Finally, the "state must ratify, help create, or at the very least, not oppose" new market governance norms (Fligstein 1996, 658; see also Lee and Jo 2011 on the role of the capitalist state in the social provisioning process). This involvement can take various forms, but often results in altered or entirely novel forms of property (see Commons [1924] 1968). For the proprietary software model, sanctioning came with the explicit extension of copyright protection of the literal and non-literal elements of code in 1980.[5] Much like a novel, play, or song, the written expression of a programmer, as well as certain, more abstract elements (for instance, the structure of the program) were protected from unauthorized copying.

As the next section will show, however, the proprietary model was found to lack the stability that firms in the industry desired. The going plant had been established and legally sanctioned by Congress; a salable product, a distinguishable artifact of the joint stock of knowledge, now existed as a business interest. Still, business control of the wider, interconnected (and rapidly changing) industrial system of computer software remained highly contentious. Not surprisingly then, the market governance norms and legal framework required refinement. Before proceeding with this history, however, it is necessary to understand that other essential component of the business enterprise, the going business.

## The going business

From an historical perspective the modern business enterprise can be understood generally as an evolution toward more sophisticated, though not necessarily more progressive or efficient, organization and greater degrees of specialization. Of chief analytical import in this regard is the separation of the industrial and pecuniary employments. The former are those discussed in the previous section, tasked most directly with the material processes of provisioning. The latter, in contrast, are concerned with the observation, creation, and manipulation of pecuniary values in property rights. Insofar as these pecuniary employments constitute their own self-perpetuating organization within the business enterprise, with concomitant norms governing them and their relation to the going plant, they can be taken together as the going business (Veblen 1901; Commons [1934] 1961, [1924] 1968; Lee 2013).

The development of a going business distinct from the going plant marks a second degree of separation between the means of the community's social provisioning and the ends toward which that provisioning process is directed through the business enterprise. Because the traffic of the industrial system is directed predominantly in terms of institutions of property, those employments whose expertise and concern most directly touch property rights will dominate the activities of the business enterprise. The industrial interests of the going plant become subordinate, and the business enterprise will be concerned chiefly with the pecuniary value of business access to the interconnected system of going plants.

Just as the relationships of the going plant involve a (re)structuring of production and consumption to facilitate stable, profitable transactions, the business enterprise as comprised of both going plant and going business requires additional efforts at stable relationships to remain a going concern as a whole. These means of generating earnings, afforded by the going business' distinct control over the industrial system, are capitalized in a distinct form of property, which Veblen referred to as intangible assets (see also Commons [1934] 1961, [1924] 1968); however, Hamilton's (1943) term, 'market equities,' cuts to their essence: capitalized exclusive rights of access to the market, which in turn is predicated on exclusive rights of access to the joint stock of knowledge (see also Rutherford 2010).

Advertising provides a clear illustration of going business behavior in this regard. As Veblen observed, the goal of these activities is in essence to create a "competitive disturbance of trade" which would "divert purchases, etc., from one channel to another" (1904, 55–57). To this view of advertising can be added Galbraith's emphasis on the exigency of such methods to the business enterprise as a going concern. Specifically, Galbraith (1967) used the term 'demand management' to denote the role of marketing in ensuring adequate demand for the firm's long-term investment plans. Such expenditures come to be part of the means by which the business enterprise, and the capitalist system as a whole, ensures its own survival and growth. Likewise, from the perspective of market competition, Gardiner Means recognized such behavior as a form of competition which is not "easily matched by strategic counter-moves" and that do not "directly threaten the corporation's financial integrity" (Lee 1998, 57; see Gagnon 2013 for a similar analysis of the pharmaceutical industry; and Lee 2012a on competition and the going enterprise).

As noted, through this behavior the interests of the business enterprise are further divorced from those of the community. "The surreal is a more valuable asset than the real, and the intangibility of information activities offers positive advantages in terms of flexibility of representation" (Macdonald 2004, 153). Macdonald here, however, is not speaking of advertising. Rather he is speaking of the strategic value of patents. Hence, returning presently to the US software industry, similar maneuvering will be shown in the businesses involved therein, especially as it regards those intellectual property rights established to stabilize going plant relations.

### Stabilizing going enterprise relationships in interoperable technologies

Owing, if nothing else, to the rapidly changing and interconnected nature of the technologies covered in the software industry, it was soon realized that the proprietary model was not stable from a business perspective. Changes were required in the governing mechanisms within and between firms to create viable markets in which to operate (Fligstein 2001). In some instances, for example a dispute between IBM and Fujitsu in the 1980s, this resulted in a reversal of the object-code-only component of the model (see Wilder 1987; Stork 1988). More broadly, however, these new mechanisms were developed through private standards consortia (see Cargill 1997; Cargill and Succi 1998; Schoechle 2009) and what Band and Katoh (1995) call the interoperability debates. These debates reflected a divergence in business strategies among business enterprises in the industry. On one side stood the 'ultraprotectionists' (Band and Katoh 1995): dominant firms controlling de facto industry standards and operating on the proprietary model described above (including IBM, Apple, and Lotus). On the other side were the 'open systems' firms. These firms, with Sun Microsystems in many ways the flag bearer (Hall and Barry 1991), adopted non-proprietary standards and contributed to the development of new standards without the intention of profiting directly from the standards as proprietary information (for example, through licensing revenues). Rather, these companies would license technologies generously to encourage adoption (Garud and Kumaraswamy 1993). Hence, their profitability, in turn, stemmed not from the perquisites of controlling de facto standards—for example, the ability to create planned obsolescence as discussed above, or to suppress or outstrip competitors' innovations (see, for instance, Band and Katoh 1995, 21–24 on IBM). Instead, open systems firms relied on their strategic contributions to the private standards-setting process, and on their reputation as experts in the resulting standards to sell their own implementations of those standards (Band and Katoh 1995; Cargill 1997).

Thus, a fundamental divergence in governing norms developed in the 1980s and 1990s, and this fell most significantly on the question of the scope of copyright protection in interface specifications. Proprietary firms believed that such protection should be extensive, allowing firms significant control over both their own technologies and the conditions under which new, connecting, and potentially competing technologies could be developed and implemented. That is, these firms sought protection of both the relationships of their own going plants as well as the market equities resulting from potential technological connections thereto. Open systems firms, on the other hand, advocated for a more limited scope of copyright protection, allowing for interoperability between technologies without compromising the system of intellectual property which afforded stability of the enterprise's own going plant.

Through a series of cases heard principally in the US Courts of Appeal, and involving numerous *amicus* briefs contributed by both sides of the industry split, various legal doctrines were developed to settle these debates (Band and Katoh 1995, 2011). Among these, the doctrines of merger and *scènes à fair* were borrowed from long-standing precedent in copyright law to ensure that software would be protected as per Congress' 1980 legislation, but would not be so broad as to prevent the development of interoperable technologies. In brief, the merger doctrine had been developed previously to hold that "where the use of an idea requires the copying of the work itself, such copying will not constitute infringement" (Leaffer 2005, 85). Similarly, *scènes à fair* ruled out copyright protection for certain aspects of a work which are dictated by external circumstances such as genre-defining plot elements in literature, and the interface specifications of connecting technologies in software.

*Computer Associates* v. *Altai* (1992) began this precedent of limiting copyright protection where the expression of software was necessary for interoperability with existing technologies. At issue was whether a software component developed by Altai to allow its applications to function across different IBM operating systems violated Computer Associate's copyright in a similar program. Reversing the district court's finding of infringement, the Second Circuit ruled that protection would not be afforded where the 'freedom of choice' of the software programmer was

> circumscribed by extrinsic considerations such as (1) mechanical specifications of the computer on which a particular program is intended to run; (2) compatibility requirements of other programs with which a program is designed to operate in conjunction; (3) computer manufacturers' design standards; (4) demands of the industry being serviced; and (5) widely accepted programming practices within the computer industry.
>
> (*Computer Associates* 1992, 709–710)

The court thus limited the scope of copyright in software. The effect, in particular, was to hold that "interface specifications were not protected expression" (Band and Katoh 1995, 126).

In doing so, the courts effectively destroyed some degree of firms' differential advantages on the going business side of the enterprise. However, it is evident just the same that the limitations of copyright protection so developed offered a degree of enterprise stability and a clear demarcation of going plant relationships in an environment of rapidly changing and highly interconnected technologies.[6] These developments thus illustrate both the hierarchical employment relationships within the business enterprise as well as the inherent conflicts of valuation within these hierarchies. Conflict then creates the potential for instability, which, in the interests of the business enterprise as a going concern, must be tamed. The development of technological processes (object-code only, private standards consortia) and legislation and court precedent (copyright, merger doctrine, scènes à fair) constitute only some of the more salient efforts to effect the governing norms necessary to stabilize relations both within and between business enterprises operating in the realm of computer software.

## Conclusion

The analysis presented above suggests that the business enterprise is comprised of overlapping and hierarchically organized groups which can be summarized as the going business and the going plant. The former consists of the technological and legal relationships which organize productive and consumptive activities such that a profitable transaction can occur at their interface. The latter consists of those relationships which deal, not directly with the technological relationships of the going plant, but with the valuation of those relationships and access to 'the market' from the business perspective. Since this hierarchy involves different modes of valuation[7]—the consumer's interest, for instance, versus the marketing director's—the business enterprise is inherently prone to conflict. These conflicts then require mitigation or suppression if the business enterprise is to remain a going concern.

Returning to Frederic Lee's social surplus approach, the above analysis illuminates the complexity of the structures that define, empower, and ultimately perpetuate the dominant classes in capitalist economies. As Lee keenly elaborated, prices, wages, profits, and the like do not organize economic activity; rather, they emerge as artifacts of the processes which create, and apportion rights of access to, the social surplus (Lee 2013). Likewise, the above analysis demonstrates that the complex technological and legal relationships that define the many forms of property, occupation, and product are chiefly the result of the decisions of the dominant classes in constructing and directing business enterprises.

Finally, an important conclusion can be drawn from this analysis. Contrary to theories of the firm in the neoclassical tradition, the size and structure of a business enterprise is not here understood as 'efficient' in the neoclassical contemplation of the term, as that concept is rejected by heterodox economics. Rather, size and structure are better characterized as the result of a gerrymandering process in the interests of the enterprise as a going concern. The structures and agency involved therein, as with pricing and other business activities, emerge through the social provisioning process, by which control over, and access to, the surplus are dictated by the ruling classes. Ultimately, the conflict innate to these processes stems from the inherent contradictions of an institutional structure—that is, capitalism—which *affords* access to the social provisioning process by means which explicitly grant the right to *prevent* access to the social knowledge requisite to carrying that process forward.

This is to say that property relations, as comprising relations of control, dependence, privilege, and oppression, must be understood as mutually constructed and constructive of our social, political, and economic world (Henry 2015). More than this, heterodox economists must be diligent in identifying these same prejudicial relations beyond the traditionally identified legal relations of property—in technological processes, occupational schema, and many other realms—as well as their consequences for the community as a going concern. In this manner the theories of the business enterprise and of social agency more generally, of social conflict and ultimately social control, can be advanced, thanks in no small part to the eminent work of Frederic Lee.

## Acknowledgments

An earlier draft of this paper was presented at a session of the Union for Radical Political Economics Annual Conference in Philadelphia, PA, January 2014. The author wishes to thank the discussant and audience there for helpful comments, as well as to the editors of this volume and Mitch Green for comments on subsequent drafts.

## Notes

1 The definition originates with Gruchy (1987, 21), although it might be taken today as the more widely accepted among heterodox economics (Dugger 1996; Lee 2009; Lee and Jo 2011).
2 Similar relationships between for-profit firms can be found elsewhere. For instance, Fisk (2009, 89–90, 122) documents engineering schools, professional societies, and periodicals developed in the nineteenth century purposed with the dissemination of technological knowledge.
3 Although usually written in all capital letters, SHARE is not in fact an acronym. See Akera (2007, ch. 7) for a more detailed history than is necessary here.
4 Stallman would go on to found the Free Software Foundation and create the GNU General Public License, both of which have been central to the free/libre open source software movement (Williams 2002).
5 See Band and Katoh (1995) and Campbell-Kelly (2003) on the decision to cover software under copyright as opposed to other forms of protection.
6 By no means, however, did this settle the issues of intellectual property rights in these technologies. Indeed, perhaps ironically, at the very time the scope of copyright was being settled, the industry was moving toward patent protection of many of its technological developments. The implications of this trend, however, cannot be explored in the present chapter.
7 As noted earlier, this method of identifying conflicting schemes of valuation is directed at dichotomizing capitalist institutions, which is methodologically distinct from the productive-unproductive labor dualism of Classical Political Economy (Todorova

2014). Hence the present analysis does not hold that the occupations of the going business do not create values (see Lee and Jo 2011). Rather, it identifies the conflict in the aims of the distinct groups, which in turn explains in part efforts to develop stabilizing governance mechanisms.

## References

Akera, A. 2001. "Voluntarism and the Fruits of Collaboration: The IBM User Group, SHARE." *Technology and Culture* 42 (4): 710–736.

Akera, A. 2007. *Calculating a Natural World: Scientists, Engineers, and Computers during the Rise of U.S. Cold War Research*. Cambridge, MA: MIT Press.

Armer, P. 1956. "SHARE—A Eulogy to Cooperative Effort." Paper presented at Electronic Business Systems Conference, San Francisco, November 8. Accessed December 2, 2014. www.dtic.mil/dtic/tr/fulltext/u2/605110.pdf.

Ayres, C. E. 1967. "Ideological Responsibility." *Journal of Economic Issues* 1 (1/2): 3–11.

Band, J. and M. Katoh. 1995. *Interfaces on Trial: Intellectual Property and Interoperability in the Global Software Industry*. Boulder, CO: Westview Press.

Band, J. and M. Katoh. 2011. *Interfaces on Trial 2.0*. Cambridge, MA: MIT Press.

Braverman, H. [1974] 1998. *Labor and Monopoly Capital: The Degradation of Work in the Twentieth Century*. 25th Anniversary Edition. New York: Monthly Review Press.

Campbell-Kelly, M. 2003. *From Airline Reservations to Sonic the Hedgehog: A History of the Software Industry*. Cambridge, MA: MIT Press.

Campbell-Kelly, M. and D. D. Garcia-Swartz. 2009. "Pragmatism, Not Ideology: Historical Perspectives on IBM's Adoption of Open-Source Software." *Information Economics and Policy* 21: 229–244.

Cargill, C. F. 1997. *Open Systems Standardization: A Business Approach*. Upper Saddle River, NJ: Prentice Hall.

Cargill, C. F. and Giancarlo Succi. 1998. "Editorial." *StandardView* 6 (2): 63–68.

Commons, J. R. 1919. *Industrial Goodwill*. New York: McGraw Hill.

Commons, J. R. [1934] 1961. *Institutional Economics: Its Place in Political Economy*. Madison: University of Wisconsin Press.

Commons, J. R. [1924] 1968. *The Legal Foundations of Capitalism*. Madison: University of Wisconsin Press.

*Computer Associates Intern. Inc.* v. *Altai, Inc. 982 F. 2d 693* (Court of Appeals, 2nd Circuit 1992).

Dean, E. 2013. "Toward a Heterodox Theory of the Business Enterprise: The Going Concern Model and the US Computer Industry." PhD diss., University of Missouri–Kansas City.

Dewey, J. 1922. *Human Nature and Conduct: An Introduction to Social Psychology*. Mineola, NY: Dover.

Dorn, P. H. 2003. "User Groups." In *Encyclopedia of Computer Science*, 4th ed., edited by A. Ralston, E. D. Reilly, and D. Hemmindinger, 1819–1821. New York: John Wiley and Sons.

Dugger, W. M. 1996. "Redefining Economics: From Market Allocation to Social Provisioning." In *Political Economy for the 21st Century: Contemporary Views on the Trends of Economics*, edited by C. J. Whalen, 31–43. Armonk, NY: M. E. Sharpe.

Fisk, C. L. 2009. *Working Knowledge: Employee Innovation and the Rise of Corporate Intellectual Property: 1800–1930*. Chapel Hill: University of North Carolina Press.

Fligstein, N. 1996. "Markets as Politics: A Political–Cultural Approach to Market Institutions." *American Sociological Review* 61 (4): 656–673.

Fligstein, N. 2001. *The Architecture of Markets: An Economic Sociology of Twenty-First-Century Capitalist Societies*. Princeton, NJ: Princeton University Press.

Forge, S. 2006. "The Rain Forest and the Rock Garden: The Economic Impacts of Open Source Software." *Info: The Journal of Policy, Regulation and Strategy for Telecommunications, Information and Media* 8 (3): 12–31.

Gagnon, M.-A. 2007. "Capital, Power and Knowledge According to Thorstein Veblen: Reinterpreting the Knowledge-Based Economy." *Journal of Economic Issues* 41 (2): 593–600.

Gagnon, M.-A. 2013. "Corruption of Pharmaceutical Markets: Addressing the Misalignment of Financial Incentives and Public Health." *The Journal of Law, Medicine & Ethics* 41 (3): 571–580.

Galbraith, J. K. 1967. *The New Industrial State*. Boston: Houghton Mifflin.

Gallant, J. 1985a. "IBM Code Rules Stir User Wrath." *Computerworld*, March 4.

Gallant, J. 1985b. "IBM Policy Draws Fire; Users Say Source Code Rules Hamper Change." *Computerworld*, March 18.

Garud, R. and A. Kumaraswamy. 1993. "Changing Competitive Dynamics in Network Industries: An Exploration of Sun Microsystems' Open Systems Strategy." *Strategic Management Journal* 14 (5): 351–369.

Gillin, P. 1984. "IBM's Object Code Policy Still Irking Users." *Computerworld*, May 14.

Goetz, M. and P. Schneider. 1988. "Object-Code Only: Is IBM Playing Fair?" *Computerworld*, 22 (6): 55.

Grad, B. 2002. "A Personal Recollection: IBM's Unbundling of Software and Services." *IEEE Annals of the History of Computing* 24 (1): 64–71.

De Gregori, T. R. 1977. "Technology and Ceremonial Behavior: Aspects of Institutionalism." *Journal of Economic Issues* 11 (4): 861–870.

De Gregori, T. R. 1987. "Resources Are Not; They Become: An Institutional Theory." *Journal of Economic Issues* 21 (3): 1241–1263.

Gruchy, A. 1987. *The Reconstruction of Economics: An Analysis of the Fundamentals of Institutional Economics*. New York: Greenwood Press.

Haigh, T. 2002. "Software in the 1960s as Concept, Service, and Product." *IEEE Annals of the History of Computing* 24 (1): 5–13.

Hall, M. and J. Barry. 1991. *Sunburst: The Ascent of Sun Microsystems*. Chicago: Contemporary Books.

Hamilton, W. 1943. "Property Rights in the Market." *Journal of Legal and Political Sociology* 1 (3–4): 10–33.

Henry, J. F. 2015. "Property and the Limits to Democracy." In *Marx, Veblen, and the Foundations of Heterodox Economics: Essays in Honor of John F. Henry*, edited by T.-H. Jo and F. S. Lee. London: Routledge.

Hobson, J. A. 1906. *The Evolution of Modern Capitalism: A Study of Machine Production*. London: Walter Scott.

Humphrey, W. S. 2002. "Software Unbundling: A Personal Perspective." *IEEE Annals of the History of Computing* 24 (1): 59–63.

"Idea: Planned Obsolescence." 2009. *The Economist*, March 23. Accessed December 2, 2014. www.economist.com/node/13354332.

Katz, M. L. and C. Shapiro. 1998. "Antitrust in Software Markets." In *Competition, Innovation and the Microsoft Monopoly: Antitrust in the Digital Marketplace*, edited by J. Eisenach and T. M. Lenard, 29–81. Norwell, MA: Kluwer Academic Publishers.

Leaffer, M. 2005. *Understanding Copyright Law*. 4th ed. Newark, NJ: Lexis Nexis.

Lee, F. S. 1998. *Post Keynesian Price Theory*. New York: Cambridge University Press.

Lee, F. S. 2002. "Theory Creation and the Methodological Foundation of Post Keynesian Economics." *Cambridge Journal of Economics* 26 (6): 789–804.

Lee, F. S. 2009. *A History of Heterodox Economics: Challenging the Mainstream in the Twentieth Century*. New York: Routledge.

Lee, F. S. 2012a. "Competition, Going Enterprise, and Economic Activity." In *Alternative Theories of Competition: Challenges to the Orthodoxy*, edited by J. K. Moudud, C. Bina, and P. L. Mason, 160–173. New York: Routledge.

Lee, F. S. 2012b. "Heterodox Surplus Approach: Production, Prices, and Value Theory." *Bulletin of Political Economy* 6 (2): 65–105.

Lee, F. S. 2013. "Post-Keynesian Price Theory: From Pricing to Market Governance to the Economy as a Whole." In *The Oxford Handbook of Post-Keynesian Economics*, vol. 1, edited by G. C. Harcourt and P. Kriesler, 467–484. Oxford: Oxford University Press.

Lee, F. S. and T.-H. Jo. 2011. "Social Surplus Approach and Heterodox Economics." *Journal of Economic Issues* 45 (4): 857–876.

Macdonald, S. 2004. "When Means Become Ends: Considering the Impact of Patent Strategy on Innovation." *Information Economics and Policy* 16 (1): 135–158.

Maguire, J. N. 1986. "Oral History of John Norris Maguire." Accessed December 2, 2014. http://archive.computerhistory.org/resources/text/Oral_History/Maguire_John/Maguire_John_1.oral_history.1986.102658223.pdf.

Marglin, S. A. 1996. "What Do Bosses Do? The Origins and Functions of Hierarchy in Capitalist Production." In *Radical Political Economy: Explorations in Alternative Economic Analysis*, edited by V. D. Lippit, 60–112. Armonk, NY: M. E. Sharpe.

Marx, K. and F. Engels. 1848. *Manifesto of the Communist Party*. Accessed December 2, 2014. www.marxists.org/archive/marx/works/1848/communist-manifesto.

Mezrich, J. L. 2001. "Source Code Escrow: An Exercise in Futility." *Marquette Intellectual Property Law Review* 5: 117.

Mills, C. W. 1951. *White Collar: The American Middle Classes*. New York: Oxford University Press.

Nyman, L., T. Mikkonen, J. Lindman, and M. Fougere. 2011. "Forking: The Invisible Hand of Sustainability in Open Source Software." *Proceedings of SOS 2011: Toward Sustainable Open Source*: 1–6.

Rutherford, M. 2010. "The Judicial Control of Business: Walton Hamilton, Antitrust, and Chicago." *Seattle University Law Review* 34: 1385.

Samuels, W. J. 1977. "Technology Vis-à-Vis Institutions in the JEI: A Suggested Interpretation." *Journal of Economic Issues* 11 (4): 871–895.

Schoechle, T. 2009. *Standardization and Digital Enclosure: The Privatization of Standards, Knowledge, and Policy in the Age of Global Information Technology*. Hershey, PA: Information Science Reference.

Stork, A. 1988. "The Use of Arbitration in Copyright Disputes: IBM v. Fujitsu." *High Technology Law Journal* 3: 241.

Sturgeon, J. I. 2009. "The Social Fabric Matrix, the Principles of Institutional Adjustment, and Individual Action." In *Institutional Analysis and Praxis*, edited by T. Natarajan, S. Fullwiler, and W. Elsner, 39–54. New York: Springer.

Todorova, Z. 2014. "Consumption as a Social Process within Social Provisioning and Capitalism: Implications for Heterodox Economics." Accessed December 2, 2014. http://papers.ssrn.com/sol3/papers.cfm?abstract_id=2355996.

Tool, M. R. 1979. *The Discretionary Economy: A Normative Theory of Political Economy*. Santa Monica: Goodyear Publishing.

Varian, M. 1991. "VM and the VM Community: Past, Present, and Future." Accessed December 2, 2014. www.cs.tufts.edu/~nr/cs257/archive/melinda-varian/neuvm.pdf.

Veblen, T. 1901. "Industrial and Pecuniary Employments." *Publications of the American Economic Association, 3rd Series* 2 (1): 190–235.

Veblen, T. 1904. *The Theory of Business Enterprise*. Clifton, NJ: Augustus M. Kelley.

Veblen, T. 1908. "On the Nature of Capital." *Quarterly Journal of Economics* 22 (4): 517–542.

Veblen, T. 1914. *The Instinct of Workmanship and the State of the Industrial Arts*. New York: Macmillan.

Wilder, C. 1987. "Fujitsu Given Key to IBM's Software Vault." *Computerworld* 21 (38): 1.

Williams, S. 2002. *Free as in Freedom: Richard Stallman's Crusade for Free Software*. Cambridge, MA: O'Reilly.

Zimmerman, E. 1972. *World Resources and Industries*, 3rd ed., edited by W. N. Peach and J. A. Constantin. New York: Joanna Cotler Books.

# 10 Analysing actually-existing markets

*Lynne Chester*

## Introduction

In the final years of this century's first decade, global financial markets went into free-fall leading to the severest economic crisis since the Great Depression. Stern's (2007) highly influential *The Economics of Climate Change* drew the world's attention to the inadequacy of 'unfettered' markets to address the economic consequences of climate change from capitalism's insatiable appetite for fossil fuels and the attendant carbon emissions. The United Nations' Food and Agricultural Organization (FAO 2011) has reported on the factors driving volatile food commodity market prices since 2003 and the implications for adequately feeding billions of people around the world. Energy prices, particularly for households, have escalated rapidly following the global liberalization of electricity markets leading to embedded energy impoverishment (Chester and Morris 2012).

These are four examples of ostensible market failure. Nevertheless, the market is still considered by mainstream economists, policymakers, and the media as being the far superior coordinating mechanism for capitalist economies. The "almost biblical status" of free market fundamentalism remains sacrosanct (Giroux 2009). Markets continue as the preferred policy solution for all economic and social problems. Debate continues about the regulation of global financial markets to prevent another crisis. Further trade liberalization and increased competition is advocated to avoid further substantive increases in food and energy prices. New markets have been created for renewable energy sources and carbon trading as the dominant policy responses to arrest the growth in carbon and other greenhouse gas emissions. This extension or "spatial spread" of markets has been "accompanied by their deepening or intensification, as more and more social spheres and an increasing range of 'necessaries of life' ... become commodified" (Streeck 2011, 155). The process of marketization denotes contemporary capitalism both in terms of the extension of market mechanisms and an intensification of commodification in established market settings such as "the ongoing reorganization of private lives, including the commercialization of household services" (155).

Public policies have become embedded with mechanisms based on economic concepts derived from the logic of perfectly competitive markets. As a consequence there has been a radical transformation of the provision of goods and services which have been the long-standing domain of the state and determine—to a very significant measure—the health, standard of living, and social inclusion of the population. These goods and services are essential to society's well-being such as education, health, public housing, electricity, water, and services for the disabled, aged, and unemployed. Essential goods and services provide a base or minimum level of provision to individuals, families, and households for protection "from misfortune and the random blows of fate by providing the most basic rights and levels of collective security and protection" (Giroux 2009). Consequently, essential goods and services are a critical element of the social provisioning process, that is,

> providing for the material means of life resulting in economic activities that generate the flow of goods and services necessary to meet the biological and socially created needs of individuals and to maintain what Veblen called the *collective life process.*
>
> (Todorova 2013, 1184, original emphasis)

Social provisioning occurs through market exchange and non-market activities (Dugger 1996).

Direct provision by the state of essential goods and services has been supplanted by, for example, the contracting out of services delivered to the unemployed through competitive tendering arrangements with private sector providers. Higher education fees, set at levels equivalent to the costs of providing higher education places, have been introduced concomitant with the reduction of state funding to institutions and the introduction of student loans. Other examples include fees being imposed for time spent in immigration detention centers, the charging of market rents to public housing tenants, the provision of infrastructure through commercial contracts with the private sector, and the framing of universal health insurance as a solution to market failure.

The rationale for market-based public policies has been presented in terms of the need for greater economic efficiency. Consequently contemporary public policies are almost exclusively framed in the abstract concepts of competition, efficiency, supply and demand, or the need to address market failures. This is the lexicon of neoclassical economics which portrays the market as a normative ideal based on a set of abstract assumptions and a market is conceived "as a space for carrying out identical transactions which bear on one well-defined product and lead to the determination of one price" (Coriat and Weinstein 2005, 2).

In addition to the widespread adoption of market-based policy instruments transforming state provisioning of goods and services essential to well-being, public sector assets have been privatized and complex new regulatory regimes have been instituted. The latter include: economy-wide regulation-*of*-competition which controls and prescribes directly the market behavior of individual firms to prevent market concentration through, for example, the reviewing of proposed mergers or cross-ownership; sector-specific regulation-*for*-competition which brings much more influence to bear on market participants and these regulatory agencies are "involved in market design and market control to an unprecedented degree" (Jordana and Levi-Faur 2004, 6); and, the regulation of price determination for monopolies such as energy transmission and distribution networks. These regulatory regimes may also include rules for the provision of consumer information, complaint handling mechanisms, dispute resolution procedures, enforcement mechanisms such as the judicial system, standards for public health, and technical standards for safety and reliability. In many respects these regulatory regimes are analogous to Lee's (2013a) concept of managed competition, that is, "a form of market governance that regulates competition ... shorn of its destructive potential" (169).[1]

Regulatory regimes are institutional 'supports' which reinforce that markets are not—as is portrayed by mainstream economics—devoid of context, operating as isolated automatons. As Polanyi (1968) observed, the economy is embedded in economic and non-economic institutions. Not only are markets supported by a range of these institutions, each market intersects with multiple other markets which blurs the boundaries of any market. "Markets are embedded in each other" (Aspers 2011, 126). Thus, the structure, functioning, and outcomes of a market, can only be revealed by considering the economic and social context in which it is embedded despite its own logic and rules.

Energy provides an example of the complex web of interdependencies and linkages between markets. For example, the electricity sector market is structured around four core markets: generation, transmission, distribution, and retail—neither market can function without each other which means that they operate in a co-constitutive manner. In addition, the operation of the generation market also depends on the functioning of markets for fossil and renewable energy fuels; and the functioning of the electricity retail market not only depends on its co-constituent electricity sector markets but is strongly influenced by the organization and operation of, for example, markets for gas and other fuel sources, meters, solar panels, hot water systems, swimming pools, heating and cooling systems, lighting, household appliances, and energy efficiency products and services.

Thus, markets are very interdependent and relate in a quite complex manner. As contended by Nelson (2011, 1) "the conception that market organisation is the best mode of economic governance is much simpler and more coherent than the complex and variegated way that economic activity is actually governed." These interrelationships also pose questions about the cumulative impact of market outcomes and the potential flow-on consequences, like a row of falling dominoes, if one particular market experiences significant disruption.

Theorizing about markets has been concerned with "the *internal* dynamics of a putative market" (Harvey 2010, 4, original emphasis) with an imbalance of attention on consumption. Yet actually-existing markets—through their interrelationships and interdependencies—determine not only consumption but also production and distribution of immeasurable commodities; actually-existing markets are also inextricably linked with markets for labor and finance.

Returning to the example of energy and more specifically the provision of electricity, production decisions are made in the generation market whereas distribution (intermediate consumption) outcomes occur in the transmission and distribution markets, and final end-use consumption is the outcome of the retail market. All four electricity sector markets are tied to finance markets through debt and borrowings, and—for generation and retail markets—with electricity derivatives. Engineers, electrical linesmen, turbine operators, mechanical maintenance technicians, systems operators, ICT (information and communication technology) specialists, meter installers, meter readers, financial traders, accountants, sales and marketing staff, are a few examples of the labor required within the electricity sector.

Given these dimensions of actually-existing markets, abstract terms, or the notions of identical transactions, one homogenous product and a single price cannot explain the functioning and outcomes of markets which characterize contemporary capitalism. Markets are not purely about relationships between inanimate objects, between goods and services, which is the strong impression evoked by any mainstream economics text or government policy statement. Nor are markets simply the intersection of demand and supply functions. Markets are highly interdependent, coordinate production, distribution and consumption decisions, and involve people and their preferences (influenced by opinions, values, and advertising). People's accessibility to, and participation in, a market will also be influenced by, *inter alia*, prices.

Accordingly, how can we understand the implications and consequences for society of marketization given that economists have, until recently, shown little interest in the "emergence and real constitution of markets" (Coriat and Weinstein 2005, 1)?

The discourse about markets has been overwhelmingly skewed towards the theoretical, "concerned more with analysing how people conceive of market systems than … with analysing the operation of those systems or the activities of market actors" (Carrier 1997, xiii). Actually-existing markets have attracted few analytical studies to determine the specific manifestation or representation of their structure, operation, participants, behaviors, rules, and/or price determination. Notable exceptions have been French strawberry and fish markets, financial and emission trading markets, Australian markets for essential goods and services, and the UK's markets for food, housing, water, telecommunications, public transport, financial services, and energy (Chester 2010, 2011; Garcia-Parpet 2007; Kirman and Vignes 1992; MacKenzie 2009; Public Services International Research Unit 2008). Similarly, 'operationalizing' the theoretical and conceptual into an analytical framework to conduct analyses of actually-existing markets has received limited attention.

This chapter seeks to address these lacunae and presents a methodological basis to conduct empirical analyses of markets which explain their structure, operation, interactions, and outcomes. Thus it "is concerned with delineating and explaining [some of] the constituent parts or sub-systems of the economy and their interdependencies" (Lee 2013b, 110). Although "organization of social provisioning is determined outside of markets ... the provisioning process itself will, in part, take place through capitalist markets" (108). Explaining the actual operation and outcomes of contemporary market provisioning and the impact on society's well-being can contribute to the development of policy options to ameliorate the adverse consequences and inequities of market provisioning and to change the social provisioning process. Empirical analysis of real-world markets aids the development of those options.

Following this introduction, the next section discusses differing conceptualizations of the market. The neoclassical conceptualization is examined because it is this lexicon which has become embedded in political rhetoric and reflected in public policies leading to radically different provisioning in essential goods and services markets during the hegemony of neoliberalism. Alternative conceptions from economic sociology and institutionalism are also examined. The chapter proceeds to review key theoretical contributions to our understanding of the organization and functioning of markets which encompass a set of propositions about different types of market in space and time, the role of property rights and contract law, the dimensions shaping the organization of exchange, and the embedded behaviors created by rules reflecting political decisions. To 'operationalize' these theoretical propositions, and thus enable concrete empirical analysis, the core essence of each proposition is distilled to reveal 12 distinctive properties of markets. These properties help us transcend from the abstract to the concrete by foreshadowing an analytical grid of questions to conduct empirical analyses. The list of properties forms a bridge between key abstract propositions and an analytical grid of questions to interrogate actually-existing markets.

## Conceptualizing the market

Since the 1970s policy debates have been framed around the role of the market vis-à-vis the state and the object of policy has become one of "efficient market design" (Galbraith 2009, 152). Government involvement has been portrayed as detrimental to efficient market operations as the ideology of neoliberalism gained ascendancy. Market discipline, competition, and commodification denote neoliberalism. Society's well-being is considered to be best achieved through private property rights, free markets, and free trade, and the role of the state is to create an institutional framework which promotes such practices. The market has primacy and virtually all economic and social problems are seen as having a market solution. Nation-states and local-states have progressively applied the neoliberalism doctrine of market solutions to a widening realm of activity.

The ideology of neoliberalism is underpinned by notions about the free market, market failure, market primacy, and interrelationships of market, state, and politics. A free market is avowed because it provides choice for a world of 'free,' independent individuals—anything restricting choice is morally bad—and choice entails competition which will generate innovation and efficiency. Market imperfections, or distortions, threaten the most efficient allocation of economic resources and lead to market failure requiring actions by the state to restore the primacy of the market, that is, the natural order of things. Finally, because of self-interested politicians and bureaucrats, the scope of the state's activities should be scaled back—through privatization and deregulation—and policy discretion eliminated (Carrier 1997; Chang 2002).

The views of neoclassical economics about the market, and its relationship with the state, are in close harmony with those of neoliberalism. Neoclassical economics presents the market as an abstract aggregate of individual choices and actions exemplified by the simple intersection of demand and supply curves, as "an allocating machine that solves the main problems of ... what to produce, how, and for whom" (Mantzavinos 2001, 162). This dominant paradigm of mainstream economics has been criticized for its increasing analytical abstraction and preoccupation with price determination resulting in the study of "a system that lives in the minds of economists but not on earth" (Coase 1992, 714). Nevertheless, neoclassical economics has successfully shaped

> the general understanding of what a 'market,' a 'market economy,' and even an 'economy' in general is, or should be ... and, thus, a *general theoretical and normative reference and benchmark* for economic analysis, economic systems and policies.... While the 'market' is an *ambiguous positive-normative ideal*, it nevertheless is considered not only an adequate reflection of the capitalist-market reality but also serves as a sound policy guideline for its reform.
>
> (Elsner 2008, 370, original emphasis)

But what does neoclassical economics tell us about the perfectly competitive market, the lexicon and logic of which now directly shape a vast array of public policies? First, the perfectly competitive market assumes that products are optimally allocated in a perfectly informed, atomistic world. Second, the market is attributed self-equilibrating properties because it is assumed to clear automatically via price adjustments, that is, prices respond to changes in demand or supply, finding equilibrium at the price at which the quantity supplied equals the quantity demanded. Accordingly, these oscillations underpin a systemic stability across markets for all goods and services and ensure an optimal allocation of resources between competing needs. Yet this self-equilibrating nature of the market rests on numerous assumptions such as identical consumers behaving rationally because they are perfectly informed about all the available alternatives, zero transaction costs, no trading at disequilibrium prices, and infinitely rapid velocities of prices and quantities (Blaug 2002, 40–41). It is also assumed that communication between market participants is solely through price signals, market participants are anonymous, interaction in the market is horizontal, virtually all transactions are commensurable, all goods are non-collective, and the market is not place sensitive (Crouch 2005, 115).

This paradigm maintains that the market should be left unfettered, as does neoliberalism, from state interventions to ensure its efficient workings are allowed to determine output and price. Free, competitive markets allocate resources and distribute income most efficiently, it is argued, because they will tend towards a (Pareto) optimal situation which occurs when no change can improve the position of one individual (as judged by herself) without a negative impact on the position of another individual (as judged by that individual).

However, six sources of market 'failure' which threaten the achievement of Pareto efficiency are deemed to warrant government action: the existence of market power; a failure to supply public goods such as defense or national security; negative externalities of production or consumption such as pollution; markets which provide incomplete goods and services (for example, insurance); imperfect information to consumers (for example, weather forecasts); and macroeconomic problems like high levels of unemployment or inflation (Stiglitz 2000, 76–90).[2] It is only these types of market 'failure'—which jeopardize the holy grail of economic efficiency—that justify any government intervention for mainstream economics.[3] Economic incentives to create the 'correct price' and reduce the negative externalities of market failure will lead to an optimum market outcome typify the neoclassical policy approach.

Many from the economics discipline have roundly challenged the neoclassical conception of the market (see, for example, Akerlof 1984; Blaug 2002; Grossman and Stiglitz 1980; Härdle and Kirman 1995; Nelson 2005; Simon 1991; Stiglitz 1987). This dissatisfaction accounts for some notable extensions to mainstream thinking (see, for example, Coase 1998; North 1990; Williamson 1975). A burgeoning literature argues that real-world markets do not emerge in a vacuum, are persistently vulnerable to failure, influence the nature and relationships of individuals, reflect socially habituated behavior, and their operation depends on highly complex non-market institutional arrangements into which they are deeply embedded (see, for example, Altvater 1993; Boyer 1997; Coriat and Weinstein 2005; Hodgson 1988; Martinez 2009; Peck and Theodore 2007; Tsakalotos 2004). In addition, Polanyi ([1944] 2001) contends that self-regulating market mechanisms cannot coordinate fictitious commodities (for example, money, labor, the environment) because their supply is not in response to changing relative prices.

Economic sociology, a major contributor to the discourse, conceptualizes markets as arenas of social interaction, a form of action (exchange) embedded in social relations which cannot exist without rules to regulate that exchange. Economic life is embedded in social relations and social structure, and therefore cannot be analyzed as separate, distinct, or isolated from social worlds (Granovetter 1985). Property rights, governance structures, conceptions of control, and rules of exchange are considered to be the institutions necessary to ensure the existence of markets (Fligstein 1996). Others have stressed the importance of networks, observed behavior, and population ecology to the social structures exerting control over the market (Granovetter 1985; Hannan and Freeman 1986; White 1981).

Sociologists have conducted detailed analyses of the creation and functioning of actual markets, especially financial markets, which have debunked neoclassical economic notions of markets being atomistic and anonymous, showing instead a range of behavioral rules, relationships, and skills required for participation (see, for example, Callon 1998; Callon *et al.* 2007; Granovetter and McGuire 1998; MacKenzie 2007a, 2007b, 2009; MacKenzie *et al.* 2007; Yakubovich *et al.* 2005).

Generally, although it is by far a unified whole, this body of work situates the market as one of a multiplicity of formal and informal capitalist institutions. "All institutions ... are defined in relation to the structure of the rights and obligations of the relevant actors" (Chang 2007, 7) which in the case of the market includes the institutional arrangements that determine and/or regulate market participants, and the objects and process of market exchange. As these 'rights and obligations' are deemed to be the result of politics, the market—like all institutions—is a political construct. Property rights, and the entitlements bestowed on market participants are not free of politics, along with numerous state actions to 'protect' market participants. Far from being natural, "markets are the fruit of complex social and historical developments" (Coriat and Weinstein 2005, 1) with politics, and thus the state, being integral to their creation and functioning. This view of the market assigns a far more active role to the state. Market outcomes result from a myriad of institutional arrangements and processes all of which are influenced by the state and politics.

## Theoretical foundations for the empirical analysis of markets

An analytical framework is inferred by Fligstein's (1996) list of market preconditions—property rights, governance structures, conceptions of control, and rules of exchange. Zelizer (1994) suggests empirical analysis is about concrete spaces, commodities being heterogeneous in time and space, money having many social uses, and the convergence of divergent interests overcoming the anonymity of market participants. For Coriat and Weinstein (2005, 2) "a market should be analysed like any institution: it is necessary to study the conditions in which it emerges, is stabilised and transformed and possibly goes into crisis." These all signal possible starting points but each requires the theoretical to be 'operationalized' for empirical application to be possible.

This task of operationalization is assisted by four contributions to the discourse: Boyer's (1997) typology of market types; Prasch's (2008) legal institutional framework of the exchange process irrespective of market type; Harvey and Randles' (2002) dimensions of the actual exchange process; and Tordjman's (1998, 2004) more concretized form of market processes of organization and exchange. The conjunction of these insights, rather than each individual contribution per se, allows us to move from the abstract to the concrete, that is, these insights provide building blocks to progress from the theoretical to a framework for empirical analysis.

Using the space and time horizon in which a market occurs, Boyer (1997, 62–66) distinguishes six different types of markets. First, markets may be periodic and/or peripatetic, presenting an embryonic form of those common to contemporary capitalist economies. These markets are authorized to occur at a specific time and location, may be wholesale or retail, and the scope of transactions is limited. A second type of market occurs as a temporary 'screening' device to procure the least costly or most 'economically advantageous' of proposals. The usual outcomes of this market are bilateral commercial contracts to supply specified goods or services by a particular time and for particular prices. This market type relies on commercial contracts and thus cannot function without a legal system. An aggregation over a geographical area or for one commodity creates a third market type: for example, the European Union single market. This market form does not hold a physical form or locale and may refer to the demand for a particular good, sector or "the economywide [*sic*] level, implying the equivalent of effective aggregate demand" (Boyer 1997, 64).

Neoclassical economics provides a fourth market type as an abstraction to make compatible a series of 'individual supplies and demands' which adjust and converge to a unique, equilibrium price to clear the market. The market is conceived as a process of rational, impersonal, discrete transactions between buyers and sellers. Boyer's fifth market type extends this abstraction to characterize an economic system dominated by market competition and a set of interdependent markets. Thus, anything that extends aspects of the market to non-market transactions is perceived as 'good' whereas anything that departs from the market model is the converse (Carrier 1997, 19). Finally, there is the metaphoric type assumed to exist whenever social actors compete for limited resources, positions, or status such as that applied by the Chicago school of economics to the social issues of marriage, crime, donations to religious orders, justice, and eternal life beliefs.

Location and time differentiate Boyer's six market types. But the nature of these different types also directly point to aspects about the structure and functioning of markets which signal a 'bridge' to empirical analysis. We can derive from the Boyer typology that markets involve repetitive—not single—transactions of commodities, there must be some form of regularity to market organization, a monetary system is required by markets to convey nominal prices and pay for transactions, and a legal regime must have the capacity to enforce commercial contracts. This latter aspect has been a specific focus for Prasch (1995, 2008).

The analytical key, for Prasch (2008), to understanding market relations lies in the evolving system of property rights and contract law which are the 'foundational institutional structures' of increasingly complex markets. A market is the organization of exchanges between transactors, a locus of repeated exchanges. Exchange is the fundamental event to take place in a market and is of "some object, promise, service or privilege" (Prasch 2008, 14). But, and this is pivotal for Prasch, not just anything can be exchanged. Before exchange can occur, one's ownership of (or legal authority over) whatever is to be sold must be established. In addition, each party to an exchange must be deemed able or competent to undertake the exchange although who is deemed a legitimate owner of property has changed over time.

Thus property ownership—and the right to exchange that property—is not simply about the relationship between "a person and a thing" but "an *artifact* of a complex set of social relations" (Prasch 2008, 14, emphasis added). Property ownership and exchange is subject to rules and law which reflect prevailing norms, values, and technology. The law has almost universally recognized a relationship to property where there is no encumbrance to disposal, that is, there is an exclusive right to control of the property which can be legitimately supported by the state's police powers. In addition, the rules or conditions of exchanging (selling) property are governed by contract law. Implicit contracts, which encompass many day-to-day activities, are not negotiated or in writing with 'completion' usually marked by a receipt. On the other hand, explicit contracts—for purchases like housing or other high cost transactions—can be quite complex documents with the negotiated terms, of a pending exchange, stipulated and, in the event of a disagreement, contract law drawing on precedent and conventional practice will resolve the matter.

Although a highly generalized synthesis of Prasch's thesis, the significance of this contribution comes from the proposition that the structure and functioning of a real-world market is based on an evolving but long-standing system of legally defined rights, property law, and contract law. This means that exchange, the fundamental event in a market, is subject to the prevailing legal regime as it applies to property and contracts. The right to exchange and conditions about the exchange transaction are embedded within implicit and explicit contracts—that is, market exchanges cannot occur without property rights and a legal regime.

Harvey and Randles (2002) extend this understanding about the exchange transaction established by Prasch. They posit that the organization of economic exchange, both market and non-market in modern capitalist economies, is framed—and thus can be discerned—through two dimensions. The first dimension is the institution of the exchange process, irrespective of the commodity exchanged, which is evident by considering the formation and differentiation of economic agents (that is, buyers and sellers) in relation to the actual exchange process. The second dimension concerns the differences in the specificities of exchange processes for any given organization of exchange. This dimension is represented by the parties to the exchange process, the commodities exchanged, and the spatial and temporal nature of the exchange. These dimensions of the exchange process introduce a different level of specificity and thus start to reveal different complexities embodied in the exchange process; for example, the criteria used to determine who may be a buyer or seller, or the multiple dimensions of any exchange process which distinguish it from others.

Tordjman (1998, 2004) develops a more concrete form of these two exchange dimensions while also extending key aspects from Boyer (1997) of repetitive transactions, regularity to market organization, and a monetary system to facilitate transactions. Tordjman (2004, 20) "envision[s] markets as institutions, i.e. sets of rules and codes of different nature organizing repeated monetary exchanges." To uncover the domain of markets, and understand their functioning as well as how they shape society, she delineates the rules which define the objects of exchange, identify market participants, and establish the market processes for exchange to take place.

Tordjman (2004) denotes those rules determining the principles of exchange (for example, the nature of the good exchanged, who are market participants) as 'constitutive' and those rules which implement exchange principles as 'procedural.' These categories also respectively contain transaction and information rules. If a market is a locus of repeated economic exchanges (posited by Boyer and Prasch) governed by property rights and law (posited by Prasch), this suggests to Tordjman that some kind of formal structures and sets of rules exist which bring together buyer–seller interactions and influence these exchanges, that is, rules governing transactions. It also suggests to her some conventions enabling sellers to propose a price and buyers to accept or negotiate another, that is, rules about the provision of information. The *conjunctive operation* of transaction and information rules induces a behavioral pattern which facilitates the continuity of a market's operation (posited by Boyer).

According to Tordjman (2004), transaction rules organize the *interaction* of buyers and sellers. In a decentralized (local) market, bilateral exchange occurs. Participants engage directly with each other and usually negotiate a price. On the other hand, there is no such direct interaction in a centralized market where an institution collects buy-and-sell orders, and determines the price until demand equals supply. Transaction rules also determine who is eligible to participate as buyers and sellers, reflect political decisions, and are enforced directly through complex regulatory regimes, competition policies, and trade practices legislation.[4] Eligibility for market participation is not decided by the individual. Specific behaviors may be prohibited by transaction rules. For example, buyers may not be permitted to be sellers concurrently to reduce the potential for collusion, insider trading, and speculation leading to 'manipulated' not market-driven transaction volumes and prices.

Tordjman's (2004) 'information rules' similarly influence the organization and operation of exchange within a market. Product guarantees, labels, standards, credit ratings, qualifications, and other types of information all convey details about the quality of product and reduce the extent of uncertainty about its quality. Thus, information about commodity quality improves market functioning but will depend upon what information is available to whom and when.

In sum, Tordjman demonstrates that rules establishing market participation eligibility, the form of interaction among participants, information about product quality as well as the property rights regime which defines what may be exchanged, induce behavioral responses to facilitate the operation of a market and its continuity.

These contributions—from Boyer, Prasch, Harvey, and Randles, and Tordjman—to our understanding of the organization and functioning of markets encompass a set of propositions about different types of market in space and time, the role of property rights and contract law, the dimensions shaping the organization of exchange, and the embedded behaviors created by rules reflecting political decision. Moreover, these propositions can be distilled to their core essence which illuminates 12 distinctive properties of markets. Ranging from the relatively simple to the more complex, and *not necessarily mutually exclusive*, these properties are:

1  A market is a location where buyers and sellers interact.
2  A market may be a physical location but does not need to be as evidenced by eBay, an internet auction, and online payment for goods and services.
3  Goods may be bought and sold on local, regional, national, or global markets.
4  A market requires a monetary system to facilitate transactions and convey prices.
5  Markets may be for intermediate or final goods.
6  The fundamental event in a market is exchange—of some object, promise, service, or privilege.
7  A market is a locus of repeated exchanges.
8  A legal system of property rights determines what may be exchanged in a market.
9  Implicit or explicit contracts govern the conditions under which property is exchanged.
10  Rules about transactions organize how buyers and sellers interact, and who may be a buyer and a seller.
11  Rules about the provision of information (including about the quality of the good) enable sellers to propose a price and enable buyers to accept or negotiate another.
12  Organized behavior, induced by transaction and information rules, provides continuity to a market's operation.

## An analytical framework to interrogate actually-existing markets

The distillation to 12 distinctive properties foreshadow a far more extensive and concrete expression of Tordjman's (2004) 'agenda of questions' which will enable us to transcend abstract notions about the market to their actualization if the object is to conduct empirical analyses of actually-existing markets. The questions that we can pose from the 12 distinctive properties of markets can be categorized according to: the process of exchange, the commodity traded in the market, market location, market participants, eligibility to market access, market behavior, price determination, the form of competition, market information, market linkages and interdependencies, institutional supports, and the role of the state (Table 10.1).

A cogent analytical grid is formed by these questions which can be used to interrogate the structure, operation, participants, behaviors, rules, price setting and more of a market and thus generate a substantive, realistic picture of actually existing markets. These questions are far more penetrating than neoclassical economic analysis which assumes a form of market organization (pure competition, duopoly, oligopoly, or monopoly) and then determines output, price, and cost outcomes within this assumed context (Sherman *et al.* 2008).

These questions are also far more penetrating than the schema proposed by Aspers (2011, 173) for a sociological analysis of markets. This schema is

*Table 10.1* Categories of analytical questions

| Category | Analytical questions |
|---|---|
| Exchange | Does the market coordinate production, distribution, or consumption decisions and outcomes? |
| Commodity | What is the commodity bought and sold? |
| | How are these goods or services defined? |
| | To what extent has the definition changed or is evolving? |
| Market location | How, and where, are market transactions performed? |
| | Must participants meet any obligations or criteria to perform market transactions? |
| | Is there a physical or virtual market location and how is this organized? |
| | Is the sphere of interaction local or global? |
| Eligibility to market access | What are the 'rules' or protocols which determine eligibility or ineligibility for ongoing access to a market? |
| | Are there legal and political decisions, or compromises, which determine who participates? |
| | What must a participant do to meet eligibility criteria and maintain ongoing market access? |
| Market participants | Who are the market participants (individuals, households, firms, groups, organizations, the state)? |
| | Who transacts with whom? |
| | Are intermediaries involved and if so, who are they? |
| Market behavior | What forms of interaction take place between buyers and sellers, and other market participants? |
| | Are particular behaviors forbidden? |
| | Are there implicit rules influencing the behavior of market participants? |
| | Are penalties imposed for breaches of market behavior and who enforces? |
| Form of competition | What is the market's form of competition? |
| | How many traders are there in the market? |
| | What is the ownership structure in the market? |
| | Is there evidence of market concentration? |
| | Is there evidence of market power? |
| Price determination | How is price determined? |
| | Are prices set outside or within the market? |
| | If it is a price-setting market, does this lead to different bilateral prices? |

| | |
|---|---|
| Information | What information is available to whom?<br>Where is it available?<br>What technology and skills are needed to access or process market information?<br>What is the impact on market participation if information access is precluded in some way? |
| Market linkages & interdependencies | What are the interrelationships with other markets?<br>Are these relationships co-constitutive?<br>How are these relationships organized?<br>What are the implications of these linkages in terms of market operation, market participation, and market outcomes? |
| Institutional supports | What are the institutions, organizations, legislation, or associations that organize the functioning of the market?<br>What are their responsibilities?<br>How do they enforce market operations?<br>To what or who are they accountable? |
| The state | What is the role of the state in terms of, but not limited to, the market's organization and operation, and determining the eligibility of participants? |

founded on three 'prerequisites': the nature of a market, its institutional foundations, and price setting. Although there are some points of commonality, such as price determination, the schema is very general and will not yield the same depth of findings about the institutional underpinnings, behavioral influences, market operation, availability and accessibility of information, forms of interaction between participants, or market interdependencies.

## Concluding comments

More and more reliance has been placed on markets by governments to solve an increasing range of issues notwithstanding the questioning by some mainstream theorists of the proclaimed efficiency of markets. Yet neoclassical economics has very successfully portrayed the normative ideal of the market, framed around a set of abstract assumptions, as synonymous with the economy and capitalism. Moreover, this normative ideal of the perfectly competitive market has become embedded in public policies, transforming markets which have traditionally been the domain of state provisioning and which determine, to a large extent, the well-being of society.

Although markets are not the only institutional arrangement for organizing economic and social life, we need to understand the market's contribution to society's well-being to inform the debate about the relative merits of different forms of provisioning. That understanding must be grounded in robust empirical analysis of the outcomes of actually-existing markets. Market outcomes reflect the organization and functioning of those markets. The normative ideal of neoclassical economics cannot elucidate the organization, functioning, outcomes, and implications of real-world markets.

The market is a physical or virtual location for repeated exchanges between buyers and sellers, which may involve intermediate or final goods, may be local or global and which is underpinned by property rights, implicit or explicit contracts, rules about transactions, and information creating organized behavior and continuity of operation. It is these distinctive properties of markets which signal a set of questions which must be addressed if the objective is a realistic understanding of the organization, functioning, and outcomes of actually-existing markets.

The analytical framework posited explicitly recognizes the different types of markets that can be discerned, the relationship to property rights, and the dimensions and behaviors shaping the organization of exchange. A distillation of these key propositions to their core essence establishes the fundamental properties of markets which enable progression from the abstract to the concrete because they indicate a cogent set of questions to frame and guide a cogent empirical analysis. The list of market properties 'operationalizes' abstract propositions into a pragmatic analytical framework.

Boyer (1997, 70) has argued that the organization of capitalist economies, which attribute a leading role to "competitive" markets, can only be explained by ascertaining: the institutions, legislation, or interactions that organize the functioning of various markets; the series of commodities for which supply and demand is heavily determined by market institutions, including regulation by the state; and the forms of competition according to the number of traders, ownership distribution, market power, and the mechanisms to resolve capacity issues or structural changes. These are indeed important 'keys' to understanding and explaining the *existence* and *operation* of markets in a capitalist economy. But to understand the impact on society's well-being, it is necessary to go to a further level of disaggregation to consider also the *interactions* and *outcomes* of actually-existing markets. To understand the relationship to, and impact on, society's well-being, market interactions and outcomes will be significant contributors. We cannot limit the analysis to a market's internal dynamics; market outcomes and interdependencies need also be included in the analysis.

The market is such a complex institution that it cannot be distilled or equated to the sum of bilateral relationships as does neoclassical economics. A market's 'constitution,' functioning, and impact on society's well-being can only be understood within the context of its empirical complexity as well as by reference to other markets given the diversity and specificities of each. The analytical framework posited in this chapter contributes a basis to do that and in that sense provides concrete expression to analyzing a component of Lee's (2013b) structure-organization-agency trichotomy to explain the capitalist social provisioning process. Markets are one of the sub-systems within Lee's organization component. If, as Fred Lee (2013b, 108) exhorted, "the ethos of heterodox economic theory is that the social provisioning process is to be accurately explained so that it can be changed" then I hope this analytical framework for understanding actually-existing markets may encourage others within the heterodox economics community to posit further frameworks to accurately explain other sub-systems of Fred's trichotomy.[5]

## Notes

1 Lee (2013a, 168) argues that 'going enterprises' construct a form of market governance that removes the pernicious and destructive nature of competition through the establishment of "trade associations, cartels, open price associations, price leadership, and government regulatory commissions; in addition, governments enact legislation that also regulates competition." I am of the view that state-led regulation and legislation, at the behest of 'ongoing enterprises,' is far more pervasive and dominant in managing the harmful effects of competition than anything established by enterprises.

2 Stiglitz (2000, 87) also argues that even if Pareto efficiency is achieved, government intervention may be warranted to achieve greater equality of income distribution and/or if the government "knows what is in the best interests of individuals."

3 Medema (2009) provides a detailed account of the dominant economic discourse, from the mid-nineteenth century to the late twentieth century, about the theory of market failure and government intervention.

4 Commons ([1924] 2007) explicitly recognized the political nature of transaction rules, and the role of the state in the process of exchange, in his *Legal Foundations of Capitalism*.

5 I would like to acknowledge the support and encouragement that Fred provided to me as a colleague and friend. Being a heterodox economist is a little like being a long-distance

runner (I am both). It can be lonely, dispiriting, and a constant test of emotional and intellectual strength. Fred understood so well the barriers and difficulties which we heterodox economists face on a day-to-day basis in terms of appointment to academic positions and promotion, publications, competitive funding grants and more but he was indefatigable in his support for us individually and for our community. I am honored and privileged to have known Fred.

## References

Akerlof, G. A. 1984. *An Economic Theorist's Book of Tales.* Cambridge, UK: Cambridge University Press.

Altvater, E. 1993. *The Future of the Market.* London: Verso.

Aspers, P. 2011. *Markets.* Cambridge, UK: Polity.

Blaug, M. 2002. "Ugly Currents in Economics." In *Fact and Fiction in Economics: Models, Realism, and Social Construction*, edited by U. Mäki, 35–56. Cambridge, UK: Cambridge University Press.

Boyer, R. 1997. "The Variety and Unequal Performance of Really Existing Markers: Farwell to Doctor Pangloss." In *Contemporary Capitalism: The Embeddedness of Institutions*, edited by J. R. Hollingsworth and R. Boyer, 55–93. Cambridge: Cambridge University Press.

Callon, M., ed. 1998. *The Laws of the Markets.* Oxford: Blackwell Publishers/The Sociological Review.

Callon, M., Millo, Y. and F. Muniesa, eds. 2007. *Market Devices.* Malden, MA: Blackwell Publishing/The Sociological Review.

Carrier, J. G., ed. 1997. *Meanings of the Market: The Free Market in Western Culture.* Oxford: Berg.

Chang, H.-J. 2002. "Breaking the Mould: An Institutionalist Political Economy Alternative to the Neoliberal Theory of the Market and the State." *Cambridge Journal of Economics* 6 (3): 539–560.

Chang, H.-J. 2007. "Institutional Change and Economic Development: An Introduction." In *Institutional Change and Economic Development*, edited by H.-J. Chang, 1–14. New York: United Nations University Press.

Chester, L. 2010. "Actually Existing Markets: The Case of Neoliberal Australia." *Journal of Economic Issues* XLIV (2): 313–324.

Chester, L. 2011. "The Participation of Vulnerable Australians in Contemporary Markets for Australian Goods and Services." *Journal of Australian Political Economy* 68: 169–193.

Chester, L. and A. Morris. 2012. "A New Form of Energy Poverty is the Hallmark of Liberalised Energy Sectors." *Australian Journal of Social Issues* 46 (4): 435–459.

Coase, R. H. 1988. *The Firm, the Market and the Law.* Chicago: University of Chicago Press.

Coase, R. H. 1992. "The Institutional Structure of Production." *The American Economic Review* 82 (4): 713–719.

Commons, J. R. [1924] 2007. *Legal Foundations of Capitalism.* New Brunswick: Transaction Publishers.

Coriat, B. and O. Weinstein. 2005. "The Social Construction of Markets." *Issues in Regulation Theory* 53: 1–4.

Crouch, C. 2005. *Capitalist Diversity and Change: Recombinant Governance and Institutional Entrepreneurs.* Oxford: Oxford University Press.

Elsner, W. 2008. "Market and State." In *International Encyclopedia of Public Policy—Governance in a Global Age, Volume 3: Public Policy and Political Economy*, edited by P. A. O'Hara, 370–389. Accessed July 27, 2011. http://pohara.homestead.com/Encyclopedia/Volume-3.pdf.

Dugger, W. M. 1996. "Redefining Economics: From Market Allocation to Social Provisioning." In *Political Economy for the 21st Century*, edited by C. J. Whalen, 31–43, Armonk, NY: M. E. Sharpe.

Food and Agricultural Organization of the United Nations (FAO). 2011. *Recent Trends in World Food Commodity Prices: Costs and Benefits.* Accessed April 23, 2014. www.fao.org/docrep/014/i2330e/i2330e03.pdf.

Fligstein, N. 1996. "Markets as Politics: A Political–Cultural Approach to Market Institutions." *American Sociological Review* 61 (4): 656–673.

Galbraith, J. 2009. *The Predator State: How Conservatives Abandoned the Free Market and Why Liberals Should Too.* New York: Free Press.

Garcia-Parpet, M.-F. 2007. "The Social Construction of a Perfect Market: The Strawberry Auction at Fontaine-en-Sologne." In *Do Economists Make Markets? On the Performativity of Economics*, edited by D. MacKenzie, F. Muniesa, and L. Siu, 20–53. Princeton, NJ: Princeton University Press.

Giroux, H. 2009. "Market-driven Hysteria and the Politics of Death." *Truthout.* Accessed November 27, 2011. www.truthout.org/1106095.

Granovetter, M. 1985. "Economic Action and Social Structure: The Problem of Embeddedness." *The American Journal of Sociology* 91 (3): 481–510.

Granovetter, M. and P. McGuire. 1998. "The Making of an Industry: Electricity in the United States." In *The Laws of the Markets*, edited by M. Callon, 147–173. Blackwell Publishers/The Sociological Review.

Grossman, S. and J. Stiglitz. 1980. "On the Impossibility of Informationally Efficient Markets." *American Economic Review* 70 (3): 393–408.

Hannan, M. and J. Freeman. 1986. "Where Do Organisations Come From?" *Sociological Forum* 1 (1): 50–72.

Härdle, W. and A. Kirman. 1995. "Nonclassical Demand: A Model-Free Examination of Price-Quantity Relations in the Marseille Fish Market." *Journal of Econometrics* 67 (1): 227–257.

Harvey, M., ed. 2010. *Markets, Rules and Institutions of Exchange.* Manchester: Manchester University Press.

Harvey, M. and S. Randles. 2002. "Markets, the Organisation of Exchanges and 'Instituted Economic Process'—An Analytical Perspective." *Revue d'Économie Industrielle* 101 (4): 11–30.

Hodgson, G. 1988. *Economics and Institutions: A Manifesto for a Modern Institutional Economics.* Cambridge, UK: Polity Press.

Jordana, J. and D. Levi-Faur. 2004. "The Politics of Regulation in the Age of Governance." In *The Politics of Regulation: Institutions and Regulatory Reforms for the Age of Governance*, edited by J. Jordana and D. Levi-Faur, 1–28. Cheltenham, UK: Edward Elgar.

Kirman, A. P. and A. Vignes 1992. "Price Dispersion: Theoretical Considerations and Empirical Evidence from the Marseille Fish Market." In *Issues in Contemporary Economics*, Volume 1, edited by K. Arrow, 160–185. London: Macmillan.

Lee, F. S. 2013a. "Competition, Going Enterprise, and Economic Activity." In *Alternative Theories of Competition: Challenges to the Orthodoxy*, edited by J. K. Moudud, C. Bina, and P. L. Mason, 160–173. London and New York: Routledge.

Lee, F. S. 2013b. "Heterodox Economics and Its Critics." In *In Defense of Post-Keynesian and Heterodox Economics: Responses to Their Critics*, edited by F. S. Lee and M. Lavoie, 104–132. London and New York: Routledge.

MacKenzie, D. 2007a. "Zero is a Clenched Fist." *London Review of Books* 29 (21). Accessed March 4, 2009. www.lrb.co.uk/v29/n21/mack01_.html.

MacKenzie, D. 2007b. "Finding the Ratchet: The Political Economy of Carbon Trading." *Post-Autistic Economics Review* 42: 8–17.

MacKenzie, D. 2009. *Material Markets: How Economic Agents Are Constructed.* Oxford: Oxford University Press.

MacKenzie, D., F. Muniesa, and L. Siu, eds. 2007. *Do Economists Make Markets? On the Performativity of Economics.* Princeton, NJ: Princeton University Press.

Mantzavinos, C. 2001. *Individuals, Institutions, and Markets.* Cambridge: Cambridge University Press.

Martinez, M. A. 2009. *The Myth of the Free Market: The Role of the State in a Capitalist Economy.* Sterling, VA: Kumarian Press.

Medema, S. G. 2009. *The Hesitant Hand: Taming Self-interest in the History of Economic Ideas.* Princeton, NJ: Princeton University Press.

Nelson, S., ed. 2005. *The Limits of Market Organization.* New York: Russell Sage Foundation.

Nelson, S. 2011. "The Complex Economic Organisation of Capitalist Economies." *Capitalism and Society* 6 (1): 1–24.

North, D. C. 1990. *Institutions, Institutional Change and Economic Performance.* Cambridge, UK: Cambridge University Press.

Peck, J. and N. Theodore. 2007. "Variegated Capitalism." *Progress in Human Geography* 31 (6): 731–732.

Polanyi, K. 1968. "The Economy as Instituted Process." In *Primitive, Archaic and Modern Economies: Essays of Karl Polanyi*, edited by G. Dalton, 139–174. Garden City, NY: Doubleday.

Polanyi, K. [1944] 2001. *The Great Transformation: The Political and Economic Origins of Our Time.* Boston: Beacon Press.

Prasch, R. E. 1995. "Toward a 'General Theory' of Market Exchange." *Journal of Economic Issues* XXIX (3): 807–828.

Prasch, R. E. 2008. *How Markets Work: Supply, Demand and the 'Real World.'* Cheltenham, UK: Edward Elgar.

Public Services International Research Unit. 2008. *Poor Choices: The Limits of Competitive Markets in the Provision of Essential Services to Low-income Consumers.* Accessed March 24, 2009. www.psiru.org/reports/PoorChoices.pdf.

Sherman, H. J., E. K. Hunt, R. E. Nesiba, P. A. O'Hara, and B. Wiens-Tuers. 2008. *Economics: An Introduction to Traditional and Progressive Views.* 7th ed. Armonk: M. E. Sharpe.

Simon, H. 1991. "Organizations and Markets." *Journal of Economic Perspectives* 5 (2): 25–44.

Stern, N. 2007. *The Economics of Climate Change: The Stern Review.* Cambridge, UK: Cambridge University Press.

Stiglitz, J. E. 1987. "The Causes and Consequences of the Dependence of Quality on Price." *Journal of Economic Literature* 25 (1): 1–48.

Stiglitz, J. E. 2000. *Economics of the Public Sector*, 3rd ed., New York: W. W. Norton & Company.

Streeck, W. 2011. "Taking Capitalism Seriously: Towards an Institutionalist Approach to Contemporary Political Economy." *Socio-Economic Review* 9 (1): 137–167.

Todorova, Z. 2103. "Conspicuous Consumption as Routine Expenditure and its Place in the Social Provisioning Process." *American Journal of Economics and Sociology* 72 (5): 1183–1204.

Tordjman, H. 1998. "Some General Questions About Markets." Interim Report IR-98–025/May, International Institute for Applied Systems Analysis, Laxenburg, Austria.

Tordjman, H. 2004. "How to Study Markets? An Institutionalist Point of View." *Revue d'Économie Industrielle* 107 (3): 19–36.

Tsakalotos, E. 2004. "Social Norms and Endogenous Preferences: The Political Economy of Market Expansion." In *Neo-liberal Economic Policy: Critical Essays*, edited by P. Arestis and M. Sawyer, 5–37. Cheltenham, UK: Edward Elgar.

White, H. C. 1981. "Where Do Markets Come From?" *The American Journal of Sociology* 87 (3): 517–547.

Williamson, O. 1975. *Markets and Hierarchies: Analysis and Anti-trust Implications.* New York: The Free Press.

Yakubovich, V., M. Granovetter, and P. McGuire. 2005. "Electric Charges: The Social Construction of Rate Systems." *Theory and Society* 34 (5/6): 579–612.

Zelizer, V. A. 1994. *The Social Meaning of Money.* New York: Basic Books.

# Part III

# Advancing the heterodox analysis of social provisioning

# 11 Advancing heterodox economics in the tradition of the surplus approach

*Nuno Ornelas Martins*

## Introduction

One of the central contributions of Professor Frederic Lee, certainly one with which his name will always be associated, concerns the development of heterodox economics. The term 'heterodox' economics indicates already a critical attitude towards 'orthodox' economics, most commonly designated as 'mainstream' economics. In this sense, we find sometimes the tendency, especially within mainstream economics, for taking heterodox economics to be essentially a criticism of mainstream economics.

Anyone familiar with heterodox economics, and most especially with Frederic Lee's contributions, will quickly realize that heterodox economics, albeit certainly critical of mainstream economics, is first and foremost a constructive project. Heterodox economists have engaged in the development of alternative theories, methods, and policies. Heterodox theories and methods, in particular, are not merely motivated by the critique of mainstream economics. Rather, heterodox theories and methods are connected to a long tradition in economic thinking—that is, the classical surplus approach.

I have argued elsewhere that the distinction between heterodox economics and mainstream economics is a contemporary form of the distinction made by Karl Marx between classical political economists who adopted a surplus approach (like Petty, Cantillon, Quesnay, Smith, and Ricardo) and vulgar political economists who subsequently distorted Ricardo's surplus theory into a scarcity theory which became often named, misleadingly, 'Ricardian' economics (see, Martins 2013a, 2013b, ch. 8). This distinction has continued and even become intensified ever since Marx's time. As Lee (2008, 2009) demonstrates in his historical study, heterodox economics in the twentieth century was organized around various critical approaches such as Marxian-radical political economics, original institutionalism, Post Keynesianism, feminist economics, and social economics. Common to these strands in heterodox economics is the rejection of scarcity, marginal analysis, equilibrium, and optimizing/isolated individual behavior. In place of the core of mainstream economics, there is a surplus approach in heterodox approaches. Marx's ([1867] 1999) critique of what he called vulgar political economy, Thorstein Veblen's (1908) critique of John

Bates Clark's (1891) marginalist framework, and the Cambridge controversies in the theory of capital which opposed the Post Keynesians to neoclassical economists (see Harcourt 1972 for the capital controversy) are all epitomes of an underlying tension between a surplus approach and a scarcity theory.

Frederic Lee and Tae-Hee Jo (2011) have recently addressed the connections between heterodox economics and the surplus approach, while showing the differences between the classical surplus approach and the surplus approach adopted within heterodox economics. In this chapter I intend to extend their analysis, but by stressing the commonalities between the classical surplus approach and the heterodox surplus approach. The central distinction to make here is that economic theories organized around the idea of production and distribution of the social surplus are in radical contrast to economic theories organized around the idea of optimization under scarcity. Rarely addressed by modern heterodox economists is the argument that present problems faced by capitalism cannot be understood adequately, if economic policy continues to be developed without an understanding of the process of reproduction and distribution of the surplus. This is the gist of the surplus approach, which was first adopted by the classical political economists and the Physiocrats, and developed to its more advanced stage within Marxian economics, original institutionalism, and Post Keynesianism.

## The classical surplus approach

Classical political economy can be best described as a set of contributions originating in the writings of William Petty, Richard Cantillon, François Quesnay, Adam Smith, and finally David Ricardo. The central analytical concept of this approach is the social surplus. The social surplus can be defined as the part of production which is not necessary for the reproduction of the existing economic system. In an economy which reproduces itself at an unchanging scale, we can distinguish between the 'basic commodities' that are necessary for the reproduction of the existing economic system (and thus are outputs of production which are also used as inputs in production), and the 'non-basic commodities' that are not necessary for the reproduction of the existing economic system (and thus are outputs of production which are not used as inputs in production) (see Sraffa 1960). This distinction is connected to the classical distinction between the commodities which are necessary for the subsistence and activity of the laborer who ensures the reproduction of the economic system, and the luxury commodities, which are not necessary for the subsistence and activity of the laborer.

In an economy that reproduces itself at an unchanging scale, the surplus simply consists of luxury commodities. However, in an economy that reproduces itself at an expanding scale, the surplus cannot be used only in the consumption of luxuries, and a part of the surplus will also be used in productive activities aimed at expanding the existing economic system, leading to economic growth. For the classical political economists, the distribution of the surplus is the key to prosperity or decadence. Prosperity occurs when the surplus is used in productive activities aimed at expanding the existing economic system (that is, leading to economic growth), and decadence comes when the surplus is squandered in luxurious consumption.

A surplus could exist even in a perfectly competitive economy, albeit such an economy does not exist in the real world. If competition drives prices down, it will also reduce the price of basic commodities, which are not only the outputs of the industries that produce them, but also the inputs of the industries which use them. David Ricardo saw agriculture as the basic sector of the economy, and corn (or other cereals, since the classical authors used the term 'corn' only as shorthand for cereals in general) as the more basic commodity. If competition drives the prices of corn down, it leads then to a reduction of input prices too, since corn is a key input in the economic process (corn can be used to produce more corn, and as a supply of food to laborers). Thus a surplus is maintained in agriculture, which enables the maintenance of a given rate of profits in agriculture. Sraffa developed this Ricardian idea, without focusing on corn specifically, and using instead an abstract notion of basic commodity.

If competition drives prices down in other sectors so that the rate of profits in those sectors would become lower than in agriculture, investment will flow into agriculture where a higher rate of profits exists. So the rate of profits in other sectors never becomes lower than in agriculture, and it is indeed the agricultural sector, or whatever sectors we consider to be the basic sectors of an economy (that is, the sectors whose outputs are used as inputs), that determines the rate of profits in this competitive economy. Ricardo's analysis of agriculture and the classical analysis of agriculture in general can be extended by including other sectors that produce basic commodities other than corn. It was reasonable for classical economists to identify agriculture as a basic sector, since agriculture was not as integrated with other sectors as it is today, with multinational firms controlling the production of various agricultural inputs and the distribution of agricultural outputs (while extracting an important part of the agricultural surplus).

In actually existing economies, perfect competition does not exist, since competition is always regulated by business enterprises and by the state, as Lee (2012a) explains. But the aim is again to obtain a surplus, in a context where prices are more often than not set by the business enterprise so that a surplus is obtained in the production process (for example, by determining a profit margin above the costs of production). In fact, the expansion of large firms throughout the development of capitalism made this type of pricing mechanism much more important (Eichner 1976; Lee 1998, 2013). This does not mean that large firms are not subject to some type of competition too. As David Harvey (2006) explains, even large firms have to compete for money capital, which means that competitive mechanisms become internalized within the very organization of large firms, rather than operating as in a market of small firms (see Moudud, Bina, and Mason 2012, for various heterodox approaches to competition).

Perfect competition never existed even at the early stage of capitalism, since large companies already played a central role. Adam Smith ([1776] 1973) and Karl Marx ([1867] 1999) trace the beginnings of modern capitalism to the Portuguese discovery of a sea route from Europe to India and the Spanish discovery of a sea route from Europe to America, which led to an integration of world markets on an unprecedented scale. The East Indies and the West Indies companies, which controlled commerce with Asia and America, respectively, were already large companies, coordinated through mechanisms of command and control (see Braudel [1979] 1982).

That is, monopolies with various degrees of control by the Crown (as we can see when comparing the Portuguese and Spanish case with the Dutch and British case) played a central role in the formation of capitalism from its very beginning, and financial capital was present from the very beginning too. The process of production and distribution of the surplus, and the way the surplus is appropriated by commercial, industrial, and financial capitalists is the essential aspect of capitalism, despite the various degrees of competition.

## Classical price theory

Piero Sraffa (1960) provides an economic system which summarizes the key tenets of the surplus approach. Sraffa says nothing about the degree of competition in the formulation of his system, and leaves this question open for further analysis. Sraffa's contribution is often interpreted as a revival of the classical surplus approach. This interpretation was first expressed in print by Ronald Meek (1961), and appears in a clearer way in Sraffa's unpublished manuscripts, which after Sraffa's death were left to his literary executor, Pierangelo Garegnani, who further developed this interpretation (see Garegnani 1984; Martins 2013b, for a discussion of this interpretation). In contrast, the orthodox interpretation of classical theory and the surplus approach contained therein is fallacious, which leads to the belief that classical theory would apply only in cases of perfect competition.

Lee (1998) convincingly argues that in modern capitalism, prices are very often (or indeed most often) formed through administrative procedures. Following the grounded theory approach as opposed to a hypothetical set of assumptions regarding the market and business activities, Lee identifies three most widely adopted pricing principles and resulting prices in modern capitalist economies. Mark-up prices are obtained by marking up normal average direct costs in order to generate a desired margin of profit, normal cost prices are obtained by marking up average direct costs in order to cover shop expenses and enterprise expenses so as to obtain normal average total costs, and then marking up those normal average total costs in order to produce a desired margin of profit, and target rate of return prices are obtained by marking up normal average total costs so that a volume of profits leads to a specific rate of return on the business enterprise's capital assets. All the prices and costs in these three pricing procedures are measured in terms of normal output and normal capacity utilization (Lee 1998, 204–205).

This approach to prices reveals that enterprises' pricing activities draw heavily upon customs and conventions prevailing in a particular market and industry. The customary (or conventional) price administered by the firm and its competitors not only persists over extended periods of time but also is a central determinant of the price to be set in the following periods. This customary price is not inconsistent with the normal price or natural price in classical political economy. For Adam Smith, the natural price is simply the ordinary or average price that persists through time and multiple transactions. This conventional price enables acting persons and organizations to form expectations, which guide economic activities. Conventional prices can emerge due to the price-setting activities of large firms, or through the interaction of several firms in a competitive market. But as long as we have conventional prices in a process of economic reproduction where a surplus is produced and distributed, the classical analysis remains relevant.

Of course, the classical authors did not engage in a detailed study of actual pricing activities as Lee does. Rather, the classical authors focused on the price that enables the reproduction of the economic system, while abstracting from the economic fluctuations that are generated through actual investment decisions. One may say that the classical authors focused on the long period trend, while abstracting from the business cycles. This needs not mean that the classical method presupposes a stationary world. As Harcourt (1981) explains, focusing on a normal position means to focus merely on what happens on average, and thereby the classical notion of center of gravitation needs not mean anything more than what happens on average and is expected to happen due to habit and custom.

Indeed, Garegnani argues that long-term growth is generated through short-term business cycles and thus the long-term averages are mere abstractions aimed at focusing on long-term growth. Garegnani and Trezzini (2010, 120) note that if we focus only on the supply side while ignoring business cycles and assuming that technological conditions provide stable long-term growth, we are then led to "a belief that short-period fluctuations in autonomous demand can only cause the level of aggregate output to oscillate around a trend determined by altogether different circumstances and thus to overlooking important phenomena."

Even authors who focus typically on the short period, like Kalecki (1971, 165), make a similar point, noting how "the long run trend is but a slowly changing component of a chain of short-period situations." The difference is that while Garegnani, following the classical method, focuses typically on the trend abstracting from cycles (without neglecting that it is through cycles that the trend and growth comes about), Kalecki focuses essentially on the business cycle, abstracting from the trend, while regretting the fact that "[b]y this separation of short-period and long-run influences I missed certain repercussions of technical progress which affect the dynamic system as a whole" (1971, 166).

In order to understand "the dynamic system as a whole," as Kalecki puts it, we must focus on the actual business activities including price-setting activities (Kalecki 1971, ch. 5; Lee 1998, 204–205), while noting that those activities generate not only economic fluctuations, but also long-term processes, not least through the formation of habit and custom concerning what is an ordinary, or normal, price, which is essential not only for the coordination of economic activity in more competitive markets, but also for the coordination of economic activities even when large firms that set prices administratively are involved. Lee (2012b) develops the surplus approach by allowing for changes in the level and composition of output (unlike Sraffa who takes the latter as given), focusing on the role of agency too, as Keynes and Kalecki did when analyzing investment decisions and the ensuing economic fluctuations.

The classical authors focused essentially on the conditions of reproduction of economic activity over the long term at a more abstract level. Their analysis must be supplemented by the more concrete analysis undertaken by, for example, Kalecki (who was influenced by Marx, and also focused on the circular process of reproduction) and Lee (who not only provided a much more detailed account of price-setting activities, but also argued that we must focus on the process of social provisioning, that is, on the distribution of the surplus, as the classical authors did).

According to the classical approach, there is a distinction between 'natural prices' and 'market prices.' Natural prices are, on the one hand, determined by the cost of production. In the classical viewpoint, the cost of production including the surplus depends upon the conditions of reproduction of the economy. Market prices are, on the other hand, actually observed prices, which are dependent upon the fluctuations of supply and demand. But the fluctuations of supply and demand mean only that the market price will gravitate around the natural price, that is, around the cost of production (remember, including the surplus). If there is excess supply, and market prices are below the cost of production, the quantity brought to the market will be reduced until the market price is again closer to the cost of production. If there is excess demand, and market prices are above the cost of production, more quantity will be brought to the market in order to take advantage of the higher process, and the market price will tend again to the cost of production.

The quantity brought to the market adjusts thus to variations in market prices, so that market prices tend to the cost of production. But for more quantity to be produced, more labor must be employed in order to produce it. The classical theory presupposes not only the production of a surplus, but also the existence of a surplus of labor. Surplus labor can exist because either people are unemployed or they are working below their potential. In both cases, the economy is below the level of full employment. The expansion of the existing economic system occurs when the surplus produced is used in productive activities, but those productive activities will be undertaken using labor time that was not previously employed.

Thomas Robert Malthus criticized this classical approach to prices. In Malthus' days, Ricardo was the main exponent of this approach. Malthus argued that natural prices are not determined by the cost of production, but rather by the interaction between supply and demand (see Martins 2013b, ch. 1). That is, it is not just the market price, but also the natural price, that is determined by supply and demand. Malthus noted that, according to Smith, the natural price can be divided into wages, profits, and rent. Malthus then argued that wages, profits, and rent are determined by supply and demand, and so must be the natural price, since it is merely the sum of wages, profits, and rents.

Malthus' approach presupposes that we can attribute a systematic and ordinary role to supply and demand forces. For Smith and Ricardo, supply and demand are merely accidental forces that take the market price away from the natural price, that is, from the cost of production. But Smith and Ricardo did not provide a systematic account of the process of gravitation of market prices around the natural prices.

By looking at the production process, Ricardo defines the wages in terms of the amount of the commodities that are necessary for achieving a certain standard of living. Although this standard of living is termed as a 'subsistence level,' the latter does not denote bare physical subsistence. Rather, it denotes a customary standard of living, according to the nature and habits of society. The surplus, for Ricardo, is the difference between the value of total production and wages necessary for the reproduction process. And rent is simply the difference between the production obtained in a given land and the production obtained in the worst land which yields no rent, but only profits. Profits are then defined as the surplus obtained in the worst land. For Ricardo, the conditions of production determine wages, profits, and rent. And these three incomes are not determined by supply and demand forces. Rather, they are determined by different aspects of the process of production, while supply and demand cause accidental deviations from the normal cost of production.

Karl Marx notes later that even if there is some sort of ordinary or average equilibrium between supply and demand (as Malthus' approach seems to presuppose), supply and demand will then cancel each other out. Thus, we must look deeper into the production process in order to understand the formation of value and prices, rather than staying only at a superficial level looking at supply and demand. According to Marx, authors from Petty to Ricardo are engaged in a scientific attempt to explain the economy. Marx thus used the term 'classical political economy' to designate the contributions of these authors, and used the term 'vulgar political economy' in order to designate those who looked only at more superficial phenomena, such as supply and demand.

The classical approach, as interpreted by Marx, fits well into the study of contemporary capitalism undertaken by Lee (1998) who stresses the role of administered prices that are set given the conditions of production. Lee, like classical political economists, focuses on the production process and how prices are formed within it, rather than taking supply and demand to be the ultimate determinant of prices as in the vulgar approach.

According to Marx, authors like Malthus and Senior, who Marx sees as 'vulgar' political economists, were no longer continuing classical political economy, which was developed into its more advanced stage by Ricardo. Rather, vulgar political economists were transforming political economy into mere apologetics of the capitalist system. In so doing, they focused on superficial phenomena such as supply and demand, rather than examining the underlying process of production as the classical authors did. The fact that the vulgar move-ment was often labeled as 'Ricardian economics' contributed to a misplaced identification of the vulgar movement with Ricardo and with classical political economy in general. While Marx was developing the classical surplus approach further, others (wrongly named as 'classical economists,' like William Nassau Senior, John Stuart Mill, and John Elliot Cairnes) had already abandoned it.

## Vulgar political economy and marginalism

Throughout the nineteenth century, the development of vulgar political economy brought important changes to economic theory. A central change was the intro-duction of subjective elements in the theory of value. Classical authors like Petty, Cantillon, and Quesnay had an objective conception of value. Petty argues metaphorically that land is the mother and labor is the father of wealth. Land and labor are the two original sources of value, which could be measured objectively (as a quantity of land, and a quantity of labor time). Petty also notes that we can measure labor in terms of the objective entities (such as food) which are neces-sary for the subsistence of the laborer. Cantillon agrees with this procedure, and Quesnay provides the first systematic objective scheme of economic circulation.

However, once we establish a relation of equivalence between land and labor (by equating the quantity of land that sustains a human being for a given quantity of time with the labor performed in that quantity of time), we can either convert labor into land or land into labor. Indeed, Petty had already advanced the idea that capital is past labor. But it is only after Adam Smith that the source of wealth and value is more clearly identified with labor.

Smith's perspective that all value comes from human labor is an objective conception of value (which switches Quesnay's emphasis on land towards labor). But Smith already introduced some ambiguity because he was not clear on how labor would be measured. Ricardo argues that the value of a commodity consists of embodied labor, that is, the labor that was spent in the production of the commodity. Marx argues instead that we should focus on socially necessary labor, that is, how much labor is necessary to reproduce a commodity given the existing mode of production.

Malthus, in contrast, argues that the measure of value of a commodity was commanded labor, that is, the unit of labor that can be purchased by the com-modity. Ricardo's approach, like Marx's, looks at the process of production. The relevant question that arises from this approach is how much labor is spent, or must be spent, in the production of a commodity. But Malthus looks at market exchange and, consequently, the important question to Malthus is how much labor can be bought in the market using the commodity, given the existing supply and demand forces.

After Malthus, vulgar political economy began to introduce subjective elements into economic theory. The purpose was to explain both the supply side and the demand side, within the supply and demand framework that replaced the classical focus on labor and the cost of production. Senior stresses the 'abstinence' of the capitalist who advances capital rather than consuming, engaging thus in what Cairnes called a 'sacrifice' representing a psychological or subjective effort that must be considered together with the labor performed by the worker as an objective effort. Therefore, the cost of production that represents the supply side starts to include subjective elements.

Subjective elements played an even more important role in demand. For the classical authors, effectual demand is the demand of those who can pay the natural price. The natural price, which depends upon the cost of production, is the ordinary price which becomes a reference for economic activity through habits and customs. Effectual demand for a given natural price is then set by institutional factors like habits and customs, which are formed throughout the reproduction of the economic process under objective costs of production. The natural price is thus a determinant of effectual demand and depends on the objective costs of production. In vulgar political economy, however, the natural price is explained by supply and demand, as Malthus argued, and thus cannot be simultaneously a determinant of demand. On the contrary, in vulgar political economy, demand is (together with supply) an independent determinant of, rather than determined by, the natural price. And like the supply side, the demand side is also explained by subjective elements.

The subjectivist perspective led vulgar political economy to the belief that economic laws could be found as a result of universal psychological laws, present themselves in the mind of every individual, and are applicable regardless of time and space (see Henry 1990, 2009). This vulgar perspective was criticized by authors like Cliffe Leslie who stressed the need of looking at historico-geographical conditions, as Adam Smith did. The subjective approach culminated in the 'marginalist revolution' brought about by Carl Menger, Stanley Jevons, Léon Walras, and Alfred Marshall. Menger, like the Austrian school he founded, also stressed the ability to derive economic laws from knowledge of the psychology of the human mind, and engaged in a debate with Gustav von Schmoller who, like the German Historical School he belonged to, criticized Menger and the Austrian approach while stressing the need to take into account historical-geographical conditions, as Leslie did in England when criticizing vulgar political economy. It goes without saying that despite these criticisms, the Historical School (British or German) never developed an objective approach to value similar to classical political economists and Marx.

Walras criticized the classical approach to value that was systematized by Ricardo. Remember Ricardo argues that under normal conditions, even if demand drives the price above its cost of production, an increase in supply will offset the increase in demand, as long as unemployed labor is available and, thereby, the price tends to the cost of production. Walras argues that this is not so, because we cannot assure that the quantity of commodities can always be increased, as Ricardo suggests and thus if demand drives the price above the cost of production, the price will not return to the previous cost of production, which means that demand is also a determinant of price together with supply (see Martins 2013b, ch. 1).

The difference at stake here is that Ricardo is presupposing a case where there is no full employment (and thus labor is available for increasing production, thus offsetting the increase in demand), whereas Walras is presupposing a case where there is full employment (and thus production cannot be increased in order to offset the increase in demand). The difference between Ricardo and Walras is symptomatic of the differences between the classical surplus approach and the marginalist scarcity approach. If we assume that all factors of production (such as land, capital, and labor) are scarce, clearly we cannot simply increase production in order to offset demand. Under scarcity, an increase in demand will have a causal influence on prices and so demand becomes a factor to be explained.

The marginalist economists explained demand in terms of the subjective preferences of consumers while presupposing scarcity. When a commodity is scarce, it has a higher marginal (or in Jevons' terms, 'final') utility, that is, the utility of an additional commodity is higher. For Ricardo, only land was seen as a scarce factor of production, which generates a rent. For the marginalist economists, in contrast, all factors of production and every commodity are scarce and, hence, priced according to their marginal productivity.

The marginalist revolution brought not just subjective elements into economic theory, but also a different economic methodology. Authors like Jevons, Walras, and Marshall thought that in order to express the marginalist ideas, a different mathematical method was required (although Menger, like other Austrian economists in general, did not find usefulness in the use of mathematics). Differential calculus, in particular, was used to express marginal utility so as to obtain a demand curve that relates prices and quantities (which is a decreasing curve, since it is assumed that marginal utility decreases when quantities increase), and also marginal costs so as to obtain a supply curve (which is an increasing curve, since it is assumed that marginal costs increase when quantities produced increase).

The ingredients necessary for the development of the marginalist revolution already existed before the 'revolution' took place. Augustin Cournot had already developed mathematical supply and demand curves. Johann Heinrich von Thünen had already used differential calculus to address the theory of value. Jules Dupuit and Hermann Heinrich Gossen had already advanced many of the marginalist ideas. But the marginalist ideas were widely and simultaneously accepted toward the end of the nineteenth century when Karl Marx was the only influential economist still working in the tradition of the classical surplus approach.

After the marginalist revolution, differential calculus became an essential method within economics. Demand curves were obtained through differential calculus based on marginal utility and supply curves were also obtained through differential calculus based on marginal cost. Production and consumption started to be theorized as optimization exercises, be it the maximization of utility or of profit.

In classical analysis, the only mathematical method used was arithmetic or 'Political Arithmetic,' as Petty called it. Like Petty, Cantillon also made extensive use of arithmetic, although the supplement with his computations has now been lost. Quesnay's Tableau also used arithmetic only. Smith was reluctant to use arithmetic, but he still used it, for example, when comparing the effects of increases in wages and in profits on prices—the first work as an arithmetic progression, the second as a geometric progression (see Smith [1776] 1993, 94). Ricardo's definition of rent is based on an arithmetic operation, namely the difference between the value of the production of a given land and the value of the production of the worst land. Likewise, Ricardo's concept of profits is the difference between the value of the production of the worst land and the value of wages.

It follows that the surplus is defined as a difference between total production and the part of production that is necessary for reproduction. This is central to the classical scheme, including Marx's version of it. Such an important concept is formulated using arithmetic. Marx, we may add, used only arithmetic in his economic analysis, in spite of the fact that he felt much more comfortable in the field of differential calculus of which he had a deep knowledge (not least of its philosophical underpinnings and historical evolution), as is evident from his Mathematical Manuscripts kept by Friedrich Engels.

In the twentieth century, the use of mathematics became widespread. It includes calculus (which is widely used in microeconomics as well as in macroeconomics), statistics and regression analysis (leading to the field of econometrics), and algebra (in particular, fixed point theorems that are used in game theory to show the existence of a Nash equilibrium, and in the reformulation of Walras's theory by Arrow, Debreu, and McKenzie in order to show the existence of a general equilibrium). The successes of the use of mathematics in science like physics throughout the twentieth century led also to the belief that mathematics is essential for economics to become a science. We may indeed say that mainstream economics is now characterized essentially in methodological terms, that is, as a commitment to mathematico-deductivist methods, as Tony Lawson (2003) explains.

## The development of the surplus approach within heterodox economics

The use of mathematical methods, like the use of any methods, carries with it ontological presuppositions concerning the nature of reality. The use of mathematical methods thus shapes the theory established to analyze reality and, ultimately, transforms our very conception of reality.

A central presupposition underlying differential calculus is that we can analyze a given part of reality while assuming that everything else remains constant. When using differential calculus to study production, for example, we can look at the marginal impact of a given factor of production in order to obtain its marginal productivity, while assuming everything else remains constant. The marginal productivity of a single factor of production (that is, capital, land, or labor) is measured by defining a production function, since the latter is taken to represent the technical conditions of utilizing those factors.

For this reason, John Bates Clark (1891) argued that the distribution of income between various classes is not a political issue, but rather a technical or theoretical issue, since the owners of factor inputs gain profits, wages, or rents according to the marginal productivity of each input. For the classical authors, in contrast, there is no mathematical criterion for the distribution of the surplus. Ricardo, for example, argues that wages are determined according to existing custom and institutions of a society. Wages further lead to a distribution of profits. For Ricardo ([1817] 1821), only rent is a result of the productivity of each land, as it was for Malthus and West too.

What Clark (1891) suggests, drawing on the results of the marginalist revolution (of which he was the greatest exponent in America), is the extension of the law of rent to the remaining factors of production: it is not just land, but also capital and labor, that would receive profits and wages according to the law of marginal productivity. That is to say, it is not only that land is scarce and thus generates a rent (as the classical authors presupposed), but rather that all factors of production are scarce, and thus all generate a rent based on their marginal productivity. For the classical authors, in contrast, only land is scarce, while it is institutional and political factors that set the distribution between wages and profits.

Although critical of what he believed to be classical political economy, Thorstein Veblen (1908) criticized J. B. Clark (1891) from the perspective of the surplus approach. For Veblen (1914, 1921), the surplus is generated in the roundabout process of production and depends upon the technological state of society. Veblen argues that what each class receives is the part of the social surplus in proportion to its institutional-social power within the society. It follows that the portion of the surplus appropriated by a leisure class does not contribute to the production of goods and services, since this surplus is used in a wasteful and conspicuous manner for the sake of signaling prestigious social status (Veblen 1899, 1914). It is not only Veblen, but also later American institutionalists like John Kenneth Galbraith (1958, 1967), who stress how modern societies are not characterized by scarcity, but rather by affluence, that is, by the creation of a surplus which is appropriated through institutional power. By focusing on the production and distribution of the surplus, authors like Veblen and Galbraith contributed much to the development of the surplus approach (see Adams 1991, for a discussion of the surplus from an institutionalist perspective).

Veblen and Galbraith were both critical of classical political economy. Veblen (1898) criticized classical political economy for being non-evolutionary or pre-Darwinian. Galbraith (1958) also argues that classical political economy focused on a world characterized by scarcity, while noting that contemporary industrial societies are characterized by abundance instead. This criticism of classical political economy is partly misleading since both Veblen and Galbraith did not have a clear distinction between classical political economy and vulgar political economy. Most of the criticisms made by Veblen and Galbraith to classical political economy apply mainly to vulgar political economy, with its emphasis on a stationary society characterized by scarcity, in which universal economic laws can be found in the human mind.

Classical political economists, in contrast, provided a theory which analyzes the normal position of the economy. As noted above, the normal position does not mean a stationary position. Rather, it focuses on what happens on average over time. Normal prices, normal profits, wages, or rents are conventional prices, conventional profits, wages, or rents. Conventional in that prices and income distribution persist on average through time and are maintained by prevailing habits and customs of society. The study of such conventional phenomena, which is central to heterodox traditions like Post Keynesianism and original institutionalism, sheds light on the formation and reproduction of the capitalist economic system (through the production and distribution of the surplus) that are controlled by large corporations or the capitalist class in general.

The analysis of large firms provided by Eichner (1976), the study of institutional mechanisms provided by American institutionalists, or the study of collective actions undertaken by business enterprises through trade associations, cartels, and the like, studied more recently by Lee (1998), can be easily combined with the classical analysis of a normal position, which need not mean a stationary long period, but rather a conventional position influenced by what has happened, on average, in the past (see Martins 2013b). As Lee (1998) shows, administered prices lead to the persistence of a given level of conventional prices maintained through time. Such a state of economy may be termed as a normal position determined by the conditions of production in the classical sense, but certainly not in the vulgar and marginalist sense (which became associated with the notion of 'normal position' after Marshall).

In neoclassical economics following vulgar political economy prices, wages and profits are determined by supply and demand curves under scarcity conditions. Supply and demand curves are an analytical tool which is radically at odds with the surplus approach, where scarcity is a particular case which usually refers to natural resources (Martins 2013c) and the emphasis is on the reproduction of a whole that can take place under various institutional settings. The activities of production and extraction of a surplus constitute an underlying process which can take place in various institutional settings, including the economic world studied by classical political economists, and the industrial society examined by American institutionalists and Post Keynesians—in particular, Lee (1998)'s theory of prices and pricing under modern corporate capitalism.

Veblen's critique of John Bates Clark's marginalist approach, like the Cambridge capital theory controversies, springs from the adoption of an approach where the distribution of the surplus depends upon institutional arrangements, rather than marginal productivities, as Avi Cohen and Geoffrey Harcourt (2003) note. Piero Sraffa and Joan Robinson argue that we cannot use a measure of capital in order to find the marginal productivity of capital without engaging in circular reasoning, since we must know the interest rate in order to compare units of capital from different time periods and reach a measure of aggregate capital. But the interest rate itself must be found using a measure of aggregate capital which in turn cannot be obtained without the interest rate (see Sraffa 1960, 38; Cohen and Harcourt 2003, 201–204).

Sraffa and Robinson point back towards the classical surplus approach in which prices are determined by the conditions of production (where the cost of production includes the surplus), not by supply and demand curves. Garegnani (1978, 1979) and Pasinetti (1993) also provide a synthesis between the thinking of Sraffa and Keynes (see Harcourt 1972, 2006). As pointed out above, Kalecki also developed an approach influenced by the idea of a circular process of reproduction, drawing upon Marx's reproduction schemes. The analysis of Kalecki and Keynes is sometimes seen as very different from Sraffa's (especially when the latter is interpreted in terms of the classical long period method following Garegnani), but such a perception springs from the fact that Kalecki and Keynes focused on economic fluctuations, and Sraffa focused on the conditions for the reproduction of economic activity while abstracting from economic fluctuations. But as noted above, both Kalecki and Garegnani stress the need of an integrated approach to the study of cycles and trends while focusing on the circular process of reproduction of the surplus.

Essentially, the history of economics running from classical political economy, institutional economics, to Post Keynesian economics reveals that the surplus approach is an integral part of heterodox economics, but also offers realistic analysis of modern capitalism that cannot be found in marginalist-mainstream economics. Once we realize that the central notion of economics is the surplus rather than scarcity, we can then see more clearly that economics is not the science which studies the allocation of scarce resources, but rather the science that studies the distribution of the surplus, and in particular the process of social provisioning (Gruchy 1987) through which the surplus is distributed, as Lee (2012b) explains.

## Concluding remarks

The surplus approach, which continues in heterodox economic traditions like Marxian political economy, original institutionalism, and Post Keynesian economics, has important political implications. If the distribution of the surplus is an institutional qua structural issue, then there is space for ethical and political debate on distribution, which lies outside the arena of market exchanges, and must take place within a broader discussion concerning social provisioning. In mainstream economics, distribution is endogenously determined, that is, mathematically and mechanically determined through marginal productivity in the context of resource scarcity. Therefore, there is no space left for ethical and political debate about distribution.

Central problems of contemporary capitalism like increasing inequality can be best addressed by a surplus approach, rather than by a scarcity cum exchange approach that goes back to, what Marx called, vulgar political economy. This particular problem of inequality becomes more crucial since it leads to the eruption of severe crises that is largely dependent upon the lack of effective demand caused by the unequal distribution of the surplus and the instability in the financial system therein (see Martins 2013b, ch. 4, for detailed discussion on this matter). As Kalecki and Keynes noted, those with higher incomes have a lower propensity to consume, and investment may not be sufficient to compensate the reduction of effective demand caused by inequality (see Martins 2011).

Marxian political economy, original institutionalism, and Post Keynesian economics provide important contributions to the surplus approach. Such contributions also raise the question of how the surplus should be distributed, that is, how should social provisioning be addressed, a topic also addressed within social economics and feminist economics. Together, these heterodox traditions challenge vulgar political economy, marginalism, or mainstream-neoclassical economics. In fact, the issue at stake in Marx's critique of vulgar political economy, Veblen's critique of Clark's marginalism, or in the Cambridge controversies on the theory of capital is connected to the distinction between a surplus approach which goes back to classical political economy and the supply and demand analysis developed within vulgar political economy and marginalism. Heterodox economic traditions have actively engaged in a critique of mainstream economics while pointing towards a return to the surplus approach, where social provisioning, that is, the distribution of the surplus, is a political and institutional issue, rather than determined by supply and demand.

In so doing, various heterodox traditions have developed the surplus approach taking into account the developments that took place in the capitalist system in the last 200 years. Indeed, a concern with the nature of economic reality is a central uniting feature of heterodox economics. At the methodological level, various strands in heterodox economics hold the common ontological orientation that is characterized by a concern with the nature of economic reality, while mainstream economics is characterized by a methodological emphasis on mathematical-deductivist methods (Lawson 2003).

The analysis of the production and distribution of the surplus vis-à-vis administered prices in the course of production continues to be essential to the understanding of contemporary capitalism. In this respect, Professor Frederic Lee's contribution is part of this grand project that started with classical political economists, and that was abandoned by vulgar political economists and then by mainstream-neoclassical economists.

If a classical economist would reappear today, s/he would quite naturally examine capitalist production and see how production processes taking place in the (contemporary) real world lead to the emergence of prices, and how the distribution of the surplus influences economic activities. This is exactly what Professor Lee has done over 30 years of his career as a heterodox economist: the analysis of the production process in the context of the capitalist social provisioning process, which is influenced by and, at the same time, advances the surplus approach. Of course, the goal of Professor Lee is not merely to return to classical political economy, but rather to advance and further develop the social surplus approach, whose origins can be found in classical political economy.

## Acknowledgments

This chapter benefited from very useful comments from Tae-Hee Jo, Zdravka Todorova, and Matias Vernengo and was written before the untimely death of Professor Frederic Lee. I would like to add that I started to learn about Fred Lee's contribution quite recently, but it quickly became extremely important to the development of my own research. In particular, it showed me how concepts which I was addressing from an history of economic thought perspective, such as surplus and prices determined by objective conditions of production, are also very relevant for a more appropriate understanding of the contemporary world, and very much in line with his own approach to the topic, as I tried to argue in this chapter. We are all in great debt to his contribution, and hope that it be extended and continued, for the continuation of his project is essential for the construction of a better world, which was in fact his lifetime purpose, always pursued with great persistency, leaving us all an impressive example of scholarly dedication.

## References

Adams, J. 1991. "Surplus, Surplus, Who's Got the Surplus? The Subtractivist Fallacy in Orthodox Economics." *Journal of Economic Issues* 25: 187–197.

Braudel, F. [1979] 1982. *Civilization and Capitalism, 15th–18th Centuries*, 3 vols., translated by Siân Reynolds. Berkeley: University of California Press.

Clark, J. B. 1891. "Distribution as Determined by the Law of Rent." *Quarterly Journal of Economics* 5: 289–318.

Cohen, A. and G. C. Harcourt. 2003. "Whatever Happened to the Cambridge Capital Theory Controversies?" *Journal of Economic Perspectives* 17: 199–214.

Eichner, A. S. 1976. *The Megacorp and Oligopoly*. Cambridge: Cambridge University Press.

Galbraith, J. K. 1958. *The Affluent Society*. Boston: Houghton Mifflin.

Galbraith, J. K. 1967. *The New Industrial State*. Boston: Houghton Mifflin.

Garegnani, P. 1978. "Notes on Consumption, Investment and Effective Demand: I." *Cambridge Journal of Economics* 2: 335–353.

Garegnani, P. 1979. "Notes on Consumption, Investment and Effective Demand: II." *Cambridge Journal of Economics* 3: 63–82.

Garegnani, P. 1984. "Value and Distribution in the Classical Economists and Marx." *Oxford Economic Papers* 36: 291–325.

Garegnani, P, and A. Trezzini. 2010. "Cycles and Growth: A Source of Demand-Driven Endogenous Growth." *Review of Political Economy* 22: 119–125.

Gruchy, A. G. 1987. *The Reconstruction of Economics: An Analysis of the Fundamentals of Institutional Economics*. New York: Greenwood Press.

Harcourt, G. C. 1972. *Some Cambridge Controversies in the Theory of Capital*. Cambridge: Cambridge University Press.

Harcourt, G. C. 1981. "Marshall, Sraffa, and Keynes: Incompatible Bedfellows?" *Eastern Economic Journal* 7: 39–50. Reprinted in P. Kerr, ed. 1982. *The Social Science Imperialists: Selected Essays of G.C. Harcourt*, 250–264. London: Routledge and Kegan Paul.

Harcourt, G. C. 2006. *The Structure of Post-Keynesian Economics: The Core Contributions of the Pioneers*. Cambridge: Cambridge University Press.

Harvey, D. 2006. *Limits to Capital.* London: Verso.

Henry, J. F. 1990. *The Making of Neoclassical Economics.* London: Unwin Hyman.

Henry, J. F. 2009. "The Illusion of the Epoch: Neoclassical Economics as a Case." *Studi e Note di Economia* 14: 27–44.

Kalecki, M. 1971. *Selected Essays on the Dynamics of the Capitalist Economy.* Cambridge: Cambridge University Press.

Lawson, T. 2003. *Reorienting Economics.* London: Routledge.

Lee, F. S. 1998. *Post Keynesian Price Theory.* Cambridge: Cambridge University Press.

Lee, F. S. 2008. "Heterodox Economics." In *The New Palgrave Dictionary of Economics*, 2nd ed., edited by S. N. Durlauf and L. E. Blume. London: Palgrave Macmillan.

Lee, F. S. 2009. *A History of Heterodox Economics.* London: Routledge.

Lee, F. S. 2012a. "Competition, Going Enterprise, and Economic Activity." In *Alternative Theories of Competition: Challenges to the Orthodoxy*, edited by J. K. Moudud, C. Bina, and P. L. Mason, 160–173. London: Routledge.

Lee, F. S. 2012b. "Heterodox Surplus Approach: Production, Prices, and Value Theory." *Bulletin of Political Economy* 6 (2): 65–105.

Lee, F. S. 2013. "Post-Keynesian Price Theory: From Pricing to Market Governance to the Economy as a Whole." In *The Oxford Handbook of Post-Keynesian Economics*, Vol. 1, edited by G. C. Harcourt and P. Kriesler, 467–484. Oxford: Oxford University Press.

Lee, F. S. and T.-H. Jo. 2011. "Social Surplus Approach and Heterodox Economics." *Journal of Economic Issues* 45 (4): 857–875.

Martins, N. O. 2011. "Globalisation, Inequality and the Economic Crisis." *New Political Economy* 16: 1–18.

Martins, N. O. 2013a. "Classical Surplus Theory and Heterodox Economics." *American Journal of Economics and Sociology* 72: 1205–1231.

Martins, N. O. 2013b. *The Cambridge Revival of Political Economy.* London: Routledge.

Martins, N. O. 2013c. "The Place of the Capability Approach within Sustainability Economics." *Ecological Economics* 95: 226–230.

Marx, K. [1867] 1999. *Capital.* Oxford: Oxford University Press.

Meek, R. 1961. "Mr. Sraffa's Rehabilitation of Classical Economics." *Scottish Journal of Political Economy* 8: 119–136.

Moudud, J. K., C. Bina, and P. L. Mason, eds. 2012. *Alternative Theories of Competition: Challenges to the Orthodoxy.* London: Routledge.

Pasinetti, L. L. 1993. *Structural Economic Dynamics: A Theory of the Economic Consequences of Human Learning.* Cambridge: Cambridge University Press.

Ricardo, D. [1817] 1821. *On the Principles of Political Economy and Taxation.* London: John Murray.

Smith, A. [1776] 1993. *An Inquiry into the Nature and Causes of the Wealth of Nations.* Oxford: Oxford University Press.

Sraffa, P. 1960. *Production of Commodities by Means of Commodities.* Cambridge: Cambridge University Press.

Veblen, T. 1898. "Why is Economics Not an Evolutionary Science?" *The Quarterly Journal of Economics* 12: 373–397.

Veblen, T. 1899. *The Theory of the Leisure Class.* New York: Macmillan.

Veblen, T. 1908. "Professor Clark's Economics." *Quarterly Journal of Economics* 22: 147–195.

Veblen, T. 1914. *The Instinct of Workmanship and the State of the Industrial Arts.* New York: Macmillan.

Veblen, T. 1921. *The Engineers and the Price System.* New York: Macmillan.

# 12 Consumption in the context of social provisioning and capitalism

## Beyond consumer choice and aggregates

*Zdravka Todorova*

### Introduction

Frederic Lee has made a case for weaving various heterodox approaches into a distinctively heterodox coherent model of the capitalist economy. He constructs a model of the economy as a whole that incorporates the social surplus approach along with the stock-flow consistent modeling, Chartalist state money theory, input-output matrix analysis, the social fabric matrix (see Hayden 2006), and the methodological articulation of the symbiotic relationship between structure and agency. Obviously, Lee exemplifies a heterodox economist who draws from a variety of heterodox traditions and methods while working towards the construction of a coherent and realistic theory of a capitalist economy. In doing that, he deems the split between microeconomics and macroeconomics as misguided and unrealistic (Lee 2008, 2009, 2011, 2012).

Analysis of aggregates cannot provide a view of the economy as a whole, and micro is not limited to individual units of analysis, but studies those in order to obtain a better understanding of the whole economy (see also Jo's chapter in this book). Thus, if consumption is to be approached as one of the aspects of the social provisioning process, it can be viewed as a process itself—that is, consumption is more than an aggregate variable or outcome of individual consumer choices.

The present chapter builds on Lee's conception of the economy as a whole and discusses consumption as a process that is part of social provisioning under capitalism. Lee's (2011) heterodox model manifests linkages among essential components of the economy as a whole: that is, (1) history and the social fabric are linked to the economic model of the social provisioning process, (2) agency is linked to structures, and (3) social provisioning is linked to social activities. The concept of social process facilitates such theorizing of the economy. The first section introduces the concept of social provisioning while stressing some analytical differences this conceptualization makes for theorizing consumption. The second section delineates a number of features of the capitalist economy that affect analyses of consumption. The third section discusses consumption as a social process. Finally, the chapter concludes by drawing implications for heterodox economics.

## A social provisioning framework of consumption

The concept of social provisioning is a basis for a social, historical, open-ended, evolutionary analysis of the economy that opens avenues to explore varieties of contexts, social divisions, conflicts, and hierarchical power relations. Continuation of the life-process, human well-being, and cultural values are central to the concept. Social provisioning allows for a broader and deeper formulation of economic activity, beyond the most visible occurrence of market exchange and beyond monetary production. It encompasses non-market activities, culture, and ecosystems (Gruchy 1987; Nelson 1993; Dugger 1996; Power 2004; Lee 2009, 2011, 2012; Jo 2011a; Lee and Jo 2011; Todorova 2013a, 2013b, 2014b). Provisioning is *social* because economic activities are based on social relations and socially generated knowledge that enables the creation of resources. Further, social provisioning is comprised of various *processes* because it involves continuous social activities and valuation that take place in historical time.

As emphasized by Fred Lee, at a most basic level the economy is founded by the interdependent production of inputs and outputs that provide for the material means of life. The volume and composition of surplus and basic goods are determined by the agency of capitalists. Households, the business enterprise, and the state consume surplus goods and services to reproduce themselves over time. Inputs and outputs are specific to the production of differentiated goods and services, and thus cannot be aggregated (Lee and Jo 2011; Lee 2011; see also Martin's chapter in this book).

Similarly, labor power embodies differentiated skills and biological bodies that ought to be reproduced, maintained, cultivated, and applied in the production of the various inputs and outputs; and consumes and produces differentiated consumption goods (Todorova 2009). Further, substitution of consumption goods is limited by biological needs, social status, perceptions, and habits and thereby substitution effects are limited (see Lavoie 1994, 2004). Thus, income, biological limitations, and agency-structures have a better explanatory power in the account of the actual provisioning process than a notion of the price mechanism as in neoclassical economics. The social surplus is produced by all agents involved in production, and is directed through the organization of monetary activities, which include monetary production and finance. In a monetary production economy the central motive of undertaking production is salesmanship or making money. Making goods that service livelihood is incidental to the monetary production process. Further, production needs not occur in money-making activities (Veblen [1919] 2005, 97; Keynes [1933] 1971; Dillard 1980; Henry 2003; Lee 2009). Finance is not directly engaged in production, but in activities that secure "vested interest," or claims on the social surplus (Veblen [1919] 2005). Those claims manifest themselves as *life-styles* with "pecuniary standards of living" that are part of class distinction (Veblen [1899] 1994, 63).

Consequently, social provisioning is theoretically explained by the surplus approach, the theory of effective demand, and the monetary theory of production. Distribution is determined outside of market exchange—by institutions rooted in class-oriented values. Markets and incomes are only manifestations of these values, meaning that distribution of income and consumption goods and services is not determined by marginal productivity. Thus, the study of consumption as one of the processes of social provisioning has the potential to unveil the underlining social fabric.

## The capitalist context of consumption

The present section delineates features of a capitalist social context of consumption inquiry. Additional characteristics could introduce context-specific variations. Delineating those features helps see that the social fabric is linked to the economic model of the social provisioning process, particularly to consumption process, that agency is linked to structures, and that social provisioning is linked to social activities.

**First**, economic activities are based on *economic class* relations stemming from the private ownership of assets that represents claims on the social product. Society's usage of tools, skills, labor power, and knowledge is always communally generated and organized. However, the private ownership of assets provides individualized income streams that claim the social product and restrain, direct, or preclude access to livelihood.

Differentiated consumption patterns emerge out of the effort to establish and maintain households as going concerns enmeshed in social networks that secure *social class* positions within the existing class relations and capitalist institutions. In the process of market expansion, business enterprises—particularly their financial branches, and financial institutions—enable households to temporarily circumvent financial constraints and to ameliorate the accompanying inequalities. This allows for households to become indebted and financially fragile in order to meet socially evolving needs that cannot be supported fully by their incomes (Tymoigne 2007; Brown 2008; Todorova 2009; Wisman 2009).[1]

The ruling class directs the generation and distribution of the social surplus, affects public policy, and influences the broader culture through a significant access to media, education, policymaking, among others, and through control over employment, production, and salesmanship decisions. Households' daily activities, livelihoods, life-styles, identities, and agency are greatly impacted by their economic class—e.g., the necessity to sell their labor power and the lack of such. Consequently, not only social class distinction based on inequality of income and socio-economic background, but economic class ought to be present in the theory of consumption.

The presence of economic class in the theory of consumption contrasts the conceptual symmetry between production/supply and consumption/demand that allows for the formulation of the mainstream notions of 'consumer surplus' and 'producer surplus.' As a result, the 'social surplus' is absent in mainstream analysis. Moreover, a discussion of economic class, conflict, and social provisioning is circumvented, and instead 'consumer sovereignty' is the norm (Todorova 2013b) and the economy is represented by harmonious and symmetric market exchanges with market imperfections as exceptions (Bharadwaj 1986). Consumer sovereignty is the conventional wisdom that workers (re-imagined as consumers) could equally partake in the direction of social provisioning that in turn is appropriately re-formulated as an asocial allocation of resources.

An analysis based on economic class does not preclude a further elaboration of social complexity, cultural and other variations among people and localities, and other ways of stratification, individuality, a variety of identities, and agency from inquiry. Indeed, economic class is the basis of theorizing the variation in agency such as between households and business enterprises as well as among households and among business enterprises. Furthermore, the recognition of various economic classes allows us to analyze the development and production of differentiated products that become part of the process of invidious distinction as well as the demarcation of social classes. In particular, the business enterprises' and sovereign states' decision to produce an array of consumption goods on a class basis also support the invidious wage structure.

**Second**, the capitalist class, the state, and global financial institutions control the *volume and composition of the output*. In addition, they simultaneously determine the level and composition of employment, wage rates, and profit mark-ups, and thus control working and financially dependent classes' access to the social surplus. Management goals formed in a particular regulatory and institutional context (which is also largely influenced by the ruling class) determine the available commodities for household activities. Working and financially dependent classes demand consumption goods out of evolving sets of commodities; they do not command the level and composition of commodities as well as the development and usage of resources utilized in the production of commodities.[2]

One implication of the above is that a critique of consumer sovereignty is not about revealing that consumers are passive victims of persuasion, but about making the point that market governance and power relations therein direct the functioning of capitalism.[3] Another implication is that the social product is not a given entity in search for realization; rather, it is determined by effective demand together with creation and articulation of consumer needs (Lee 2011; Lee and Jo 2011). A corollary implication is that the production of the social surplus is not constrained by households' savings. On the contrary, households' activities and their financial positions including the ability to save are constrained by the desire of the business enterprise and the state to produce the social surplus.

Household consumption includes commodities produced through monetary production as well as goods and services that are not commodities, but the provision of which may necessitate commodities. Both commodities and non-commodities reproduce labor power which enters into the production of the social product, and thus of the social surplus, a portion of which again goes to support households' social activities. Those activities produce non-commodities that sustain labor power as well as other aspects of human life. In a capitalist economy to support activities not motivated by making money, households need money to buy commodities, and thus consumption could not be fully met outside of monetary production (Todorova 2009). Thus, commodity production emerges out of effective demand and non-commodity production is affected by effective demand, because as pointed out social provisioning activity not directed towards the market still depends on incomes and commodities subject to market participation.

Working and financially dependent classes do have a room for *agency* in consumption through collectively organized social activities of provisioning that attempt to reduce the reliance on commodities by cultivating non-market forms of social relations. Within the social provisioning framework, agency exists in the possibility of *"non-invidious recreation of community"* (Tool [1979] 1985, 299, emphasis added) and is restricted by the class structure, inequality, and the structure of employment (see Wisman 2011). It is important to note that the possibility for such agency can be articulated only if it is recognized that the social surplus is comprised of both commodities as well as of goods and services that are produced outside of a money-making motive (including, but not limited to, households and the state). In fact in a monetary production economy commodities and non-commodities cannot be neatly separated from each other.

**Third**, class power relations are masked by *inequality of life-styles* within the working class as well as by the notions of *consumer* and *taxpayer*. Differentiated consumption goods are produced in accordance with income differences. Variation in consumption activities define various life-styles and are central to invidious distinction (Veblen [1899] 1994; Todorova 2009, 2013b; Wisman 2009). Social categories such as 'middle class,' 'upper middle class,' 'professionals,' and 'the creative class' emerged historically to denote belonging to a certain lifestyle. They are reference categories that signify *groups* of people on the basis of consumption patterns, education, living quarters, neighborhoods, and occupations—in other words *social class*.

Individuals have many *identities* and strive for belonging to a number of reference groups by performing various *behaviors* to express their identities, but at any point in time they occupy a position in the economic class structure which determines *the extent* of their actions. Consequently, the role of an economic class process cannot be understated especially with respect to determination and directing of the social surplus, and the economic compulsion—e.g., to sell one's labor. This does not mean that individual lives are predetermined, but that individual actions (expressed for example by choices and patterns of behavior) are always in the context of institutions that precede the particular individual(s). Obviously, there are degrees of agency—some individuals make decisions that direct the social surplus and others choose between a paper or plastic bag at the cash register; dress provocatively; others set prices; select who to hire; vote; or a combination of these, among others.

The emergence of consumers and taxpayers as analytical categories and discourse are historically specific phenomena (Perelman 2005; Trentmann and Taylor 2006). Formulating problems in terms of taxpayers and consumers narrows the articulation of conflicts of social provisioning to matters of exchange. While as Ben Fine (2006, 306) points out the politics of consumption is limited in its radical content as "putting politics into consumption can serve to focus on the individual at the expense of the collective and immediate delivery at the expense of the broader parameters of provision and provisioning." Consumer politics, he argues, reflects a corresponding "consumerisation of politics." This is expressed by the marketization of non-commodities and the discourse of consumers and clients in education, healthcare, and social programs (Fine 2006; Galbraith 2008, ch. 11).

The reliance on the concept of consumers and taxpayers thus has a purpose as well as a consequence. It redirects a discourse from class relations and the degree of agency to market exchanges, from collective life process to privatization and individual costs/benefits, and from social provisioning to *neoliberal subjectivity* (Todorova 2013c, 10). When class relations and the degree of agency are out of the picture the theoretical focus is exclusively on subjective valuation which justifies asocial individualism and the politics of neoliberalism.

**Fourth**, the activities of the business enterprise as a going concern are tied to the cultivation of *growth of needs* (Lavoie 1994) and *chronic dissatisfaction*—that is, a social habit of life and thought, rather than an idiosyncratic individual state of mind (Hamilton 1987). "If production is to increase, the wants must be effectively contrived" (Galbraith 1958, 129).

Thus, business enterprises do not respond passively to autonomous consumer needs, but actively seek to create wants and needs through the development of new products and marketing campaigns. In doing so they are not acting independently from the rest of society. Rather, they seek to incorporate and respond in various ways to social attitudes, beliefs, and events. For example, business enterprises engage in social activities of "corporate social responsibility" as part of their market governance strategy (Brei and Böhm 2011; Jo 2011b).

Chronic dissatisfaction generates *systemic and growing waste*—a concept referring not only to unused by-products, but to "expenditure that does not serve human life or human well-being on the whole ... and occurs on the ground of an invidious pecuniary comparison" (Veblen [1899] 1994, 60) and represents a vested interest corresponding to a "free income." Individuals and going concerns deem such incomes, products, and activities necessary, deserving, and of worth, rather than wasteful, since they help secure social status. For that reason, waste can be discussed and addressed only in view of social provisioning and not in view of individual choices (Todorova 2013a). This is also valid for "conspicuous consumption"—that is, a particular form of waste (Todorova 2013b) since the expansion of the capitalist economy depends on the generation of "conspicuous waste" (Veblen [1899] 1994, 60).

**Fifth**, the state is active in creating and organizing markets that support the existing power relations. Consumption activities take place within a given infrastructure, and the development of public infrastructure could be prompted by the goal of selling commodities. Thus, public infrastructure enables and affects consumption of commodities (Galbraith 1958; Todorova 2013a). One method of organizing markets is the creation of mass consumers or 'middle-class' with expanding purchasing power through the growth of the wage bill including public goods and services that reduce household expenditures (Glickman 1997). Another method is through privatization and marketization of space, resources, social activities, and institutions such as media, education, and financialization resulting in growing household indebtedness and precarious wages (Wray 2008; Bayliss, Fine, and Robertson 2013). Neither entails maintaining full employment. Instead, both sustain existing power relations (Kalecki [1943] 1990; Todorova 2013b).

While the first method has disappeared through the "Keynesian devolution" (Galbraith 2008, 61), the second is contributing to the expansion and entrenchment of capitalist relations in all elements of life. The state adopts pecuniary criteria of valuation, which lead to what J. K. Galbraith called "social imbalance": "Every corner of the public psyche is canvassed by some of the nation's most talented citizens to see if the desire for some merchantable product can be cultivated. No similar process operates on behalf of the non-merchantable services of the state" (Galbraith 1958, 205).

Yet, the generation of monetary flows is supported by 'non-market' relations and by nature. In efforts to secure its position, the ruling class seeks to control those relations, the public, and nature by continuous enclosures, extraction, and marketization (Veblen 1923; Polanyi [1944] 1957; Marx 1990; Robertson 2008; LeBaron 2010) that determine the composition and level of the output available for consumption.

The delineated features of the capitalist economy prompt the analysis of consumption that goes beyond theories of consumer choice and aggregate consumption expenditures. The following section introduces the concept of social process which facilitates micro-macro analysis of consumption as part of theorizing social provisioning under capitalism.

## Consumption as a social process and the economy as a whole

The concept of *social process* is consistent with Fred Lee's formulation of micro-macro analysis of the economy as a whole (see, for example, Lee 2009, 2011) to the extent that it can capture action and agency taking place at the micro level as well as the continuity and interconnectedness of activities and outcomes within the whole economy. Furthermore, *process* as a concept in heterodox economics also exemplifies the connections among approaches within heterodox economics as it can be found in various institutional, Marxist, feminist, social structure of accumulation analyses, or combinations of those (Veblen 1898; Nelson 1993; Fraad *et al.* 1994; Power 2004; Todorova 2009).

Social process enables theorizing the social provisioning process that takes place in historical time generating stable institutional arrangements and power relations, and thus encompasses analysis of agency and structures. Individuals' purposeful actions (expressed for example by choices, strategic decision-making, and patterns of behavior) take place in the context of institutional settings that precede particular individual(s) and groups. The advantages of utilizing the concept of social process is that the social context and agency gain explanatory power, that is, agency is not formulated in terms of methodological individualism, nor is it lost within aggregate analyses.

*Social process* emerges out of the evolution and interaction of conventions (working rules and procedures), discourse, symbols, norms of valuation, standards, personal attitudes, rituals, and customs that emerge out of the activities of going concerns. Together with specific going concerns those categories comprise an *institution*: the business enterprise, the household, the state, global organizations, religion, schooling and research, the foundation, the stock exchange, the beauty pageant, military, media, unions, cooperatives, and collectives. Institutions embody collective action that is connected to the class structure. Table 12.1 delineates the elements of social processes, expanding on (Todorova 2014a), and provides examples with a particular reference to the process of consumption.

*Social activities* are organized and carried out by going concerns on the basis of historically established institutional settings. Thus, the individual *act* of socializing is a part of a particular social activity that is organized by a *going concern* (the household, the business enterprise, the state). Going concerns engage in continuous, relatively stable social activities through which they exercise agency that help create symbols and discourse, promote norms of valuation, social beliefs, and personal attitudes, and help establish conventions. *Conventions* consist of procedures and working rules. For example, the conventions of 'reduced margins of safety' in lending and borrowing, and the shorter planning span of business enterprises are based on the *procedures* of: securitization; flexibility of labor and subcontracting; reliance on credit scoring in lending; and the switch to define contribute retirement plans (Brown 2008; Kregel 2008). *Working rules* include legal statutes, contracts, legislation, tax codes, and regulations (such as consumer protection provisions, financial regulation, and tax structure).

Diverse individual *perceptions* and multidimensional *identities* underline collective action. Identities may not be clearly formed and recognized, and are not purely subjective in the sense that they are also based on relatively stable social arrangements—institutions or structures. For example, the debt-credit process cannot be transcended by subjective perception. Theorizing an objective existence of debtor-creditor relations need not harm the conceptualization of diverse identities and perceptions. Discourse, social beliefs, standards, norms of valuation, and symbols affect perceptions. *Discourse* includes sign, conventional wisdom, and expert discourse. *Sign* is a depiction or image that conveys a message or status, such as a logo of a brand. It acts as a shortcut for a complex social statement. *Conventional wisdom* represents a knowledge claim and a widely accepted matter of fact understanding of how things work based on 'myth.' For example, it is a conventional wisdom for freedom to be equated with the opportunity to shop and to choose among variety of products (Galbraith 2008, ch. 2). Conventional wisdom is reinforced by *expert discourse* including by specific academic theories, concepts, and methods, such as marginal productivity theory of distribution, consumer sovereignty, and utility maximization. Unlike social belief, conventional wisdom is a knowledge claim, even if those who profess it may not be aware of its theoretical underpinnings.

A *social belief* is a shared conviction that does not necessarily make knowledge claims, rather it serves as a center of gravity for a sense of unity among

Table 12.1 Elements of social process with reference to consumption process

| Element | Examples with reference to consumption process |
|---|---|
| acts | eating |
| consumption activities | eating out; preparing food at home; celebration |
| going concerns | households; business enterprises; universities; state; unions; collectives |
| conventions | bottled water; individualized packaging; reduced margins of lending and borrowing; sexualized advertising |
| working rules | food safety regulations; water pumping laws; financial deregulation |
| procedures | packaging and distribution methods; securitization |
| perceptions | perceptions about health, prestige, product benefits; expectations about income |
| identities | masculinity; beauty; good parenting; success |
| discourse | freedom through commodity consumption |
| conventional wisdom | variety of products equated with freedom; expressing individuality/agency through products |
| expert discourse | consumer sovereignty; healthy dietary needs; necessary water intake |
| rhetorical constructs | consumers |
| sign | brand name/logo |
| social belief | American Dream |
| norms of valuation | 'pecuniary strength'; 'pecuniary beauty'; 'pecuniary reputability'; sustainability of the life-process |
| standards | nutrition and health norms; 'standards of pecuniary decency': 'middle-class' consumption standards, including number, size, and kind of rooms in homes |
| symbols | shopping centers; store/restaurant chains; engagement rings; lawn; reusable drinking bottle |
| customs and rituals | gifting of commodities; special food preparation; themed commodities/marketing; consumption to feel good and to go on |
| personal attitudes | importance of brand names for personal self-esteem |
| habits of life and thought (an amalgamation of particular developments in the above elements) | conspicuous consumption; fashion; tourism; standardized consumption; gated consumption; sexism; racism; ageism. |

people, as mechanism of coping, and as motivation and justification for (in) action. A social belief could be interpreted and acted upon in varieties of ways. For example, the American Dream is a social belief that has been articulated in a particular way in the politics of 'the ownership society' (Todorova 2014a; see Wray 2005 for a detailed discussion of the politics of ownership society). In turn, the 'ownership society' is *rhetorical construct* used as a justification for financial deregulation and privatization. Emerging out of social beliefs, rhetorical constructs not only manifest social beliefs but also are directly connected to *norms* such as "pecuniary strength," "pecuniary beauty," and "pecuniary reputability" (Veblen [1899] 1994, 63) that signify success and social worthiness. Norms of valuation are connected to specific *standards*, such as "pecuniary canons of taste" and "decency" used in the judgment of acceptable and distinct consumption thresholds and product specifications (Veblen [1899] 1994, 71). The existence of various lifestyles is concurrent to the evolution and persistence of varieties of consumption standards, including size of yards, rooms, and houses, as well as amenities and product specifications that are deemed minimally adequate. Such standards are also symbolized. The proper lawn today is a symbol of 'middle class living standards' (another rhetorical construct). While *symbols* serve as visualization of standards, moral norms, social beliefs, and rhetorical constructs, they can also be conventions as they involve procedures and rules. Capitalist activities produce symbols in terms of monetary valuation. Thus, the institution of the stock exchange promotes specific norms of social worthiness. Further it communicates appropriate behavior and personal attitudes via its symbols that are present in everyday life. For example, ubiquitous stock price tickers help establish a social belief that 'watching the market' is not only beneficial but also important for everybody's livelihood. *Rituals* (e.g., ringing the bell at the stock exchange) are also symbols that embody, express, and reinforce social values. More general rituals could also be delineated. For example, the BBDO advertising company defines ritual as "sequences that are developed over time" and as "series of actions that move people emotionally from one place to another" (Brady 2007).[4] *Customs* involve many people routinely engaging in specific type of activities with shared meaning, albeit with variations (e.g., celebrations). Both rituals and customs involve the consumption of particular class-specific goods and services.

The concept of social process encompasses all of the analytical categories delineated above. Agency exercised within specific institutional arrangements, gives rise to specific *habits of life and thought*. Thus, financialization, conspicuous consumption, fashion, standardization of consumption, sexism, racism, austerity, tourism, and gated consumption can be defined as habits of life and thought, which represent ideas and action. Habits of life and thought become instituted through the organization of social activities and agency exercised by going concerns such as business enterprises, households, the state, trade unions, non-for-profit organizations, and international organizations, among others; and also through the creation of conventions—e.g., sexualized advertising, individualized packaging, reduced margins of safety in lending and borrowing (Todorova

2014a). Habits of life and thought are different from *personal attitudes*. In order for personal attitudes to become habits of life and thought, a *collective action* ought to take place. Such a distinction allows for a micro-macro analysis of the economy as a whole. For example, personal attitudes towards the importance of brand status for one's self-esteem are only part of the conspicuous consumption as habits of life and thought.

Social processes unfold in historical time and form an open system with full of uncertainty but no finality. All social processes involve cognition, learning, and the formation of expectations. While individuals are integral in the analysis, the delineated categories of social processes are not limited to individuals and groups. Consequently, the delineated conception of social process supports non-reductionist micro-foundations that are not based in methodological individualism (Lee 2009, 2011; Jo 2011a; Lee and Jo 2011).

Table 12.2 depicts social processes based on *social provisioning activities* and suggests ways that consumption of commodities and non-commodities are part of those processes. To emphasize, those are not two separate worlds, but two dimensions of social provisioning. The distinction is useful for recognizing the distinct motivation and valuation associated with the production of commodities and non-commodities (for more details on each one of those processes, see Todorova 2014b).

The outlined social processes and their application to consumption provide a starting point for a context-specific analysis. Social processes are not fixed or universal. Some of the social processes may be delineated on the basis of identifiable social activities that take place at the micro level and affect the composition and distribution of the social surplus at the macro level. Social activities are delineated on the basis of acts that emerge in the course of the life-process. Thus, such activities as caring, working, recreation, studying, inquiry, organizing, aggression, lending/borrowing, gifting, consumption, disposal, traveling, migration, and transportation are all social activities that address the continuation of life-process in particular and non-interchangeable ways. For example, one cannot fully replace care for somebody by purchasing commodities. Neither could one care about somebody without commodities (given a capitalist context). Specifically, a consumption process is defined in terms of consumption activities that are centered on consumption acts. Consumption activities are intertwined with other social activities such as care, leisure, work, and business negotiation. For example, leisure activities (e.g., wine tasting, restaurant tours, practicing various sports, traveling, and craft-making) could be simultaneously recreation, business, and consumption activities (Todorova 2014a).

Social processes based on social provisioning activities are part of a broader *culture-nature life-process* (see Todorova 2014b). Consumption process then is connected also to: geography, landscapes, physical spaces/buildings, and biological life-processes (bodies, biophysical processes, and ecosystems). Moreover, consumption process is based in and affects social processes, such as gender, race/ethnicity, social class, language, economic class, citizenship and legal residency, ownership, contracts, worship, and kinship. Thus, consumption ought to be

Table 12.2 Other social processes and consumption of non-commodities and commodities

| Social processes | Consumption of non-commodities | Consumption of commodities |
|---|---|---|
| Labor | subsistence production; cooking and other unpaid work contributing to maintaining consumption life-styles | monetary production; labor power used in 'salesmanship' activities such as advertising and product differentiation |
| Care | non-commodities supporting paid and unpaid care provision | commodities used in the provision of paid and unpaid care |
| Recreation | public space and access to means of recreation such as nature and art | art for sale; commercial sports and exercise consumption activities; conspicuous leisure; gated consumption |
| Mobility and residence | public spaces; publicly supported goods | individualized automobile transportation; tourism; internet used for consumption purchases; gated communities; invidious distinction through housing and vehicles |
| Communication, expression, and persuasion | non-commodity inputs for art; downshifting campaigns; promotion of non-commodity production and life-styles | corporate media promoting life-styles; advertising; art for sale and commodity inputs for art |
| Undertaking | non-commodities supporting mobilization and community organizing | conspicuous consumption of commodities in developing business partnerships, entrepreneurship, investment (golf, business presents; business entertainment) |
| Cultivation and transmission of knowledge, memories/tools | development and preservation of non-commodity production techniques (such as food preparation); destruction of resources; invention and technology | technology; invention; patents; destruction of memory through commercialization; folklore appropriation for commercial purposes |
| Resource creation and usage | financially feasible innovations and innovations in not-for market production and activities; sharing of non-commodity output | financially feasible innovations and consumption commodities; patents; transforming non-commodities into commodities |

*continued*

Table 12.2 Continued

| Social processes | Consumption of non-commodities | Consumption of commodities |
|---|---|---|
| Machine process | sharing of non-commodities | purchase of domestic 'labor-saving' appliances; standardization of products |
| Supervision, direction, surveillance | national and international of subsistence production; management of household or other non-commodity production | marketing surveys, profiling, business data mining and surveillance for the purpose of salesmanship |
| Threat and punishment | 'proper' domesticity, (wo)manhood, or parenting; stigmatization based on those | welfare system; austerity policies; advertising and consumption based on fear; credit scoring; censorship of harmful product features or effects |
| Distribution | based on obligations, needs, and access to money for purchasing commodity inputs | based on administered prices and incomes, property rights, conventions, and notions of productivity |
| Gift/exchange | gift of non-commodities | gifting commodities |
| Deprivation | malnutrition; enclosures preventing self-subsistence, or production of non-commodities | sabotage of 'industrial efficiency' in the design of products, and their level (unemployment); destruction of resources; austerity policies; promotion of mis-information about products |
| Waste | reuse; repurposing; disposal; conspicuous waste | business practices of recycling and reuse; cost cutting disposal; conspicuous waste |
| Debt-credit | | consumer debt and credit; mortgage debt |
| Violence | obligation to provide non-commodity output invidious comparison based on moral/physical judgment about personal worth; using non-commodities for invidious practices of femininity, masculinity, parenthood, and nationalism; communitarianism | invidious comparison based on money/wealth; displacement; ecological destruction |

theorized as part of the social provisioning process as well as more broadly as a part of a *social fabric* embedded in nature.

## Conclusion: implications for heterodox economics

The proposed formulation of consumption as a social process encompasses individual decision-making as well as the generation of consumption expenditure flows in the economy, while broadening the terrain of heterodox analysis of consumption. Consumer choice is an aspect of the consumption process that is part of social provisioning. Aggregate consumption expenditures also have a limited role in understanding the social provisioning process. In order to obtain a fuller discussion of consumption within the capitalist economy, the starting point ought to be the logic of the capitalist system and the conception of the economy as social provisioning. Economic analysis of consumption should not be limited or reduced to either an aggregated macro analysis or a micro theory of consumer choice. The proposed approach is neither micro nor macro. Consumption is viewed as a process in conjunction with other processes constituting social provisioning, a part of a culture-nature life process.

One of the implications is that an inquiry into consumption as a process could start with any institution, not just the household or the individual consumer. A further implication is that behavior, choice, and identity are only parts of the picture. Focusing exclusively on those elements could lead consumption analysis straight into subjectivism and relativism on which neoliberalism thrives. In the presented approach there is no division between cultural and material—social provisioning is both.

The concept of the consumption process enables an analysis of consumption activities within the delineated characteristics of capitalism. As a result, the utilization of the analytical category of *consumers* needs to be critically examined within heterodox economic theory. On the one hand the process of consumption is important to heterodox economic theory since people consume as part of their material survival and social lives. On the other hand, whenever the 'consumer' is deployed as an actor, it is hard to avoid the symmetry of exchange that is constructed for the purpose of obscuring social conflict and the existence of distinct economic classes. Similarly, the neoliberal construct of 'consumer choice' has little significance for the development of heterodox economic theory.

Historically a discourse on consumers was used to promote collective actions of consumer groups, women's movements, and unions. However, it has become entirely neoliberal and individualistic and thus it runs counter to heterodox economics. The proposition of this chapter is that 'consumers' is a *rhetorical construct* and *not* an *analytical category* that is suitable for heterodox economic theory. People engage in consumption as well as in a multiplicity of other activities. Still, they cannot escape the economic compulsion pointed out by Marx; why would we describe them/us as consumers?! Consequently, one task for heterodox economists is to bring back 'labor' (in its broadest form) into the popular and academic discourse through a non-universalizing formulation of social provisioning as a cultural-material process. Perhaps abandoning the concept of 'consumers' altogether and instead focusing on processes would have a liberating potential for heterodox economics, consumption inquiry, and beyond.

## Acknowledgments

I am grateful to Tae-Hee Jo and William Waller for valuable suggestions. I am also thankful to Wright State University, the Raj Soin College of Business, and Dean Joan Lee for providing a sabbatical support, as well as to the Gender Studies department at the Central European University, where I spent my sabbatical and wrote this chapter.

## Notes

1 See Mishel *et al.* (2012) for the distribution of wealth and class mobility in the USA; Wolff (2007) for wealth inequality and rising US household debt; and Wolff and Zacharias (2013) for class and inequality. For a discussion of the various economic classes see Lee (2009) and Todorova (2013b).
2 Given capitalist economic class relations, unions, consumer organizations, and community groups are only in the position to *respond* to business decisions. Responses are the function of collective action, such as unionization. The US Bureau of Labor Statistics reports that in 2013, the union membership rate was 11.3 percent; in 1983, the first year for which comparable union data are available, the union membership rate was 20.1 percent. While workers do participate in various degrees in political processes, their power in the distribution of the social surplus—its level and composition—and in the generation of income flows is very limited.
3 For a critique of consumer sovereignty and the use of "the imagery of choice" see for example Joan Robinson ([1933] 1969, xii) and J. K. Galbraith (1973, 223).
4 According to the report *BBDO—The Ritual Master* rituals that by definition "make people feel good" include: "preparing for battle: transforming us from the cocoon to 'ready to face the day'"; "feasting: the pleasure of eating … transforming us from alone to connected"; "sexing up: a highly pleasurable and indulgent ritual, though not without stress (particularly for women), that transforms us from our everyday selves to our most fabulous selves"; "returning to camp: that moment when we unwind and exhale, transforming us from tense to relaxed"; "protecting yourself for the future: that last ritual of the day that moves us from relaxed to feeling safe and secure before the next day comes around" (Brady 2007).

## References

Bayliss, K., B. Fine, and M. Robertson. 2013. "From Financialisation to Consumption: The Systems of Provision Approach Applied to Housing and Water." FESSUD Working Paper 02. Accessed December 4, 2014. http://eprints.soas.ac.uk/16844/1/FESSUD-Working-Paper-02-.pdf.
Bharadwaj, K.1986. *Classical Political Economy and the Rise to Dominance of Supply and Demand Theories.* Calcutta: Universities Press.
Brady, D. 2007. "BBDO—The Ritual Masters: The Secret is to Become a 'Fortress' Brand." *Business Week*, May 10. Accessed December 23, 2014. www.aef.com/on_campus/classroom/research/data/7000.

Brei, V. and S. Böhm. 2011. "Corporate Social Responsibility as Cultural Meaning Management: A Critique of the Marketing of 'Ethical' Bottled Water." *Business Ethics: A European Review* 20 (3): 233–252.

Brown, C. 2008. *Inequality, Consumer Credit, and the Savings Puzzle*. Cheltenham: Edward Elgar.

Bureau of Labor Statistics. 2013. "Union Members Summary." Economic News Release, January 23, USDL-13-0105. Accessed November 1, 2013. www.bls.gov/news.release/union2.nr0.htm.

Dillard, D. 1980. "A Monetary Theory of Production." *Journal of Economic Issues* 16 (2): 255–275.

Dugger, W. 1996. "Redefining Economics: From Market Allocation to Social Provisioning." In *Political Economy for the 21st Century*, edited by C. Whalen, 31–43. Armonk, NY: M. E. Sharpe.

Fine, B. 2006. "Addressing the Consumer." In *The Making of the Consumer: Knowledge, Power Identity in the Modern World*, edited by F. Trentmann, 291–311. New York: Berg.

Fraad, H., S. Resnick, and R. Wolff. 1994. *Bringing It All Back Home: Class, Gender, and Power in the Modern Household*. Boulder, CO: Pluto Press.

Galbraith, J. K. 1958. *The Affluent Society*. Bombay: Asia Publishing House.

Galbraith, J. K. 1973. *Economics and the Public Purpose*. Boston: Houghton Mifflin.

Galbraith, J. K. 2008. *The Predator State*. New York: Free Press.

Glickman, L. 1997. *A Living Wage: American Workers and the Making of Consumer Society*. Ithaca, NY: Cornell University Press.

Gruchy, A. 1987. *The Reconstruction of Economics: An Analysis of the Fundamentals of Institutional Economics*. New York: Greenwood Press.

Hamilton, D. 1987. "Institutional Economics and Consumption." *Journal of Economic Issues* 21 (4): 1531–1554.

Hayden, G. 2006. *Policymaking for a Good Society: The Social Fabric Matrix Approach to Policy Analysis and Program Evaluation*. New York: Springer.

Henry, J. F. 2003. "Say's Economy." In *Two Hundred Years of Say's Law: Essays on Economic Theory's Most Controversial Principle*, edited by S. Kates, Northampton, MA: Edward Elgar.

Jo, T.-H. 2011a. "Social Provisioning Process and Socio-Economic Modeling." *American Journal of Economics and Sociology* 70 (5): 1094–1116.

Jo, T.-H. 2011b. "Heterodox Critiques of Corporate Social Responsibility." MPRA Working Paper 35367. Accessed December 4, 2014. http://mpra.ub.uni-muenchen.de/35367.

Kalecki, M. [1943] 1990. "Political Aspects of Full Employment." In *Collected Writings of Michal Kalecki, Vol. I, Capitalism: Business Cycles and Full Employment*, edited by J. Osiatynski, translated by C. A. Kisiel, 347–356. Oxford: Clarendon Press.

Keynes, J. M. [1933] 1971. "Monetary Theory of Production." In *The Collected Writings of John Maynard Keynes*, Vol. XIII, *The General Theory and After: a Supplement*, Part I: *Preparation*, edited by D. Moggridge, 408–411. London: Macmillan.

Kregel, J. 2008. "Using Minsky's Cushions of Safety to Analyze the Crisis in the U.S. Subprime Mortgage Market." *International Journal of Political Economy* 37 (1): 3–23.

Lavoie, M. 1994. "A Post Keynesian Approach to Consumer Choice." *Journal of Post Keynesian Economics* 16 (4): 539–562.

Lavoie, M. 2004. "Post-Keynesian Consumer Theory: Potential Synergies with Consumer Research and Economic Psychology." *Journal of Economic Psychology* 25 (5): 639–649.

LeBaron, G. 2010. "The Political Economy of the Household: Neoliberal Restructuring, Enclosures, and Daily Life." *Review of International Political Economy* 17 (5): 889–912.

Lee, F. S. 2008. "Heterodox Economics." In *The New Palgrave Dictionary of Economics*, 2nd ed., edited by S. N. Durlauf and L. E. Blume. London: Palgrave Macmillan.

Lee, F. S. 2009. "Alfred Eichner's Missing 'Complete Model': A Heterodox Micro-Macro Model of a Monetary Production Economy." In *Money and Macrodynamics: Alfred Eichner and Post-Keynesian Economics*, edited by M. Lavoie, L.-P. Rochon, and M. Seccareccia. Armonk, NY: M. E. Sharpe.

Lee, F. S. 2011. "Modeling the Economy as a Whole: An Integrative Approach." *American Journal of Economics and Sociology* 70 (5): 1282–1314.

Lee, F. S. 2012. "Heterodox Surplus Approach: Production, Prices, and Value Theory." *Bulletin of Political Economy* (6) 2: 65–105.

Lee, F. S. and T.-H. Jo. 2011. "Social Surplus Approach and Heterodox Economics." *Journal of Economic Issues* 45 (4): 857–876.

Marx, K. 1990. *Capital*, Vol. 1. London: Penguin.

Mishel, L., J. Bivens, E. Gould, and H. Shierholz. 2012. *The State of Working America, Wealth*, 12th ed. Economic Policy Institute. Accessed December 4, 2014. www.stateofworkingamerica.org/files/book/Chapter6-Wealth.pdf.

Nelson, J. 1993. "The Study of Choice or the Study of Provisioning? Gender and the Definition of Economics." In *Beyond Economic Man: Feminist Theory and Economics*, edited by M. Ferber and J. Nelson, 23–37. Chicago: University of Chicago Press.

Perelman, M. 2005. *Manufacturing Discontent: The Trap of Individualism in a Corporate Society*. Ann Arbor, MI: Pluto Press.

Polanyi, K. [1944] 1957. *The Great Transformation: The Political and Economic Origins of Our Time*. Boston: Beacon Press.

Power, M. 2004. "Social Provisioning as a Starting Point for Feminist Economics." *Feminist Economics* 10 (3): 3–21.

Robertson, M. 2008. "Discovering Price in All the Wrong Places: The Work of Commodity Definition and Price under Neoliberal Environmental Policy." In *Privatization: Property and the Remaking of Nature-Society*, edited by B. Mansfield. Malden, MA: Blackwell.

Robinson, J. [1933] 1969. *The Economics of Imperfect Competition*. London: Macmillan.

Todorova, Z. 2009. *Money and Households in a Capitalist Economy: A Gendered Post Keynesian–Institutional Analysi*s. Northampton: Edward Elgar.

Todorova, Z. 2013a. "Connecting Social Provisioning and Functional Finance in a Post Keynesian–Institutional Analysis of the Public Sector." *European Journal of Economics and Economic Policies: Intervention* 10 (1): 61–75.

Todorova, Z. 2013b. "Conspicuous Consumption as Routine Expenditures and its Place in Social Provisioning." *American Journal of Economics and Sociology* 72 (5): 1183–1204.

Todorova, Z. 2013c. "Consumption as a Social Process within Social Provisioning and Capitalism: Implications for Heterodox Economics." MPRA Working Paper 51516. Accessed December 4, 2013. http://mpra.ub.uni-muenchen.de/51516.

Todorova, Z. 2014a. "Consumption as a Social Process." *Journal of Economic Issues* 48 (3): 663–679.

Todorova, Z. 2014b. "Social Provisioning within a Culture-Nature Life-Process." Unpublished working paper.

Tool, M. [1979] 1985. *The Discretionary Economy: A Normative Theory of Political Economy*. Boulder, CO: Westview Press.

Trentmann, F. and V. Taylor. 2006. "From Users to Consumers: Water Politics in Nineteenth-Century London." In *The Making of the Consumer: Knowledge, Power Identity in the Modern World*, edited by F. Trentmann, 53–58. New York: Berg.

Tymoigne, E. 2007. "A Hard-Nosed Look at Worsening U.S. Household Finance." *Challenge* 50 (4): 88–111.

Veblen, T. 1898. "Why is Economics not an Evolutionary Science?" *Quarterly Journal of Economics* 12 (4): 373–397.

Veblen, T. [1899] 1994. *The Theory of the Leisure Class*. New York: Dover Publications.

Veblen, T. [1919] 2005. *The Vested Interests and the Common Man*. New York: Cosimo Classics.

Veblen, T. 1923. *The Absentee Ownership and Business Enterprise in Recent Times: The Case of America.* New York: Huebsch.

Wisman, J. 2009. "Household Saving, Class Identity, and Conspicuous Consumption." *Journal of Economic Issues* 43 (1): 89–114.

Wisman, J. 2011. "Inequality, Social Respectability, Political Power, and Environmental Devastation." *Journal of Economic Issues* 45 (4): 877–900.

Wolff, E. 2007. "Recent Trends in Household Wealth in the United States: Rising Debt and the Middle-Class Squeeze." Levy Economics Institute Working Paper 502.

Wolff, E. and A. Zacharias. 2013. "Class Structure and Economic Inequality." *Cambridge Journal of Economics* 37 (6): 1381–1406.

Wray, L. R. 2005. "The Ownership Society: Social Security Is Only the Beginning…" Public Policy Brief 82, Levy Economics Institute.

Wray, L. R. 2008. "Demand Constraints and Big Government." *Journal of Economic Issues* 42 (1): 421–431.

# 13 Social provisioning process, market instability, and managed competition

*Tuna Baskoy*

## Introduction

I met Professor Frederic S. Lee at the University of Missouri–Kansas City (UMKC), while attending the Seventh Post Keynesian Summer School as a PhD candidate in June 2002. After dinners, he would come to the dormitory's lobby where I and other students were staying and chat with us about Post Keynesian micro- and macro-economic issues for hours. He was so passionate and still highly energetic after long days of lectures that he would scream occasionally to keep us awake! He would lament that many Post Keynesian economists privilege macroeconomic issues such as monetary, fiscal, and trade policies over microeconomic themes of business enterprise, competition, and market governance.

For him, studying macroeconomic issues is not fully complete without understanding their microeconomic roots. Professor Lee situates macro and micro issues within a broader theoretical framework of what he calls the *theory of the social provisioning process*. This is the approach he was about to develop after more than 30 years of researching market prices and business competition. His goal was to put forward a scheme that would make possible a relational way of studying microeconomic topics such as markets, instability, business competition, and market governance with macroeconomic themes like fiscal and monetary policy. He completed the groundwork for this task in his recent publications over the past several years. However, his untimely death prevented him from putting his scattered ideas together and presenting them as a unified framework.

This chapter primarily focuses on Lee's writings to accomplish this task of describing his theory of the social provisioning process and locating business competition within it as a way of creating a springboard that future studies may use different components of his theory to understand the real world. The underlying hypothesis in this chapter is that not only does Lee provide a vision of the economy as a whole with his theory of the social provisioning process within the Post Keynesian economic tradition, but also he characterizes business competition as a dynamic process of rivalry that carries the elements of instability and stability simultaneously. The innovative aspect of Lee's contribution is in how he explains business competition and resulting market (in)stability and how they are connected to the social provisioning process in an empirically and historically grounded manner.

This chapter is structured as follows. The next section reviews the literature on business competition in Post Keynesian economics. The third section analyzes Lee's theory of the social provisioning process, followed by his contribution to business competition, market instability, and how business enterprises work together to manage competition in the fourth section. The fifth section discusses Lee's originality in the Post Keynesian tradition before summarizing the findings as a way of conclusion.

## Literature review

Business competition is one of the areas that is relatively less developed in Post Keynesian economics. For instance, Amitava Dutt contends that there is no widely-accepted theory of business competition in the Post Keynesian tradition (Dutt 1994). Similarly, Mark Glick and Donald Campbell note that there is no single Post Keynesian approach to competition, but it is possible to identify a set of common characteristics in the writings of Post Keynesians (Glick and Campbell 1994). Others argue that Post Keynesians synthesize different approaches to competition (Walters and Young 1997; Tsaliki and Tsoulfidis 1998). At best, a number of Post Keynesians take oligopolistic markets as given and build their macroeconomic models on such markets (Arestis and Milberg 1993–1994; Lavoie 2001). Malcom Sawyer identifies two prevalent approaches to competition: that is, "monopoly capital" and "investment-based pricing." Both views share a common premise that business enterprises have market power to set prices (Sawyer 1994, 3). Surprisingly, many Post Keynesians who investigate the causes of the global financial crisis barely mention the role of business competition (e.g., Wray 2009, 2014; Arestis and Karakitsos 2013; see Baskoy (2011) that links business competition to the financial crisis from the Post Keynesian perspective).

Theories of imperfect and monopolistic competition that were developed in the early 1930s set the stage for Post Keynesian approach to business competition. Joan Robinson's theory of imperfect competition was an upheaval against neoclassical theory of perfect competition, after a growing dissatisfaction with Alfred Marshall's analysis of increasing returns to scale in perfectly competitive industries (Triffin 1947, 3). According to Robinson, the average cost of production falls rapidly due to economies of large scale but the decline in the supply price is less than expected. Big business enterprises tend to improve the techniques of production considerably. At the same time, there is a question of whether they share cost savings with consumers. Business enterprises have market power to keep prices artificially high (Robinson 1932, 544). In the words of Robinson: "Thus a monopolist could hope not only to raise the price of the commodity by restricting output, but also to lower costs by improving the organization of the industry" (Robinson 1933, 170). From Robinson's viewpoint, market power became a reality in capitalist economies with the emergence of the modern corporation—especially in the manufacturing sector. Furthermore, it pertains to politics: "The problem of the world of monopolists thus resolves itself into the familiar dilemma between efficiency and justice" (324). Post Keynesian economists have tried to strike a balance between efficiency and justice in income distribution when they investigate the macroeconomic implications of oligopoly.

At the same time, Edward H. Chamberlin underlined the significance of quality and product competition with his theory of monopolistic competition. Business enterprises compete not solely on price competition, but on quality and product competition (Chamberlin 1950, 1961). To be more specific, business enterprises differentiate their products and compete against each other with slightly differentiated products. Similarity of products in their functions limits the market power of monopolies, since their products are substitutes and compete against each other (Chamberlin 1937, 572). In short, market power is here to stay and keep prices higher, while creating waste.

In this broader intellectual milieu, Post Keynesian economists characterize business competition as a dynamic and evolving process full of uncertainties that are caused by mainly demand and constant rivalry to get the highest share from limited demand. For instance, Nicholas Kaldor emphasizes the nature of interaction of the price and output policy of rival producers for the reason that each producer's equilibrium position with respect to price and output is dependent on its own anticipation of its competitor's behavior which also has implications for marketing costs (Kaldor 1934).

In a similar way, Michał Kalecki emphasizes the dynamic nature of competition when business enterprises set their individual price in oligopoly: "In fixing the price the firm takes into consideration its average prime costs and the prices of other firms producing similar products" (Kalecki 1971, 44). His notion of the degree of monopoly is not solely based on the quantity conception of competition, as in the case of neoclassical perfect competition. The degree of monopoly depends on the size of business enterprises, sales promotions, and advertising by individual enterprises, price leadership, tacit agreement and cartels, and the strength of trade unions. The degree of monopoly as a concept captures the structural as well as behavioral dimensions of competition in individual markets. Price and non-price competition exists in oligopoly. Yet, cartels are frequent to prevent cut-throat competition (28). For instance, changes in the level of overheads in relation to prime costs, influence the degree of monopoly—especially in times of depression during which demand is low, and business enterprises increase their price through a tacit agreement to protect their profits (49–51).

Both Kaldor and Kalecki approach business competition from the perspective of individual business enterprises in relation to their competitors. There is a significant difference in the size of individual business enterprises in that there are few dominant and powerful ones which are surrounded by a number of smaller competitors. There is always a possibility that some of the smaller competitors may have new technologies and grow faster than their powerful counterparts. Besides, new entry is always possible, as long as profit rate is attractive. In short, Kaldor's and Kalecki's views are useful in understanding how individual enterprises act alone or collectively to maintain a certain price level to recover their cost and make a profit. It is important to qualify the fact that their analysis stops short of relating profit to funding explicitly. Alfred Eichner and Adrian Wood investigate how business enterprises fund their investment by choosing pricing policies in competition with other enterprises.

Eichner's main concern was creating funds for investment. The big business enterprise or what he calls the "megacorp" is the key player in oligopoly. The primary goal of the megacorp is to expand at the highest rate possible, and decisions are made through a managerial hierarchy. Unlike the representative enterprise in the orthodox theory, the megacorp operates several plants in each of the industries to which it belongs and usually starts up or shuts down plant segments over the business cycle (Eichner 1985, 30–31). In oligopoly, the business enterprise's market power is the distinguishing feature, not the number of players per se. The source of market power is the size and the institutional structure of the business enterprise. There are a few large players with market power to determine the level of production and price, while smaller competitors follow them by adjusting their cost margins to price leaders. Eichner describes the Post Keynesian vision of market competition as follows:

> In a post-Keynesian analysis, competition need involve no more than a continual effort by business firms to exploit the most profitable investment opportunities. It is only competition in this limited sense that generally prevails throughout the world—a fact that the classical economists clearly recognized.
>
> (Eichner 1979, 16)

Competition is mainly about investment, advertising, and other discretionary expenses (Eichner and Kregel 1975, 1305). Emphasis on competition shifts from price to non-price elements (Eichner 1969). The megacorp competes with its counterparts not on the basis of price, but through the various types of investment it undertakes. Change in the market-position of business enterprises over time is highly possible and occurs primarily as a result of non-price forms of competition (Eichner 1983, 138–148). Price competition is not completely ruled out. It is still a factor to be considered, but it is rare, and yet bloody whenever it happens, because the megacorp has financial power to sustain price wars for a long time, thereby, inflicting serious financial damage to themselves as well as to their competitors. As part of its effort to minimize its material losses, the megacorp avoids using price as a weapon in competition. In Eichner's view, oligopolistic markets are so dynamic that a dominant business enterprise may lose its position over time, as its smaller competitors grow at their expense with new investment, technology, and advertising efforts (Eichner 1976).

Not unlike Eichner's line of logic, Adrian Wood maintains that business enterprises which want their sales to grow need to expand their productive capacity through investment in fixed assets and stocks. They can finance new investment through their retained profits or through external borrowing. At the end of the day, their borrowing ability to finance any new investment project depends on the perceived profitability of new investment to compensate the rate of interest on the loan plus some extra income for business enterprises. Otherwise, banks are hesitant to finance any new investment project, especially uncertain and risky ones. The required amount of funding to finance a planned investment governs the business enterprise's decision on profit margin, which is also dependent on competition. "In particular, competition from other firms limits both the rate of expansion of its sales, and its ability to make profits" (Wood 1975, 4). Business enterprises always compete for a limited aggregate demand at any moment of time and their urge to grow as fast as possible instigates them to compete against their rivals by innovation, price policy, advertising, forming alliances with other firms, and other means (108–110).

Furthering Eichner's and Wood's line of thinking, Nina Shapiro and Tracy Mott underline the significance of pricing power of business enterprises, as it is an important ability for them to recover the costs of a plant and equipment, or to invest in new product or process development (Shapiro and Mott 1995). Business enterprises have power to price their products, but their power is not absolute. Rather, it is limited by how competitors and potential entrants behave. Shapiro admits that competition is limited in oligopolies: "The entry barriers of industries increase and stabilize the investment in products, and while they also lessen competition, they do not end it" (Shapiro 2012, 94). Product competition is the dominant form of competition in oligopolies. Competition improves their production as well as increases investment with increasing research and development spending, an observation made by Joan Robinson in her theory of imperfect competition a long time ago. Shapiro argues that product competition is the dominant form which does not mean that there is no price competition. Price reductions, which expand markets and increase market shares, are also practiced occasionally (Shapiro 2012).

Overall, Post Keynesians economists are realistic in their approach to competition in that they admit that the modern corporation or the megacorp has changed the structure of the market as well as the behavior of competitors. As a dynamic and evolving process full of uncertainties owing to demand and competitors' behavior, competition takes place through investment, research and development, new technology, new products, product differentiation, advertising and other forms of selling efforts. Although Eichner, Wood, and Shapiro and Mott developed a macroeconomic analysis from the vantage point of the megacorp, Lee proposes to analyze micro- and macro-economic issues in a relational way, by offering an innovative theoretical framework, which situates business competition in its broader economic, social, cultural, and political environment.

## Theory of the social provisioning process

Lee (2013a) classifies Post Keynesian economics as part of heterodox economics and defines the latter as "*a historical science of the social provisioning process*"

(108, original italics). The social provisioning process is continuous, and a carefully thought and planned series of "production-based, production-derived economic activities" taking place through historical time to cater to the needs of individuals and families within the context of broader cultural and social environment (Lee and Jo 2011, 859). In Post Keynesian economics, the discipline of economics is mainly concerned with explicating the process that provides the flow of products required by society to meet the needs of those participating in its activities, i.e., the social provisioning process in a capitalist economy (Gu and Lee 2012, 456).

The theory of the social provisioning process draws from various heterodox approaches and treats human agency as embedded in a transmutable and uncertain world. Human beings have fallible knowledge and changing expectations shaped by a specific culture in which they live. The social processes that they involve take place in historical time and affect resources, consumption patterns, production and reproduction, plus the meaning of the market, state and non-market activities. Interdependent social context for understanding human agency as well as the relations between the parts of the whole replace the image of isolated individuals and solitary decision-making process, as assumed in neoclassical economics (Lee 2013a, 108).

Echoing the theory of the social provisioning process which is conceived as an emergent theoretical system with several theoretical subsystems, Lee views the economy as an evolving system with different sub-parts. Instead of dividing the economy into disjointed subsystems of microeconomics and macroeconomics, he proposes a theoretical approach consisting of three analytical and interdependent segments—structure, organization, and agency—that constitute the whole capitalist society. Consequently, "the model rejects the microeconomics-macroeconomics divide; rather, there is the economy as a whole, which has emergent interconnected components that can be studied" (Lee 2011, 1311). The first component is the productive and monetary structures of the social provisioning process that is the material basis of a capitalist economy. According to Lee (2010):

> The schema of production of the economy can be represented as a circular production input-output matrix of material goods combined with different types of labor power skills to produce an array of goods and services as outputs. Many of the outputs replace the goods and services used up in production, and the rest constitute a surplus to be used for consumption, private investment, and government usage.
>
> (25)

Through this productive structure of the economy, an array of outputs in the forms of intermediate ("basic") and final ("surplus") goods and service is produced. While the basic goods are directly tied to the production of goods and services in the following production period, the surplus goods render the reproduction the provisioning process possible over time, since they are used for meeting consumption needs of individuals, families, government, private invest-ment, and needs of other countries through exporting them. The surplus is the source of wages, profits, and government taxes. In other words, it is this produc-tion process, where distribution of wealth takes place in a capitalist society (Lee 2013a, 109–110). Thus, theoretically, the social provisioning process is consist-ent with the theory of monetary production, the surplus approach, and the theory of effective demand (Lee and Jo 2011).

The second part of the theory of the social provisioning process is organiza-tion. Lee delineates three categories of economic organizations and institutions within the broader structures of the capitalist market economy. Markets organ-ized around particular goods and services, make up the first category of eco-nomic organizations and institutions. In this "market-specific" category, there are business enterprises, private and public market organizations including cartels and government regulatory agencies, trade unions, and institutions such as minimum wage laws that set and control wages. Business competition takes place in this category in Lee's theoretical classification. The second category is the state and its various organizations such as parliament and the central bank that spread across markets and products and make decisions about government expenditures, taxation, and interest rate (Lee 2013a, 109–110). The business enterprise and the state organize as well as direct the social provisioning process. The business enterprise affects economic activity and therefore the social provi-sioning process for its own interest of survival and continuity by setting prices, making investment, and deciding the level of production as well as employment (Lee 2010, 30). Non-market organizations and institutions (households, the state, charities) that promote social reproduction make up the last category of organ-ization (Lee 2013a, 109–110).

In the theory of the social provisioning process, agency is the final com-ponent. Lee (2011) defines agency as "socialized individuals" because they are located in organizations. Individuals make decisions through organizations that are embedded in instrumental as well as ceremonial institutions which are part of the broader social fabric:

> The social fabric, as noted above, consists of cultural values, norms and beliefs, societal institutions, and technology; and they influence the actions of the acting organizations and institutions. In turn, the acting organizations and institutions act on the social provisioning process and social activities, and the latter has an impact on the provisioning process.
>
> (Lee 2011, 1308)

Social relationships are the means that facilitate individuals' decisions. Lee dis-tinguishes two major social forces with reference to economic activity: those who own the means of production and those who do not own or control the means of production. The means of production provides privileged access to incomes for those who own them in addition to giving them social power in deciding about the level of economic activity, and thus social surplus and employment (Lee 2010, 30). Within this broader framework, Lee identifies three major classes. These are the ruling class made up of business people/corporate enterprise and members of board of directors/senior management as the capitalist class, the political elite, the working class, and the dependent class such as retirees, children, and others (Lee 2011, 1293–1295). As a result, workers do not control their own social provisioning process in the absence of their direct control and command over the production of their consumption goods. The capitalist class and the dependent capitalist state together decide the amount and composition of the surplus for a society as a whole.

Broader context of the capitalist market economy serves as a reference point for the theory of the social provisioning process. Class, power, hierarchical domination, inequalities, social-economic discontent and conflict are the fundamental characteristics of the capitalist society. The goal of public policy is to improve human dignity through enhancing the social provisioning for all members of the society and particularly for the disadvantaged groups by either recommending incremental or radical redistributive economic and social policies to eradicate racial, gender, and other forms of discrimination. The social provisioning process takes place through the capitalist market, but the organization of social provisioning is determined outside markets (Lee 2013a, 108).

To reiterate, in the theory of the social provisioning process the economy is characterized as a disaggregated interdependent system and changes in one part of the economy result in alterations in other parts as well as in the economy as a whole. Delineating and explaining the constituent parts or subsystems of the economy is the key for studying the economy as a whole and the changes in various parts of the economy (Lee 2013a, 110). Households, business enterprises, and the state are the three actors that have access to the surplus. The surplus is produced by workers, while it is appropriated by the business enterprise in the form of profits with the help of the state.

> Thus, the origins of profits are found in the possibility and capability of capitalists and the state to force workers to produce surplus goods and services for them; and since profits consist of non-scarce reproducible goods, they are not based on scarcity and hence are not technologically constrained.
>
> (Lee 2010, 34)

Nevertheless, the capitalist class and the dependent capitalist state—which Lee calls the ruling class—decides the material basis of the social provisioning process for the whole society (Lee 2013a, 111).

In short, Lee believes that the trappings of market forces function as a veil to obscure the real social relationships sustaining the ruling class through the creation and distribution of the surplus. Markets and the price system obscure how the social relationships of the capitalist class and the political elite of the dependent state make decisions about the creation as well as the distribution of the surplus. That the capitalist class is strong as a collective actor does not mean that individual going business enterprises do have a secure place as a result of instability created by competition, even after they try to manage it to reduce instability, as the next section elaborates.

## Business enterprise and competition

A representative business enterprise in Lee's theoretical framework is the going concern or the modern corporation. Lee (2013b) notes that:

> The concept of the going concern refers to business enterprises with con-tinuity of economic activity and an indefinite life span (as opposed to a ter-minal venture or an enterprise in the process of liquidation). It consists of a going plant or productive capabilities and a going business which referred to managerial activities, such as investment, research and development, and pricing, that affect the enterprise's market transactions over time.
>
> (166)

The going concern has an organizational component, a production and cost com-ponent, and management. It has several plants to produce goods and services as well as an established bureaucracy to oversee productive activities. It is hierar-chical and authoritarian in nature; it produces multiple products. Profit is not the end goal for management. It is rather an intermediate aim that helps realize dif-ferent objectives. The ultimate goal is the survival, continuation, and if possible expansion of the enterprise (Lee 2010, 30). The going business enterprise's pro-ductive and managerial capabilities, working rules that include pricing proced-ures, enable it to control its environment and determine its future, to a certain extent, rather than being powerless. In other words, the going enterprise's cap-abilities are the source of its power to affect market transactions (Lee 2013b, 166).

In the broader picture of the theory of the social provisioning process, the going business enterprise is an organizational mechanism as well as a legitimate institution that enables the capitalist class to gain continuous access to the state-monetized social provisioning process in the form of profit-derived dividends and salary income. The business enterprise is an organic entity living in histor-ical time with goals of survival and growth. Maintaining and augmenting positive business income or profit is the primary objective of the going business enterprise, as it ensures both its survival and the capitalist class to have access to the social provisioning process continuously. This takes place in the process of competition with other business enterprises in a marketplace. Competition is the source of instability, even though going business enterprises attempt to stabilize instabilities by means of "managed competition" (Lee 2013b, 166).

For Post Keynesians the market is an abstract concept and denotes all the transactions of a specific product between buyers and sellers. Lee notes that "[r]ejecting the attribute of market clearing, Post Keynesians define market as a concept that simply refers to all the exchanges of a specific good" (Lee 1990–1991, 258). His understanding of the market takes product and its exchange for money as a reference point. Transaction lies at the center of his conceptualization of the market. "Hence, a market exists simultaneously with the product in the abstract and disappears when the transactions of the product cease" (Lee 1998, 228). The number of markets depends on the number of products. Hence, there are as many markets as there are products, in Lee's view (2010, 31). In simple terms, markets revolve around products and their transactions.

Markets also have their social basis interwoven with institutions to bring stability and orderliness. Business enterprises that operate in specific markets actively create, alter, and recreate rules and market institutions as part of their efforts to establish a stable market price which they believe does not hinder market transactions. The type of rules and institutions are context and time dependent in that social, legal, and economic factors together with customs, conventions, and traditions play a major role. The going business enterprise operates in an institutional environment in competition with other going enterprises. These institutions help the business enterprise to manage competition and prices. "The market price is consequently set and the market managed for the purpose of ensuring continual transactions for those enterprises in the market, that is for the benefit of the business leaders and their enterprises" (Lee 1998, 228). As a result, Lee claims that the division among monopoly capitalism, competitive oligopoly, and competitive capitalism does not have any firm foundation under corporate capitalism over the last hundred or more years. Market prices are not market clearing prices; they are rather enterprise, and transaction-reproducing prices. In a way, they reproduce the business enterprise, and hence of the capitalist market economy as a whole. Detailed historical studies that examine changing economic, social, and political environments are essential for understanding the determination of the profit markup (Lee 1998, 228–330).

Lee defines business competition as follows:

> Competition between enterprises in the production and the sale of goods involves the use of these capabilities [of setting their own prices and engage in other competitive activities] in the attempt to make a profitable volume of sales in the face of the offers of other enterprises selling identical or closely similar products.
>
> (Lee 2013c, 476)

To achieve its goals of survival and growth, the business enterprise carries out appropriate and timely measures of investment to come up with new production processes, new products and markets. Only in this way, can it fight against current and prospective competition. It does not mean that there are no constraints beyond the reach of individual business enterprise:

> Admittedly, the imperatives of the present in terms of markets, technology, and business practice must constrain the behavior of the firm at any point in time. Thus markets dictate limits to prices in terms of what are currently

competitively possible; technology and its embodiment in capital limits the products and markets which can currently be exploited; and business practice in terms of contractual stipulations and the need to maintain goodwill imposes service obligations upon the corporation.

(Davies and Lee 1988, 13)

Business competition compels individual going business enterprises to make decisions about their investment, advertising, research and development, production process, and new products, instead of engaging in competitive activities through price wars. Competition functions as a mechanism to pressure them. This, in turn, creates instability in the market, as such decisions may result in the deterioration of the relative position of competitors and hence bankruptcy of some going enterprises for two reasons. In the first place, research and development may result in new and innovative production processes to cut down the cost of the going enterprise vis-à-vis its rivals, thereby diverting the surplus in favor of innovative enterprises that will have more capital for research and development in future. High-cost business enterprises are naturally driven out of the market. Second, research and innovation that result in new product may destroy existing product markets or make it difficult for other enterprises to enter new markets. Consequently, business enterprises that do not have any ability to offer new products may eventually disappear from the market (Lee 2013b, 169). Competition creates instability for individual going concerns, as their competitors' decisions destabilize market positions constantly. After all, they compete for the limited amount of demand at any given point in time.

Competitive conditions may be effective enough to seriously disturb the going enterprise's ability to generate revenues and profits essential for reproduction and expansion. With their capability to set their own prices and engage in other types of competitive activities, there is a high possibility that business competition may be destructive. If rivalry eliminates positive net cash flows of some going enterprises, there may be casualties. Lee (2013c) makes the following observation:

Because the going enterprise exists in markets with other competing enterprises, competitive conditions may generate market prices that seriously affect the going enterprises' ability to reproduce and expand. That is, since they have capabilities of setting their own prices and engage in other competitive activities, going enterprises have the ability to inflict unacceptable consequences upon competitors. In particular, they have the ability to eliminate positive cash flows, insofar as the cash flows are derived from, or depending upon, activities in the markets in which they participate.

(476)

Price is not the only weapon the going business enterprise has in its arsenal. In producing and selling identical or closely similar products, aspects of competition include advertising, service, and product development (Lee 2013c, 476).

Price war is the last weapon to use for going enterprises, since it has an imme-diate impact on their profit markups and cash flows. To remain profitable, the going business enterprise adopts a number of strategies such as increasing its market share by advertising or reducing cost, increasing profit markup by enhancing its revenues or cutting costs, developing new products and creating new markets, entering new geographic markets, forming alliances to determine prices and/or seeking government support (Lee 2013b, 166).

Price competition may still be imminent. To avoid immediate and dire con-sequences of price wars and destructive competition, going enterprises prefer to establish market governance organizations and maintain a stable market price. Not surprisingly, business enterprises always look for and attempt to regulate competition and establish orderly markets collectively by cooperating as a group. In a sense, competition is managed by the going business enterprise. Trade associations, cartels, price associations, price leadership, government regulatory commissions, and government legislations are some of the tools of market gov-ernance as a way of regulating business competition (Lee 1994a, 321; 2013c, 476).

Overall, competition is managed and serves both as a mechanism that pres-sures competitors to follow certain types of actions and as an action that mani-fests behaviors of individual going concerns in response to rivalry individually as well as collectively. Individually, they carry out research and development activities to develop new processes, new products, advertise or differentiate their products to better position themselves in the market. Collectively, they form cartels, associations, joint ventures for new product development or marketing, or merge voluntarily or take over one another in a friendly or hostile way to manage the market. In Lee's view, therefore, market stability and instability exist side by side; both are consequences of deliberate enterprise activities embedded in the capitalist social provisioning process. Lee (2013b) notes that: "These heightened degrees of regulated 'creative' competition only occur in a few markets at any one time in the economy; so the capitalist economy simultan-eously exhibits market instability and stability" (169). Security for individual going business enterprises is a relative term and there is no guarantee for their existence in the future, even if they have the most secure market position today.

## Discussions and conclusions

Frederic S. Lee's contribution to Post Keynesian economics is significant in a number of ways. First, he locates business competition within the broader social provisioning process, unlike his mentor Alfred S. Eichner and other Post Keyne-sians. At the systemic level, the first function of competition in general and com-petitive activities in particular is to obfuscate the true nature of social relations such that capitalists as the ultimate decision makers in producing surplus goods, setting wage rates, prices and profit markups, and creating their profits through the going business enterprise disappear from the radar (Lee 2013b, 169). Busi-ness competition is a legitimation mechanism for capitalists to justify their appropriation of the surplus created by workers. Lee pictures business competition as a smokescreen that disguises how the surplus is produced and distributed for the benefit of the ruling class in general. Business competition and the price system play a secondary role of regulating the access of particular capitalists and workers to social provisioning, and ensuring the reproduction of the business enterprise, in addition to helping the capitalist class maintain its dominance over the working class which is necessary for capitalism to exist. In the end, the ruling class consisting of the capitalist class and the state decides the production of the surplus, and hence wage rates, profit markups, and state money, thereby managing the real direction of the capitalist economy by controlling the volume of and access to the social provisioning process (Lee 2013a, 111). With the theory of social provisioning process, Lee advances a new way of picturing business competition in Post Keynesian economics.

Second, Lee dismisses the distinction between competitive and oligopolistic markets in contrast to his mentor Eichner and other theorists who influenced his thoughts such as Gardiner C. Means (Lee 1994b). For him, markets are always competitive with varying degrees and competition does not depend on the number of players—that is, it is the agency of the business enterprise and the state that controls the market, rather than the stylized "structure" of the market as in the conventional theory of the competition. Flexible market shares and profit rates are indications of healthy competition (Lee 1998, 73). Furthermore, Lee posits that there is no relationship between the degree of monopoly and the magnitude of markup (Lee 2013b, 160). He offers a new approach to business competition that explains why some business enterprises go into bankruptcy, whereas others expand at the same time without relying on price-cutting. For Lee, it is clear that business competition has no fundamental role in influencing pricing or profit markups. The magnitude of profit markup is either independent of the level of economic activity or there may be a positive correlation between them (161). Lee's claim regarding the significance of downward price adjustments in business competition contradicts the conventional Post Keynesian approaches to competition (e.g., Sen and Vaidya 1995, 42; Shapiro and Mott 1995, 44; Ong 1981, 103; Atesoglu 1997, 646; Shapiro 2012). By moving beyond the theoretical boundaries of conventional Post Keynesian approaches to business competition such as Kalecki's degree of monopoly, Robinson's theory of monopolistic competition, and Eichner's theory of the megacorp, Lee's historically and empirically grounded approach advances Post Keynesian economics toward an integrated heterodox economic research in general.

Regardless of competition in the market, the going business enterprise uses normal cost, markup, and/or target-rate-of-return to determine its price outside the market (Lee 1985, 206). This does not mean that there is no regard for competitive process. Lee places the going enterprise in competition with other business enterprises in the market. Competitor-motivated markup pricing as one of the methods of cost-plus pricing procedures emphasizes how going enterprises position themselves in setting their markup rates and hence prices. Gu and Lee (2012, 460) delineate four possible tactics for business enterprises—that is, leader pricing, parity pricing, low-supplier price, and opportunistic pricing—depending on their position in the relevant market as price leader or price follower. Again, the position of a market leader(s) is not necessarily determined by their size, but by their superiority in technology. In place of the price adjustment mechanism that does not play a significant role in terms of enterprise activities and competition, Lee (2013b, 169) finds the importance of cost differences between business enterprises and of product innovation, which are the two sources of market instability that may result in the disappearance of high cost and technologically backward competitors. With such an account of business competition, Lee overcomes the structuralist and quantitative theory of competition that haunted his mentor and many other Post Keynesians for many years. Besides, his approach to competition is more dynamic and open-ended in that both stability and instability exist side by side, which makes his analysis original.

Finally, Lee brings up a new dimension to the understanding of the state. Many Post Keynesians perceive the state as an institution that promotes the public interest. For instance, Richard P. F. Holt (2013) provides the following summary for the role of the state: "The essence of the post-Keynesian approach is a set of public investments to stabilize the economy and provide merit goods and to deal with economic and social problems" (307). Because the lack of demand in the economy is seen as the source of unemployment, public policy in particular and the state in general has a role to decrease unemployment. In a way, the state is seen as an institution to serve the public. Contrary to this view, Lee contends that the state is dependent on the market because it is not a major producer or a surplus generator. Capitalists and political elite make up the ruling class who, in turn, make all decisions regarding the social provisioning process. He makes a distinction between the political elite and the state—the latter possesses its own activities and 'property,' whereas the former is the acting persons who have the legal authority to steer and direct the activities of the state (Lee 2011, 1293–1294). In a way, Lee has an articulated conception of the state in his framework which requires further development, which is a weak point in Post Keynesian economics in general.

In conclusion, this chapter has demonstrated that Frederic S. Lee makes a significant theoretical contribution to Post Keynesian theory. His theory of the social provisioning process offers an encompassing picture of the capitalist market economy and its dynamics delineating strict borders between microeconomics and macroeconomics. Lee develops a theoretical foundation to explain market and economic stability as well as instability. In a way, his theory emphasizes class, power, hierarchical domination, inequalities, social-economic discontent and conflict as the prevalent features of capitalism. Within this broader milieu, he offers a dynamic view of business competition and explains how it functions at the macro as well as micro levels. In his framework market governance plays an important role, but requires further work to explain what it means and how it works. Finally, it is equally important to study how business enterprises work in different stages of a full business cycle, as outlined by Kalecki. All in all, the theory of the social provisioning process is an encompassing approach that provides more realistic explanation for instability and stability caused by business competition together with its distributional implications. Applying this framework to examine competition in individual industries is the next task to continue Lee's legacy in Post Keynesian economics.

## References

Arestis, P. and E. Karakitsos. 2013. *Financial Stability in the Aftermath of the 'Great Recession.'* New York: Palgrave Macmillan.

Arestis, P. and W. Milberg. 1993–4. "Degree of Monopoly, Pricing, and Flexible Exchange Rate." *Journal of Post Keynesian Economics* 16 (2): 167–188.

Atesoglu, S. H. 1997. "A Post Keynesian Explanation of U.S. Inflation?" *Journal of Post Keynesian Economics* 19 (5): 639–649.

Baskoy, T. 2011. "Business Competition and the 2007–08 Financial Crisis: A Post Keynesian Approach." In *Heterodox Analysis of Financial Crisis and Reform: History, Politics, and Economics*, edited by J. Leclaire, T.-H. Jo, and J. Knodell, 124–136. Cheltenham, UK: Edward Elgar.

Chamberlin, E. H. 1937. "Monopolistic or Imperfect Competition?" *Quarterly Journal of Economics* 51 (4): 557–580.

Chamberlin, E. H. 1950. *The Theory of Monopolistic Competition: A Re-Orientation of the Theory of Value.* 6th ed. Cambridge, MA: Harvard University Press.

Chamberlin, E. H. 1961. "The Origins and Early Development of Monopolistic Competition Theory." *Quarterly Journal of Economics* 75 (4): 515–543.

Davies, J. E. and F. S. Lee. 1988. "A Post Keynesian Appraisal of the Contestability Criterion." *Journal of Post Keynesian Economics* 11 (1): 3–25.

Dutt, A. 1994. "Classical Competition and Post-Keynesian Monopoly Power: A Possible Synthesis." In *Competition, Technology and Money: Classical and Post-Keynesian Perspectives*, edited by M. Glick, 40–51. Aldershot, UK: Edward Elgar.

Eichner, A. S. 1969. *The Emergency of Oligopoly: Sugar Refining as a Case Study.* Baltimore: John Hopkins Press.

Eichner, A. S. 1976. *The Megacorp and Oligopoly: Micro Foundations of Macro Dynamics.* Cambridge: Cambridge University Press.

Eichner, A. S. 1979. "Introduction." In *A Guide to Post-Keynesian Economics*, edited by A. S. Eichner, 3–18. White Plains, NY: M. E. Sharpe.

Eichner, A. S. 1983. "The Micro Foundations of the Corporate Economy." *Managerial and Decision Economics* 4 (3): 136–152.

Eichner, A. S. 1985. *Toward a New Economics: Essays in Post-Keynesian and Institutionalist Theory.* Armonk, NY: M. E. Sharpe.

Eichner, A. S. and J. A. Kregel. 1975. "An Essay on Post-Keynesian Theory: A New Paradigm in Economics." *Journal of Economic Literature* 13 (4): 1293–1314.

Glick, M. and D. Campbell. 1994. "Post-Keynesian and Classical Theories of Competition." In *Competition, Technology and Money: Classical and Post-Keynesian Perspectives*, edited by M. Glick, 24–39. Aldershot, UK: Edward Elgar.

Gu, G. C and F. S. Lee. 2012. "Prices and Pricing." In *The Elgar Companion to Post Keynesian Economics*, 2nd ed., edited by J. E. King, 456–463. Cheltenham, UK: Edward Elgar.

Holt, R. P. F. 2013. "The Post-Keynesian Critique of the Mainstream Theory of the State and the Post-Keynesian Approaches to Economic Policy." In *The Oxford Handbook of*

*Post-Keynesian Economics, Vol. 1: Theory and Origins*, edited by G. C. Harcourt and P. Kriesler, 290–309. Oxford: Oxford University Press.

Kaldor, N. 1934."Mrs. Robinson's 'Economics of Imperfect Competition'." *Economica* 1 (3): 335–341.

Kalecki, M. 1971. *Selected Essays on the Dynamics of the Capitalist Economy 1933–1970.* London: Cambridge University Press.

Lavoie, M. 2001. "Pricing." In *A New Guide to Post Keynesian Economics*, edited by R. P. F Holt and S. Pressman, 21–31. London: Routledge.

Lee, F. S. 1985. "Full-Cost Prices, Classical Price Theory: A Critical Evaluation and Long Period Method Analysis." *Metroeconomica* 37 (2): 135–240.

Lee, F. S. 1990–1. "Marginalist Controversy and Post Keynesian Price Theory." *Journal of Post Keynesian Economics* 13 (2): 252–263.

Lee, F. S. 1994a. "From Post-Keynesian to Historical Price Theory, Part I: Facts, Theory and Empirically Grounded Pricing Model." *Review of Political Economy* 6 (3): 303–336.

Lee, F. S. 1994b. "Introduction: Means and the Making of an Anti-Keynesian Monetary Theory of Employment." In *A Monetary Theory of Employment: Gardiner C. Means*, edited by W. J. Samuels and F. S. Lee, xvii–xxxix. Armonk, NY: M. E. Sharpe.

Lee, F. S. 1998. *Post Keynesian Price Theory.* Cambridge: Cambridge University Press.

Lee, F. S. 2010. "Alfred Eichner's Missing 'Complete Model': Heterodox Micro-Macro Model of a Monetary Production Economy." In *Money and Macrodynamics: Alfred Eichner and Post-Keynesian Economics*, edited by M. Lavoie, L.-P. Rochon, and M. Seccareccia, 22–42. Armonk, NY: M. E. Sharpe.

Lee, F. S. 2011. "Modeling the Economy as a Whole: An Integrative Approach." *American Journal of Economics and Sociology* 70 (5): 1282–1314.

Lee, F. S. 2013a. "Heterodox Economics and Its Critics." In *In Defense of Post-Keynesian and Heterodox Economics: Responses to Their Critics*, edited by F. S. Lee and M. Lavoie, 104–132. London: Routledge.

Lee, F. S. 2013b. "Competition, Going Enterprise, and Economic Activity." In *Alternative Theories of Competition: Challenges to the Orthodoxy*, edited by J. K. Moudud, C. Bina, and P. L. Mason. 160–173. London: Routledge.

Lee, F. S. 2013c. "Post-Keynesian Price Theory: From Pricing to Market Governance to the Economy as a Whole." In *The Oxford Handbook of Post-Keynesian Economics, Vol. 1: Theory and Origins*, edited by G. C. Harcourt and P. Kriesler, 467–484. Oxford: Oxford University Press.

Lee, F. S. and T.-H. Jo. 2011. "Social Surplus Approach and Heterodox Economics." *Journal of Economic Issues* 45 (4): 857–875.

Ong, N.-P. 1981. "Target Pricing, Competition, and Growth." *Journal of Post Keynesian Economics* 4 (1): 101–116.

Robinson, J. 1932. "Imperfect Competition and Falling Supply Price." *Economic Journal* 42 (168): 544–554.

Robinson, J. 1933. *The Economics of Imperfect Competition.* London: Macmillan.

Sawyer, M. 1994. "Post-Keynesian and Marxian Notions of Competition: Towards a Synthesis." In *Competition, Technology and Money*, edited by M. A. Glick, 3–23. Aldershot, UK: Edward Elgar.

Sen, K. and R. R. Vaidya. 1995. "The Determination of Industrial Prices in India: A Post Keynesian Approach." *Journal of Post Keynesian Economics* 18 (1): 29–52.

Shapiro, N. 2012. "Competition." In *The Elgar Companion to Post Keynesian Economics*, 2nd ed., edited by J. E. King, 92–95. Cheltenham, UK: Edward Elgar.

Shapiro, N. and T. Mott, T. 1995. "Firm-Determined Prices: The Post-Keynesian Conception." In *Post-Keynesian Economic Theory*, edited by P. Wells, 35–48. Boston: Kluwer Academic Publishers.

Triffin, R. 1947. *Monopolistic Competition and General Equilibrium Theory.* Cambridge, MA: Harvard University Press.

Tsaliki, P. and L. Tsoulfidis. 1998. "Alternative Theories and Competition: Evidence from Greek Manufacturing." *International Review of Applied Economics* 12 (2): 187–204.

Walters, B. and D. Young. 1997. "On the Coherence of Post Keynesian Economics." *Scottish Journal of Political Economy* 44 (3): 330–348.

Wood, A. 1975. *A Theory of Profits.* Cambridge: Cambridge University Press.

Wray. L. R. 2009. "The Rise and Fall of Money Manager Capitalism: A Minskian Approach." *Cambridge Journal of Economics* 33 (4): 807–828.

Wray, L. R. 2014. "Lessons Learned from the Global Financial Crisis: A Minskian Interpretation of the Causes, the Fed's Bailout and the Future." In *Financial Stability and Growth: Perspectives on Financial Regulation and New Developmentalism*, edited by L. C. Bresser-Pereira, J. A. Kregel, and L. Burlamaqui, 109–126. London: Routledge.

# 14 The embedded state and social provisioning

## Insights from Norbert Elias

*Bruno Tinel*

## Introduction

Norbert Elias (1897–1990) is one of the giants in the social sciences in the twentieth-century. His rich contributions are, however, not much discussed by economists—mainstream and heterodox economists alike. It might be because the topics he dealt with seem barely related to the 'economy' as we understand now. Titles like *The Loneliness of the Dying* or *The Court Society* appear to be more akin to an analysis of Faulkner or Shakespeare. But Elias has also made some major contributions to topics like individualism, sport, social norms, knowledge, and behavior. *The Civilizing Process* is probably the core of his works. In 1998, it was listed by the International Sociological Association as the seventh most important book of the twentieth century.[1] The idea of this book is very ambitious. Elias' plan is to explain the emergence and the structuration of the modern state throughout a very long historical overview that goes from the end of the Carolingian Empire to absolute monarchy in Europe. He considers that the civilizing process involves a deep historical transformation of social habits, including the most trivial ones like everyday life manners, where self-restraint behavior is more and more internalized by individuals with the growth of social differentiation and interconnection. This internalization process is related to the change in the social access to violence which is increasingly centralized and monopolized through the formation and development of the state system. Initially the book was made of two volumes; the first one discusses the historical development of social attitudes and the second volume analyzes the state formation. The latter part is directly related to the concerns of heterodox economics as it focuses on the emergence of the modern state but, strangely enough, such an important book remains overlooked by heterodox economics.[2] Note that in other disciplines, like medieval history or sociology, Elias' global framework of analysis on the modern state formation is considered as a kind of model.[3]

In mainstream economics, the state is something that exists *in order to* solve (only partially) market failures. In most of the Keynesian traditions, the state is something that exists *in order to* lead the economy to full employment. In Marxist economics, the state is something that exists *in order to* maintain and reproduce the capitalist class as the dominant class in the society. Nevertheless, it is dubious that the state exists and has been able to perpetuate through centuries only to fulfill a specific and/or such a simple functionalist purpose. One of the important features in Elias' framework is to analyze the modern state formation without resorting to a purposive or deterministic argument. In particular, he shows that the state is not an immutable entity but an evolving set of elements, which are themselves subject to transformations, that exercise altogether a *contradictory* role in the process of social provisioning and of social (or class) reproduction. The state cannot be understood as an entity situated out of the economy and its development. Neither can it be interpreted as a pure economic entity created to achieve one form of efficiency or another. The aim of this chapter is to present the basic line of argument that Elias develops and to point out some elements that can be of crucial importance for heterodox economics as defined by Frederic Lee in his constructive book, *A History of Heterodox Economics*, and some other papers.

This chapter should be considered as an engagement with Lee's endeavor to build an integrative and pluralist approach to the social provisioning process. His pioneering work and energetic commitment to heterodox economics contributes to the invaluable bedrock that opens up a range of opportunities to advance heterodox economics. Lee rejects indeed the mainstream explanation of the economy as it considers asocial and ahistorical individuals and uses fictitious concepts based on a deductivist and closed-system methodology (Lee 2009, 7). Such a dismissal is actually based on a long series of critiques which form together a general structured critique and which Lee considers also as providing a way to do heterodox economics in a very different fashion from mainstream. He defines heterodoxy as being

> concerned with explaining the process that provides the flow of goods and services required by society to meet the needs of those who participate in its activities. That is from a heterodox perspective, economics is the science of the *social* provisioning process.... The heterodox explanation involves human agency in a cultural context and social processes in historical time affecting resources, consumption patterns, production and reproduction, and the meaning (or ideology) of market, state, and non market/state activities engaged in social provisioning. Thus heterodox economic theory is a theoretical explanation of the historical process of social provisioning within the context of a capitalist economy.
>
> (Lee 2009, 8, emphasis in original)

Lee has developed this view in several recent papers (Lee 2008, 2011a, 2011b, 2011c). Besides these empirical grounds of the heterodox economic theory, he shows that heterodoxy is a community of economists who contribute to develop approaches such as Austrian economics, feminist economics, Institutional-evolutionary economics, Marxian-radical economics, Post Keynesian and Sraffian economics, and social economics. Lee emphasizes that all of these approaches overlap as heterodox economists do engage most of the time with several traditions and develop integrations and synthesis between them. The outcome of all these crossings, borrowings, and combinations (or "cross-approach engagement") is a pluralistic integrative research program, which is "now an established feature on the disciplinary landscape and the progressive future of economics" (Lee 2008). Lee himself has played an important role to make the heterodox community more aware of itself (Jo 2013) and his global argument has been resumed and expanded notably by Jo (2011) and Todorova (2013). Elias is among those forgotten precursors of the heterodox approach in economics as described by Lee, which will be one day or another fully acknowledged as such. He is himself an heir to a long tradition mainly from the sociology and the history of both Max Weber and the German school but a careful reading shows that he had also a solid background in economics. His (socio)economics, as we shall see, was not made of equilibrium, interdependent markets through the price system only and asocial individuals maximizing their utility in an ahistorical context, but rather a historical process combining various mechanisms where individuals are largely constrained by the institutions and the development level of the economic and technological forces they get from the past. His economics has necessarily both a political and a sociological side, and vice versa. These methodological features of Elias' work make of him a genuine forerunner of what Fred Lee later described as heterodoxy. In addition, his work is of some interest for heterodoxy also because just as Marx did with the analysis of the emergence of capitalism, Elias gives insights notably on the emergence of the modern state and, related to it, economic competition and the diffusion of monetary exchanges before the advent of capitalism. His analysis brings light on some major notions that heterodoxy has often to take for granted. He shows how some significant social facts of the capitalist system are not eternal truth but evolving and contingent entities connected one with another through relations changing irreversibly and more or less rapidly.

This conception of social change takes a clear and telling form in the analysis of the process of monopolization. Elias emphasizes the historical link between the monopoly over violence, initially pointed out by Max Weber (1968), and over taxes in the genesis of the modern form of the state, which has important implications for the preconditions of economic activity such as production, exchange, and money. The method looks inductive because Elias is permanently referring to historical facts but he considers this historical case as a general and representative narrative on state formation. He presents a dynamic analysis describing the step by step mechanism that progressively led from feudalism, characterized by an extreme decentralization of society in which numerous warriors were the real rulers, to the emergence of absolutism in Western Europe, characterized by a relatively "stable and centralized government apparatus" (Elias 2000, xii). To Elias, the latter is the first stage of the modern state. The military and social competition mechanism at stake is supposed to apply with more or less accuracy to every nation state and, interestingly, it appears as a metaphor of economic activity: indeed one of his key arguments is that competition leads progressively to monopoly by the successive elimination of competitors.

The twin accumulation of military and financial potential, which in the final analysis rests upon the possession of territories, led to the domination of whole continents by modern states.

The remaining chapter is organized as follows. The second section presents the basic principles of competition associated with the monopolization mechanism which implies a 'no tax, no state' rule discussed in the third section. The fourth section presents the intuition that the administration is the result of reciprocal dependence. The fifth section examines the relation between taxes and money. The sixth section addresses the mutual effects of centralization and economic development. The final section concludes.

## A movement of monopolization: eat or get eaten

In the feudal system, after the fragmentation of the Carolingian Empire which occurred progressively during the ninth century, any territory (a dukedom for example) would include several warrior families which enjoyed the privilege to use arms and to possess land. The House which dominated a territory was also the richest as it possessed the vastest landed estate. Its domination disappeared if it did not succeed in militarily outclassing the other warrior families on this given territory. Military domination of a feudal lord was grounded on property income and on the number of his vassals and feudatories installed in its territory.[4] As soon as predominance of a House was ensured in the limits of its domain a new struggle for hegemony started over a larger area. This mechanism gives us one of the most fundamental keys to explain the struggle of the great lords to control the Kingdom as a whole. The unification movement among several distinct seigneuries occurred in the same way that led to the domination of a knight or a feudal lord over and inside a given territory. This process of progressive concentration and centralization of military and political power unfolded during the five centuries constituting the second part of the middle ages in the big countries of Western Europe and led to the formation of nation states.

In the early phase of the process, small territorial entities of the future state played a very decisive role. Those dominant units were relatively small and relatively loosely structured just like in every place in the world where the division of labor and exchanges (internal as well as external) are not well developed. For Elias, the Dukedom of France at the beginning of the twelfth century is a good example.[5] He mentions a few feudal seigneuries which also transformed into small Kingdoms, Dukedoms, or Counties in the German Empire; the same process applied also to the Scottish Kingdom before being integrated to the UK along with England and Northern Ireland. Basing his analysis mainly on French medieval history, Elias shows how 'at the beginning' it was not obvious that the House of the Capet would 'in the end' (i.e., three or four centuries later) impose and centralize its domination monopoly over the territory of the West Frankish Kingdom. Capet was one of many lords in this era. As a king, although he enjoyed more spiritual prestige, his effective force was not at all significantly superior to many other lords of his realm; for instance, Louis VI 'the Fat' (1081–1137) was undeniably weaker than his vassal, the Duke of Normandy, who had also been King of England since 1066, 42 years before Louis' coronation in 1108.

No less conscious of their own interest than dominant classes nowadays, medieval lords and knights were spurred towards internal and external expansion for livelihood issues. The forms of competition were imposed on feudal lords, they had to extend their domain through neighbor subjugations in order not to be themselves defeated. Defeat was equivalent to an elimination of the scene of potential competitors by loss of territory and military control or even by physical destruction: they had to grow to avoid declining. The ones who merely wanted to preserve their possessions seriously imperiled themselves by enabling a more bellicose neighbor to absorb them. Such kind of social competition inevitably triggered monopolist mechanisms. At the beginning, a lot of free competitors were present in the arena. Their means of competition were not much different from each others'. After many victories and defeats, only a few competitors were left on the scene. Even though the defeated competitors could still enjoy important social influence they became secondary protagonists. The decisive struggle opposes the last two defeaters who are already close to a monopoly position. Norbert Elias puts these thoughts forward in the following terms:

> Precisely because estate owners were in a certain sense opposed to one another, just as states today, the acquisition of new land by one neighbour represented a direct or indirect threat to the others ... [A]nyone who declines to compete, merely conserving his property while others strive for increase, necessarily ends up 'smaller' and weaker than the others, and is in ever-increasing danger of succumbing to them at the first opportunity.
>
> (Elias 2000, 219)

This observation is important for heterodox economics because it cleverly dismisses the idea of a 'competitive equilibrium.' Indeed, each individual unit involved in a competitive process has to constantly undertake new actions in order to simply try to reproduce its position in the competition. Hence at the individual level, each unit is continually constrained to struggle not to disappear from the scene: "in a society with such competitive pressures, he who does not gain 'more' automatically becomes 'less'" (Elias 2000, 263). Those who are unable to provide enough resources or to timely renew their strategies in order to sustain this competitive process are pushed out. Consequently, more resources and power accrue to some of the remaining competitors. Elias thus argues that there is no competitive equilibrium in this historical process:

> If we assume that to begin with all the people in this area fight one other for the available opportunities, the probability that they will maintain this state of equilibrium indefinitely and that no partner will triumph in any of these pairs is extremely small ... and the probability that sooner or later individual contestants will overcome their opponents is extremely high.
>
> (Elias 2000, 269)

Of course the estate of the eliminated competitors were not equally shared among the survivors, since the estate itself was one of the objects of competition. At the social level, the combination of all these individual hectic activities could hardly be named an 'equilibrium.' On the contrary, the combination of these frenetic individual behaviors produced a tumultuous and unpredictable environment for everyone. This competition process that generated constantly and endogenously changing surroundings had only one outcome: the reduction in the number of actual participants and the growth of their power. No doubt such a process of competition was not confined to the political and military spheres:

> The mechanism leading to hegemony is always the same. In a similar way—through the accumulation of property—a small number of economic enterprises in more recent times have slowly outstripped their rivals and competed with each other, until finally one or two of them control and dominate a particular branch of the economy as a monopoly.
>
> (Elias 2000, 260)[6]

## The exclusive control over physical violence and tax imposition

For Elias, the monopolist position of modern central power is defined by a twofold monopoly: (i) monopoly over military means and (ii) monopoly over tax levying. Those two monopolies go along together and support each other: the financial means accruing to the central power enables it to maintain military and police monopoly, which, in turn, ensures the effectiveness in taxation. Modern societies based on a sophisticated division of labor are also characterized by a permanent administrative apparatus specialized in running both monopolies. Elias considers this twofold monopoly as a key element among the broader set of monopolies, which altogether form the state. If one of the two key monopolies fails then the state starts to decline. The complementarity between military power and tax power has to be emphasized: these two powers are the two sides of the same coin in the hands of the one who rules. Tax is hence a compulsory phenomenon, which is related to the existence of a united ruling entity within a given territory: their relative acceptance is therefore ontologically related to the relative acceptance of the ruler by the rest of the society. In other words, the ability of a central authority to raise taxes on the society determines the ability of this authority to reproduce itself as the central power which could be summed as 'no tax, no state.'

This basic principle can find some possible applications in contemporary economic problems. For example, in advanced capitalist countries, tax reductions induce higher rates of public debts (for a given level of expenditures) which make the state more dependent on financial markets: part of the contemporary sovereign debt 'problems' are due to a weakening of the tax system which eventually undermines the whole state apparatus. Another possible field of application relates to the role of the state in developing countries. The contemporary literature on the 'state failure' is prolific. Issues like development strategy, institutional capacities, and service-delivery tasks are widely treated but very little reflection is actually devoted to the analysis of the twofold monopoly constitution. Very often, one can read papers advocating sophisticated plans for the development and the 'governance' of countries in which the state is so non-existent that the ruling class is constrained to delegate the levying of taxes like tariffs to private companies. Elias shows that the formation of the state is a pre-condition to modern economic development, which is too often overlooked by the profession and international organizations. A third possible application of the 'no tax, no state' principle could be named the 'Dutch disease problem' of the state: those developing countries which possess a great quantity of natural resources like petrol, gas, or diamonds for instance are not encouraged to develop a genuine tax system and the state apparatus that is supposed to go with it. The absence of a real state organization is then an incentive for rent seeking strategies like guerillas and mafias to appropriate the natural resources. As a consequence, permanent instability, underdevelopment, and patron/client relations are prevalent.

## Administration as reciprocal dependence

Elias explains how and why those 'twin' monopolies emerged in West Francia (former western Frankish Empire) a 1,000 years ago during the eleventh century. As already noticed, his starting point corresponds to a situation where each warrior exercises all government functions over the limited piece of land under the warrior's control. A warrior can start a war when he wants to protect or to extend his possessions. Conquest and domination functions over owned land are both reserved to the private initiative of each warrior. The victorious lord increases his potential power by appropriation of at least a part of the military and economic means of the defeated until only one individual concentrates all this potential in his hands. Defeated competitors are eliminated and become dependent on remaining competitors. But this should not be interpreted naively. In fact, dependency develops reciprocally from a certain threshold of concentration onwards, at least in sufficiently differentiated societies. The more the number of individuals who lost their independency increases, the more their collective social power increases to face up to the decreasing number of monopolists.

The social power of dependent people is based on two pillars: (i) the increasing number of dependents and (ii) the monopolist's need of the dependents to maintain and use effectively its monopoly potential. Elias explains that the accumulation of great quantities of land, soldiers, and financial means in a few hands makes their control more difficult. In other words, the monopolist cannot handle his increasing power on his own as it grows. He is constrained to delegate his decision power to specialized people who depend on him. Hence the monopolist progressively becomes embedded in the social network of those who are depending on him because he has to organize his power through a more and more complex network of relations and procedures, which progressively crystallize into an administration:

> The more people are made dependent by the monopoly mechanism, the greater becomes the power of the dependent, not only individually but also collectively, in relation to the one or more monopolists. This happens not only because of the small number of those approaching the monopoly position, but because of their own dependence on ever more dependents in preserving and exploiting the power potential they have monopolized.
>
> (Elias 2000, 270)

This process was very slow and lasted over centuries. The development and the concentration of the twin monopolies lead to a differentiation of activities and to an increasing division of labor inside the organizations which are meant to maintain and enforce the monopoly. At one point, those organizations start to have their own weight and their own rules to which the holder of the monopoly has to submit to. The possession of such a monopoly requires establishing a large administration and a well developed division of labor which imply more and more formal rules and procedures for appointment, promotion, and activity fulfillment:

> the more comprehensive a monopoly position becomes and the more highly developed its division, the more clearly and certainly does it move towards a point at which its one or more monopoly rulers become the central functionaries of an apparatus composed of differentiated functions, more powerful than others, perhaps, but scarcely less dependent and fettered.
>
> (Elias 2000, 271)

The monopoly holders are thus increasingly transformed into conveyors or servants of an administrative apparatus with multiple functions. Those servants are certainly more influential than many other people but they are nevertheless dependent and bound by numerous contingencies, rules, laws, and functional dependence vis-à-vis the society they dominate. With the growth of the central monopoly, power slides from the private hands of the lord to numerous hands of dependent people in charge of monopoly administration. The private monopoly of a few isolated individuals becomes socialized. Controlled by whole stratums of the society, the private monopoly transforms into a public entity, the state. The monopoly is less and less arbitrarily exploited by a few individuals because the network of interdependent and differentiated functions is ruled by its own principles which progressively prevent private monopolization of the elements constituting the twin monopolies. The switch from private to public is considered by Elias as a result of an increasing social interdependency:

> the power first won through the accumulation of chances in private struggles, tends … to slip away from the monopoly rulers into the hands of the dependents as a whole, or, to begin with, to groups of dependents, such as

the monopoly administration. The privately owned monopoly in the hands of a single individual or family comes under control of broader social strata, and transforms itself as the central organ of a state into a public monopoly.

(Elias 2000, 271)

So a new type of competition arises, a social competition among dependents to obtain places inside the monopoly with its own rules and system of selection: "the struggle for monopolies no longer aims at their destruction; it is a struggle for control of their yields, for the plan according to which their burdens and benefits are to be divided up, in a word, for the keys to distribution" (Elias 2000, 275; see also Bourdieu 1996). Elias considers this "unfree" regulated competition (i.e., without the force of arms) inside the monopoly as a crucial element of a "democratic regime" and he emphasizes that such a regime is in fact not the freest possible competition but "presupposes highly organized monopolies, and it can only come into being or survive … in a very specific social structure at a very advanced stage of monopoly formation" (Elias 2000, 276).[7]

In the previous period, competition was free as victory went to the strongest, once the centralization process reaches its turning point competition then depends on the function and the activity that each individual is able to fulfill for the monopolist: individuals hence compete for a position in the state apparatus. From now on competition is ruled by a central administration which selects types of men and women differently from those of the previous period. The goal is no longer to abolish or to redistribute the central monopoly power but, by contrast, to reallocate charges and benefits inside the monopoly. This competition is 'pacific'; it consists in periodical 'play-offs' and supposes the creation of control procedures. All these elements of monopolization are preconditions to the contemporary 'democratic' regimes.

Be it a modern state apparatus or an absolute monarchy, the central monopoly is always weaker than the society as a whole. If the totality or a great part of the society united and rebelled against it, then the central authority would not be able to resist the pressure (Elias 2000, 353). An important condition for the reproduction of the central monopoly, not only under the form of an absolute monarchy, is hence that the acceptance or the legitimacy of the sovereign authority must be wide enough in the society. But this political element is not sufficient. Elias also emphasizes that social interests of the different parts composing the society must be sufficiently ambivalent and contradictory to ensure a maximum of strength to the central entity. The compensation or mutual neutralization of class interests inside the society plays a major role in the enforcement of the central monopoly (the well-known 'divide to rule' principle). In other words, a government structure simply based upon a narrow social basis would not be able to reproduce and last for a long period of time.

This allows us to say a few words about the Marxist conception of the state, which is so often misunderstood and caricatured by its detractors as well as by its proponents (on the Marxist conception of the state, see Barrow 2000; Lenin 1917; Herrera 2001; Poulantzas 1978). To put it briefly, for Elias the state is the expression of a class domination resulted from the long-time struggle within the warrior class for the monopoly over violence and taxation—that is, the monopoly over the domination (hence the stabilization or even the reproduction) of the society as a whole. It is thus conceivable from Elias' perspective that the state is a crucial element that contributes to the class structure formation and reproduction.[8] Furthermore, if his analysis is correct then the key elements of the 'modern state' already were in place prior to the development of the capitalist system. This implies that most of the elements of the 'capitalist state' identified by, for example, Poulantzas (1978) are in fact not specific to capitalism, although the idea that an autonomous organization progressively emerges to manage the twin monopoly is very close to Poulantzas' idea of a relative autonomy of the state from the capitalist class.

Such a conception of the state is akin to a Kaleckian view of the political economy—that is, a Post Keynesian view that acknowledges the importance of class struggle, and which is also shared by Fred Lee (Lee 2011a, 18).[9] From this perspective, the government is likely to implement decisions favorable to lower classes only if it does not threaten the dominant position of ruling classes. The government is also able to implement some decisions against some fractions of dominant classes in order to preserve the collective interests of the ruling classes—for example, in the face of crisis the government arbitrates in favor of dominating classes as a last resort even if the consequences are really bad for the whole society. In this regard, the state is the watchman of the class order.

In short, Elias' analysis appears as highly compatible with the Marxist conception of the state as well as a Post-Keynesian approach to the state. The socio-economic approach developed by Elias is also very close to the institutionalist tradition with its emphasis on the dynamic interactions between rules, behaviors, and mental representations.[10] Thus it appears that Elias offers an important insight into the theory of the state from which an integrative and pluralistic heterodox approach could benefit greatly. Elias' analysis would become more interesting for heterodox economists if his analysis of taxes and money is considered.

## Taxes and money

Before the emergence of the twin monopolies, princes and kings could not actually impose taxes directly on the population all over the Kingdom. The ability to impose taxes was based on land ownership: each lord could impose taxes on people of his own territory; in case of resistance, he could resort to his local monopoly over violence. Central taxation remained casual until the fourteenth century. Unlike regular taxation in a developed market economy, such kind of levying could be more than burdening mainly because it could be hardly predictable. As it was not a normal institution, nobody could include it in his/her calculus: trade, prices, and individual wealth could then be seriously perturbed by a tax imposed by the central authority. This is all the more true that such a kind of central taxation was often required in money: less advanced countries, where monetary exchange was not well developed, could have considerable problems meeting the central demand, which could hence turn into a tragedy.

During the middle ages, government expenditures were supposed to be financed only through the revenue of the dynastic possessions of the central lord (the 'ordinary'). Even when the king started to become more than a big warrior among other big warriors from the end of the twelfth century onwards, he could not afford to impose taxes as he wished on his whole sphere of influence. He had to gather the representatives of the three orders (Nobility, Church, and Third Estate) into States-General (*Etats Généraux*, or simply the 'States'). The king had to justify the reasons of an extraordinary tax raising (the 'extraordinary' also called the 'helps' or *aides*) and to be authorized by the States to do so. With the Hundred Years' War (1337–1453), the need for money to finance the war became permanent which forced the States to be in session more and more often. In 1362, John the Good was taken as a captive to England. The necessity to pay a huge ransom compelled the States to plan annual taxes in the whole Kingdom over 20 years, which greatly accelerated the extension process of levying taxes regularly at the monopoly level. In 1436, King Charles VII was able to impose taxes without the States convening. This indicates that the king already gained sufficient social power. From then on, the king was able to raise funds through taxation on the whole Kingdom territory, beyond his own dynastic domain, without resorting to any formal authorization (Elias 2000, 348 and passim). Through wars, the link between monopoly over violence and monopoly over taxes is particularly obvious: the need to spend money for war requires more and more taxes beyond the individual domain of the king which reinforces in turn the army and the police of the central power. Just as efficiency requires the command of war to be centralized, the war resources have become also more and more centralized.

The cities developed against local lords and got early special protection from the central power. Normally, just like any feudal lord, city *bourgeois* should provide military units to the king if an enemy was to threaten the Kingdom. Very early, instead of sending their sons to be killed for the home-land, *bourgeois* of cities started to give money to the central power. On the one hand, military service could be bought. This kind of monetary transaction helped develop the double monopoly and extend the tax systems initially created by independent cities. This replacement of military service by monetary tax also shows the profound and explicit link which existed between both monopolies six or seven centuries ago. On the other hand, the central power found it useful to collect money through the tax system because it was easy to hire mercenaries among poor people and to command armament and war equipment directly from manufacturers at a massive scale. Monetary-fiscal resources were preferred to payment in kind since the latter gave less freedom to the central monopoly. For this reason and also because they quickly under-stood that they could practice seigniorage if they could impose their own money, lords started to demand taxes in money. This contributed greatly to develop monetary exchanges. Instead of remaining more or less self-sufficient and to sell only the surplus necessary to get enough money for the provision of commodities produced elsewhere, people were enforced to obtain more money in order to be able to pay their taxes and hence to sell more. As more money was flowing into the Treasury chests, more money was also used in the whole economy to buy commodities. Here again, monetary exchanges, trade, and markets were greatly stimulated, if not created, by the development of a central monopoly and its demand for taxes in money. Money taxes can therefore be said to have contributed to the institutionalization and stimulation of money market exchanges. Obviously, this conception of money is very close to the chartalist tradition initiated notably by Georg Friedrich Knapp who may have influenced Elias during his training in Germany. This state money tradition continues in Post Keynesian economics through John Maynard Keynes and his followers, and Fred Lee advocates this view of money in his integrative approach to the economy as a whole (Lee 2011c, 1293).[11]

## Power centralization and economic development

Until the rise of centralized taxes paid in money, the central power had to reward its main partisans and the closest members of the royal family with fractions of its domain. Indeed, the lord or the king used to give his sons and daughters castles, counties, or duchies because they had to live in accordance with their rank and hence maintain the prestige of their royal origin. This system of appanage was thus a counter-movement to monopolization. It was a factor of decentralization, fragmentation, and disintegration of the family domain, though the basis of the monopoly power until the absolutist period. With the huge increase in monetary resources that occurred with systematic money taxation, this counter-movement disappeared because the central power could then distribute prebends in money. This further rendered servants more dependent and devoted to the Prince that they did not possess their own piece of land. On this aspect again, demanding taxes in money considerably contributed to the reinforcement of the central monopoly because (i) the royal domain ceased to be divided and (ii) the persons integrated into the central administration became monetary dependent and hence more loyal. The necessity to develop an administration system for the twin monopoly thus stimulated the payment of taxes in money and the development of monetary exchanges in turn facilitated the development of the administrative structure.

Lastly, Elias establishes an interesting link between the level of development of the economy and the form of the state. He distinguishes a "barter economy" from a "money economy" (Elias 2000, 205–206). A barter economy is not an imaginary economy without money that is usually presented to students to tell the tale of the origins of money as a commodity. For Elias, there is money even in a barter economy and such an economy refers actually

> to a society in which the transfer of goods from the person who gets them from the soil or nature to the person who uses them takes place directly, that is without intermediaries, and where they are worked up at the house of one or the other, which may well be the same.

> (Elias 2000, 207)

He considers that "as long as barter relationships predominated in society, the formation of tightly centralized bureaucracy and a stable apparatus of government working primarily with peaceful means and directed constantly from the centre, was scarcely possible" (Elias 2000, 205). In other words, the fragmentation and the predominance of short distance domestic exchanges prevent the centralization process of the twin monopoly from occurring. With the development of a money economy the feudalization of states (centrifugal forces) can step back. It is easy to imagine the relationship going from the development of the money economy to the development of the modern state: the diffusion of money allows the diffusion of money taxes, which in turn reinforces the centralization process. According to this view, the development of the modern state is subject to the rise of private market exchanges. Here the state remains as a result of the economy which appears as a distinct and autonomous force but this is not exactly the idea developed by Elias in his book. For him, the state is actually embedded in the economy. Both the state and the economy co-evolve because the development of the state itself has an influence on the development of the economy: the relation goes both ways. Not only does the state need the economy for tax raising, but the economy also cannot expand before the state has reached a certain degree of development:

> economic struggles ... presuppose the secure existence of certain very advanced monopolies. Without the monopoly organization of physical violence and taxation ... the restriction of this struggle for 'economic' advantages to the exertion of 'economic' power, and the maintenance of its basic rules, would be impossible over any length of time even within individual states. In other words, the economic struggles and monopolies of modern times occupy a particular position within a larger historical context.
>
> (Elias 2000, 277)

Besides, Elias insists on the idea that before the advent of centralization in the form of a genuine state apparatus each lord used to consider his estates as his private property like a "small family enterprise" (Elias 2000, 291), which gave them an autarkic character. Each warrior house was hence induced to focus on the consolidation of its control over its possessions and its internal development to increase its revenues, which must have had an impact on the development of activities and of internal connections and transports. He considers that the merging of different possessions even stimulated economic integration:

> their union under one and the same house and partly under the same administration, did remove a whole series of obstacles in the way of fuller integration. It corresponded to the tendency towards an extension of trade relations, the intensification of links beyond the local level, which was already discernible in small parts of the urban population.
>
> (Elias 2000, 287)

And he adds a few lines further that, under the protection of the princes' houses, towns and trade flourished and profited from the concentration of power which in turn relied on the concentration of human and financial resources offered by urban strata and growing commercialization.

This kind of positive feedback between the development of the money economy and the centralization process logically implies the idea of a cumulative causation. But this framework can also be pushed a step further and viewed as a macro-economic understanding, and closing off, of the monetization of taxes in relation with the development of money economy. As for taxes, not only is the state able to levy money taxes more easily when monetary exchanges develop but the fact that taxes are no longer payable in kind also stimulates the economy because it induces people to bring to the market more commodities in order to obtain more money inter alia to pay taxes with money. As for 'public' spending, the central power is now able to give a monetary revenue to the 'civil' servants, instead of endowing them with a piece of land; this new class of money earners has hence to spend at least a part of its income for its everyday life which creates a new demand for consumption goods. The same reasoning applies to direct spending by the central power, for instance, for the equipment of its armies. Now that it receives more taxes in the state money form, the government is henceforth able to buy more supplies, equipments, arms, horses, manufactured goods from the private sector which stimulates economic activities and allows suppliers to get the money they need to pay their taxes. Thus it appears more clearly how the state develops through the monetization of taxes and state spending is a vector of economic development which steers both supply and demand on markets. For this reason an economic theory that considers the economy and the state separately is fallacious. The state and the economy appear as profoundly interlocked to each other. The reader must have noticed that the present argument of the embeddedness of the state in the economy is not based upon the classical Smithian contention that the state provides pacification (defense, justice) services or 'public goods' which are supposed to have a positive effect on private business. Of course, these elements presented by Adam Smith in the first chapter of the fifth book of the *Wealth of Nations* are not contradictory to Elias' viewpoint but, merely, *The Civilizing Process* goes much further in the understanding of, among other things, the state embeddedness.

## Conclusion

This chapter has emphasized that Norbert Elias' view of the economic development and socio-economic relations on the emergence of the state is very close to Fred Lee's conception of heterodoxy. The second section has shown that for Elias the competition for power and land leads necessarily to monopoly. He considers that this type of competition process dismisses any notion of competitive equilibrium and applies to modern economic activities and not only to middle ages' political and military struggles. The third section highlighted the double nature of the monopoly power that forms the very core of the state: monopoly over violence and over taxes. The fourth section developed the idea that administration and bureaucracy are unavoidable outcomes of the centralization process. The fifth section on taxes and money showed that, according to Elias, the development of the state and monetary exchanges are stimulating each other. This state money approach is also shared by Fred Lee in his integrative model of the economy as a whole. The sixth section exposed that the development of the economy has to be understood as the development of the state as well and vice versa: one is impossible without the other. Fred Lee addressed this view in his last lecture in April 2014 that building a macro model without the state amounts to writing fairy tales (Lee 2014).

## Acknowledgments

The author is grateful to Tae-Hee Jo, Zdravka Todorova, and an anonymous referee for most helpful comments and suggestions.

## Notes

1  See the Top 10 list here: www.isa-sociology.org/books/books10.htm.
2  See Elias ([1939] 2000) for any reference and also the HyperElias© WorldCatalogue[HTM], http://hyperelias.jku.at/.
3  In France, see for instance Alain Guéry's works in the tradition of the Annales school of Georges Duby and Jacques Le Goff, cf. Descimon and Guéry (2000). On the analytical side of the issue, see the imposing work of Pierre Bourdieu (2012). Check also the website of the Norbert Elias Foundation, www.norberteliasfoundation.nl/.
4  A feudatory holds an estate in land (fiefdom) granted by a lord to his vassal on the condition of homage and service. A vassal can be the owner of his land.
5  At this time these possessions represent not much more than Paris and Orléans plus a few small cities around Paris like Senlis.
6  On the general character of the monopoly mechanism and the fact that some would call it a 'law,' see Elias (2000, 264). See also page 269 for a global and synthetic formulation.
7  For a contemporary application of 'regulated competition,' see Lee (2012, 168).
8  Of course this idea is profoundly shocking as it does not match well with the modern ideal of freedom and equality. It goes without saying that this observation is not a normative but a historical and positive statement.
9  Note that Post Keynesians in general do not have a clear view of the state and class and while Kalecki had a class analysis, some later Kaleckians do not have it. For the Post Keynesian theory of the state, see Pressman (2006b).
10  Neither the contribution on the institutionalist perspectives on the state by Waller (2006) nor the 'Polanyian' article by Stanfield and Stanfield (2006) in Pressman's edited book (2006a) on the theories of the state noticed the importance of Elias for their field of research.
11  See for instance the contribution of Wray (1998) for a recent chartalist and historical approach of money.

## References

Barrow, C. W. 2000. "The Marx Problem in Marxian State Theory." *Science & Society* 64 (1): 87–118.
Bourdieu, P. 1996. *The State Nobility: Elite Schools in the Field of Power.* Cambridge: Polity Press.

Bourdieu, P. 2012. *Sur l'État, Cours au Collège de France (1989–1992)*. Paris: Raisons d'Agir/Seuil.

Descimon, R. and A. Guéry. 2000. "Un État des Temps Modernes?" in *Seuil Histoire de la France. La longue* durée *de l'*État, edited by Jacques LeGoff, vol. 1, 209–503. Paris: Éditions du Seuil.

Elias, N. 2000. *The Civilizing Process*. Oxford: Blackwell Publishing (originally published as *Über den Prozess der Zivilisation*, as two separate volumes in 1939 by Haus zum Falken; English translation: *The History of Manners*, 1978, Basil Blackwell and *State Formation and Civilization*, 1982, Basil Blackwell).

Herrera, R. 2001. "Brève introduction à la théorie de l'État chez Marx et Engels." *Cahiers de la MSE*, série rouge, n°R01001.

Jo, T.-H. 2011. "Social Provisioning Process and Socio-Economic Modeling." *American Journal of Economics and Sociology* 70 (5): 1094–1116.

Jo, T.-H., ed. 2013. *Heterodox Economics Directory*, 5th ed. Accessed December 19, 2014. http://heterodoxnews.com/directory/hed5.pdf.

Lee, F. S. 2008. "Heterodox Economics." In *The New Palgrave Dictionary of Economics*, 2nd ed., edited by S. N. Durlauf and L. E. Blume. London: Palgrave Macmillan.

Lee, F. S. 2009. *A History of Heterodox Economics*. London: Routledge.

Lee, F. S. 2011a. "Heterodox Microeconomics and the Foundation of Heterodox Macroeconomics." *Economia Informa* 367: 6–20.

Lee, F. S. 2011b. "Heterodox Surplus Approach: Production, Prices, and Value Theory." MPRA Working Paper 31824. Accessed December 19, 2014. http://mpra.ub.uni-muenchen.de/31824.

Lee, F. S. 2011c. "Modeling the Economy as a Whole: An Integrative Approach." *American Journal of Economics and Sociology* 70 (5): 1282–1314.

Lee, F. S. 2012. "Competition, Going Enterprise, and Economic Activity." In *Alternative Theories of Competition: Challenges to the Orthodoxy*, edited by J. K. Moudud, C. Bina, and P. L. Mason, 160–173. London: Routledge.

Lee, F. S. 2014. "The Role of Microeconomics in Heterodox Economics: A View of a Heterodox Micro Theorist." Unpublished transcript of Fred Lee's last lecture at the University of Missouri–Kansas City, April 24, 2014. The video of this lecture is available at http://heterodoxnews.com/leefs/fred-lee-lecture-at-umkc.

Lenin, V. 1917. *The State and Revolution*. Accessed December 19, 2014. www.marxists.org/archive/lenin/works/1917/staterev/index.htm.

Poulantzas, N. 1978. *Political Power and Social Classes*. London: Verso.

Pressman, S., ed. 2006a. *Alternative Theories of the State*. New York: Palgrave Macmillan.

Pressman, S. 2006b. "A Post Keynesian Theory of the State." In *Alternative Theories of the State*, edited by S. Pressman, 113–138. New York: Palgrave Macmillan.

Stanfield, J. R. and J. B. Stanfield. 2006. "The Protective Response and the Evolution of the Capitalist State." In *Alternative Theories of the State*, edited by S. Pressman, 34–63. New York: Palgrave Macmillan.

Todorova, Z. 2013. "Connecting Social Provisioning and Functional Finance in a Post-Keynesian–Institutional Analysis of the Public Sector." *European Journal of Economics and Economic Policies: Intervention* 10 (1): 61–75.

Waller, W. 2006. "The Pragmatic State: Institutionalist Perspectives on the State." In *Alternative Theories of the State*, edited by Steven Pressman, 13–34. New York: Palgrave Macmillan.

Weber, M. 1968. *Economy and Society*. New York: Bedminster Press.

Wray, L. R. 1998. *Understanding Modern Money*. Northampton, MA: Edward Elgar.

# 15 Analogies we suffer by

## The case of the state as a household

*Huáscar Pessali, Fabiano Dalto, and
Ramón Fernández*

### Introduction

We had the opportunity to meet with Frederic Lee on various academic occasions and his wit and provocative enthusiasm always invigorated us. His relentless message that we should not give up using our full capacities to improve the lives of many and his consistent example shall be with us vividly, as we intend to show in this chapter. We have experienced the aggravation in the lives of many whenever the idea of 'sound finance' is put into action. It is our responsibility, thus, to scrutinize it. Sound finance economists and politicians proclaim that fiscal austerity gives confidence to financial markets and allows governments to pay lower interest rates on their debts. This arguably leads to a safer environment for investments as the reduction in inefficient government spending gives room to efficient private spending. As a result, it is said, production and employment increase. In order to legitimate their view and to gain social assent, those economists and politicians use analogical reasoning to claim that managing the central government's budget is like managing the household finances.

Analogical reasoning infers that one phenomenon is similar to another one in a certain respect on the basis that both phenomena are known to be similar in other respects. When applied in political and economic discourses, an analogy helps legitimate our views of "the on-going economic process that provides the flow of goods and services required by society to meet the needs of those who participate in its activities" (Gruchy 1987, 21). The functioning of a social provisioning process sets the institutional conditions by which burdens and provisions are distributed throughout all going concerns involved (Lee 2011a; Todorova 2007). Government spending, for instance, is crucial in the provisioning process of modern capitalism. It can be used to promote full employment and to drive transactions closer to socially desired values, beliefs, and ethical standards (Todorova 2013). Yet, the understanding of such a potential is obstructed by the state-as-household analogy, of which examples abound in the political arena.

Margaret Thatcher (1975) once said "What is right for the family is right for Britain. The first priority is to cut Government spending drastically." Decades later across the Atlantic Ocean, President Obama (2011) unveiled the US budget and stated: "That's what families across the country do every day—they live within their means and they invest in their family's futures. And it's time we did the same thing as a country. That's how we're going to get our fiscal house in order." Similarly, Republicans have stated: "We believe the state should live within its means and budget just like families do every day" (Republican Caucus 2011).

Public figures like Cindy Chafian agree: "I really equate it [federal government] to the family" (Mencimer 2011). Elsewhere, Gustavo Franco, President of the Brazilian Central Bank during President Cardoso's first term (1995–1998), remarked about Brazil's privatization program: "The economic logic of privatization has never been difficult to grasp. The family has huge debts, earnings disputed by relatives, and assets that create more costs than earnings. Selling some of these assets to pay debts is a very good idea to improve the family's finances" (Franco 2004). Similarly, the Finance Minister of President Lula's first term (2003–2006) Antonio Palocci said:

> One should not doubt the fiscal commitment of this government, which will deal with the budget just like the worker deals with his. He spends only what he earns, pays his debts, and keeps a balanced life to preserve his reputation.
>
> (Beck 2004)

Yet, during the 1990s and early 2000s, there was slow economic growth, falling average wages, increasing rates of unemployment and of household debt (Quadros 2003).[1]

Those examples show an analogy presented in both direct and indirect form. The latter form starts with a wider association between entities through metaphorical reasoning. In a metaphor, resemblance between entities is suggested without a particular reference to one or another respect. On occasion, the institution of the state is compared to other aspects of the institution household—as in expressions like 'tidy up the mess,' 'put order to one's house,' or 'citizens are consumers of the products of the state.' Whenever these metaphors drive our thoughts to the specific analogy of the central government's budget being like the budget of a household, we will refer to them interchangeably as the state-as-household analogy. The distinctive inference of this reasoning by sound finance advocates is the imperative that, as in a household, the state should not spend more than it earns.

This chapter evaluates the aptness of the state-as-household analogy in improving our understanding of the functioning of the state in modern economies. To do this, we first discuss the role of metaphors and analogies in the construction of understanding. We then show some of the rhetorical strengths of the analogy. Next, we show some of its weaknesses—especially those based on economic arguments that help to conceal the nature of the state as a peculiar institution. Concluding remarks follow.

## Metaphors and analogies as argumentation and practice

As we try to understand what is unknown or too complex, we put it in most familiar terms. Aristotle (1984) suggested that to explain is to reduce the unknown to the already known. A physician explains to a patient how blood circulation works by comparing blood vessels to pipes and the heart to a pump, while business people refer to a CEO as the head of an organization. Producing economic understanding is no different (Henderson 1994). This demands attention to how we build and present our reasoning and our arguments through models, stories, facts, logic, and other persuasion devices (McCloskey 1990).

In this context, metaphors and analogies are no longer a fancy and superfluous use of language but an inherent necessity, indispensable to our conceptual system and, thus, to knowledge production. As reasoning mechanisms, they shape how we perceive and think about our daily interaction with the world (Lakoff 1999; Lakoff and Johnson 1980). On the one hand, metaphors try to establish similarities between different entities, suggesting an understanding of one of them based on the other (Black 1993). On the other hand, metaphors avoid differing aspects between them (Lakoff and Johnson 1980). The latter aspect is especially relevant for economists and other social scientists. As Lakoff and Johnson (1980, 236) argue:

> Like all other metaphors, political and economic metaphors can hide aspects of reality. But in the area of politics and economics, metaphors matter more, because they constrain our lives. A metaphor in a political or economic system, by virtue of what it hides, can lead to human degradation.

In the early 1980s, some authors called attention to the importance of metaphors in the work of economists (Henderson 1982; McCloskey 1983). The subject has since been explored.[2] Today we are much more aware of the framing role of metaphorical reasoning in economics and economic policy issues.

The daily usage of a metaphor usually produces variants in more specific similarities or analogies. An analogy transfers specific relations believed to be valid on a certain context to other. A certain element 'A' is for 'B' in one context just like 'C' is for 'D' in a different context (Perelman and Olbrechts-Tyteca [1958] 1969, 373). If we say that the finances (A) of a household (B) are like the budget (C) of the state (D), we use an analogy to claim a specific similarity between two different things. This is a condensed form of the state-as-household analogy. The household budget is used as a mirror for the ideal and necessary budget policy for the state.

According to Burke (1954), a danger in analogies is to turn a claim of similarity into evidence of identity. In the analogy examined here, the similarity is that both entities register (or can register) their financial flow on a budget. The danger is to conclude that the nature and consequences of their budget management are identical. Seen as an identity, the analogy suggests that state deficits necessarily lead to debt increase and, finally, to insolvency—the equivalent to a bankrupt household.

In order to avoid such danger, it is expected that metaphors and analogies used in a scientific debate, unlike poetic ones, be worked and reworked to exhaustion, extended and questioned (Mirowski 1988). By definition, an analogy frames the debate around specifically claimed similarities and keeps off issues claimed to be irrelevant, inexistent, or dissimilar. The state—the entity that receives the normative load of the state-as-household analogy—is a peculiar entity with distinctive goals, resources, responsibilities, and operating logic. This is what the analogy helps us forget.

## The rhetorical strengths of the state-as-household analogy

One of us once asked a first year class of economics undergraduates: "Do you think the state can or must spend more than it collects?" One of them answered very confidently: "No, if the state spends more than it collects, it goes bust." A supportive humming quickly followed. Students seem to have formed an opinion before being exposed to the sound finance arguments coming mainly from neo-classical economics. They probably read or heard about the issue somewhere else and in a simpler frame that associated certain elements they think they understand better (their household or their business enterprises for instance) to other elements they do not understand (the intricate role of the state in an economy).

In order to produce engagement and eventual assent, arguments must contain some shared cognitive elements with the audience at sight. This is something easily prompted by the state-as-household analogy. There is comfort in understanding a more abstract issue by making direct correspondence to the everyday experiences of family life.

As Frederic Lee has extensively argued (Lee 2005, 2010, 2011b), for their own good, students should be presented to contesting ideas. This implies enabling them to leave their comfort zones. The dominant curricula of economics do little in that direction. It is thus hard to dispute the common analogical reasoning used by our students and many others when looking for an answer to the question above. That is the task, nevertheless (Hodgson, Mäki, and McCloskey 1992). We shall start by exploring the strength of the analogy in the similarities claimed, and then move on to its weaknesses by showing the differences it helps to hide.

When the state is viewed as a household, for instance, the latter's usual hierarchies can be easily transferred to it. The state shall become the 'head p[erson]'. Although households may show different degrees of 'democracy' [or 'oligarchy],' it is common for their head persons to have discretionar[y power] without having to justify it with arguments other than the [appeal to] hierarchy. If the head of the household is responsible fo[r ...] in all circumstances, then the state head (no matter h[ow different the] context) must simply do the same.

As argued earlier, analogies offer a closed set o[f ... 'don't spend more than] what you earn' seems to be a principle consistent[ly ...]

## The rhetorical weaknesses of the state-as-househo[ld analogy]

In a highly specialized, market oriented, and money based cap[italist] process of social provisioning involves extensive interactions be[tween] entities with systemic consequences (Jo 2011). In such a complex e[conomy,] analogical reasoning is a helpful cognitive tool if used with care. A grea[t deal] lies in invoking sameness when all we have is a claimed similarity. Insti[tutional] research has shown that emergent institutions are irreducible to any other e[ntity,] comforting analogy, thus, is not the ending point of our understanding but t[he begin-]ning. The very interaction between emergent entities, like households an[d the state,] opens new ground for contesting reasoning about social provisioning (Lee [...]).

One critical factor put aside by the analogy is the power of the stat[e ...] widely accepted money (Lerner 1943, 1947; Wray 2004), something [that house-]hold cannot do. Were such power irrelevant, why should states [and other] organizations) care to establish it under different forms of govern[ment through] history? Or why should one, suspicious of the state, want to m[...] policy a task of independent (from the state) central banks? Of c[ourse, govern-] that new money can be created to pay for government expens[es ...] questions about when, how much, and, most importantly, to [...] spending is granted. That is why many are concerned with the [...] austerity. After all, as put by Frederic Lee (2011a, 1294–129[5 ...] public spending and public debt, inflation, income, unemplo[yment ...] necessary for access to social provisioning', and so control ov[er ...] ditions the survival of families and firms as going concerns.

According to Lee's stock-flows accounting and the c[...] private surplus can only happen with equivalent governme[nt ...]

terms, public debt must accumulate as private sector assets (Lee 2011a, 1296–1299). It follows that, in order to have access to social provisioning, households and firms need that the public sector operates deficits in its own money or issues debt in other forms. In line with Lee's approach, imagine what would happen with social provisioning if government attempted to operate under continuous budget surpluses instead. The state collected taxes from individuals and organizations and continuously its expenditures were lower than its revenues. Firms and households should expect a difficult time for the government sector would have more financial claims on the private sector, which would eventually lead to lower effective demand. Would the state be any better? Why would the state run a fiscal surplus after all, saving in its own money? In practical terms, every sovereign state budget surplus is bound to go to waste. A surplus in one period, unlike that of a family, cannot be carried over to the next year. It is misleading to justify lower state expenditures on healthcare and education today in order to save money to be spent in healthcare and education tomorrow.

In 2010, for example, President Obama announced a two-year freeze in pay for federal civilian workers as a sacrifice to get public deficits under control. Although President Obama (2010) argued that "small businesses and families are tightening their belts" so "that sacrifice must be shared by the employees of the federal government," military personnel were not included. President Obama made civil servants' pay a pliable part of the state budget, but not the military's. In Brazil, the analogy usually stresses the need of primary surpluses—a positive balance account that excludes financial expenses. Economists may know what that means, but most ordinary citizens do not. Households pay interest on debts and worry about paying all that is due, *including* interest. Those who use the analogy often speak about the state's primary balance surplus, but rarely invoke the so called nominal balance that includes interest paid and received (a major burden for the state in Brazil and other countries). This selective use of the analogy seems to be an institutional mechanism by which the ruling class directs social provisioning through its control of the access to state money, as Lee argues (2011a, 1295).

What would ordinary households do when burdened with debt and interest payments? Some will experience cuts on expenditures for schooling, healthcare, shelter, and even on food. Others will try to renegotiate debt terms with their creditors. In terms of both short and long term wellbeing, it seems sensible for households to follow the latter option. After all, this strategy seems less harmful to their current living standards and preserves their position to increase future income. Users of the analogy, however, seem to ignore what households actually do. Health, food, shelter, education, safety, and all else are treated as secondary in a 'sound finance' approach to government deficits. Is this actually valid within the household analogy? Is this what a reasonable head of household does? The importance conferred to debt payments relates also to the means a creditor uses to warrant them. Households whose creditors are drug dealers prioritize payments of those debts for fear of death, but creditors of modern states usually behave differently.[5] Thus, it seems that the use of the analogy conceives of a state in panic, as if it were a household dealing with a violent mafia and thus willing to do anything to escape murder.

Advocates of the state-as-household analogy maintain that primary balance is necessary for paying up existing debt, reducing its total, and thus making it easier to manage. State deficits require resources from the financial system to be covered. As a result, public debt becomes uniquely a function of the increasing primary account imbalances. This reasoning is maintained even in face of conflicting evidence. In 1994, for instance, the Brazilian government took advantage of global liquidity and launched a series of anti-inflation measures (the Real Plan). Annual inflation was brought down from four to one digit figures. Official statistics showed, however, that treasury debt increased about 800 percent in the following four years. Users of the analogy would logically claim that primary balance deficits were the culprit. If so, then primary deficits should have grown just as much. Figures, however, tell a different story. The Treasury recorded primary or nominal balance surpluses every year but two during President Cardoso's terms (1995–2002). And they were far more significant as a percentage of GDP than deficits.

It is a conventional wisdom that government deficits cause inflation.[6] With presumed scarce resources, or an economy operating at full employment, government deficits are seen as pushing prices up through expanding demand. However, it is not only state expenditures that push prices up. At full employment, any increase in spending by private investors would drive interest rates and prices up or reduce other investments, even if state expenditures remained the same. That would not happen if families decided to save more out of their current incomes. The issue, framed by Keynes (1936), is to know whether entrepreneurs will get loans to invest more—and commit themselves to future interest payments—while seeing current sales and profits going down. After all, state purchases become the revenue and profits of firms, which can be used to pay old debts and fund new investments.

Mainstream economists claim that firms can sell more by simply lowering prices, but firms know that this can risk meeting their financial commitments and compromise their future as a going concern. With his empirically grounded approach, Lee (1998) argues that "pricing procedures are used by pricing administrators to establish prices which will cover costs, hopefully produce a profit, and, most importantly, permit the enterprise to engage in sequential acts of production and transactions" (228). Instead of varying prices to maximize a utility function, actual business enterprises adopt some sort of conventional pricing procedure which will "produce prices that are stable for many sequential transactions and variations in sales" (228). As a result, such "market prices are not market clearing or profit-maximizing prices, but rather are enterprise-, and hence transaction-reproducing, prices" (228). Pricing is thus a surviving and growing strategy for the firm and one should expect price stability within a wider range of demand variation than neoclassical pricing theory supposes (see Eichner 1976; Harcourt and Kenyon 1976; Lee 2013).

Sovereign governments spend by crediting vendors' and service providers' bank accounts (Wray 2000). This increases bank reserves, which means *ceteris paribus* an increase in banking liquidity. Banks may want to lend this bigger amount of funds by reducing interest rates on loans or easing credit conditions. In order to shun off volatility on interest rates, central banks may want to issue bonds to dry out excessive bank reserves. In other words, state spending does not increase public debt directly; it is the central bank's decision to issue bonds to drain reserves that makes it a debt.[7] If state spending is equally accompanied by an increase in credit demand by the private sector, then security issuing by central banks would concur with private debt.

Consider now that the government issues bonds in order to drain liquidity and to avoid demand inflation (assuming that there is full employment and demand is the cause of increasing prices). Conventional theory says that the state should issue bonds if its spending causes no inflation. In doing so, the state would only dislodge resources from the private sector without adding to total product. When this reasoning is applied to the private sector under the same assumptions, private expenditures like investments also cause inflation if financed by 'new' money (for example, by foreign loans). State or private debts imply interest payments which would increase money in the hands of creditors. More money in the hands of creditors, whose propensity to spend is surely inferior to their debtors', would not necessarily lead to corresponding increases in investment, employment, and economic growth. When an economy works below full employment, however, increased demand can mean employing idle resources.

In face of logic and opposing evidence, restrictive economic policies based on the household-as-state analogy are often justified with two kinds of arguments. One refers to a promise for the future. As Perelman and Olbrechts-Tyteca ([1958] 1969, 245) explained, "in general, pictures of a golden age, past or future, of paradise lost or hoped for—work to the disadvantage of the time or the country in which one is actually living." Fabio Erber (2002), for instance, identified the mythical content of policymaking in the 1990s as the saga of crossing the desert. Recurrent negative results are the natural suffering of the arid path towards the Promised Land (economic growth, employment, social justice, and so on). They come from external factors that affect all (e.g., globalization) and tie the hands of those leading the crossing. But there, in the future, lies the Promised Land of austerity policies. Sacrifices imposed by such policies today will be rewarded at some indefinite point in time. The state-as-household analogy, combined with the image of crossing the desert, puts a carrot in front of the horse while the stick operates.

Justification also comes with a variant of the *limited development argument.* According to Perelman and Olbrechts-Tyteca ([1958] 1969, 287), this kind of argument "insists on the possibility of always going further in a certain direction without being able to foresee a limit to this direction, and this progress is accompanied by a continuous increase of value." If sound finance has not produced the good we expect from it, it is because we have not had enough of it yet. While all eyes are kept on the carrot, key issues are overlooked. For instance, governments in surplus do not need to issue securities to finance their spending. Why do they do so? Where have public savings gone? Do governments 'save' in the same way a private agent does? How can one, using the analogy, explain the contrasting evidence? We cannot deal with all questions here, so we illustrate the point with some macroeconomic arguments that the analogy helps to conceal.

Consider this sequence of events often implied in the analogy:

1   Some families and firms save money, keeping it in their bank accounts. The counterpart, not mentioned, is that increasing savings means decreasing spending;
2   Banks, thus, have more money and so are able to lend more;
3   The increased capacity to supply credit pulls interest rates down;
4   Other families and firms may take new cheaper loans to finance increased spending;
5   Increased spending and investments by these families and firms increase employment and production, that is, lead to economic growth.

To start with, this reasoning neglects agents' expectations: Why have these agents, at instance 1, decided to spend and invest less? On instance 4, why should firms want to produce more if families and other firms signal that they want to spend less? Surely, one reason why one spends less out of a given income is to hold assets relatively more secure to face uncertain future events. However, one may spend less simply for a lack of interest in buying anything at a given time, or for any of a lengthy list of additional motives ignored by traditional economics. Be it as it may, with reduced spending and no compensating investments, one can be sure of at least two results. First, on aggregate terms, households would have lower incomes and be unable to keep or increase their consumption levels unless they contracted new debts. Second, firms would not be able or inclined to keep or increase current levels of production. They would expect or experience a decrease in sales, or they may deem an expansion too risky. Such a lack of interest by firms to keep production levels or to increase investment, in turn, sends a message to others in the supply chain: no new or bigger orders to come. As soon as firms notice the slowing down of their consumers' spending (or their increasing interest in saving), they feel that it is time to review downwards production, employment, and investment plans. In such case, even if the rate of interest comes down, there seems to be no reason for firms to take new loans to increase investment. Some may do it, as instance 4 above suggests, but most likely for the purpose of substituting new cheaper debts for old ones. Moreover, why would families with increased savings take loans that charge more interest than their financial assets pay?

If the 1–5 circuit is expected to work, there needs to be a perfect balance between the amount firms and families desire to save and the amount other firms and families want to borrow in order to invest and consume. The gloomy expectations of some firms must be exactly compensated by the glowing expectations of others. However, if glowing expectations cannot simply come from more savings and less demand, the spending of a few firms should have a null result. The circuit depends on the absolute realization of instance 5. The state plays a key role in its forcefulness. By spending, the state can ease the financing of firms by increasing liquidity and, furthermore, can also create effective demand directly.

Reasoning based on the analogy leads one to think that government indebtedness (debt which carries interest) is the only way to finance state deficits, as it happens to households. Households can only change the form of their indebtedness, although all forms involve redemptions in money issued by the state. As Lee argues, "exchange ... arises from the need of households to gain access to a state-money monetized social provisioning process" (2011a, 1294). For the state, except for debts in foreign currency, any debt liquidation involves the money it issues.

Mainstream theory holds that new money must grow in line with productivity growth if prices are not to go up. Such linear association, however, has found little empirical support. For example, money supply (as measured by reserves or M1) in Brazil has increased by a factor of 32.6 between 1994 and 2013 (BCB 2014). Nominal income has grown by a factor of 13.6 and prices by a factor of 4.1 in the same period (BCB 2014; IBGE 2014).

Conventional theory holds also that all willing and able workers are employed at all times (or become so quickly, driven by equilibrating market forces). Unemployment is either frictional or voluntary. If that is not the case, however, the assumed causation between money supply and inflation is lost. If no one else is willing to buy unemployed resources, then the state can do it at an administered price *with* price stability (Lerner 1943; Wray 1998).

The composition of government expenditure is also central. State spending happens in specific contexts and in the face of structural conditionings. Economies may present bottlenecks as, for example, economic sectors with more or less idle capacity, growth potential, or skilled workers. This allows us to explore the different roles state spending may play in the economy according to different situations. Prices are likely to go up if state purchases increase the demand in sectors working at full capacity, for example. At the same time, however, state provided education may enlarge the supply of skilled labor and may help increase capacity in such sectors.

The way in which the state spends is also relevant. Paying for goods and services with new money, for instance, may avoid certain knotty relations within which states get involved in the financial circuits. And paying without borrowing from private banks increases the relative autonomy of the state and expands banks' reserves. One can see important developments from such circumstances. For one, the so called monetary multiplier would work in response to payments for production, not for financial securities. Banks would have to look for borrowers other than the state, like firms in expansion and families increasing consumption, encouraging economic growth. The question is where governments are willing and able to use such a capacity, one that makes them quite different from a household.

## Concluding remarks

Is the state like a household? Can we think of the state revenues (taxes) in the same way as we think of our wages? Does the state, like us, need to save for its holidays? We have made an effort to show that the state-as-household analogy conceals important differences between the two institutions. If the peculiar qualities of the state are ignored, then our persuasions about economic policy can be seriously misguided and harmful consequences ensue.

The first and crucial difference is that the state can pay its expenses directly with new currency. Families cannot do that, and must 'tighten their belts, 'cut the fat,' and 'put the house in order' when illiquid. In spite of that, users of the analogy focus on 'spending' to try to equalize the entities.

This issue often leads to questions about the quality of government spending. Mainstream economists usually claim that governments make poor decisions on what to purchase and at what price. However, particular kinds of expenses seem protected from such criticism. The choice of the primary surplus as a key objective of economic policy, for instance, decides that the payment of debt services to bondholders has primacy over other expenses. Would sound finance economists claim that this is also a poor decision by governments? Or, as Todorova (2013, 69) puts it, is it "the qualitative direction of the government deficits that is kept in check"?

To question the use of the analogy in economics is not to replace it with the idea of a state that spends for its own sake or that deficits will always correlate unitarily to economic growth and welfare increase. The point is that deficits are not an evil in itself. The state-as-household analogy can be more helpful if limited to defending the idea that the two institutions are similar in caring for the welfare of their members, leading us to take a social provisioning approach to the economy (Lee 2011a). With regard to spending, states and household are simply different institutions.

The state can use new money to pay for its purchases and thus spend more than it collects without debt. The argument that any currency issuing is inflationary has low face value in situations of high unemployment and falling incomes, but this is often forgotten. Even Milton Friedman (1948, 258–259) realized that the budget deficit

> is a net contribution by the government to the income stream which directly offsets some of the decline in aggregate demand, thereby preventing unemployment from becoming as large as it otherwise would and serving as a shock absorber while more fundamental correctives come into play.

The capacity of the state to spend should be analyzed in light of its position as the main or sole buyer in various sectors of activity, including of labor power, and thus as a price maker. When this special capacity of the state is taken into account, new forms of non-inflationary spending can be discussed. None of them needs to be seen as a panacea or undertaken without limits. The state can use a ceiling, non-inflationary reserve price in its bids, for instance, and lead buyers to adjust to it, or make large scale purchases that stimulate the production of goods and services with reduced average costs. Government deficits can be run in a given year, as long as there are unemployed productive resources. As idle resources lessen, state surpluses become more likely. This is done by the well known income multiplier. All this is consistent with the arguments of long term fiscal balance. In the end, the balance of state accounts becomes a result of the functioning of the economy where resources are either underused or used to its full.

## Acknowledgments

Huascar Pessali and Ramón Fernandéz are grateful for funding from CNPq, the Brazilian Research Council, under grant agreement PQ 306568/2012–8.

## Notes

1 You will notice by the previous quotes that 'family' is also a term used in the analogy, interchangeably with 'household.' We will stick to 'household' for it stands closer to a budgeting unit.
2 See for instance Cosgel (1996), Dolfsma (2001), Klamer and Leonard (1994), Pessali (2009), and Shulman (1992).
3 The search for such 'natural laws' in economics is accounted for by Clark (1992). See also Henry (1990, 2009).
4 In Brazil, the idea has also been supported by an analogy. It is usually said that if a policy or an institution in Brazil has no parallel in developed countries, then it should not exist in Brazil. The policy or institution is metaphorically (and belittlingly) compared to a jaboticaba (*Myrciaria cauliflora*)—a fruit native to Southeast Brazil and found nowhere else—suggesting that uniqueness is enough reason to consider them improper or wrong.
5 This has been institutionalized in international relations since the Drago Doctrine established that creditor countries could not declare war to debtor countries for that very reason.
6 We use the expression 'conventional wisdom,' following Galbraith (1971) and Block (1996), to speak of a widely held set of beliefs about the economy that appear in the comments of the economic sections of the newspapers, TV and radio news, magazines, and so on, most of which are also held at the academy.
7 The same happens with other determinants of money supply like, for instance, foreign capital inflows.

## References

Aristotle. 1984. *Rhetoric*. Edited as *The Rhetoric and the Poetics of Aristotle*. New York: Modern Library.
BCB (Banco Central do Brasil). 2014. "Séries temporais." Accessed October 3, 2014. www3.bcb.gov.br/sgspub/consultarvalores/telaCvsSelecionarSeries.paint.
Beck, M. 2004. "Palocci: será difícil corrigir o IR como querem as centrais sindicais." *O Globo*, May 18. Accessed July 28, 2010. http://oglobo.globo.com.
Black, M. 1993. "More about Metaphor." In *Metaphor and Thought*, edited by A. Ortony, 19–41. Cambridge: Cambridge University Press.
Block, F. 1996. *The Vampire State and Other Myths and Fallacies about the U.S. Economy*. New York: New Press.
Burke, K. 1954. *Permanence and Change*. Berkeley: University of California Press.
Clark, C. 1992. *Economic Theory and Natural Philosophy*. Aldershot: Edward Elgar.

Cosgel, M. 1996. "Metaphors, Stories, and the Entrepreneur in Economics." *History of Political Economy* 28 (1): 57–76.

Dolfsma, W. 2001. "Metaphors of Knowledge in Economics." *Review of Social Economy* 59 (1): 71–91.

Eichner, A. S. 1976. *The Megacorp and Oligopoly: Micro Foundations of Macro Dynamics.* Cambridge: Cambridge University Press.

Franco, G. 2004. "Parcerias Complicadas." *Veja*, 1863, July 21. Accessed July 28, 2014. www.econ.puc-rio.br/gfranco/VEJA124.htm.

Friedman, M. 1948. "A Monetary and Fiscal Framework for Economic Stability." *American Economic Review* 38 (3): 245–264.

Galbraith, J. K. 1971. *The Affluent Society.* 2nd ed. Boston: Houghton Mifflin.

Gruchy, A. G. 1987. *The Reconstruction of Economics.* New York: Greenwood Press.

Harcourt, G. C. and P. Kenyon. 1976. "Pricing and the Investment Decision." *Kyklos* 29 (3): 449–477.

Henderson, W. 1982. "Metaphor in Economics." *Economics* (Winter): 147–153.

Henderson, W. 1994. "Metaphor and Economics." In *New Directions in Economic Methodology*, edited by R. Backhouse, 343–367. London: Routledge.

Henry, J. F. 1990. *The Making of Neoclassical Economics.* London: Unwin Hyman.

Henry, J. F. 2009. "The Illusion of the Epoch: Neoclassical Economics as a Case Study." *Studi e Note di Economia* 14 (1): 27–44.

Hodgson, G., U. Mäki, and D. McCloskey. 1992. "Plea for a Pluralistic and Rigorous Economics." *American Economic Review* 82 (May): xxv.

IBGE (Instituto Brasileiro de Geografia e Estatística). 2014. "Séries históricas." Accessed July 28, 2014. www.ibge.gov.br/home/estatistica/indicadores/precos/inpc_ipca.

Jo, T.-H. 2011. "Social Provisioning Process and Socio-Economic Modeling." *American Journal of Economics and Sociology* 70 (5): 1094–1116.

Keynes, J. M. 1936. *The General Theory of Employment, Interest and Money.* London: Macmillan.

Klamer, A. and T. Leonard. 1994. "So What's an Economic Metaphor?" In *Natural Images in Economic Thought*, edited by P. Mirowski, 20–51. Cambridge: Cambridge University Press.

Lakoff, G. 1999. *Philosophy in the Flesh.* New York: Basic Books.

Lakoff, G. and M. Johnson. 1980. *Metaphors We Live By.* Chicago: University of Chicago Press.

Lee, F. S. 1998. *Post Keynesian Price Theory.* Cambridge: Cambridge University Press.

Lee, F. S. 2005. "Teaching Heterodox Microeconomics." *Post-Autistic Economics Review* 31: 26–39.

Lee, F. S. 2010. "A Heterodox Teaching of Neoclassical Microeconomic Theory." *International Journal of Pluralism and Economics Education* 1 (3): 203–235.

Lee, F. S. 2011a. "Modeling the Economy as a Whole: An Integrative Approach." *American Journal of Economics and Sociology* 70 (5): 1282–1314.

Lee, F. S. 2011b. "The Pluralism Debate in Heterodox Economics." *Review of Radical Political Economics* 43 (4): 540–551.

Lee, F. S. 2013. "Post-Keynesian Price Theory: From Pricing to Market Governance to the Economy as a Whole." In *The Oxford Handbook of Post-Keynesian Economics, Volume 1: Theory and Origins*, edited by G. C. Harcourt and P. Kriesler, 467–484. Oxford: Oxford University Press.

Lerner, A. 1943. "Functional Finance and the Federal Debt." *Social Research* 10 (1): 38–51.

Lerner, A. 1947. "Money as a Creature of the State." *American Economic Review* 37 (2): 312–317.

McCloskey, D. 1983. "The Rhetoric of Economics." *Journal of Economic Literature* 31: 482–517.

McCloskey, D. 1990. *If You're So Smart: The Narrative of Economic Expertise.* Chicago: University of Chicago Press.

Mencimer, S. 2011. "Memo to Tea Party: The US Government's Budget is not Like a Family's." *MotherJones*, July 28. Accessed May 4, 2013. www.motherjones.com/mojo/2011/07/government-budget-vs-family-budget.

Mirowski, P. 1988. "Shall I Compare Thee to a Minkowski-Ricardo-Leontief-Metzler Matrix of the Mosack-Hicks Type? (Or Rhetoric, Mathematics and the Nature of Neoclassical Economic Theory)." In *The Consequences of Economic Rhetoric*, edited by A. Klamer, D. McCloskey, and R. Solow, 117–145. Cambridge: Cambridge University Press.

Obama, B. 2010. "President Obama on the Federal Pay Freeze: Getting this Deficit Under Control is Going to Require Broad Sacrifice." The White House Blog, November 29. Accessed October 4, 2013. www.whitehouse.gov/blog/2010/11/29/president-obama-federal-pay-freeze-getting-deficit-under-control-going-require-broad.

Obama, B. 2011. "Remarks by the President on Unveiling of the Budget in Baltimore, Maryland." The White House, Office of the Press Secretary, February 14. Accessed October 9, 2013. www.whitehouse.gov/the-press-office/2011/02/14/remarks-president-unveiling-budget-baltimore-maryland.

Perelman, C. and L. Olbrechts-Tyteca. [1958] 1969. *The New Rhetoric: A Treatise on Argumentation.* Notre Dame, IN: University of Notre Dame Press.

Pessali, H. 2009. "Metaphors of Transaction Cost Economics." *Review of Social Economy* 67 (3): 313–328.

Quadros, W. 2003. "Classes sociais e desemprego no Brasil dos anos 1990." *Economia e Sociedade* 12 (1, 20): 109–135.

Republican Caucus. 2011. "Budget Forecast: State Still Spending More Than It Takes In." Minnesota House of Representatives, March 1. Accessed October 8, 2013. www.minnesotahousegop.com.

Shulman, S. 1992. "Metaphors of Discrimination: A Comparison of Gunnar Myrdal and Gary Becker." *Review of Social Economy* 50 (4): 432–452.

Thatcher, M. 1975. "Speech to Shipley Conservatives." Thatcher Archive: CCOPR 643/75 (2); originally published in *Yorkshire Post*, June 30, 1975. Accessed February 23, 2015. www.margaretthatcher.org/document/102726.

Todorova, Z. 2007. "Deficits and Institutional Theorizing about Households and the State." *Journal of Economic Issues* 41 (2): 575–582.

Todorova, Z. 2013. "Connecting Social Provisioning and Functional Finance in a Post-Keynesian–Institutional Analysis of the Public Sector." *European Journal of Economics and Economic Policies: Intervention* 10 (1): 61–75.

World Bank. 1994. *Brazil: An Agenda for Stabilization.* October, Report 13168-BR.

Wray, L. R. 1998. *Understanding Modern Money.* Cheltenham: Edward Elgar.

Wray, L. R. 2000. "The Neo-Chartalist Approach to Money." Working Paper no. 10, Center for Full Employment and Price Stability.

Wray, L. R., ed. 2004. *Credit and State Theories of Money.* Cheltenham: Edward Elgar.

Wray, L. R. 2006. "Teaching the Fallacy of Composition: The Federal Budget Deficit." Policy Note 06/01, Center for Full Employment and Price Stability.

# 16 Technological-institutional foundations of the social economy

## A framework for the analysis of change in the social provisioning process

*Henning Schwardt*

## Introduction

The composition and technological foundation of economic activity is constantly changing. This change manifests, for instance, on the level of connected production structures and consumption patterns. Agents' individual actions shape these foundations, structures, and patterns. Their actions are, in turn, shaped by the institutional framework that represents their social environment. The direction of change of technological as well as institutional characteristics of the system thus depends on the institutional framework. Institutional frameworks differ, and there is not one single path for such processes of change. Potential paths emerge as a result of preceding paths and their circular and cumulative causation dynamics. Impulses from the overall technological-institutional space have to arise continuously for a long-term instrumentality of processes to be possible. Such impulses rely on individuals' ability to learn and to utilize acquired knowledge. Consequently, how knowledge creation and transmission is valued is a crucial component for processes of change, and their more instrumental or ceremonial overall character.

We shall categorize the main factors that have an impact on changing technological foundations of economic activity for the purpose of discussing the relations between the factors in the delineated categories. The resulting framework draws on an understanding of interdependent technology and institutions, and allows us to stress the following features of institutional-technological change.

- Socio-economic systems create the paths they follow. Institutional framework and technological capacity jointly shape these paths. Systems' paths can differ from one another.
- The institutional framework within which agents make their decisions embeds their activities and exerts influences on the kinds of activities agents pursue. The institutional framework cannot be severed from the level of technology accessible to agents. They change jointly.
- Dynamics of change can be described by a circular and cumulative causation among institutions and technology. Change manifests on different levels and in different aspects of socio-economic environments.

- Narrowly economically motivated activity, as a subset of economically relevant activity, relies on a number of factors that are not necessarily economic
in nature. Hence, a separation of an economic sphere and economic motives
from the rest of social reality can be very misleading for analytical purposes,
and damaging for policy purposes. The treatment of knowledge creation and
education are critical areas in this regard.

A system may evolve following a range of potential paths. A path may be
selected by collective agency. Such a selection is shaped by the institutional
framework, which influences how existing capacities are used and where
changes can be and are sought and introduced. Different institutional environments can lead agents to emphasize different objectives and different ways for
reaching these. Their emphases, in turn, have an impact on the technological
foundations of activities and, thereby, on the possibilities for further changes.
Consequently, trajectories of change can differ noticeably between groups. Additionally, it is not only technological capacities that expand or contract along the
paths that can serve to describe the changes observed. The institutional framework itself can also change, with possible repercussions on the effectiveness and
use of technology.

The connection of economic activity, such as production, distribution, and
consumption, and the related exchanges and transactions, to other social activities and influences has repeatedly been pointed out (e.g., Polanyi 1968; Lee and
Jo 2011; Todorova 2013). It is a part of the overall social environment. Economic activity is structured and shaped not solely by economic factors and constraints, but by a broader set of political, social, and cultural influences as well,
which are themselves overlapping. For example, people are citizens, not only
consumers and taxpayers. The direction and nature of individuals' activities
respond to social structures (Archer 1995; Lawson 1997; Lee 2011).

The socio-technological environment of agents shapes a gamut of possibilities from which production processes can be selected. It lies behind rules of
exchange, patterns of distribution, possibilities for the logistics of distributing
products, and the consumption space that agents can explore, amongst others.
Patterns of production, distribution, and consumption, as well as exchanges,
emerge from technological potential. The specific institutional environment in
which these activities are undertaken directs agents' focus and awards them
meaning. Economic activities are occurring in a social context. They are part of
on-going processes. Consequently, economic activities are understood as a
'social provisioning process,' as the historical process that provides agents with
the means for satisfying needs that are amenable to economic exchanges (e.g.,
Gruchy 1987; Dugger 1996; Jo 2011; Lee 2011, 2012; Lee and Jo 2011). The
integration of economic activity and its technological foundation as a part of the
overall social environment are proposed in order to offer the foundation for an
understanding of endogenous dynamics in the system and open-ended, non-
teleological processes of change (see, e.g., Veblen 1898; Ayres [1944] 1996; Lee
2011; Elsner 2012).

The following section discusses the concepts of institutions and technology, and the relationship between them. This provides the foundation for a classification of factors influencing and shaping the technological base of economic activity and its change over time delineated in the third section. The categories of 'development effects' introduced to that end offer a convenient way to structure the relations between the constitutive factors of resulting processes of change. The fundamental influence of the social sphere and social structures will become apparent, and will be further discussed focusing on knowledge creation and transmission in the fourth section. The fifth section concludes.

## The relationship between institutions and technology

Very suitable for our purposes here, institutions have been defined as 'correlated patterns of thought' that have emerged in and from individual interactions and eventually become habituated (Veblen [1899] 2010; Waller 1982; Bush 1987; Elsner 2012). They manifest in common rules and norms, possibly codified in laws, as well as related habits and behavioral routines, including those regarding social hierarchies. Institutions structure social processes by directing agents' attention and delimiting the space of acceptable behavior, as well as stabilizing expectations regarding others' behavior. They thus constrain individual activity at the same time that they enable interactions and coordinate activities in interdependent decision-making, as "collective action in control, liberation and expansion of individual action" (Commons 1931, 241). Values shape the motivations underlying behavior in this understanding. Institutions and values are joined this way (Bush 1987). Behavior is thus motivated by objectives that draw on specific sets of values; a noticeable source of change is related to this aspect of institutions. It entails changes in the motivations and values keeping institutions in place, from the instrumental (problem-solving) to the ceremonial (status-conserving). Increasingly ceremonial motivations have, amongst others, significant effects on resource-use and resource-allocation patterns, pushing the system in a direction where its problem-solving potential can be expected to be reduced.

Technology entails both skill and equipment (Ayres [1944] 1996). Knowledge embeds both of these aspects of technology, as technology is knowledge brought to specific applications. Knowledge and skill components can be the almost exclusive aspects of certain technologies (as in a number of service sector activities, for instance).

Equipment is needed for performing acts of skill. Skill is exercised in the use of equipment. Skill also shapes the effectiveness with which tools can be wielded, and altered for that matter. Behavioral patterns developed in technological applications link technology to the institutional sphere. The application of technology relies on institutional provisions, and in turn influences these over time. Technological change builds on existing capacities and structures, with new technology coming about as a combination of already existing skills and equipment. It relies on knowledge expansion. The existing technological framework shapes the path that is open for further changes, by providing the foundation for possible new combinations (Schumpeter [1912] 1997; Ayres [1944] 1996). The institutional framework influences which of these paths is actually taken by shaping in which direction change is sought.

Ceremonial and instrumental characteristics may be viewed as part of all institutions and inform an understanding of dynamics and dimension of institutional change in a technological-institutional space (Waller 1982). The instrumental drives of workmanship, idle curiosity, and parental bent can provide the foundation for and motivate attempts to improve individuals' situation. Learning undergirds instrumental valuation and entails using existing tools better, improving upon tools, applying skills and tools in areas where they had not been developed originally, or finding something entirely new. However, the scope for learning and change is limited by the institutional framework that allows or constrains detection of problems, the ability to recognize a problem, formulation of permissible solutions given the value structures in place and so on. How solutions can be communicated depends on the institutional structures in place, as well.

## Technology and institutions and changes in the technological foundation of economic activity

Through the influence on individuals' behavior, the institutional framework shapes activity, directions of change in institutions and technology, and possibilities for communicating changes and thus possibly establishing an altered foundation on which economic activity rests and draws. Technological use, development, and change are embedded in the institutional environment. Still, technology as skill and equipment entails two components that are changing following an impetus from different aspects of the socio-economic sphere. And just as institutional change can have an eventual impact on the technological environment, so can technological change have an impact on the institutional sphere (for instance, in the changes in social structures following the emergence of suburban lifestyles enabled by enhanced transportation options; in the changes in social behavioral patterns following the recent changes in communication technologies; or, on a larger scale, in the vast disruption of values around the industrial revolution, as described by Mokyr (1990) or Heilbroner ([1953] 1999)).

With this background, we formulate categories to capture the processes that shape the technological base of economic activities. Manifesting within the space that institutional framework and technological capacity have opened, these *development effects* have repercussions in the technological environment, mediated by institutional influences, and eventually shift the boundaries of the existing technological capacity. Single effects have the potential to have an impact on each other and provide the foundation and input to developments in their own and in other categories. They cannot be expected to have a lasting and noticeable overall impact unless other factors change, either in response, or in parallel. The categorization will help identify and stress relations, influences, and causations giving shape to the processes of change referred to, and hence the changing shape of the social provisioning processes, as well as underline the role of the social environment in these processes (for an application, see Schwardt 2013).

### The relation between different factors shaping the technological foundation of economic activities

We can capture the different factors affecting the technological foundation of activity by categorizing them as belonging to what we term Veblenian development effects, Smithian development effects, Schumpeterian development effects, Arrovian development effects, and Solovian development effects.[1] As pointed out earlier, changes in the institutional-technological environment provide the foundation for further institutional and technological change, influencing in how far an existing knowledge base is drawn on in activities, or following an expansion of knowledge that is in fact drawn upon. The development effects formulated here—and the impulses that can be subsumed under one heading or another—integrate these changes into a framework that lays the foundation for analyses of said processes of change. That the original impetus may emerge in dynamics we place primarily on the demand or the supply side, respectively, is therefore important only insofar as it allows distinguishing the different areas in which changes are required, or may have been forthcoming in a particular pattern. All of these effects eventually result in contributing to a broadening of the technological base on which economic activity rests, and thereby the basis for future technological development. For a continuous process of change, effects on supply and demand sides will have to come together.

Briefly, Veblenian development effects capture effects that result from changes in the institutional environment that are reflected in behaviors and attitudes. Concerning changes of socio-economic systems, they cover those which are permitting a more effective use of technologies. Smithian development effects are those that can be realized because an extension of markets permits the use, or broader use, of already existing technologies; they can also have their foundation in changes in institutions. However, separating them from the direction of institutional change-based impulses in Veblenian development effects promises increased clarity of analyses. The change in effectiveness of technology applications and the change in market extensions are treated separately in the formulation of the framework proposed here. Schumpeterian development effects result from radical innovation, and Arrovian development effects from incremental innovation. Solovian development effects, finally, emerge from a spread of available equipment. They contribute to changes in technological capacity by changing the composition of production structures.

Veblenian development effects serve to capture that as a result of institutional changes, existing potential technological capacity may subsequently be utilized differently. The changes focused on in this category refer to attitudes and related behavior. First, there emerge possibilities for a more effective utilization of existing technologies. Examples may include instances where technology has become available through learning and transfer processes from elsewhere, which has been developing in a specific institutional environment and therefore includes certain behavioral aspects and notions that agents in the new environment do not (yet) show. This may for instance entail communication cultures, or relations between agents at different hierarchical levels in organizations, amongst others. In such circumstances, changes in accepted behavioral patterns, or the values underlying and motivating these, may result in more effective means for using a technology. This may in turn have knock-on effects in other areas, or for the application, extension of use, or integration of other aspects of technologies. A second possibility is that changes in institutions lead to an increasingly ceremonial motivation in making decisions about the utilization of existing potential, reducing the problem-solving capacity of activities in the socio-technological sphere. An example for this kind of dynamic may be found in the increasing orientation of company strategies on short-term financial indicators and share price manipulations over the past three decades with concurrent negative effects on productive investment and capacity utilization (see, for example, Minsky 1993; Lazonick 2009, 2010; Wray 2009). A third aspect bridges to the Smithian development effects discussed in the following paragraph, as markets may also open up as a result of institutional changes that have an impact on consumption patterns. For instance, products may become more attractive to consumers copying higher-status consumption patterns from other groups, domestic or foreign.

Smithian development effects result from structural changes in markets, which in turn make specific technologies more worthwhile to use than before. Institutional changes lie behind such changes, as markets are always and everywhere institutional structures; in this case, institutional changes that have an impact on the rules of exchange, which may furthermore be connected to technological development. In particular, effects in this categorization mean a usability of technologies that have been known but not in use due to disadvantageous cost-benefit expectations, whereas Veblenian development effects focus on aspects of behavior and values of agents. Behind Smithian development effects, we can therefore expect to find extensions of demand due to growth, extensions of demand due to new territorial reach, possibly as a result of infrastructural change, or changes in rules structuring exchanges and transactions (including cross-border), as well as extensions of demand due to changes in consumption patterns, amongst others. The subsequent crossing of a certain threshold in cost-structures, due to economies of scale, for instance, may then further support resulting dynamics.

Schumpeterian development effects result directly from the extension of the economically accessible technology space that results from innovation. In this category, innovations refer to radical innovations (as opposed to incremental innovations taken up below), in Schumpeter's categories (e.g., Schumpeter [1912] 1997) of new products, new production processes, new markets, new organizational forms, or new inputs. In the process towards innovations, inventions precede innovations. The invention refers to the finding of a novel concept of making use of existing relations and a novel way of combining knowledge (as such, or embodied in tools) for creating known outcomes or new outcomes. Out of this pool, economic agents select novelties for the introduction in the economic sphere—that is, innovations. This process may entail the creation of and pushing of products into new markets; potential new offers and supply precede the demand for them. The organization of processes in management, marketing, logistics, and the like is a component of the dynamics entailed here. Technology entails a whole body of ideas, and the structuring of processes is a core aspect of the way towards the achievement of certain outcomes.

For Schumpeterian development effects to actually be realizable, a pool of inventions has to exist and access to this pool has to be possible. Factors that influence the capacity for inventions as well as the ability to make inventions known to potential users, therefore, play a significant role for the continued impetus Schumpeterian development effects can give. Room for curiosity and communication abilities, as aspects of the institutional framework, have a significant impact here. Furthermore, there have to be motivations for agents to actually transfer inventions to economic activity, and thus require a certain value set to be adopted by the agents. The process from invention to innovation and economic activity involves uncertainty. For an individual inventor, curiosity and joy in experimentation may be more than enough for motivating inventive activity. However, for the transfer to economic uses—that is, innovation—additional factors play a part, and a widespread impact of novelties in an actually noticeable change of the technological foundation of activities requires supportive factors from the institutional environment.

Innovations that persist can be understood as economically viable novelties that serve companies' vested interests. There is no reason to assume that innovations should necessarily be advantageous to the larger group of agents they are introduced into. This is true for innovation in production processes—one might think of novelties strengthening the position of owners over workers, for instance. It is also, and possibly more so, true for innovations in the service sector that may be supporting production activity, or, probably especially in the case of financial market innovation, increasingly just distributing value created in other sectors to itself. There is no reason, therefore, to assume that innovations should always be instrumental.

Arrovian development effects result from incremental changes in technologies already in use. Once people start using things, they may become aware of possibilities for improving their effectiveness. Hence, these effects induce extensions of knowledge emerging as learning-by-doing (Arrow 1962), learning-by-using (Rosenberg 1982), or learning-by-interacting (Lundvall 1988). Arrovian development effects can and do have significant and cumulatively noticeable effects on the effectiveness of technology. However, for an impact on the overall effectiveness of technological processes in a larger area, sector, or even an entire economy, the improvements they may bring about have to be communicated between different users. Not infrequently, processes behind this type of development effects will entail tacit knowledge components, which make the transferability dependent on exchanges of people. Nevertheless, eventually, technology may become more standardized, embodied in new machines, and amenable to transfers on a more abstract level of communication (as seen in, for example, Chang's (2008) discussion of technology transfers in Europe).

Solovian development effects, finally, result from the spread of available knowledge throughout the production fabric, specifically through their embodiment in investment. To the degree that investment depends on the permission to use available knowledge while making it profitable to the owners of capital equipment, this is strongly linked to the institutional framework. Novelties, or changes on a more detailed level of the functioning of processes, have to spread in order for them to have an impact on the overall technological capacity of the economic agents in a territory. Once standardized and codified, this spread takes the form of investment (see the next paragraph). At this point, skills that are connected to the related equipment can spread as well, changing the technological foundation of activities and, possibly, broadening the foundation for further changes to draw on.

We can distinguish different kinds of investment shaping the development capacity in an economy. The first would be *replacement investment*. Depreciated equipment has to be replaced to maintain productive capacity; a side-effect is, of course, that skills can be maintained and thus the level of technology stabilized. In order for related skills to be maintained, and the foundation for improvements to remain intact, the general availability of structures to exercise these skills and to serve as inputs for new combinations in economic activity is required. Beyond replacement investment, we can point to *imitation investment*, which provides the foundation for the spread of improvements in the effectiveness of processes that may have been found and standardized. Those are in fact Solovian development effects. Finally, there is *innovation investment* undertaken for introducing novelties into the economic realm—for example, investment for setting up new production structures for established products (or in established product categories), or investments undertaken with an eye on the production of new products. Schumpeterian development effects entail this type of investment. All of these types of investment are necessary for maintaining the innovation capacity of a system and for introducing and spreading novelties. Whether and how agents are willing to engage in these activities depends on the institutional framework.

### Circular and cumulative causation patterns of influence

In practice it is often difficult to clearly distinguish between different development effects. After an initial impetus, processes usually require additional impulses for dynamics to continue. For instance, we find that the embodiment of novelties is carried into a broader economic use through investment that is imitating prior changes. The technological framework in the broader economy changes as a consequence. This in turn means that the foundation for further changes becomes wider and new paths may emerge. It is the invention that stands at the outset of structural changes, but it has to spread through various stages of innovation and imitation, and demand has to be created in order to allow its economic viability. The overall process of economic development or the structural change in the social provisioning process requires permissiveness or changes in different areas of society, and these changes enable, and are in turn enabled by, further changes elsewhere. Circular and cumulative causation patterns can be identified behind the continuation of processes of change.

Even though not easily separable in practice, the organization of these development effects appears rather useful for analytical purposes. We can group the

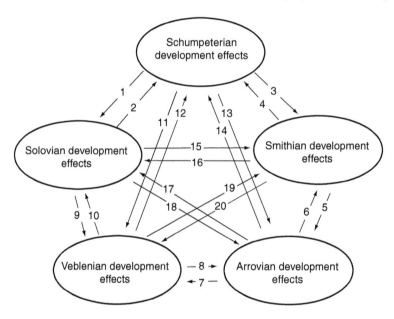

*Figure 16.1* Examples for relations between categories of development effects (DE).

Notes
  1  Schumpeterian DE required for Solovian DE
  2  Solovian DE enable new input to Schumpeterian DE
  3  Schumpeterian DE required for Smithian DE
  4  Smithian DE enable new input to Schumpeterian DE
  5  Smithian DE provide foundation for Arrovian DE
  6  Arrovian DE increase effectiveness, enable Smithian
  7  Arrovian DE as learning may open new perspectives
  8  Veblenian DE may open mind for experimenting
  9  Solovian DE can foster changes in skills
10  Veblenian DE maybe lead to investment willingness
11  Novelty may change mindset
12  Changed mindset may permit novelty
13  Schumpeterian DE provide foundation
14  Cumulated improvements leads to new input
15  Investment increases market
16  Increased market fosters investment
17  More effectiveness makes investment worthwhile
18  Foundation for further improvement
19  Institutional change may open new markets
20  New markets may foster changes in mindset

diverse factors that jointly influence the technological foundation of economic activity, and stress their connection to the institutional framework relevant for agents. For instance, Schumpeterian development effects will open space for Arrovian development effects. The necessary spread of technology relies on Solovian development effects. The effective introduction and application of this technology possibly needs Veblenian development effects as well as Smithian development effects which in turn may have resulted from newly available markets, or related purchasing power increases that have opened up following the initial change in activity. This is true in different strengths and emphases for the relation between development effects from all categories proposed. Technological change as an overall phenomenon relies on impulses from different categories taking effect and can only become noticeable if factors in different development effect categories are jointly affected (for some examples for the dual relations between all factors, see Figure 16.1).

### *Trade-offs between different objectives*

In more specific areas, trade-offs in fostering different aspects of processes of change are also possible. This may amongst other things depend on the objectives pursued, the timeframe chosen under which objectives are formulated, the direction found desirable, or the interests and interest groups taken into account, as well as the emphasis on stimulating selected factors that may differ and shift over time.

From the policy-maker's perspective trade-offs arise in their structuring of the framework for economic activity, as the attempt to achieve a furthering of one set of objectives may well rely on measures that simultaneously result in situations in which it is less attractive to pursue other objectives. Possible conflicts of interests or objectives include, but not are limited to, opening space for imitation versus a guarantee to exploit rents accessible through innovation; an ease of the flow of information versus restrictions to these in order to grant, at least temporal, monopoly rents; a domestic capacity development versus more opening for accessing external sources of information, knowledge, or learning; or capacity development versus exploitation of existing technological capacities (especially where this entails exploiting economies of scale with concurrent small numbers of suppliers). In none of these, or other conceivable areas, can we expect to find undisturbed reference points against which to evaluate measures, in an environment where the public agent may decide to abstain from specific measures.

Trying to gain some degree of control over the socio-economic environment is an attractive course of action for private business enterprises (as for instance pointed out by Berle 1967; Galbraith [1967] 2007; Means 1967; Kapp 2011). We can expect business enterprises to strive for enhancing control of their environment (e.g., Lee 1998; Fligstein 2002). A concentration of power can generally be assumed to be an attractor in the process of socio-economic change. Socio-economic change may be suppressed once a sufficient degree of control has been obtained by agents. In fact, a general tendency appears to be that stable institutional environments tend towards a ceremonialization of structures (Ayres [1944] 1996). Such stability may enhance a feeling of security through a per-ceived reduction of risks for individual agents.

Private agents on their own are unlikely to be able to set up the structures and guarantee the conditions needed for keeping the process of change instrumental. The control of private power becomes a necessary task, albeit difficult to imple-ment it. A conscious decision is required concerning a treatment of the counter-weight that public power may provide. An advantage of public power is that it can bring a legitimization process into effect within a society. It is in principle more amenable to oversight, and offers clearly defined channels for its exercise. Private power is, however, fuzzier and more difficult to foresee; and it is harder to control and counterweigh for other private agents, and much more so for a group or society at large (see also, e.g., even though from a different angle, Olson [1965] 1971). Coordination and cooperation of private agents may con-sequently be more likely to be forthcoming if public agents can exercise some influence responding to broadly based interests. A counterweighing dynamic between the public and private agents is expected to support a continuous, suffi-cient instrumentality of institutional structures. A public agent, properly embed-ded in a participatory democratic system, appears to be needed in the process of socio-economic change (Elsner 2001).

## Faultiness of the narrowly defined economy: knowledge, education, and skills

The development effects introduced in the preceding section capture influence factors that shape the technological foundation of an economy. While they are formulated to trace influences on a stylized technological level, we argued that the institutional framework is crucial for their emergence and impact on a broader level in a real-world economy. That is to say, the foundation of eco-nomic activity emerges in a technological-institutional space. Economic activity proper is then situated in a space that is defined, delineated, and enabled by social and political decisions; for instance, through decisions concerning what can be exchanged, and decisions on the conditions under which transactions can take place. How economic activity is interpreted and given a particular meaning depends on the institutional framework. However, as discussed, the influence goes beyond the structuring and shaping of exchange and transactions, and their perception. Therefore, the institutional framework is crucial for (the analysis of) the trajectory of change.

The embeddedness of economic activity is briefly addressed in this section, with a view on the necessity to draw on structures, conditions, and inputs that are in place as an outcome of non-economic processes and structures. Comple-menting Polanyi's ([1944] 2001) unproduced inputs (labor, land, and money; or fictitious commodities), and Kapp's (2011) unpaid and unaccounted imports from the natural environment and exports in terms of unaccounted negative impacts on natural and social environments, we stress the treatment of the know-ledge fund (or a joint stock of knowledge in Veblen's terms) of societies as it relates to their socio-political environment.

Like any social activity, economic activity always requires knowledge, which is translated and systematized into technology, be it productive, social, or other. The foundation for purposeful activity is the ability to filter information from data, and put this information into a context. In social environments, knowledge about the institutional framework serves to structure behavior. The emergence of institutions requires capability for purposeful action in interdependent settings, and an understanding of social environments that is in either abstract and spe-cific knowledge pertaining to interactions between agents. The technological-institutional space developed above changes based on the specific tools agents have acquired for shaping these abilities. Knowledge extension and application depend on the values influencing agents. Education, knowledge, and skill are attributes of the individuals participating in economic relations through activity that becomes labor, where knowledge in this case refers to the part of the know-ledge fund that an individual has learned.

The creation of knowledge, either directed in research or based more broadly in general curiosity and learning, is often not a direct outcome of economically motivated activities. 'Workmanship' and 'idle curiosity' are not rooted in profit-driven behavior (Veblen [1899] 2010; [1921] 1990). The foundation for indi-viduals to actually be able to acquire knowledge does not usually respond to agents' economic considerations. The foundation for acquiring further know-ledge and developing skills that is offered in education structures is a social component and input to social activity. Education enables agents to partake in social activities. Thus basic social abilities are obtained in social settings. Under such a perspective on education, a marketable skill-set is a side-product of an education process through which agents have acquired and can build on means that is found in economic settings.

The provision and extension of basic knowledge—that is, basic research—is not something with which business enterprises are particularly concerned. Rather, they tend to focus their activities on later development (and then market-ing) and imitation. Input for more significant changes tends to be emerging from public sector activity (Lazonick 2010; Milberg and Shapiro 2013). Of course, as these authors also point out, this is not so by necessity. Especially the shift in business strategies over the last few decades reflect shifts in values, in a direc-tion we can interpret as reducing problem-solving and increasing ceremonial motivations, in an increasingly strong weight for motives that are separated ever further from production and serviceability (for the basic mechanism of such a transition, see already Veblen [1904] 1978, [1921] 1990; also, Sturgeon 2010).

A reorientation of the education sector towards a narrow evaluation crite-rion—money and earning capacity as a reflection of this—is likely to limit the scope of non-economic motivations behind knowledge acquisition. Placing the profit motive at the center of knowledge acquisition limits the natural area of focus to existing structures. Likewise and accordingly, a reorientation of instrumental values onto ceremonial values is likely to be more pronounced in these circumstances.

In fact, this process takes effect in a dual fashion: Through individuals' decision regarding the content of their education pursuits, as well as through educational organizations' capacity to focus on their activities. An expected result from such dynamics will be a reduction in the instrumentality of education structures in general, as these will offer less space to the acquisition of knowledge in open-ended approaches once a business motive becomes more prominent in its structures.

Regarding the individuals' decisions, in this context, under a monetary motive they are expected to be oriented on existing structures, and on the resulting ability to find a place within those structures. The focus will be more on acquiring skills that are related to such existing structures and activities, than on open or 'idle' knowledge acquisition. Such open knowledge acquisition, however, is most likely to give an impetus for a continued countering of ceremonial tendencies. The distinction is not a black-and-white one, for sure, but the tendencies are expected to hold. The trend towards ceremonial motivations is also found in educational institutions providing 'employability' over other objectives. Such a focus will shape values—reflected in the acceptability of a narrower outlook for educational institutions—and expectations in the course of public discourses. A narrowing of the educational scope to a skill-transmission for functioning in economic relations would be centered on offering the ability to fill positions in existing structures, which will require an orientation on existing and known structures. In such situations, instrumental changes that counter dynamics towards a ceremonialization are expected to become less likely over time, as agents have fewer tools to explore possibilities for such changes and fewer reasons to respond to the possibility of such changes.

## Conclusion

Longer-term processes of change in economic activity and in its foundation can be addressed in a framework that integrates original institutionalists' conceptions of technology and institutions. The development effects introduced above offer a way to bring some structures to the relation between the different factors playing a role for the shape, direction, and pace of processes in which the technological and institutional foundations for activities in socio-economic spaces change. Individual motivation and values remain the principal factors on which dynamics build, embedding the process into the existing institutional framework. Economic activity draws on a number of areas, structures, or even inputs that are not located in a narrowly conceived economic space. Amongst others, these include the informal institutional framework, the formal framework of rules, the stabilization of the economic sphere, knowledge and knowledge creation, infrastructure provisions, and communication ability. The resulting system of technology and institutions creates its own future paths from the provisions, attitudes, abilities, and capacities that are in place. Which of these paths is followed is not predetermined but is rather the outcome of collective agency.

Subsuming 'non-economic' factors into a narrowly defined economic framework can lead to attitudes and dynamics, which may be resulting in reductions of problem-solving potential more generally. A narrow and single-dimensional evaluation criterion in which individual decisions—through, for instance, a shift of increasing numbers of decisions to a 'one dollar one vote' rule—that are detrimental to the collective well-being can more easily be taken and justified, shifts attitudes away from more broadly based decision-criteria. Specifically, behaviors carried and motivated by invidious distinction, in predation or emulation, through for instance an increased importance of pecuniary gain for the individual agent may be expected to emerge (for an example, see Galbraith [1958] 1998). That the system provides the foundation for its change and takes the process into a certain direction means that an environment shapes what is seen as successful so that agents within the system may be expected to move further in that direction (Schmookler 1993). For instance, reduced innovation capacity, negative productivity effects, and increased unemployment have been observable in more 'flexible' labor relations (Vergeer and Kleinknecht 2012). Still, this flexibility, being the outcome of conventional wisdom, accepted values, and predominant ideology, is not questioned, but pursued further for addressing the problem it has helped create. A narrowing of the scope of treatment and valuation of knowledge that aims at finding places within existing structures is expected to further such developments even more.

We might well come to the conclusion that this is part of a larger project of redistribution stabilized by fear and the threat of taking away the last options of gaining one's livelihood, as Robert Reich, for example, has repeatedly posited. We can certainly identify how increasingly ceremonial attitudes and values are reflected in the behavior driving this development and employed for advancing it further, and how this has had an adverse impact on the social provisioning process and its technological foundations if assessed in terms of their serviceability for individuals. One area in which this trend currently finds a pronounced reflection is education. Maintaining a socio-economic system's instrumental character requires continued action, collective agency, and vigilance. This appears to be a message well-worthy of a chapter in a book dedicated to the memory and life's work of Professor Frederic S. Lee.

## Acknowledgments

I thank Zdravka Todorova, Tae-Hee Jo, F. Gregory Hayden, and two anonymous reviewers for their comments on earlier drafts of the chapter. The usual disclaimers, of course, apply.

## Note

1 We find a similar terminology in Mokyr (1990, 4–6). He distinguishes Solovian growth that results from investment, Smithian growth that results from commercial expansion, and Schumpeterian growth that results from "[i]ncreases in the stock of human knowledge, which includes technological progress proper, as well as changes in institutions."

The categorization of development effects we propose here is thus more detailed, and the addition of Arrovian development effects and Veblenian development effects permits to explicitly integrate additional factors that can have a determining influence on the trajectory of an economy. Different influence factors and sources of development effects, and their relations during the process can thereby be identified more clearly.

# References

Archer, M. S. 1995. *Realist Social Theory: The Morphogenetic Approach*. Cambridge: Cambridge University Press.

Arrow, K. 1962. "The Economic Implications of Learning by Doing." *Review of Economic Studies* 29 (3): 116–131.

Ayres, C. E. [1944] 1996. *The Theory of Economic Progress*. Accessed January 21, 2015. http://cas.umkc.edu/econ/Institutional/Readings/Ayres/tep/TEP.html.

Berle, A. 1967. "Property, Production and Revolution." In *The Modern Corporation and Private Property* by A. Berle and G. C. Means (Preface to the 1967 edition). New York: Harcourt, Brace, and World.

Bush, P. D. 1987. "Theory of Institutional Change." *Journal of Economic Issues* 21 (3): 1075–1116.

Chang, H.-J. 2008. *Bad Samaritans: The Myth of Free Trade and Secret History of Capitalism*. New York: Bloomsbury Press.

Commons, J. R. 1931. "Institutional Economics." *American Economic Review* 21: 648–657.

Dugger, W. M. 1996. "Redefining Economics: From Market Allocation to Social Provisioning." In *Political Economy for the 21st Century*, edited by C. J. Whalen, 31–43. Armonk, NY: M. E. Sharpe.

Elsner, W. 2001. "Interactive Economic Policy: Toward a Cooperative Policy Approach for a Negotiated Economy." *Journal of Economic Issues* 35 (1): 61–83.

Elsner, W. 2012. "The Theory of Institutional Change Revisited. The Institutional Dichotomy, Its Dynamic, and Its Policy Implications in a More Formal Analysis." *Journal of Economic Issues* 46 (1): 1–44.

Fligstein, N. 2002. *The Architecture of Markets: An Economic Sociology of Twenty-First Century Capitalist Societies*. Princeton, NJ: Princeton University Press.

Galbraith, J. K. [1958] 1998. *The Affluent Society*. Boston: Houghton Mifflin.

Galbraith, J. K. [1967] 2007. *The New Industrial State*. Princeton, NJ: Princeton University Press.

Gruchy, A. G. 1987. *The Reconstruction of Economics: An Analysis of the Fundamentals of Institutional Economics*. New York: Greenwood Press.

Heilbroner, R. [1953] 1999. *The Worldly Philosophers: The Lives, Times, and Ideas of the Great Economic Thinkers*. New York: Touchstone.

Jo, T.-H. 2011. "Social Provisioning Process and Socio-Economic Modeling." *American Journal of Economics and Sociology* 70 (5): 1094–1116.

Kapp, K. W. 2011. *The Foundations of Institutional Economics*, edited by S. Berger and R. Steppacher. London: Routledge.

Lawson, T. 1997. *Economics and Reality*. London: Routledge.

Lazonick, W. 2009. *Sustainable Prosperity in the New Economy? Business Organization and High-tech Employment in the United States*. Kalamazoo, MI: W. E. Upjohn Institute for Employment Research.

Lazonick, W. 2010. "Innovative Business Models and Varieties of Capitalism: Financialization of the U.S. Corporation." *Business History Review* 84: 675–702.

Lee, F. S. 1998. *Post Keynesian Price Theory*. Cambridge: Cambridge University Press.

Lee, F. S. 2011. "Modeling the Economy as a Whole: An Integrative Approach." *American Journal of Economics and Sociology* 70 (5): 1282–1314.

Lee, F. S. 2012. "Heterodox Economics and its Critics." *Review of Political Economy* 24 (2): 337–351.

Lee, F. S. and T.-H. Jo. 2011. "Social Surplus Approach and Heterodox Economics." *Journal of Economic Issues* 45 (4): 857–876.

Lundvall, B.-A. 1988. "Innovation as an Interactive Process: From User-Producer Interaction to National Systems of Innovation." In *Technical Change and Economic Theory*, edited by G. Dosi, C. Freeman, R. Nelson, G. Silverberg, and L. Soete. London: Pinter Publishers.

Means, G. C. 1967. "Implications for Economic Theory." In *The Modern Corporation and Private Property* by Adolf Berle and Gardiner Means (Preface to the 1967 edition), New York: Harcourt, Brace, and World.

Milberg, W. and N. Shapiro. 2013. "Implications of the Recent Financial Crisis for Innovation." Schwartz Center for Economic Policy Analysis, SCEPA Working Paper 2013–2.

Minsky, H. P. 1993. "Schumpeter and Finance." In *Markets and Institutions in Economic Development: Essays in Honor of Paulo Sylos Labini*, edited by S. Biasco, A. Roncaglia, and M. Salvati, 103–115. New York: St. Martin's.

Mokyr, J. 1990. *The Lever of Riches, Technological Creativity and Economic Progress*. Oxford: Oxford University Press.

Olson, M. [1965] 1971. *The Logic of Collective Action*. Cambridge, MA: Harvard University Press.

Polanyi, K. 1968. "The Economy as Instituted Process." In *Primitive, Archaic and Modern Economies: Essays of Karl Polanyi*, edited by G. Dalton, 59–77. Boston: Beacon Press.

Polanyi, K. [1944] 2001. *The Great Transformation: The Political and Economic Origins of our Time*. Boston: Beacon Press.

Rosenberg, N. 1982. *Inside the Black Box: Technology and Economics*. Cambridge: Cambridge University Press.

Schmookler, A. B. 1993. *The Illusion of Choice: How the Market Economy Shapes Our Destiny*. Albany: The State University of New York Press.

Schumpeter, J. A. [1912] 1997. *Theorie der wirtschaftlichen Entwicklung, Eine Untersuchung über Unternehmergewinn, Kapital, Kredit, Zins und den Konjunkturzyklus*. München: Verlag von Dunckel und Humblot.

Schwardt, H. 2013. *Institutions, Technology, and Circular and Cumulative Causation in Economics*. Basingstoke: Palgrave Macmillan.

Sturgeon, J. I. 2010. "Explorations in Institutional Economics: The Kansas City Approach." Evolutionary Social Theory Work Group Spring 2010 Working Papers. Accessed October 1, 2014. http://cas.umkc.edu/econ/_researchCommunity/EVOworkgroup/.

Todorova, Z. 2013. "Consumption as a Social Process within Social Provisioning and Capitalism: Implications for Heterodox Economics." SSRN Working Paper. Accessed October 1, 2014. http://dx.doi.org/10.2139/ssrn.2355996.

Veblen, T. 1898. "Why is Economics Not an Evolutionary Science?" *Quarterly Journal of Economics* 12: 373–397.

Veblen, T. [1899] 2010. *The Theory of the Leisure Class*. Bremen: Europäischer Hochschulverlag.

Veblen, T. [1904] 1978. *The Theory of the Business Enterprise*. New Brunswick, NJ: Transaction Books.

Veblen, T. [1921] 1990. *The Engineers and the Price System*. New Brunswick, NJ: Transaction Books.

Vergeer, R. and A. Kleinknecht. 2012. "Do Flexible Labor Markets Indeed Reduce Unemployment? A Robustness Check." *Review of Social Economy* 70 (4): 451–467.

Waller, W. 1982. "The Evolution of the Veblenian Dichotomy: Veblen, Hamilton, Ayres, and Foster." *Journal of Economic Issues* 16 (3): 757–771.

Wray, L. R. 2009. "The Rise and Fall of Money Manager Capitalism: A Minskian Approach." *Cambridge Journal of Economics* 33: 807–828.

# Part IV

# The heterodox economics of Frederic S. Lee

# 17  Predestined to heterodoxy or how I became a heterodox economist[1]

*Frederic S. Lee*

How I ended up being a heterodox economist did not involve a flash of light on the road to Damascus or some similar event. Rather, in hindsight, I was 'predisposed' to becoming one. The journey started before I was born. My father's father was a lawyer working in Washington D.C. for the federal government in the 1920s and early 1930s. Much of his time was spent writing legislation for Congressmen, especially in the area of agriculture price supports. As a result he was called upon by the Roosevelt Administration in 1933 to help write the Agricultural Adjustment Act, which was an attempt to establish a governmental mechanism to manage and stabilize the farm sector. Consequently, for my father, the 1930s was not a time of desperation, but being a child growing up in an affluent home where important figures from the Roosevelt Administration visited and discussed pressing economic and social issues. However, the Great Depression did catch his attention and he became interested in Marxism (and nearly joined the Communist Party at one time). He acquired many of the writings of Marx, Engels, Lenin, and Stalin; and his parents contributed to the collection by, for example, giving my father for his 20th birthday in 1944 Lenin's *State and Revolution*.[2]

In 1942 my father went off to Hamilton College where, after military service in the Pacific, he graduated in 1947. While at Hamilton, he took an economics course from John Gambs, the well-known Institutionalist economist and one of the co-founders of the Association for Evolutionary Economics. After graduating, my father went to Columbia University Law School, where he found time to take an economics course given by that arch neoclassical economist, Fritz Machlup. However, my father found the subject matter such nonsense that he left the course and has never taken another economics course since. Finally, while attending the Columbia Law School he happened on a couple of occasions to have coffee with Paul Sweezy. My father became a labor lawyer and worked for the National Labor Relation Board.

My mother's father was born in London and his father, as the unsubstantiated family story goes, was a member of the Independent Labor Party who left England for Canada and then the United States to escape the class system. Thus, her father grew up politically aware and in circa 1916 acquired Marx's three volumes of *Capital* which were displayed prominently on his bookshelves as I was growing up.[3] My grandfather had another significant feature: he obtained a Ph.D. in political science in 1921 from Columbia University.[4] My mother was a politically active, progressive Democrat. So between my mother and father I grew up in a house where progressive politics and civil and workers' rights were considered the norm and the book shelves were filled with Joan Robinson's *Introduction to the Theory of Employment, Accumulation of Capital*, and *Collected Economic Papers*, Piero Sraffa's *Production of Commodities by Means of Commodities*, Paul Baran's and Paul Sweezy's *Monopoly Capital*, Robert Brady's *Business as a System of Power*, Clarence Ayres's *The Problem of Economic Order*, the works of Marx, and the books of other heterodox economists.

When I went to university in 1968 I majored in history and did not take a single economics course. Mostly apolitical in my first two years, the Vietnam War, civil rights, and the women's movement made little impression on me. But this changed during the summer of 1970 when, for reasons lost to memory, I began reading books more intensely and expanding my intellectual horizons. So in my final year at university (1970–1971) I became interested in philosophy because, for me, it dealt with issues that were relevant to my own intellectual growth. It also helped me, after a fashion, to start comprehending the social and political turmoil around me.

I continued taking philosophy classes after graduation, especially in the area of the philosophy of science. But my interest in the subject began to wane once I realized that after 1800 the really interesting social questions were not being examined by philosophers, but by economists. Consequently, I started reading books on economics, one of the first being Robert Heilbroner's *The Worldly Philosophers*, followed by Thorstein Veblen's *The Theory of the Leisure Class*, and then followed by various books on dialectical materialism and Marxism, and ending with the first volume of *Capital*.[5] However, in retrospect, I am not sure that I understood much of what I had read, but I certainly thought so at the time. So by the end of 1972 I had a little knowledge of what constituted heterodox economics which I knew from my father was different from neoclassical economics; but I did not really know what neoclassical economics was.

The next two years were significant in my embryonic development as a heterodox economist. In the summer of 1973 I got my first economic publication as a letter in a local Marxist-Leninist paper critically evaluating the role of cartels in the definition of imperialism as the highest form of capitalism.[6] That autumn I got married to a very sensible woman, Ruth Buschman, and hence became a socially responsible and civilized person overnight. In addition, my wife thought that a life without books, learning, social activism, and international travel was not a life worth living. Hence, she has supported materially, emotionally, and intellectually my long trek to becoming a heterodox economist and obtaining a Ph.D. in economics; has provided significant financial support for my terrible habit of buying lots of economic books no matter what the costs; and has enjoyed with me international travel and living overseas. Finally, I began to seriously and systematically read economic texts and books. At the time I was married I was working in New York City as a supply clerk for the US Army

Corp of Engineers. The job was not difficult; thus I was able to read extensively on the job. Using Joseph Schumpeter's *A History of Economic Analysis* as a guide (see his 'List of Books Frequently Quoted'), I read in succession Adam Smith, David Ricardo, Alfred Marshall, William Stanley Jevons and finished the year out with Keynes's *General Theory* and Joan Robinson's *Economic Heresies*.

Feeling confident of my knowledge of economics, I decided to enroll in two graduate classes in economics at New School for Social Research in January 1974, one on 'Reading and Using Capital' taught by Frank Roosevelt and the second on 'Theory of the Business Cycle' taught by Alfred Kahler. In the former class, Marx and the first volume of *Capital* were the focal points; but in the latter, Kahler who did pioneering work on input-output economics, had the class read articles by Friedrich Hayek, Ralph Hawtrey, Hans Neisser, Nicholas Kaldor, Michal Kalecki, and Schumpeter. Much of the class was over my head, but I still obtained an A– and an abiding interest in input–output economics. At the same time I continued my historical reading of economics, starting with Richard Cantillon and ending with Knut Wicksell.

In September 1974, I transferred to a two-year supply clerk position with the Corp of Engineers in Riyadh, Saudi Arabia. By the time I took the position I knew that I wanted to get a Ph.D. in economics and become a professor. However, I had heard horror stories of how professors treated their graduate assistants. To avoid this, I took the position in Saudi Arabia in order to accumulate enough savings so that I would not have to be a teaching assistant (and the chance to live overseas was also a plus). And I achieved this end.

While in Saudi Arabia, I took correspondence courses in introductory micro and macroeconomics, labor economics, international economics, and calculus. I also continued my reading, taking in Jacob Viner on 'Costs,' John Bates Clark on 'Distribution,' John R. Hicks on 'Wages,' and a phalanx of heterodox economists including Maurice Dobb's *Theories of Value and Distribution Since Adam Smith*, V. K. Dmitriev's *Economic Essays on Value, Competition and Utility*, Paolo Sylos-Labini's *Oligopoly and Technical Progress*, Robinson's *Essays in the Theory of Employment*, and Kalecki's *Theory of Economic Dynamics*. I even started Sraffa's *Production of Commodities by Means of Commodities* but after reading a few pages and understanding very little I gave up. During this time my most memorable experience was reading Roy Harrod's *The Life of John Maynard Keynes* while spending an afternoon and early evening in a Beirut jail.

Returning to New York City in August 1976, I entered the School of General Studies at Columbia University in order to complete my undergraduate education in economics in preparation for going to graduate school. Thus, I took the conventional courses in macroeconomics, economic development, industrial organization, mathematical economics, and mathematics. I also took a course in the history of economic thought from Alexander Erlich and a course from John Eatwell on 'the theory of effective demand.' It was during this period that I began to delve deep into heterodox economics, especially heterodox microeconomics. Immediately upon returning to the States, I acquired and read Adrian

Wood's book *A Theory of Profits*; and I continued with reading articles and books on pricing, costs, and the business enterprise by Hall and Hitch, Philip Andrews, Nicholas Kaldor, Josef Steindl, Michal Kalecki, Gardiner Means, and Alfred Eichner. From these readings I wrote papers for my classes that formed the beginnings of my life-long agenda of developing a heterodox alternative to neoclassical microeconomic theory. One paper was simply titled 'Micro-economics' while a second was titled 'Competition and Classical Economics'; and my paper for Eatwell's class was titled 'Price Theory, the Firm and Manu-facturing Business.'

In addition to classes there was one other significant event while at Columbia and perhaps the most important in my entire academic career. It was my dis-covery of Alfred Eichner. In November 1975 I had bought his book *The Mega-corp and Oligopoly* and started reading it. Then in February one of my teachers who knew of my interests suggested that I should go and talk to Eichner who happened to work close by. So in February 1977 I walked into Eichner's office and said "Professor Eichner, I would like to talk about the determination of the mark-up." And Eichner and I commenced to discuss it for the next hour. It was at this point that I got ushered into Post Keynesian economics officially so to speak. Eichner became my mentor, dissertation advisor, and friend. That evening at home I told my wife about the meeting and she was relieved that there existed somebody like me in economics—that I was not alone.[7]

While at Columbia, I decided to pursue my Ph.D. at Edinburgh University because the economics department offered a specialization in industrial eco-nomics. Eichner told me I was making a mistake and suggested that I go to Rutgers University where Paul Davidson and Jan Kregel taught. He was right; so after a year at Edinburgh, I entered Rutgers in Fall 1978. However, I spent my year at Edinburgh obtaining a better understanding of neoclassical theory and developing a more extensive understanding of Post Keynesian-heterodox micro-economics. My readings included Davidson's *Money and the Real World* and Kregel's *The Reconstruction of Political Economy: An Introduction to Post-Keynesian Economics*; and I even subscribed to the first issue of the *Journal of Post Keynesian Economics*.[8]

When I entered Rutgers I was a Post Keynesian-heterodox economist; and with Davidson, Kregel, Eichner, and Nina Shapiro as my professors, there was no chance that I would deviate. Over the three years at Rutgers I wrote papers on various themes in Post Keynesian-heterodox microeconomics, such as the relationship between market prices and prices of production in the context of a Sraffian price model, the net profit margin, and the general theory of industrial prices. In addition, as a result of a course I took with Kregel, I wrote my first major economics article, 'The Oxford Challenge to Marshallian Supply and Demand: The History of the Oxford Economists' Research Group,' which appeared in the November 1981 issue of *Oxford Economic Papers*. Finally, in my second year at Rutgers, 1979–1980, I taught an introductory micro-economics course. Given some leeway in what to teach I put together a set of lecture notes that was also the basic text for the students.[9] The notes introduced microeconomics in terms of a Sraffian input-output framework, delineating a Post Keynesian approach to the business enterprise, pricing, and markets along with a discussion of neoclassical micro. In the final section of the notes a Sraffian input-output pricing model was used to examine questions such as market prices and convergence to prices of production, changes in prices of production due to changes in wage rates, profit margins, and technology, and changes in distribution due to changes in profit margins and wage rates. I entered Rutgers as a Post Keynesian-heterodox economist with an overriding interest in developing a Post Keynesian-heterodox microeconomic theory that would completely replace neoclassical microeconomic theory; and I left it, thanks to my professors, infinitely more capable of achieving that goal.

## Notes

1 Editors' note: This autobiography was written in 2004 for the *EAEPE (European Association for Evolutionary Political Economy) Newsletter* 32 (July).
2 Much of the collection now resides on my bookshelves.
3 I acquired them in 1972 upon his death and have read all three volumes.
4 His dissertation was on 'The Pressure of the Interests on Government: A Study of the Political Activities of the National Trade Board.'
5 Starting in June 1971, I have maintained a record of all the books, articles, and papers that I have read by month and year. To date I have read 9,260 books, articles, and papers (some more than once) over the past 33 years or approximately 280 per year.
6 To this day, I am still interested in cartels as a capitalist-collective form of market governance.
7 Editors' note: Fred Lee edited 'Tributes in Memory of Alfred S. Eichner' (1991, available at http://heterodox-economics.org/archive/eichner/1991-eichner-tributes.pdf). In his own tribute to his mentor, Fred Lee notes that:

> he [Eichner] was the first economist I met who really encouraged me in my work on pricing and thought that I was not a complete fool. This was important, because until I met Al, my wife was wondering whether I was the only person in the United States who thought like this. She was relieved to know that there was somebody who even had a Ph.D. who thought like me. When I mentioned to Al one day, he remarked that Barbara [Eichner's wife] wondered about him in the same manner and was greatly relieved when he began corresponding with Joan Robinson. The intellectual relief and support that Robinson gave Al in the dark days of 1969–71 clearly comes out in the correspondence that Al gave to me.

Robinson's influence on Eichner is demonstrated by Eichner's dedication of his last (unfinished) work, *The Macrodynamics of Advanced Market Economies* (1987), to Joan Robinson: "To Joan Robinson who, by first putting together into a coherent whole the alternative post-Keynesian paradigm, showed us the path out of the Valley of Darkness that is the neoclassical theory."
8 Editors' note: The list of books and articles Fred Lee read between 1975 and 1979 is available here: http://heterodoxnews.com/leefs/books-articles-1975-9/. In 2014 Fred Lee was either a member or subscriber of 29 associations and journals.
9 Editors' note: Fred Lee's introductory microeconomics lecture notes are available here: http://heterodoxnews.com/leefs/intro-micro-1979/.

# 18  Frederic Sterling Lee (1949–2014)

*John E. King*

On October 23, 2014 the heterodox micro theorist Fred Lee, a tireless advocate of heterodox economics for more than three decades, succumbed to lung cancer at the absurdly early age of 64. He is survived by his wife, Ruth, their daughter Sally, and two granddaughters. He also leaves behind a magnificent legacy of published work and substantial organizational achievements, not to mention many friends and colleagues.[1]

When he entered Rutgers, Fred recalled, he already thought of himself as a Post Keynesian-heterodox economist.[2] In the late 1970s Rutgers was a stronghold of heterodoxy. He was taught by Eichner, Paul Davidson, Jan Kregel, and Nina Shapiro, who were members of the faculty, and in Fall 1978 he took a course in the history of economic thought with Alessandro Roncaglia, who was a visiting professor. In his second year at Rutgers (1979–1980), Fred himself taught an introductory microeconomics course. He was already working on his first major article, on the Oxford Economists' Research Group (Lee 1981). The Post Keynesian group at Rutgers was soon dispersed (see Lee 2009, 88–89, 93–94), but not before Fred had benefited very greatly from it.

After this unusual, and unusually late, beginning, Fred's academic career lasted barely a third of a century. Between 1981 and 1991 he taught, in rapid succession, at the University of California Riverside, at Roosevelt University in Chicago, and across the Atlantic at Staffordshire Polytechnic (now the University of Staffordshire). In 1991 he moved a short distance further east, to what would soon be De Montfort University (then still Leicester Polytechnic), where Peter Riach was making a brave attempt to create a pluralistic economics department on 'the zoo principle—two of everything.' Sadly Riach could only afford *one* of everything, and he then succumbed to managerial pressure and moved the department from the city campus in Leicester to a new building in the suburban wastelands of Milton Keynes (emphatically no relation!), where the brave experiment ended badly.

In a sense its failure was good for Fred, who was now able to spend the second half of his career in the much more hospitable environment provided by the University of Missouri–Kansas City. It was certainly good news for his new employer. Between 2001 and 2014 Fred was 'Mister Micro' to Randall Wray's 'Mister Macro' at UMKC—an allusion, of course, to the roles played by George

Stigler and Milton Friedman 40 years earlier in Chicago. Between them Fred, Randall, and their colleagues established Kansas City as the global capital of Post Keynesian economics. Fred's own detailed account of his department's organization, ideals and progress (Lee 2012) ends by listing some of its brightest young graduates, all of whom he had taught: Flavia Dantas, Gyun Cheol Gu, Tae-Hee Jo, Joëlle Leclaire, Yeva Nersisyan, Robert Scott, Pavlina Tcherneva, Zdravka Todorova, and Éric Tymoigne. As Jo noted in his obituary for Fred, "he will be remembered as an inspirational teacher and wonderful mentor who taught students how to do heterodox economics in a pluralistic, realistic, and integrative manner, and who cared about his students from the bottom of his heart."

As if teaching and research were not enough, Fred also played an important role in the institutions that sprang up around heterodox economics in the final quarter of the twentieth century. In the United Kingdom he set up the Association for Heterodox Economics in 1999, angered by the refusal of the august and ultra-orthodox Royal Economic Society to permit a heterodox presence at its annual conferences (Lee 2009, 197–200; see Chapter 2 in this volume for the subsequent history of the AHE). Fred's achievement inspired heterodox economists around the world, not least Peter Kriesler of the University of New South Wales, who established the Society of Heterodox Economists in Australia a couple of years later.

Fred remained involved with the AHE after his return to the United States. In 2004 he was one of the academics who took part in the third postgraduate workshop in Manchester on advanced research methods organized by the AHE, coordinated by Paul Downward and funded by the United Kingdom's Economic and Social Research Council. Fred had recently published a paper on the use of grounded theory (Lee 2002), and his session at the workshop was on the application of grounded theory research methods to the study of pricing. One of the student participants, Therese Jefferson, found all the sessions to be extremely useful for a doctoral student interested in heterodox economics and research methods—Fred's most of all (see Chapter 4 of this volume). "Fred was also very generous with his time," she recalled ten years later,

> and seemed to be present at any gathering that was officially part of the workshop or otherwise. Several other academics at the workshop were similarly generous, but it was Fred who had engaged seriously with debates about grounded theory and this definitely left its mark.
>
> (personal communication, November 17, 2014)

On his return to the United States, Fred had moved into cyberspace as the publisher and founding editor of the *Heterodox Economics Newsletter*, which soon became an indispensable source of information and mutual support for dissident economists all over the world. He edited the *Newsletter* from 2004 to 2009, when two of his former students, Tae-Hee Jo and Ted Schmidt at SUNY Buffalo State, took over (it is now in the capable hands of Jakob Kapeller of the University of Linz), and was then editor of the *American Journal of Economics and Sociology* between 2009 and 2013. Somehow Fred also found time to become deeply involved in the activities of other heterodox societies, including the Association for Evolutionary Economics (AFEE), the Association for Institutional Thought (AFIT), the Association for Social Economics (ASE), the European Association for Evolutionary Political Economy (EAEPE), the International Confederation of Associations for Pluralism in Economics (ICAPE, of which he was Executive Director from 2006 to 2010), and the Union for Radical Political Economics (URPE). He was also a member of the Business History Conference, the (UK) Conference of Socialist Economists, the Progressive Economics Forum, and history of economic thought associations on three continents. In 2000 Fred was honored by EAEPE with its Gunnar Myrdal Prize, awarded for his theoretical achievements, in particular for Lee (1998), and in 2009 he received the Ludwig Mai Service Award from the ASE for exceptional service. At the time of his death he was president-elect of AFEE.

In England, an old friend remembered, Fred was a member of the Leicester Secular Society and had at one time been its president, holding it together in quite difficult times. Back in Chicago, in 1989, he had joined the Industrial Workers of the World, the anarcho-syndicalist organization also known as the 'Wobblies.' He played a key role in reviving a moribund Wobbly organization in the British Isles while he was teaching there, served as chair of the IWW's General Executive Board in the United States, and spearheaded the successful effort to liberate Joe Hill's ashes from the National Archives, where the federal government was quietly holding them captive, and to scatter them around the world in accordance with Joe Hill's last wishes. In 2005 Fred organized a small conference at UMKC to celebrate the centenary of the IWW's foundation, and co-edited the volume in which the proceedings were published (Lee and Bekken 2009). He never doubted the profound gap that separated the interests of employers and workers. "Those of us with an IWW background," he reminded me, "have never thought that capitalism changed its stripes from the 1930s to the 1970s—there was no labor-capitalist accord, just a time period until the capitalists could again show their claws" (personal communication, April 22, 2014).

I cannot remember exactly when Fred and I first began to correspond with each other, or who initiated our first contact. It would have been in the early 1980s, and the occasion would have been our common interest in the maverick British price theorist P. W. S. Andrews (1914–1971), my first boss and one of Fred's earliest intellectual heroes. I do remember that he shared with me not just his ideas but also his sources—large quantities of unpublished documentary material soon arrived (in those pre-digital days) in the post. Fred was a true socialist, not just in theory but also in his attitude to intellectual work: he really did believe that knowledge was a public good, and should be distributed as widely as possible. We met every now and then at conferences in Britain, and I stayed with him and Ruth in Leicester in 1992 when I was presenting a paper at the (then) Polytechnic. We kept in contact over the next 20 years, first by post and then by email. I think our last meeting was in Ballarat in 2006, when he was the invited keynote speaker at the 19th conference of the History of Economic

Thought Society of Australia (see Lee 2007). He was fascinated by the dark secrets of the Australian labor movement, as revealed by the custodian of the Melbourne Trades Hall. And I have a photograph of the two of us in a bushland setting with an emu standing between us—presumably my wife Mary and I had taken him to the Healesville Sanctuary outside Melbourne and introduced him to the native wildlife.

Nature (and labor history) aside, Fred's interests centered on two areas, one very broad and the other slightly narrower: the first was heterodox economics and its history, and the second was Post Keynesian microeconomics (especially pricing theory) and its history. (Agreeing with Hegel that to know a thing is to know the history of that thing, Fred was incapable of divorcing economic theory from the history of economic thought.) Thus his pugnacious and controversial interpretation of what heterodox economics is all about cannot be dissociated from his equally combative and contentious history of the movement(s) in the United States and Britain in the twentieth century (Lee 2009). This was based on many years of meticulous research into the overlapping memberships of the various heterodox associations (AFEE, AFIT, ASE, URPE, and IAFFE, the International Association for Feminist Economics) and—in the absence of a formal association of Post Keynesians—subscriptions to the *Journal of Post Keynesian Economics*, which led him to conclude that "heterodox economists in the United States [had] coalesced into a professional community by 2000" (Lee 2010, 25). There was also clear evidence of theoretical integration, he claimed, citing a substantial volume of published work between 1990 and 2006 that engaged two or more heterodox approaches (27, Table 1.3). From all this he proclaimed the emergence of "a group of broadly commensurable economic theories—specifically Post Keynesian-Sraffian, Marxist-radical, Institutional-evolutionary, social, feminist, Austrian, and ecological economics" (19). He also documented the damage done to this community in the United Kingdom by the government's pernicious Research Assessment Exercise. The often-cited paper by Harley and Lee (1997) warned us in Australia of the consequences when our own authorities introduced an even less defensible scheme early in the new century.

Fred's important contributions to the theory of pricing in Post Keynesian microeconomics can be found in his *magnum opus*, *Post Keynesian Price Theory* (Lee 1998) and in his more recent entries in handbooks (Gu and Lee 2012; Lee 2013b), but these should all be read in conjunction with his earlier analyses of the work of Andrews (Lee 1981), Eichner (Groves, Lee, and Milberg 1989), and Gardiner Means (Lee and Samuels 1992). His last published contributions on pricing remain within the Andrews–Eichner–Means tradition, since they emphasize that prices do not just *happen* in 'the market,' and are not announced by some omniscient Walrasian auctioneer, but instead are *administered* by companies. Hence prices do not vary continuously with day-to-day fluctuations in demand, and are almost invariably determined by the imposition of a profit mark-up over some estimate of normal unit cost. Fred went into great detail on the ways in which firms allocated overhead costs between different products, the role played by product life-cycles, and the effects of business decisions to target specific classes of consumers. He stressed the need for Post Keynesian theorists to take account of "recent developments in accounting systems and pricing practices in the business world since the early 1990s" (Gu and Lee 2012, 457), especially the emergence of 'activity-based costing' (ABC). Fred himself drew on such unlikely sources as the *Journal of Business-to-Business-Marketing*, the *Journal of Comparative Accounting and Finance*, the *Journal of Applied Accounting Research,* and *Management Accounting Quarterly* (Lee 2013b, 482–484).

Despite his exhaustive research into business pricing decisions, many important questions appeared to him to remain open. As he told me, shortly before his death:

> The Harcourt–Eichner argument that enterprises vary their profit mark-up to finance investment has never had much empirical support. My position is that we really do not know how the profit mark-up is really determined because no one has done the hard work of going into enterprises to find out—also no one has done the archival work as well.
>
> (personal communication, April 22, 2014)

He had already made this point in print. Post Keynesians, he noted, had tended to stress the importance of market structure and internal finance for investment plans in the determination of the mark-up. "However," he concluded, "neither argument has much empirical support. Thus the mark-up remains theoretically unexplored in Post Keynesian theory" (Gu and Lee 2012, 461). And so "the major area" for future research "lies in detailed, enterprise-specific case study work on the determination of the profit markup" (Lee 2013b, 481).

Somehow, despite the huge workload that he had imposed upon himself, Fred always found time to keep in touch with old friends. He and I continued to debate by email about the nature of heterodox economics and the case(s) for pluralism in economics; see King (2013) and Lee (2013a) for our—very different—views on these fundamental questions. He was working on his forthcoming text on heterodox microeconomics almost until the end, synthesizing his work on the business enterprise, its behavior and governance, and its role in the social provisioning process; at the time of writing it is unclear whether he had made enough progress on the manuscript for it to be published. However, there are certainly two further books to look forward to, one a co-edited handbook on heterodox research techniques (Lee and Cronin 2015) and the other a festschrift for his long-time friend and colleague, John Henry (Jo and Lee 2015).

Fred travelled to England for one last time in July 2014 and was able to present a keynote lecture to the AHE conference at the University of Greenwich. Then he went north. "Ironically," he told me in the last message I was to receive from him, "the best day I have felt was when I was in Kirkcaldy visiting Adam Smith—sort of coming around in a full circle" (personal communication, October 5, 2014). Fred's circle is now complete, and I will not be able to have the protracted and vigorous argument with him that I was looking forward to on the implications of financialization and the rise of Shareholder Value Maximization for the Post Keynesian theory of the firm and its pricing and investment decisions (see Lazonick 2013). But I can imagine what his position would have been: clear, firm, and vigorously expressed, but always open to fresh arguments and new evidence. He will not be soon forgotten.

## Acknowledgments

This is an abridged version of an obituary that first appeared in the April 2015 issue of the *Review of Keynesian Economics* 3 (2): 226–232. The author is grateful for corrections and comments from John Henry, Therese Jefferson, and Tae-Hee Jo. The usual disclaimer applies.

## Notes

1 Biographical information, along with a brief autobiography, a complete list of Fred's publications, a number of anecdotes and more extended tributes from friends and colleagues, and details of how contributions can be made to the Frederic S. Lee Heterodox Economics Scholarship Fund, can be found at http://heterodoxnews.com/leefs (consulted November 12, 2014).
2 Details of Fred's life before he became a student at Rutgers University in the fall of 1978 are given in his autobiography in this book.

## References

Groves, M., F. S. Lee, and W. Milberg. 1989. "The Power of Ideas and the Impact of One Man: Alfred Eichner 1937–1988." *Journal of Post Keynesian Economics* 11 (3): 491–496.

Gu, G. C. and F. S. Lee. 2012. "Prices and Pricing." In *The Elgar Companion to Post Keynesian Economics*, 2nd ed., edited by J. E. King, 456–463. Cheltenham, UK: Edward Elgar.

Harley, S. and F. S. Lee. 1997. "Research Selectivity, Managerialism, and the Academic Labor Process: The Future of Nonmainstream Economics in U.K. Universities." *Human Relations* 50 (11): 1427–1460.

Jo, T.-H. and F. S. Lee, eds. 2015. *Marx, Veblen, and the Foundations of Heterodox Economics: Essays in Honor of John F. Henry*. London and New York: Routledge.

King, J. E. 2013. "Post Keynesians and Others." In *In Defense of Post-Keynesian and Heterodox Economics: Responses to Their Critics*, edited by F. S. Lee and M. Lavoie, 1–17. London and New York: Routledge.

Lazonick, W. 2013. "From Innovation to Financialization: How Shareholder Value Ideology is Destroying the US economy." In *The Handbook of the Political Economy of Financial Crises*, edited by M. H. Wolfson and G. A. Epstein, 491–511. Oxford: Oxford University Press.

Lee, F. S. 1981. "The Oxford Challenge to Marshallian Supply and Demand: The History of the Oxford Economists' Research Group." *Oxford Economic Papers* 33 (3): 339–351.

Lee, F. S. 1998. *Post Keynesian Price Theory*. Cambridge: Cambridge University Press.

Lee, F. S. 2002. "Theory Creation and the Methodological Foundation of Post Keynesian Economics." *Cambridge Journal of Economics* 26 (6): 789–804.

Lee, F. S. 2007. "Making History by Making Identity and Institutions: The Emergence of Post Keynesian-Heterodox Economics in Britain, 1974–1996." *History of Economics Review* 46 (Summer): 62–88.

Lee, F. S. 2009. *A History of Heterodox Economics: Challenging the Mainstream in the Twentieth Century*. London and New York: Routledge.

Lee, F. S. 2010. "Pluralism in Heterodox Economics." In *Economic Pluralism*, edited by R. Garnett, E. K. Olsen, and M. Starr, 19–35. London and New York: Routledge.

Lee, F. S. 2012. "University of Missouri-Kansas City." In *The Elgar Companion to Post Keynesian Economics*, 2nd ed., edited by J. E. King, 571–577. Cheltenham, UK: Edward Elgar.

Lee, F. S. 2013a. "Heterodox Economics and Its Critics." In *In Defense of Post-Keynesian and Heterodox Economics: Responses to Their Critics*, edited by F. S. Lee and M. Lavoie, 104–132. London and New York: Routledge.

Lee, F. S. 2013b. "Post-Keynesian Price Theory: From Pricing to Market Governance to the Economy as a Whole." In *The Oxford Handbook of Post-Keynesian Economics, Volume 1: Theory and Origins*, edited by G. C. Harcourt and P. Kriesler, 467–484. Oxford: Oxford University Press.

Lee, F. S. and J. Bekken, eds. 2009. *Radical Economics and Labor: Essays Inspired by the IWW Centennial*. London and New York: Routledge.

Lee, F. S. and B. Cronin, eds. 2015. *Handbook of Research Methods and Applications in Heterodox Economics*. Cheltenham, UK and Northampton, MA, USA: Edward Elgar.

Lee, F. S. and W. J. Samuels, eds. 1992. *The Heterodox Economics of Gardiner C. Means: A Collection*. Armonk, NY: M. E. Sharpe.

# 19 In memoriam

## Frederic S. Lee, 1949–2014[1]

*Jan A. Kregel and L. Randall Wray*

Fred Lee's mentor, Alfred Eichner, sent him to do graduate work at Rutgers University, hoping that he could benefit from the Post Keynesian faculty that was growing up around Paul Davidson including Jan Kregel, Nina Shapiro, Lourdes Beneria, and Bruce Steinberg at Rutgers' Livingston College—and which subsequently came to include Eichner himself. His early interest in Post Keynesian price theory was evidenced in his objection to the dominance of monetary and macro phenomenon in Post Keynesian growth and distribution theory.

When it was suggested to him by one of us who served as his graduate instructor and supervisor, that Roy Harrod, a major contributor to growth and dynamic theory, was also involved in the imperfect competition revolution, inventing the marginal revenue curve, as well as having been a participant in the Oxford Economists' Research Group which engaged in the investigation of real world business and pricing decision, he quickly followed this lead to concentrate on what would become the focus of his work in developing a Post Keynesian approach to pricing and production. Indeed, as a result of this background to his research he resolutely refused to recognize the standard dichotomy between microeconomics and macroeconomics.

The first fruits of this investigation produced a paper on the Oxford Economists' Research Group which was accepted for publication in *Oxford Economic Papers*.[2] A March 1980 letter reporting on his progress on his thesis sets out a schematic representation of the various influences on the work of the Oxford group (see Figure 19.1) and notes that

> further work such as on the influence of the Balfour Committee on Industrial Efficiency and on the influence of MacGregor (who was Professor of Political Economy at Oxford) might provided [*sic*] better evidence of the eclectic nature of Oxford economics. (This would support my contention that in the underworld of economics of the 1920–30s, there lurked the basis for an non-supply & demand approach to a theory of prices and the firm.)

In section II of the letter he reports that

> I have also done a bit of work on pricing in the American literature. Surprisingly, I am finding quite a bit of information in accounting and cost accounting

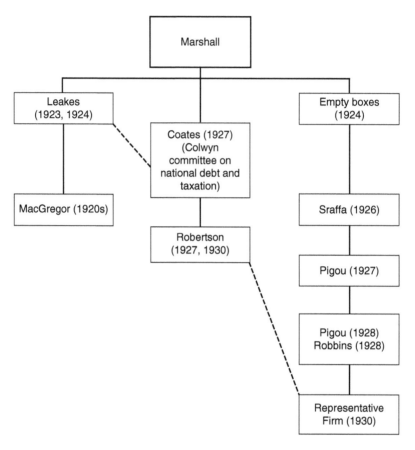

*Figure 19.1* Fred Lee's schema of Marshall's influence (source: Fred Lee's letter to Jan Kregel (March 1980). Kregel's personal collection).

Notes

This schema is reproduced by the editors. Along with this schema, Fred Lee also wrote a note that "The 1st group['s] response to Marshall was to discard (or at least ignore) the supply-demand theoretic aspect and to develop conceptions of the firm and pricing which drew upon the non-supply and demand part of Marshall. The 2nd group accepted Marshall with all the logical inconsistencies and, in the case of Coates, tried to provide Marshall's Representative Firm concept with an empirical basis. The 3rd group is well known—they 'perfected' the supply and demand theoretic aspect of Marshall's work and discarded the rest. I call this group Marshallian, the 2nd group Marshall, and the 1st group? Each one of these groups had an influence on OERG."

journals and management journals.... I am getting an inkling that it will be relevant or useful for what I want to do—but then I am probably wrong.

Fred was not usually prone to self-doubt and in this case he was clearly wrong as the study of cost accounting practices and the US approach led to a highly fruitful line of research and publications.

His analytical and historical research on administered and mark-up pricing culminated in his *Post Keynesian Price Theory* (1998). Shortly after the publication of this important contribution, he moved to the University of Missouri at Kansas City where he devoted much of the rest of his life to promoting and protecting heterodox economics and economists from the onslaught of rankings and 'research assessments' that would eliminate variety from the economics discipline by enforcing conformity with established orthodoxy.

To those who came in contact with him, Fred had a deserved reputation for principled argumentativeness. When he came to UMKC, he announced that he was through with fighting orthodoxy and intended to work quietly in his office for the remainder of his career. He kept the first part of that promise for about a week, after which he took on innumerable causes to right the multitude of wrongs within the university and the profession at large. However, his commitment to the second never varied. Fred was in his office from 9 to 5 like any union employee—albeit a Wobbly—punching a clock. He volunteered for every service commitment that came along. His door was always open to students. He hesitated only if a commitment was to extend into the weekend—which was always set aside for his family.

Fred never gave up the idea of writing a *magnum opus* on Post Keynesian micro—indeed over the years he found traditional Cambridge Post Keynesian theory to be far too constraining as he pursued a microeconomic foundation for all heterodoxy. Indeed, he insisted that traditional micro was too constraining since the behavior of households, firms, and governments must be grounded in the historically specific capitalist economy—a non-ergodic, monetary, circular, capitalist process of surplus production. He needed to include not only the Sraffian version of Post Keynesian economics, but also Marxian and Institutionalist insights as well as the economic sociology and historical literature. In his vision, the firm as well as the monetary production process itself must be treated as a 'going concern' that reproduces itself with a surplus to support growth.

UMKC was an excellent home for Fred. It already had an Institutionalist tradition that stretched back more than four decades—to John Hodges, who was later joined by Bob Brazelton, Jack Ward, Jim Sturgeon, Ben Young, Bill Williams, and Jim Webb. John Henry also joined the faculty, with interest in uncovering the similarities between Marx and Veblen. Fred had a large group of PhD students on which he could practice his ideas—students with a background in heterodox micro, Institutionalist theory, and also heterodox macro.

At first, there was some inconsistency between the micro and macro theory taught within the department—with Fred insisting that firms internally finance investment, while the macro theorists stressed the Kaleckian reverse causation in which investment creates the profits, as well as Minskyan financial fragility that results from the addition of external to internal finance of investment.

However, over the years, Fred gradually reconciled the differences as he continued to develop his theory of the surplus production economy. He knew production begins with money and ends with more money, so he had to learn about money and banking. Fred was stubborn but he also cared deeply about getting it right. He would meet for hours with the macroeconomists to discuss how to get money into his models. As what would become 'modern money theory' was developed, Fred began to realize that this was perfectly consistent with his arguments. He had long rejected the 'supply and demand' and scarcity approaches of neoclassical economics. Money could not be introduced into his microeconomics as a scarce commodity. Money is not a commodity and it is not scarce. Why does it have value, and why is 'more money' the object of production? Fred pursued solutions to these puzzles within his search for heterodox economic foundations.

In the final years of his life, Fred worked to complete a manuscript[3] that would integrate his pricing theory, his view of the enterprise as a 'going concern,' and his model of circular production of a surplus. That production process is directed by an elite composed of the capitalist class and the political elite. The state, as issuer of the state money and as supporter of the capitalist class, plays the deciding role. There is no capitalism without a state, and no money without state money. While exchange is carried out in markets, it takes place in what Fred called "state money prices" that are correlated with "state money incomes and the social rules governing the continually changing provisioning process."

Fred's analysis begins with state creation of "its own money income for spending by crediting the bank accounts of enterprises and employees with state money that are located in bank corporate enterprises that constitute the banking sector." But why would enterprises produce for state money? Because taxes "create demand for the state's fiat money—in short taxes are the 'cost' of having state money."

Fred argues that by

> [a]ccepting state money for its goods and services, the capitalist class in turn demands that all market exchanges for its goods, services, and resources are carried out in state money and the working class is paid with state money. By requiring all payments be made with state money, the capitalist class makes their own as well as the working class access to the provisioning process dependent on having it.

He concludes "every exchange, every transaction that involves state money prices is a public manifestation of the dominant-subordinate social relationship between the ruling and the working-dependent classes." In this way, Fred brings together his approach to heterodox pricing theory and the Marx-Veblen-Keynes monetary theory of production approach—with "state money prices" at the micro level and reproduction at the macro level accomplished through receipt of "more state money" than production had started with.

In an important sense, Fred's foundation reunites the micro and macro theories that were separated after Keynes's *General Theory*. The Bastard Keynesians had tried to synthesize neoclassical microeconomics based on scarcity prices with a Keynesian theory of effective demand. Fred had always rejected neoclassical pricing in favor of cost-plus pricing to ensure survival of firms as going concerns. But how could that be placed in a Keynesian monetary theory of production, in which social provisioning occurs within a social, political, and economic system that is directed by capitalists and their representatives in the state? The coordination is largely accomplished through the monetary *system*—a system that is dominated by the state because it is the issuer of its own currency.

What Fred has attempted is to see through the same "haze where nothing is clear and everything is possible"[4] that Keynes noticed in the conventional theory—the division between the 'Theory of Value' and the 'Theory of Money and Prices.' Which side of the moon are we on? How can we "escape from this double life" and "bring the theory of prices as a whole back to close contact with the theory of value"? It would be too much to claim that Fred has resolved the issue, but he has certainly pointed us in the right direction by linking "the theory of state money prices" with the theory of the operation of the monetary system as a whole.

## Notes

1 This is an expanded version of Editors' Corner in *Journal of Post Keynesian Economics* 37 (3): 528–531, published in 2015.
2 Lee, F. S. 1981. "The Oxford Challenge to Marshallian Supply and Demand: The History of the Oxford Economists' Research Group." *Oxford Economic Papers* 33 (3): 339–351.
3 *Microeconomic Theory: A Heterodox Approach.* Manuscript, preliminary draft, September 2013. All quotes here are from that draft.
4 J. M. Keynes. 1936. *The General Theory of Employment, Interest, and Money.* Chapter 21.

# The bibliography of Frederic S. Lee's writings

## 1978

"The Empirical Basis for Constructing Post Keynesian Models," with A. S. Eichner. Conservation of Human Resources Project, Working Paper 2, Columbia University.

## 1981

"The Oxford Challenge to Marshallian Supply and Demand: The History of the Oxford Economists' Research Group." *Oxford Economic Papers* 33 (3): 339–351.

## 1983

"Full Cost Pricing: A Historical and Theoretical Analysis." PhD Diss., Rutgers University, New Brunswick, New Jersey.

## 1984

"The Marginalist Controversy and the Demise of Full Cost Pricing." *Journal of Economic Issues* 18 (4): 1107–1132.
"Full Cost Pricing: A New Wine in a New Bottle." *Australian Economic Papers* 23 (32): 151–166.
"Whatever Became of the Full Cost Principle?" In *Economics in Disarray*, edited by P. Wiles and G. Routh, 233–239. Oxford: Basil Blackwell.
"The Marginalist Controversy and the Demise of Full Cost Pricing." Department of Economics, Working Papers Series No. 72. University of California, Riverside.

## 1985

"'Full Cost' Prices, Classical Price Theory, and Long Period Method Analysis: A Critical Evaluation." *Metroeconomica* 37: 199–219.
"Kalecki's Pricing Theory: Two Comments." *Journal of Post Keynesian Economics* 8 (1): 145–148.

# 1986

"P. W. S. Andrews's Theory of Competitive Oligopoly: A New Interpretation," with J. Irving-Lessmann, P. Earl, and J. Davies. *British Review of Economic Issues* 8 (19): 13–40.

"Post Keynesian View of Average Direct Costs: A Critical Evaluation of the Theory and the Empirical Evidence." *Journal of Post Keynesian Economics* 8 (3): 400–424.

"Comment: Reply to Basile and Salvadori." *Journal of Post Keynesian Economics* 9 (1): 161–162.

A new edition of "On the Relations Between Cost and Quantity Produced" by P. Sraffa (with G. Langer). Unpublished working paper.

# 1987

"A Post Keynesian Approach to a Theory of Industrial Organization." *The Keizai Hyoron*, June (in Japanese).

# 1988

"A New Dealer in Agriculture: G. C. Means and the Writing of *Industrial Prices*." *Review of Social Economy* 46 (2): 180–202.

"A Post Keynesian Appraisal of the Contestability Criterion," with J. Davies. *Journal of Post Keynesian Economics* 11 (1): 3–25.

"Costs, Increasing Costs, and Technical Progress: Response to the Critics." *Journal of Post Keynesian Economics* 10 (3): 489–494.

# 1989

"G. C. Means's Doctrine of Administered Prices." *Thames Papers in Political Economy*, Summer. Reprinted in *Theory and Policy in Political Economy: Essays in Pricing Distribution and Growth*, edited by P. Arestis and Y. Kitromilides. Cheltenham, UK: Edward Elgar, 1990.

"The Power of Ideas and the Impact of One Man: Alfred Eichner, 1937–1988," with M. Groves and W. Milberg. *Journal of Post Keynesian Economics* 11 (3): 491–496.

"D. H. MacGregor and the Firm: A Neglected Chapter in the History of the Post Keynesian Theory of the Firm." *British Review of Economic Issues* 11 (24): 21–47.

"The Full Cost Principle After 50 Years: A Review of its History and Speculation of its Future." Working Papers in Economics and Political Economy 89–3, Roosevelt University.

# 1990

"Symposium: The Marginalist Controversy and Post Keynesian Price Theory: Introduction." *Journal of Post Keynesian Economics* 13 (2): 233–235.

"Marginalist Controversy and Post Keynesian Price Theory." *Journal of Post Keynesian Economics* 13 (2): 252–263.

"From Multi-Industry Planning to Keynesian Planning: Gardiner Means, the American Keynesians, and National Economic Planning at the National Resources Committee." *Journal of Policy History* 2 (2): 186–212.

"*The Modern Corporation* and Gardiner Means's Critique of Neoclassical Economics." *Journal of Economic Issues* 24 (3): 673–693. Reprinted in *Corporate Governance*, edited by T. Clark. London: Routledge, 2005.

"The Marginalist Controversy and the History of the Normal Cost Prices Doctrine." *Les Cahiers d'Economie Industrielle*, Working Paper 1990–6.

## 1991

"The History of the Oxford Challenge to Marginalism, 1934–1952." *Banca Nazionale Del Lavoro Quarterly Review* 179 (December): 489–511.

*Tributes in the Memory of Alfred S. Eichner.* Private printing, available at http://heterodox-economics.org/archive/eichner/1991-eichner-tributes.pdf.

Review of *A Century of Economics: 100 Years of the Royal Economic Society and the Economic Journal*, edited by J. D. Hey and D. Winch. *British Review of Economic Issues* 13.

## 1992

*The Heterodox Economics of Gardiner C. Means: A Collection*, edited with Warren J. Samuels. Armonk. NY: M. E. Sharpe.

"Gardiner C. Means 1896–1988," with Warren J. Samuels, for the Introduction of *The Heterodox Economics of Gardiner C. Means: A Collection.*

"The Fate of an Errant Hypothesis: The Normal Cost Prices Doctrine," with J. Irving-Lessmann, *History of Political Economy* 24 (2): 273–309.

"Gardiner C. Means, 1896–1988." In *Biographical Dictionary of Dissenting Economists*, edited by Philip Arestis and Malcolm C. Sawyer. Cheltenham, UK: Edward Elgar.

Review of *Mr Sraffa on Joint Production and Other Essays* by B. Schefold, and *Essays on Piero Sraffa: Critical Perspectives on the Revival of Classical Theory*, edited by K. Bharadwaj and B. Schefold, *British Review of Economic Issues* 14.

"Philip Walter Sawford Andrews: An Industrial Economist and Creator of a Realistic Theory of Prices." Leicester Business School Occasional Paper 6.

## 1993

*Oxford Economics and Oxford Economists 1922–1971: Recollections of Students and Economists* (edited), Oxford: Bodleian Library (MS. Eng. c. 4819).

"Introduction." In *Oxford Economics and Oxford Economists 1922–1971: Recollections of Students and Economists*. Oxford: Bodleian Library.

*Oxford Economics and Oxford Economists*, co-authored with Warren Young. New York: Macmillan.

*The Economics of P. W. S. Andrews: A Collection*, edited with Peter E. Earl. Cheltenham, UK: Edward Elgar.

"Philip Walter Sawford Andrews, 1914–1971." In *The Economics of P. W. S. Andrews: A Collection*, edited by Frederic S. Lee and Peter E. Earl. Cheltenham, UK: Edward Elgar.

"Facts, Theory and the Pricing Foundation of Post Keynesian Price Theory." In *Dynamics of the Firm, Strategies of Pricing and Organisation*, edited by J. Groenewegen. Cheltenham, UK: Edward Elgar.

Review of *Thorstein Veblen and his Critics, 1891–1963*, by Rick Tilman. *History of Economic Ideas*.

"Directing Economic Research, Philanthropic Foundations and the Rehabilitation of Big Business, 1930–1980: Summary with Discussion." *History of Economic Thought Newsletter* 51 (Autumn).

Review of *Theories of Political Economy*, by J. A. Caporaso and D. P. Levine. *Journal of Economic Issues* 27 (4): 1292–1293.

## 1994

*A Monetary Theory of Employment* by Gardiner C. Means, edited with Warren Samuels. Armonk, NY: M. E. Sharpe.

"Means and the Making of a Anti-Keynesian Monetary Theory of Employment." In *Gardiner C. Means's A Monetary Theory of Employment*, edited with Warren J. Samuels. Armonk, NY: M. E. Sharpe.

"From Post Keynesian to Historical Price Theory, Part I: Facts, Theory, and Empirically Grounded Pricing Model." *Review of Political Economy* 6 (3): 303–336.

"Gardiner C. Means," with Warren J. Samuels. In *The Elgar Companion to Institutional and Evolutionary Economics*, edited by W. J. Samuels, G. Hodgson, and M. Tool. Cheltenham, UK: Edward Elgar.

"Full Cost Pricing." In *The Elgar Companion to Institutional and Evolutionary Economics*, edited by W. J. Samuels, G. Hodgson, and M. Tool. Cheltenham, UK: Edward Elgar.

"Administered Prices." In *The Elgar Companion to Institutional and Evolutionary Economics*, edited by W. J. Samuels, G. Hodgson, and M. Tool. Cheltenham, UK: Edward Elgar.

Review of *Income Distribution in a Corporate Economy*, by Russell Rimmer. *The Manchester School* 62.

Review of *Pricing & Growth: A Neo-Ricardian Approach*, by Stanley Bober. *Eastern Economic Journal* 20 (3): 372–373.

"Grounding Post Keynesian Price Theory: Recollections of Economists." Unpublished working paper.

## 1995

"From Post Keynesian to Historical Price Theory, Part II: Facts, Theory, and Empirically Grounded Pricing Model." *Review of Political Economy* 7 (1): 72–124.

"The Academic Labour Process and the Research Assessment Exercise: Academic Diversity and the Future of Non-Mainstream Economics in UK Universities," with S. Harley. Leicester Business School Occasional Paper 24.

"Conversation with J. E. King." In *Conversations with Post Keynesians*, edited by John E. King. New York: Macmillan.

"The Death of Post Keynesian Economics?" *PKSG Newsletter* (January).

## 1996

"Pricing, the Pricing Model, and Post Keynesian Price Theory." *Review of Political Economy* 8 (1): 87–99.

"Pricing and the Business Enterprise." In *Political Economy for the 21st Century: Contemporary Views on the Trend of Economics*, edited by C. J. Whalen. Armonk, NY: M. E. Sharpe.

"Gardiner C. Means." In *International Encyclopedia of Business and Management*, edited by M. Warner. London: Thomson Business Press. Reprinted in *IBEM Handbook of Management Thinkers*, edited by M. Warner. London: International Thomson Publishing, 1998.

Review of *Ownership and Control: Rethinking Corporate Governance for the Twenty-First Century*, by M. M. Blair, and *Managers vs. Owners: The Struggle for Corporate Control in American Democracy*, by A. Kaufman, L, Zacharias, and M. Karson. *Journal of Economic Issues* 30 (4): 1193–1195.

"PKSG Attendance Data." *PKSG Newsletter* (October).

"The Future of Post Keynesian Economics: A Response." *PKSG Newsletter* (October).


# 1997

"Research Selectivity, Managerialism, and the Academic Labor Process: The Future of Nonmainstream Economics in U.K. Universities," with S. Harley. *Human Relations* 50 (11): 1427–1460.

"Philanthropic Foundations and the Rehabilitation of Big Business, 1934–1977: A Case Study of Directed Economic Research." *Research in the History of Economic Thought and Methodology* 15: 51–90.

"Research Assessment Exercise and Dictating Economic Research: The Case of Economics," with S. Harley. *Radical Philosophy* 85. Reprinted as "The Economic Cleansing of Economics." *Lib Ed: A magazine for the liberation of learning* 29 (Autumn 1998).

Review of *Competition, Technology and Money: Classical and Post-Keynesian Perspectives*, edited by Mark A. Glick. *Review of Radical Political Economics* 29 (1): 172–175.

Review of *Beyond Competition: The Economics of Mergers and Monopoly Power*, by Thomas Karier. *Review of Radical Political Economics* 29 (2): 110–112.

Letter, *PKSG Newsletter* (December).


# 1998

*Post Keynesian Price Theory*. Cambridge: Cambridge University Press. Reprinted in paperback in 2006.

"Peer Review, the Research Assessment Exercise and the Demise of Non-Mainstream Economics," with S. Harley. *Capital and Class* 22 (66): 23–51.

"Economics Divided: The Limitations of Peer Review in a Paradigm Bound Social Science," with S. Harley. In *The New Higher Education: Issues and Directions for the Post-Dearing University*, edited by D. Jary and M. Parker. Stoke-on-Trent: Staffordshire University Press.

"Gardiner Means and the Dissent of Administered Prices." In *Economics and its Discontents: Twentieth Century Dissenting Economists*, edited by R. Holt and S. Pressman. Cheltenham, UK: Edward Elgar.

"Alfred Eichner, Joan Robinson and the Founding of Post Keynesian Economics, 1969–1983: Summary with Discussion." *History of Economic Thought Newsletter* 61 (Winter).

Review of *Post-Keynesian Economic Theory*, edited by Paul Wells. *Review of Radical Political Economics* 30 (1): 130–132.

Letter. *The Times Higher Education Supplement*, January 30.

"Pricing and Big Business: The Brookings Institution Contribution to the Doctrine of Administered Prices." Unpublished working paper.

## 1999

"Re-Testing Gardiner Means's Evidence on Administered Prices," with P. Downward. *Journal of Economic Issues* 33 (4): 861–886.

"Administered Price Hypothesis and the Dominance of Neoclassical Price Theory: The Case of the *Industrial Prices* Dispute." *Research in the History of Economic Thought and Methodology* 17.

Review of *Economics and the Historian*, by Thomas G. Rawski *et al. Review of Radical Political Economics* 31 (2): 116–118.

"Market Governance in the American Gunpowder Industry, 1865–1880." Unpublished working paper.

## 2000

"The Organizational History of Post Keynesian Economics in America, 1971–1995." *Journal of Post Keynesian Economics* 23 (1): 141–162.

"Inflexible Prices and the Great Depression." *Cuadernos de Economia* 19 (32) (in Spanish).

"Gardiner C. Means, 1896–1988." In *Biographical Dictionary of Dissenting Economists*, 2nd edition, edited by Philip Arestis and Malcolm C. Sawyer. Cheltenham, UK: Edward Elgar.

"Caroline Ware," with W. J. Samuels. In *A Biographical Dictionary of Women Economists*, edited by R. W. Dimand, M. A. Dimand, and E. Forget. Cheltenham, UK: Edward Elgar.

"On the Genesis of Post Keynesian Economics: Alfred S. Eichner, Joan Robinson and the Founding of Post Keynesian Economics" (edited). In *Research in the History of Economic Thought and Methodology*, Volume 18-C, *Twentieth-Century Economics*, Amsterdam: JAI/Elsevier.

"Alfred S. Eichner, Joan Robinson and the Founding of Post Keynesian Economics." In *Twentieth-Century Economics*, Amsterdam: JAI/Elsevier.

Review of *The Market: Ethics, Knowledge and Politics*, by John O'Neill. *Capital and Class* 24 (2): 171–172.

## 2001

"Conference of Socialist Economists and the Emergence of Heterodox Economics in Post-War Britain." *Capital and Class* 25 (3): 15–39.

"Post Keynesian Pricing Theory 'Reconfirmed'? A Critical Review of 'Asking about Prices'," with P. Downward. *Journal of Post Keynesian Economics* 23 (3): 465–483.

"Means, Gardiner (1898–1988)." In *Biographical Dictionary of Management*, vol. 2, edited by M. Witzel. Bristol: Thoemmes Press.

"Macroeconomics, Post-Keynesian Microeconomics Foundations," "Mark-up, Post-Keynesian Literature," and "Microeconomics, Post-Keynesian." In *Reader's Guide to the Social Sciences*, vol. 2, edited by J. Michie. London and Chicago: Fitzroy Dearborn Publishers.

"Gardiner C. Means." In *International Encyclopedia of Business and Management*, 2nd edition, edited by M. Warner. London: Thomson Learning. Reprinted in *The IEBM Handbook of Economics*, edited by W. Lazonick. London: Thomson.

"History of Heterodox Economics as a History of Failure: Comment on Geoff Hodgson." *EAEPE Newsletter* 26 (July).


## 2002

"The Association for Heterodox Economics: Past, Present, and Future." *Journal of Australian Political Economy* 50.

"Mutual Aid and the Making of Heterodox Economics in Post-War America: A Post Keynesian View." *History of Economics Review* 35 (Winter): 45–62.

"Theory Creation and the Methodological Foundation of Post Keynesian Economics." *Cambridge Journal of Economics*, 26 (6): 789–804. Reprinted in *Realist Methodology*, edited by W. Olsen. Los Angeles: SAGE Publications, 2010.

"Post Keynesian Economics (1930–2000): An Emerging Heterodox Economic Theory of Capitalism." In *Understanding Capitalism*, edited by D. Dowd. London: Pluto Press.

"Graduate Programs for Radical Political Economists." *URPE Newsletter* 34 (1).


## 2003

"Post Keynesian Economics Since 1936: A History of a Promise that Bounced?" with E. Tymoigne. *Journal of Post Keynesian Economics* 26 (2): 273–287.

"Theory Creation and the Methodological Foundations of Post Keynesian Economics." In *Applied Economics and the Critical Realist Critique*, edited by P. Downward. London: Routledge.

"Pricing and Prices." In *The Elgar Companion to Post Keynesian Economics*, edited by J. King. Cheltenham, UK: Edward Elgar.

Review of *A History of Post Keynesian Economics Since 1936*, by John King. *Journal of the History of Economic Thought* 25 (4): 523–526.

Review of *Economics and its Enemies: Two Centuries of Anti-Economics*, by William O. Coleman. *History of Economics Review* 38: 76–77.

"Heterodox Journals." *URPE Newsletter* 35 (1).

"Heterodox Book Series." *URPE Newsletter* 35 (1).


## 2004

"To be a Heterodox Economist: The Contested Landscape of American Economics, 1960s and 70s." *Journal of Economic Issues* 38 (3): 747–763.

"The Incoherent Emperor: A Heterodox Critique of Neoclassical Microeconomic Theory," with S. Keen. *Review of Social Economy* 62 (2): 169–199.

"History and Identity: The Case of Radical Economics and Radical Economists, 1945–1970." *Review of Radical Political Economics* 36 (2): 177–195.

"Philip W. S. Andrews." In *Dictionary of British Economists*, edited by Donald Rutherford. Bristol: Thoemmes Continuum.

"David H. MacGregor." In *Dictionary of British Economists*, edited by Donald Rutherford. Bristol: Thoemmes Continuum.

"Sidney Ball." In *New Dictionary of National Biography*, vol. 3, edited by H. C. G. Matthew and B. Harrison. Oxford: Oxford University Press.

"Predestined to Heterodoxy or How I became a Heterodox Economist." *EAEPE Newsletter* 32 (July).

Review of *The Crisis in Economics: The Post-Autistic Economics Movement: The First 600 Days*, by Edward Fullbrook. *Journal of Economic Issues* 38 (3): 880–882.

"Economics as a Disabling Myth." *Industrial Worker* 101 (2).


## 2005

"Teaching Heterodox Microeconomics." *Post-Autistic Economics Review* 31 (May).

"Grounded Theory and Heterodox Economics." *The Grounded Theory Review: An International Journal* 4 (2): 95–116.

"Pasinetti, Keynes and the Multiplier," with A. B. Trigg. *Review of Political Economy* 17 (1): 29–43.

Review of *Political Economy from Below: Economic Thought in Communitarian Anarchism, 1840–1914*, by Rob Knowles, *History of Economics Review* 42 (Summer); also appeared in *Industrial Worker* 102 (9).

Review of *Post Keynesian Econometrics, Microeconomics and the Theory of the Firm*, edited by S. C. Dow and J. Hillard. *International Journal of Social Economics* 32 (2).

*Informational Directory for Heterodox Economists: Journals, Book Series, Websites, and Graduate and Undergraduate Programs*, compiled and edited with S. Cohn, G. Schneider, and P. Quick, 1st edition (January) and 2nd edition (May).

"Undergraduate Programs for Heterodox Economists." *URPE Newsletter* 36 (2).


## 2006

"The Ranking Game, Class and Scholarship in American Mainstream Economics." *Australasian Journal of Economics Education* 3 (1–2): 1–41.

"Introduction to the Special Issue on the History of Heterodox Economics." *Review of Radical Political Economics* 38 (4): 497–498.


## 2007

"Making History by Making Identity and Institutions: The Emergence of Post Keynesian-Heterodox Economics in Britain, 1974–1996." *History of Economics Review* 46 (Summer): 62–88.

"Research Assessment Exercise, the State, and the Dominance of Mainstream Economics in British Universities." *Cambridge Journal of Economics* 31 (2): 309–325.

"The Role of Oral History in the Historiography of Heterodox Economics," with T. Mata. In *Economists' Lives: Biography and Autobiography in the History of Economics*, edited by E. R. Weintraub and E. L. Forget. Durham, NC and London: Duke University Press.

"Teoria Microeconomica Heterodoxa." In *Microeconomia Heterodoxa: Lecturas del Primer Seminario de Microeconomia Heterodoxa*, edited by Gustavo Vargas Sanchez. Mexico City: Editorial Castdel.

"The Industrial Workers of the World." In *The Encyclopedia of the Age of the Industrial Revolution 1700–1920*, edited by Christine Rider. Westport, CT: Greenwood Press.

## 2008

"Heterodox Economics." In *New Palgrave Dictionary of Economics*, edited by L. E. Blume and S. Durlauf. New York: Palgrave Macmillan.

"Publishing, Ranking, and the Future of Heterodox Economics—Introduction." *On The Horizon* Special Issue of *On the Horizon* 16 (4): "Publishing, Refereeing, Ranking, and the Future of Heterodox Economics," edited with W. Elsner.

"A Case for Ranking Heterodox Journals and Departments." *On the Horizon* 16 (4): 241–251.

"Heterodox Economics." *The Long Term View* 7 (1): 23–30.

"Series Forward." In *Future Directions for Heterodox Economics*, edited by J. T. Harvey and R. F. Garnett. Ann Arbor: University of Michigan Press.

Review of *Economics Confronts the Economy*, by Philip A. Klein. *Journal of Economic Issues* 42 (1): 276–277.

"A Comment on 'The Citation Impact of Feminist Economics'." *Feminist Economics* 14 (1): 137–142.

*Informational Directory for Heterodox Economists: Graduate and Undergraduate Programs, Journals, Publishers and Book Series, Associations, Blogs, and Institutes and other Websites*, compiled and edited, 3rd edition (September).

## 2009

*A History of Heterodox Economics: Challenging the Mainstream in the Twentieth Century*. London: Routledge. Reprinted in paperback in 2011.

*Radical Economics and Labor: Essays Inspired by the IWW Centennial*, edited with Jon Bekken. London: Routledge.

"The Economics of the Industrial Workers of the World: Job Control and Revolution." In *Radical Economics and Labor: Essays Inspired by the IWW Centennial*, edited by F. S. Lee and J. Bekken. London: Routledge.

"Radical Economics and the Labor Movement," with J. Bekken. In *Radical Economics and Labor: Essays Inspired by the IWW Centennial*, edited by F. S. Lee and J. Bekken. London: Routledge.

"Alfred Eichner's Missing 'Complete Model': A Heterodox Micro-Macro Model of a Monetary Production Economy." In *Money and Macrodynamics: Alfred Eichner and Post-Keynesian Economics*, edited by M. Lavoie, L.-P. Rochon, and M. Seccareccia. Armonk, NY: M. E. Sharpe.

"Foreword" (with L. R. Wray) to *Money and Households in a Capitalist Economy*, by Z. Todorova. Cheltenham, UK: Edward Elgar.

## 2010

*Evaluating Economic Research in a Contested Discipline: Ranking, Pluralism, and the Future of Heterodox Economics*, edited with W. Elsner. Malden, MA: Wiley-Blackwell. Also appears as the 2010 November issue of *the American Journal of Economics and Sociology*.

"Editor's Introduction," with W. Elsner. *American Journal of Economics and Sociology* 69 (5): 1334–1344.

"Ranking Economics Departments in a Contested Discipline: A Bibliometric Approach to Quality Equality Between Theoretically Distinct Sub-disciplines," with T. C. Grijalva and C. Nowell. *American Journal of Economics and Sociology* 69 (5): 1345–1375.

"Research Quality Rankings of Heterodox Economic Journals in a Contested Discipline," with B. C. Cronin, assisted by S. McConnell and E. Dean. *American Journal of Economics and Sociology* 69 (5): 1409–1452.

"A Heterodox Teaching of Neoclassical Microeconomic Theory." *International Journal of Pluralism and Economics Education* 1 (3): 203–235.

"Pluralism in Heterodox Economics." In *Economic Pluralism*, edited by R. Garnett, E. K. Olsen, and M. Starr. London: Routledge.

"Assessing Economic Research and the Future of Heterodox Economics: Failures and Alternatives of Journals, Departments, and Scholars Rankings," with W. Elsner. *Intervention: European Journal of Economics and Economic Policies* 7 (1): 31–41.

"Heterodox Production and Cost Theory of the Business Enterprise," with Tae-Hee Jo. MPRA Working Paper 27635. Available at http://mpra.ub.uni-muenchen.de/27635.

# 2011

*Social Provisioning, Embeddedness and Modeling the Economy* (edited), Malden, MA: Wiley-Blackwell. Also appears as the 2011 November issue of the AJES.

*Social, Methods, and Microeconomics: Contributions to Doing Economics Better* (edited), Malden, MA: Wiley-Blackwell. Also appears as the 2011 April issue of the AJES.

"Être ou ne pas être hétérodoxe: réponse argumentée aux détracteurs de l'hétérodoxie." *Revue Francaise De Socio-Economie* 8.

"Modeling the Economy as a Whole: An Integrative Approach." *American Journal of Economics and Sociology* 70 (5): 1282–1314.

"Social Surplus Approach and Heterodox Economics," with Tae-Hee Jo. *Journal of Economic Issues* 45 (4): 857–875.

"The Pluralism Debate in Heterodox Economics." *Review of Radical Political Economics* 43 (4): 540–551.

"Heterodox Economics, Tolerance and Pluralism: A Reply to Garnett and Mearman." *Review of Radical Political Economics* 43 (4): 573–577.

"Heterodox Microeconomics and the Foundation of Heterodox Macroeconomics." *Economia Informa* 367: 6–20.

"David H. MacGregor and Industrial Economics at Oxford, 1920–1945." In *Marshall and Marshallians on Industrial Economics*, edited by T. Raffaelli, T. Nishizawa, and S. Cook. London: Routledge.

Review of *Economists and Societies: Discipline and Profession in the United States, Britain & France, 1890s to 1990s*, by Marion Fourcade. *Journal of Socio-Economics* 40 (5): 717–718.

Review of *Issues in Heterodox Economics*, edited by Donald A. R. George, *Economica* 78 (312): 791–792.

"The Making of Heterodox Microeconomics." MPRA Working Paper 30907. Available at http://mpra.ub.uni-muenchen.de/30907.

"Old Controversy Revisited: Pricing, Market Structure, and Competition," MPRA Working Paper 30490. Available at http://mpra.ub.uni-muenchen.de/30490.

## 2012

*In Defense of Post-Keynesian and Heterodox Economics: Responses to Their Critics*, edited with Marc Lavoie. London: Routledge.

"Heterodox Surplus Approach: Production, Prices, and Value Theory." *Bulletin of Political Economy* 6 (2): 65–105.

"Heterodox Economics and its Critics." *Review of Political Economy* 24 (2): 337–351.

"Introduction to the Symposium: The Future of Post-Keynesian Economics and Heterodox Economics contra their Critics," with M. Lavoie. *Review of Political Economy* 24 (2): 303–304.

"Competition, Going Enterprise, and Economic Activity." In *Alternative Theories of Competition: Challenges to the Orthodoxy*, edited by J. K. Moudud, C. Bina, and P. L. Mason. London: Routledge.

"Preface," with M. Lavoie. In *In Defense of Post-Keynesian and Heterodox Economics: Responses to their critics*, edited by F. S. Lee and M. Lavoie. London: Routledge.

"Heterodox Economics and its Critics." In *In Defense of Post-Keynesian and Heterodox Economics: Responses to Their Critics*, edited by F. S. Lee and M. Lavoie. London: Routledge.

"Pricing and Prices," with G. C. Gu. In *The Elgar Companion to Post Keynesian Economics*, 2nd ed., edited by J. King. Cheltenham, UK: Edward Elgar.

"University of Missouri-Kansas City." In *The Elgar Companion to Post Keynesian Economics*, 2nd ed., edited by J. King. Cheltenham, UK: Edward Elgar.

"Critical Realism, Grounded Theory, and Theory Construction in Heterodox Economics." MPRA Working Paper 40341. Available at http://mpra.ub.uni-muenchen.de/40341.

Review of *At the Edge of Camelot: Debating Economics in Turbulent Times*, by Donald W. Katzner. *OEconomia—History/Methodology/Philosophy*, 2 (3). Also on *Weboeconomia*, The *OEconomia* Book Review Online, May 2012. Available at http://weboeconomia.org/bro_lee_katzner.pdf

## 2013

*Markets, Competition, and the Economy as a Social System* (edited). Malden, MA: Wiley-Blackwell. Also appears as the 2013 April issue of the AJES.

"The UK Research Assessment Exercise and the Narrowing of UK Economics," with Xuan Pham and Gyun Gu. *Cambridge Journal of Economics* 37 (4): 693–717.

"Post Keynesian Price Theory: From Pricing to Market Governance to the Economy as a Whole." In *Handbook of Post-Keynesian Economics*, edited by G. C. Harcourt and P. Kriesler. Oxford: Oxford University Press.

Review of *The Microfoundations Delusion: Metaphor and Dogma in the History of Macroeconomics*, by John E. King. *Economic and Labour Relations Review* 24 (2): 255–260.

Translation of Burchardt, F. (1931, 1932), *The Schemata of the Stationary Circuit in Böhm-Bawerk and Marx*. Translated by Christian Spanberger and Frederic S. Lee. Unpublished.

"State Funding of Research and the Narrowing of Economics in the United Kingdom." *Global Labour Column* 150 (October 2013). Available at http://column.global-labour-university.org.

## 2014

Review of *The Making of a Post-Keynesian Economist*, by G. C. Harcourt. *Journal of the History of Economic Thought* 36 (4): 508–509.
"Heterodox Theory of Production and the Mythology of Capital: A Critical Inquiry into the Circuit of Production." Unpublished Working Paper.

## 2015

*Handbook of Research Methods and Applications in Heterodox Economics*, edited with Bruce Cronin. Cheltenham, UK: Edward Elgar.
*Marx, Veblen, and the Foundations of Heterodox Economics: Essays in Honor of John F. Henry*, edited with Tae-Hee Jo. London: Routledge.
"Marx, Veblen, and Henry," with Tae-Hee Jo. In *Marx, Veblen, and the Foundations of Heterodox Economics: Essays in Honor of John F. Henry*, edited by T.-H. Jo and F. S. Lee. London: Routledge.
"Introduction," with B. Cronin. In *Handbook of Research Methods and Applications in Heterodox Economics*, edited by F. S. Lee and B. Cronin. Cheltenham, UK: Edward Elgar.
"Critical Realism, Grounded Theory, and Theory Construction." In *Handbook of Research Methods and Applications in Heterodox Economics*, edited by F. S. Lee and B. Cronin. Cheltenham, UK: Edward Elgar.
"Modeling as a Research Method in Heterodox Economics." In *Handbook of Research Methods and Applications in Heterodox Economics*, edited by F. S. Lee and B. Cronin. Cheltenham, UK: Edward Elgar.
"Predestined to Heterodoxy or How I Became a Heterodox Economist." In *Advancing the Frontiers of Heterodox Economics: Essays in Honor of Frederic S. Lee*, edited by T.-H. Jo and Z. Todorova. London: Routledge.

## 2016

"Social Provisioning Process," with Tae-Hee Jo and Zdravka Todorova. In *The Routledge Handbook of Heterodox Economics*, edited by T.-H. Jo, L. Chester, and C. D'Ippoliti. Routledge.

## Incomplete monographs

*Microeconomic Theory: A Heterodox Approach.*
*Neoclassical Microeconomics from a Heterodox Perspective.*
*Topics in Heterodox Theory of Production: Burchardt, Circular Production, Kalecki, and Scarcity.*

# Index

Page numbers in *italics* denote tables, those in **bold** denote figures.

fety Concerns and Information please contact our EU
GPSR@taylorandfrancis.com
is Verlag GmbH, Kaufingerstraße 24, 80331 München, Germany

Frederic S. Lee (1949–2014)